Capitalism since World War II

Philip Armstrong is a principal research fellow at the Technical Change Centre. He previously worked at the OECD and the Department of Economic Affairs.

Andrew Glyn is fellow and tutor in economics at Corpus Christi College, Oxford. He is the co-author with Bob Sutcliffe of *British Capitalism, Workers and the Profits Squeeze* (1972) and, with John Harrison, of *The British Economic Disaster* (1980).

John Harrison is senior lecturer in economics at Thames Polytechnic. He is the author of *Marxist Economics for Socialists* (1978) and co-author, with Andrew Glyn, of *The British Economic Disaster* (1980).

Philip Armstrong
Andrew Glyn
John Harrison

Capitalism since World War II

The making and breakup
of the great boom

Fontana Paperbacks

First published in 1984 by Fontana Paperbacks
8 Grafton Street, London W1X 3LA

Copyright © Philip Armstrong, Andrew Glyn and John Harrison
1984

Set in Linotron Plantin
Reproduced, printed and bound
by Hazell Watson and Viney Ltd,
Member of the BPCC Group, Aylesbury, Bucks

Contents

List of Charts   9
List of Tables   11
Preface   15

PART I: Postwar Reconstruction, 1945–50

1 Chaos and Despair   21

2 Behind the Chaos   24

The means to produce 25   *Workers* 25   *War damage* 26
Investment 26   *Bottlenecks* 28   Capital and labour 30
The United States and the United Kingdom 31
Japan and Germany 37   *Italy and France* 41
International relations 44   *Relations between the advanced
countries* 44   *The colonies* 46   *Relations with
the USSR* 47

3 Great Power Policies   50

Uncle Sam out for himself 50   *Aid to Europe and
Japan* 52   *International money and trade systems* 53
US occupation policy 55   Uncle Joe in control 60
People's democracy 61   *The Czech case* 64
East and West 67

4 The First Two Years   69

Investment and wages 70   Japan 72   Germany 80
Italy 86   France 91   The United Kingdom 96

5 Marshall Aid: the United States Changes Tack   106

Europe's crisis? 106   Economic problems in the
United States 112   US labour 115
How the Marshall Plan worked 119

6 The New Turn in Europe and Japan   123

France 128   Italy 132   Japan 136   Germany 140
The United Kingdom 149   Summary 154

7 Towards the Boom   156

The US recession 156   The 1949 devaluations 157
The Korean upswing 158   Investment and the boom 160

PART II: The Great Boom, 1950–74

8 The Golden Years   167

Workers and means of production 168   Profits 170
Profit shares and rates 170   Production and realization 173
Wages 174   Why wages rose 177   Exports 179
Government spending 181   Investment 182
The Japanese economic miracle 183

9 A New, Managed Capitalism?   193

The welfare state 194   German codetermination 199
French economic planning 202   Japanese industrial policy 206
Conclusions 211

10 The Eclipse of US Domination   212

The growth of trade 214   International oligopoly 216
US business slips back 218   *Low accumulation at home* 222
Investment abroad 224   The boom, Bretton Woods and
the dollar 227   *US gains* 228   *Costs of maintaining the dollar* 231
International monetary reform 232

11 Overaccumulation   235

Development of the working class 236   The late 1960s: the
problem of full employment 239   Tight labour markets 239
Accumulation and the demand for labour 241   The profits
squeeze 245   Productivity growth 248   Product wages 251
International competition 251   Falling output-capital ratio 253
Falling rate of profit 255   Post-tax profits 258
Did workers gain? 259   Inflation 263

12 Overheating   269

Overaccumulation sets in 269   Strike waves and wage
explosions 271   *Italy's Hot Autumn* 276   *May 1968* 282
Clampdown and the 1970–1 recession 290   The breakup of
Bretton Woods 291   *Dollar devaluation* 294   *The surplus
countries* 295   *US competitiveness and payments* 297
The 1972–3 mini-boom 300   *The commodities boom* 303
The grain market 305   *End of an era* 307

13 Oil and the Crash of 1974   309

The oil crisis 309   The crash 314

PART III: Things Fall Apart, 1974–

14 Unemployment Mounts   323

Unemployment 323   The structure of jobs 327
Who is out of work? 329

15 Unemployment and Accumulation   332

New technology 332   Real wages 334   The stagnation of
output 335   Consumers to blame? 335   . . . or foreigners? 337
. . . or governments? 338   Investment and accumulation 339
Profits 340   Profits, finance and confidence 342
Accumulation and productivity 346   Living standards
and inflation 348

16 International Relations   351

The Eastern bloc 351   The less developed countries 353
The oil producers 355   *The newly industrializing countries* 357
Debt 361   The advanced countries 364
Uneven development 364   *International money* 367
Trade 371   *Protectionism* 374

17 Capitalists and Workers   378

Labour in retreat 378   After Japan? 382
Relocating production 392   Reorganizing work 396

18 Thatcherism and Reaganomics   402

Rhetoric 403   Political economy 403   The real project 405
Restrictive monetary policy 407   *Dismantling welfare* 410
Tax cuts 413   *Privatization and deregulation* 415
Union bashing 418   Militarism 423   Is it working? 424

19 The Left Alternative   426

Obstacles to full employment 427   Jobs 431
Wages 434   Industrial democracy 436   Industrial policy 439
Conclusion 448

20 Future Prospects   449

Data Appendix   457
Sources   473
Bibliography   483
Index   497

Charts

5.1   Europe's trade with the United States, 1946–50   107
5.2   US aid to Europe, 1946–50   121
6.1   Gross domestic product, 1947–51 *(by bloc)*   123
6.2   Gross fixed investment, 1947–51 *(by bloc)*   124
6.3   Industrial productivity, 1947–51 *(by bloc)*   127
6.4a Profitability, 1945–51 *(by country)*   153
6.4b Profitability, 1946–51 *(by country)*   154
8.1   ACC production, capital stock, productivity and employment, 1952–70   169
8.2   ACC profit rates, 1955–68   171
8.3   ACC business productivity and product wages, 1955–68   172
8.4   ACC business mechanization and output-capital ratio, 1955–70   173
8.5   ACC consumption, 1952–70   176
8.6   ACC components of government spending, 1952–70   180
8.7   ACC components of investment, 1952–70   183
8.8   Japanese business capital stock, mechanization, output-capital ratio, 1955–61   187
8.9   Japanese business productivity and product wages, 1955–61   188
8.10 Japanese business investment and profits, 1955–61   189
10.1 Shares of ACC production, 1952–70 *(by bloc)*   213
10.2 Share of manufacturing output produced by top firms, 1960, 1970 *(by bloc)*   217
10.3 Shares of ACC exports of manufactures, 1953–71 *(by bloc)*   218
10.4 Business capital stock, 1952–70 *(by bloc)*   220
10.5 Mechanization: manufacturing capital-labour ratio, 1955–70 *(by bloc)*   221
10.6 Ratios to US business productivity, 1952–70 *(by bloc)*   222

11.1a	Unemployment rates, 1965–75 *(by bloc)*	240
11.1b	Job vacancies, 1965–75 *(by country)*	241
11.2	Business accumulation, 1960–73 *(by bloc)*	242
11.3	ACC business accumulation and employment, 1962–71	243
11.4	Business profit shares, 1960–73 *(by bloc)*	247
11.5	Manufacturing profit shares, 1960–73 *(by bloc)*	248
11.6	ACC business productivity and product wages, 1962–71	252
11.7	Business profit rates, 1960–73 *(by bloc)*	255
11.8	Manufacturing profit rates, 1960–73 *(by bloc)*	256
13.1	World foreign exchange trading volume, 1970–9	318
15.1	ACC manufacturing accumulation and profit rates, 1951–80	342
15.2	ACC business accumulation and profit rates, 1951–81	343
15.3	ACC money wages and prices, 1973–83	349
16.1	Business accumulation, 1970–82 *(by bloc)*	365
16.2	Manufacturing accumulation, 1970–80 *(by bloc)*	366
16.3	Real competitiveness, 1970–82 *(by country)*	368

Tables

2.1	Wartime changes in the stock of means of production *(by country)*	28
4.1	Production and investment, 1937–47 *(by country)*	69
4.2	Profits, wages and productivity: Japan, 1936–47	75
4.3	Productivity and wages: Italy, 1938–47	87
4.4	Productivity and wages: France, 1938–47	94
4.5	The British welfare state, 1938–51	100
5.1	Receipts of US non-military grants and government long-term capital, 1946–50 *(by country)*	119
6.1	Accumulation: growth of the business capital stock, 1947–51 *(by country)*	125
6.2	Volume of trade, 1947–51 *(by bloc)*	126
6.3	Consumer prices, 1947–51 *(by bloc)*	128
6.4	Productivity and wages: France, 1947–50	129
6.5	Productivity and wages: Italy, 1947–51	132
6.6	Profits, wages and productivity: Japan, 1947–51	137
6.7	Productivity and wages: Germany, 1948–51	144
6.8	Profits and wages: Britain, 1938–51	150
7.1	Prices and exchange rates, end of 1949 *(by country)*	158
7.2	Real share prices, 1929–59 *(by country)*	161
8.1	Long-term growth, 1820–1973	167
9.1	Growth of ACC welfare spending in the 1960s	197
10.1	Weight of the US economy, 1950–70	212
10.2	Exports of manufactures, 1950–71 *(by bloc)*	215
10.3	Import penetration by manufactures, 1913–71 *(by bloc)*	215
10.4	Growth of export volumes, 1953–71 *(by country)*	219
10.5	Hourly labour costs in manufacturing, 1960–70 *(by country)*	221
10.6	Growth of sales of giant firms, 1962–72 *(by bloc)*	226
10.7	US balance of payments, 1950–67	229

11.1	ACC sector growth rates, 1955–68	237
11.2	ACC growth of employment, 1955–68	237
11.3	Civil employment, 1960–73 *(by bloc)*	244
11.4	Sources of labour, 1968–73 *(by bloc)*	245
11.5	Profit shares, 1960–73 *(by bloc)*	246
11.6	Productivity and mechanization, 1960–73 *(by bloc)*	249
11.7	Output-capital ratios, 1960–73 *(by bloc)*	254
11.8	Profit rates, 1960–73 *(by bloc)*	257
11.9	Effective tax rates on profits, 1960–73 *(by country)*	258
11.10	Productivity, real wages and the profits squeeze, 1960–73 *(by bloc)*	260
11.11	ACC price changes, 1961–73	261
11.12	Public expenditure, 1960–73 *(by bloc)*	262
11.13	Business borrowing as a percentage of fixed investment, 1962–73 *(by country)*	265
11.14	Government surpluses, 1965–73 *(by bloc)*	265
12.1	The European wage explosions, 1965–70 *(by country)*	272
12.2	US balance of payments, 1968–74	298
13.1	Business profit rates, 1968–75 *(by bloc)*	320
13.2	Manufacturing profit rates, 1968–75 *(by bloc)*	320
14.1	Unemployment rates, 1973–83 *(by bloc)*	324
14.2	Population, labour force and employment, 1960–82 *(by bloc)*	325
14.3	ACC participation rates, 1960–82	326
14.4	Sectoral employment changes, 1973–81 *(by bloc)*	327
14.5	Youth unemployment rates, 1973–82 *(by country)*	330
15.1	ACC productivity and wages, 1965–81	334
15.2	ACC contributions to increased sales, 1960–82	336
15.3	Profit rates, 1960–81 *(by bloc)*	341
15.4	UK manufacturing shares of gross output, 1973–5	343
15.5	Internal funds as a percentage of fixed investment, 1973–81 *(by bloc)*	344
15.6	Taxation and distributions as a percentage of gross profits, 1973–81 *(by bloc)*	345
15.7	Real share prices, 1973–81 *(by bloc)*	345
15.8	The productivity slowdown, 1960–81 *(by bloc)*	347

16.1	Growth rates of less developed countries, 1960–80	354
16.2	Oil producers' investment growth, 1960–79	356
16.3	Investment growth in the newly industrializing countries, 1960–79	357
16.4	Newly industrializing countries' trade balances, 1980	359
16.5	Trade controls, 1983 *(by bloc)*	360
16.6	US balance of payments, 1975–81	370
16.7	Manufacturing export shares, 1973–81 *(by bloc)*	371
16.8	Imports and net exports of manufactures, 1973–81 *(by bloc)*	372
16.9	Net exports of manufactures to various markets, 1973–81 *(by bloc)*	374
16.10	Share of imports in apparent consumption of manufactures, 1970–80 *(by bloc)*	375
17.1	Days occupied in strikes, 1953–82 *(by country)*	378
17.2	Real wages, productivity and terms of trade, 1972–82 *(by bloc)*	382
17.3	Profits, wages and productivity: Japan, 1970–82	383
17.4	Manufacturing plant size, 1958–73 *(by country)*	392
19.1	French nationalization, 1982	443
19.2	French nationalization by industry, 1982	444

Preface

This book is about the economic history of the advanced capitalist countries since 1945. It is not a history of the capitalist system as a whole, since attention is largely confined to the United States, Western Europe and Japan. We have limited consideration of the less developed economies to events which impinged forcefully on the advanced countries. We believe that the advanced countries constitute a group with its own dynamics, and even five hundred pages is little enough space into which to compress forty years of the development of a substantial part of the world.

We have divided the period into three distinct phases: postwar reconstruction (1945–50), the great boom and its disintegration (1950–74) and the years of mass unemployment (1974 onwards). The very different character of the three periods has dictated a distinct approach to each.

Reconstruction involved the formation of the basic relationships between labour and capital within each country, and of the relations between the various countries, which were to underpin the subsequent boom. Part I discusses in detail developments in each of the six biggest advanced capitalist countries – the United States, the United Kingdom, Germany, Italy, France and Japan – during those five years. This crucial and exciting period of history is not widely known about, despite many excellent studies of particular countries, on which we have drawn heavily. We have also included many eye-witness accounts. Reports from the *Economist*, in particular, show how events were assessed at the time by a magazine devoted to providing serious information for those concerned to preserve capitalism. The discussion ventures beyond the economic indices to grapple with political programmes, international relations and many other issues. We hope to have shown that the generation of the boom was neither preordained nor trouble-free.

The great boom of the 1950s and 1960s displayed capitalism in full swing. Political differences became submerged into a social-democratic consensus, accepted more or less enthusiastically by parties of both left and right. Part II reflects the reduced political turmoil of this period and focuses on the economic dynamics of the boom. Here, the advanced countries are considered as a group, rather than as individual countries. For this purpose we have constructed data for the seven largest capitalist countries taken together (the six on whose development we focus in Part I plus Canada), which contribute some 85 per cent of the output of the twenty-four countries which comprise the Organization for Economic Cooperation and Development (OECD). Figures for the advanced capitalist countries as a whole (ACCs) in the tables refer to those seven countries; those in the text sometimes refer to the OECD as a whole. Attention is paid, however, to changing relations between the different blocs (the United States, Europe and Japan), especially to the eclipse of US domination and to the rise of Japan. Figures for Europe in the tables refer to the four largest Western European economies taken together (West Germany, France, Italy and the United Kingdom); those in the text sometimes refer to all of Western Europe. Figures for the EEC refer to the total for member states.

The beginning of the breakup of the boom in the late sixties is examined in a more blow-by-blow fashion. For it was in those years that the ideas generated by the boom – of the end of class conflict, the permanence of prosperity – were shattered. The forces undermining them and the turbulent events which these forces unleashed are discussed in some detail.

Since 1974 accumulation has faltered and mass unemployment returned. Part III analyses these developments, and discusses their implications for relations between the advanced countries and for those between labour and capital. Japan – regarded by other capitalist countries as a model for industrial relations – is examined in some detail.

The outstanding political development of the 1970s and early 1980s was the breakup of the social-democratic consensus. Right-wing parties adopted aggressive policies to rectify the position of business, and workers' parties sought alternatives capable of preserving and extending gains made during the boom. To exemplify these developments we discuss the policies of Thatcher and Reagan on the one hand and those of the British Labour government (1974–9) and French Socialist government (1981–) on the other.

We have tried to explain economic terminology and, more importantly, real economic mechanisms as we go along, although some sections may still prove difficult for somebody with no knowledge of economics. Many of the more important economic facts are presented in tables, but these can safely be skipped by readers who find them distracting. We have presented the more important trends in charts. We have seldom contrasted our interpretation with other writers', even those on whose work we have drawn heavily. This is not because such differences do not matter. Important debates rage about many events discussed: the role of Marshall Aid, the causes of falling profitability in the late sixties, the gains for the United States from the international position of the dollar, the role of government policies of deficit spending in sustaining the boom and so forth. But numerous subplots involving differences of interpretation would make it harder to keep hold of the main strands of an already complex story. The notes on sources indicate where some rival interpretations can be found. The Appendix describes in some detail the data we have constructed, which form the statistical background for Parts II and III. It also gives the various and diverse sources for statistics used in Part I. Since the text frequently refers to flows of exports, loans and so on in billions of dollars, it also contains a table of benchmark values.

We began work on the subject matter of this book in 1972 when we were working on a project on 'Profitability and Capital Accumulation in the Advanced Capitalist Countries'. We are grateful to the Social Science Research Council for financing the project and to the Oxford University Institute of Economics and Statistics for housing the project and for continuing to provide research facilities to Andrew Glyn. While working on this project we wrote a preliminary draft of Part I and developed our shared approach to the analysis of capital accumulation.

Over the past two years, when the bulk of this book was written, circumstances dictated a division of labour. Andrew Glyn did the research for, and wrote the first drafts of, most of the chapters. John Harrison contributed the other drafts and rewrote the whole into its present form. Philip Armstrong assembled the data on profitability and capital accumulation. The final result is the product of endless discussions.

We have been enormously helped by the staff of the Oxford Institute and thank Sybil Owen for typing hundreds of pages of scrawl, Gillian Holiday for computing tables and charts, Catherine Fitzharris for computations, and John Watson, Doreen Monger, John Power and Alison Bates of the excellent library.

Steve McDonnell carried out the research on France for Chapter 19. Wendy Carlin contributed material on German reconstruction for Part I and commented extensively on the whole. We drew heavily on David Soskice's work on industrial relations in Europe in Chapters 12, 17 and 18. As a result of many discussions, and his comments on drafts, we have pillaged many of Bob Rowthorn's ideas, especially on employment in Chapter 14 and trade in Chapter 16. Bob Sutcliffe was involved in the early stages of our work, especially on the reconstruction period, and provided detailed comments on the draft. We are very grateful for all of this help and to the many other people who commented on parts of the draft and who helped in other ways, including Felicity Armstrong, Wlodek Brus, Bunt Ghosh, Marcus Giaquinto, Lucy Glyn, Teresa Hayter, Steven Howe, Makoto Itoh, Alan Kramer, Jill Paterson, Pascal Petit, Hideo Totsuka, Tom Weisskopf and Vera Zamagni.

Part I

Postwar Reconstruction 1945–50

1. Chaos and Despair

Japan and continental Europe were in chaos as hostilities ceased in 1945. Millions of people were on the move: occupying troops, defeated troops, evacuees, slave labourers, those expelled as borders were redrawn, refugees of every description. Food was hopelessly insufficient. The military administrations were ill-equipped to deal with huge civilian problems. Civilian administrations were inexperienced, disorganized and often without much authority.

In Japan, half the housing in the major cities had been destroyed. Evacuation had reduced the number of people living in Tokyo, Osaka and Kobe by one-half. Food supplies had broken down. The black market was the main source for food other than rice. On one Sunday in September 1945, a month after the end of the war, nearly a third of Tokyo's 3 million people left the city to try and buy food in the countryside. Since the purchasing power of wages was less than one-tenth of the prewar level, savings were run down and possessions sold in order to obtain food. Many failed in this struggle to survive, as a survey of the period explains:

'Indeed food was in extreme shortage, and many people were literally starving. In the days immediately after the war it was not uncommon at all to see hungry and malnourished people collapse and die on the streets. On 18 November 1945 the major Tokyo dailies reported that since the end of the war a total of 300 people had starved to death in Kyoto, 148 in Kobe, 100 in Fukuoka, 72 in Nagoya and 42 in Osaka. . . .

'Most of them were homeless and jobless people who had become extremely weak and infirm. In the daytime they wandered around towns in search of leftover food, and at night they slept on the bare concrete floor or railway stations or underground tunnels with only a thin blanket to keep warm. Even if there were a job for them, the result was much the same. As a day labourer a man could not get paid more than 1 or 2 yen a day – but a small rice ball cost 10 yen and a bun 15 yen' (quoted Moore, pp. 89–90).

In Europe there was a deficiency of 16 million houses, due to war damage and dilapidation. A reported 8 million refugees were in the Berlin area, where the struggling German administration could only try to minister to the dying, while pushing the rest on into the countryside. *Picture Post* published photographs of German women and children hunting for food on a vast US army garbage dump, and predicted, 'German misery this winter will be on a scale unknown in Europe since the Middle Ages' (8 September 1945). But the desperate situation that winter was not confined to Germany, as the *Economist*'s description makes clear:

'. . . the tragedy is vast. It may vary in intensity; the peasantry are reasonably well provided and the rich can use the black market, but the poor urban populations of Europe, perhaps a quarter of its 400 millions, are all condemned to go hungry this winter. Some of them will starve. The plague spots are Warsaw, where, according to Mr Lehman, Director-General of UNRRA [the United Nations Relief and Rehabilitation Administration], ten thousand people will die of starvation; Hungary, particularly Budapest, where deaths from famine may reach a million; Austria, particularly Vienna and Lower Austria, where the rate of calories is below 1000 a day (the rate needed to maintain reasonable health is well over 2000), and where in some towns, Wiener-Neustadt for instance, there is already starvation; the Saar, where children are reported to be dying of hunger; Northern Italy, the Ruhr, Berlin, and most large towns in Germany, where it is proving difficult to keep the calorie rate up to 1200. Greece and Western Holland are improving, but are still below full subsistence level. Paris and the larger towns of France face a new food crisis. Nor does this bare recital of calories and diets cover those grisly companions of starvation – tuberculosis, dysentery, typhoid and typhus, rickets – nor the appalling figures for maternal and infant mortality.

'One person in ten in Poland has TB – the figure for Warsaw is one in five – it is rampant in Jugoslavia, and the Czechs say that out of 700,000 needy children 50 per cent have been discovered to be tuberculous. Infant mortality in Berlin has doubled. In Budapest it has risen from 16 to 40 per cent since September. There are no figures for the Ruhr, but English visitors have been told that very few newborn babies are expected to live this winter' (26 January 1946).

Nor, for those with time to think about such matters, were the precedents for postwar economic reconstruction and recovery en-

couraging. The years immediately after the First World War had
seen a feverish postwar boom quickly collapse, in some countries
after degenerating into hyperinflation. In Europe as a whole,
manufacturing production fell by 9½ per cent between 1920 and
1921. In the United Kingdom, earliest and worst affected, unemployment rose from 2 per cent to 11 per cent; in the United
States, where the fall in production was 20 per cent, unemployment reached 11½ per cent. Between 1920 and 1922 prices
fell by 27 per cent in the United Kingdom; over the same period
they rose by nearly fifteen times in Germany. Since conditions
immediately after the First World War were reckoned, in a classic
history of the period, to be 'on the whole not so bad as in 1946'
(Lewis, p. 16), the prospects at the end of the Second World War
were distinctly ominous. Paul Samuelson, who later wrote the
bestselling economics textbook published in the postwar years,
raised in 1943 the probability of a 'nightmarish combination of the
worst features of inflation and deflation', fearing that 'there would
be ushered in the greatest period of unemployment and industrial
dislocation which any economy has ever faced' (Samuelson, p. 51).
He was speaking, it should be remembered, about the United
States, which was relatively unscathed by hostilities.

The political precedents from the period around the end of the
First World War were equally suggestive of turbulence. Not only
was the Bolshevik revolution in Russia carried through and consolidated, but enormous social turmoil shook every major country.
There had been a real possibility at the end of the war that the
revolution against the imperial regime in Germany would follow
the same path as that in Russia. In Italy revolutionary workers had
occupied the factories in an explosive challenge to capitalist rule.
In the United Kingdom the level of industrial and political unrest
in the years after 1918 had been without parallel. In the United
States, Joseph Schumpeter, an eminent economist, summed up
the mood of alarm in 1945: 'The all but general opinion seems to
be that capitalist methods will be unequal to the task of reconstruction.' He regarded it as 'not open to doubt that the decay of
capitalist society is very far advanced' (Schumpeter, p. 120).

2. Behind the Chaos

This chapter documents the deep disorganization of the capitalist system at the end of the war and the resulting volatile situation that lay beneath both the celebrations of victory in some countries and the miseries brought by defeat in the others. The pattern of reconstruction proved to be the basis of the greatest boom in the history of capitalism. In 1945, however, no one knew how the process of reconstruction would proceed and under whose control it would be.

Even in Europe and Japan the fundamental problem for post-war recovery was not the physical destruction wrought by the war. As this chapter shows, destruction of the stock of industrial plant was comparatively minor. Nor were war casualties the major constraint on production. The war had certainly left very serious bottlenecks in the productive process, most importantly in fuel, transport and food, which would have catastrophic consequences if not removed. But they could be cleared away fairly rapidly if the available resources were mobilized with sufficient authority.

Much more serious for the long-term prospects of the capitalist system than the *physical* destruction was the challenge to its effective functioning as a *social* system. In the defeated countries the war had discredited the capitalist class: its association with the horrific consequences of fascism and war had undermined its authority in the political sphere and industrially. It could no longer control a government in the capital city nor the workers in the factories. At the same time, organized labour was enormously strengthened in the victorious countries. Everywhere, with gathering momentum, people were demanding radical social and economic improvements.

Moreover, it was not only the internal structure of many of the capitalist states which was in turmoil. The old hierarchy of nation states was overturned, the continued domination of the colonial world was under challenge, and capitalism was confronting a hostile social system, that of the USSR, whose prestige had been enormously increased by the war.

The means to produce

The prerequisites for producing goods in any social system are workers and the means of production (factories, equipment, machinery – the capital stock) for them to operate. Only if the war had destroyed a significant part of the labour force or capital stock would the capacity to produce have been seriously diminished. During the war, governments had tried to maintain morale by exaggerating the extent of damage inflicted on the enemy; airforces connived in order to obtain a bigger share of resources. Newsreels of flattened cities seemed to confirm the picture of massive destruction of plant and machinery. Yet, more dispassionate studies have shown that in most capitalist countries the capacity to produce was as great or greater at the end of the war as at the beginning. This claim is so contrary to popular ideas about the economic effects of the war, and so important in our interpretation of what happened subsequently, that it must be backed up in some detail.

Workers

Despite the appalling numbers of people killed and wounded, none of the advanced capitalist countries (ACCs) ended the war with a significantly reduced labour force. Three factors account for this. First was the 'natural' increase in the population of working age which exceeded casualties by a substantial margin everywhere except Germany. Second, wartime mobilization raised the proportion of the population of working age at work. In the United States civilian employment rose by 5 million between 1940 and 1945. Despite an 11 million expansion of the armed forces, male civilian employment fell by only 1 million as previously unemployed men took jobs. Female employment rose by 6½ million as women were encouraged to take jobs outside the home. In the United Kingdom increased female employment made up for 1 million of the 5 million men transferred to the forces. In Japan as many as 2 million extra women may have been employed. Many of these women, who under prewar conditions would not have looked for jobs, were available for postwar employment. In Germany fascist ideology dictated a far smaller increase in wome workers. Finally, at the end of the war huge influxes of people started moving west. By 1948, 8 million expellees and refugees from areas incorporated into Poland, Czechoslovakia and the

Soviet zone of Germany had flooded into Germany's Western zones. Six million refugees from Japan's Asian empire had also returned home, contributing to a rise of 15 per cent in Japan's labour force as compared to before the war. In the United States, the labour force had increased by a similar percentage. In Germany the labour force of the British and American zones rose by 7 per cent. In the United Kingdom the rise was about 5 per cent. France and Italy's number of workers remained more or less stable.

War damage

Industrial war damage was almost certainly heaviest in Japan where around one-quarter of the factory buildings and one-third of plant and equipment were destroyed. The incidence of the damage was very uneven. About one-seventh of electricity-generating and steel capacity was destroyed, but as much as six-sevenths of oil-refining capacity. In Germany during 1944 when air attacks were heaviest, about 6½ per cent of machine tools were damaged or destroyed, but most of them (one estimate is 90 per cent) were repaired at the time. Around 10 per cent or less of steel capacity appears to have been lost. The most careful estimate puts Germany's total war damage at 17½ per cent of the prewar capital stock.

In Italy the steel industry lost about one-quarter of its capacity and engineering 12 per cent, but destruction in most other sectors was put at only 4–5 per cent. The Bank of Italy estimated damage to the total capital stock at 8 per cent. In France, industry lost around 10 per cent of its capital stock, 15 per cent in engineering. War damage in the United Kingdom was described by the UN as negligible. From August 1940 to December 1941 when air raids were at their peak, only 1.7 per cent of machine tools was damaged or destroyed.

Investment

The damage inflicted by hostilities is only one aspect of the way in which the war affected the stock of means of production. Another is that much new plant and machinery was installed. The expansion of munitions production required heavy investment, as well as a diversion of capacity from civilian to military uses.

In Japan throughout the period 1939–44 private industrial investment ran at around double the rate of the mid-thirties. In

Germany between 1936 and 1943 the volume of investment in industry grew continuously to an unprecedented level. By 1945 this investment, allowing for normal scrapping of old equipment but not war damage, would have increased the capital stock by 38 per cent. At the beginning of 1945 34 per cent of equipment was five years old or less as compared to only 9 per cent in 1935.

In the United States investment grew rapidly during the early years of the war. The peak in 1941, however, still represented a lower level than that achieved in 1929, and it then declined and stayed at a rather low level (less than half the 1929 peak) for the remainder of the war. Investment in plant and machinery in the United Kingdom rose by nearly one-half between 1938 to 1940, but then declined to well below half the previous rate for the last three years of the war. In Italy a high rate of investment was recorded until 1942, after which it sank to very low levels. In France investment declined earlier, averaging only half the 1929 peak (or two-thirds the immediate prewar level) for the whole period 1940–4.

The change in the stock of equipment during the war depended on the net effect of additions, through investment, and losses, through war damage and scrapping. Estimates are at best rough and ready, but nevertheless indicate how the stock of machine tools and total means of production changed during the war period (Table 2.1).

Clearly engineering capacity increased substantially in many of the major countries despite war damage. Even in Britain, where the increase in the number of machine tools was quite small, the total engineering capital stock doubled. Numbers of machine tools are obviously a crude indicator. In Japan, in particular, shortage of materials led to deteriorating quality – one manufacturer put the life expectancy of machines produced in the last years of the war at only six to twelve months – and in France the average age of machine tools was twenty-five years, the more modern ones 'having taken the road to Germany' (Rioux, p. 35). But even by the end of the war only 15 per cent of Japanese machines were special-purpose and therefore hard to convert to peacetime production. In Germany many technical advances resulted from increased specialization, introduced to facilitate the mass-production techniques made necessary by the shortage of labour (especially skilled labour). Assembly-line production was extended in a variety of industries ranging from machine tools to furniture and clothing.

Table 2.1 Wartime changes in the stock of means of production[1]

Percentage change

	Machine tools	Total stock of fixed capital
USA	100	10
UK	15	0
France	5	n.a.
Italy	40	0
Germany	50	20
Japan	25	0

1. Figures show percentage change between 1938 and 1945 and are only very approximate.

Source: see Appendix.

Conversion to peacetime production proved less difficult than expected, despite the fact that engineering sectors were very heavily biased away from civilian production. In the United States, for example, by 1945 only 30 per cent of the industry's output was of the kind delicately titled '1939-type goods'. Other sectors inevitably suffered from the concentration on munitions. Perhaps the most dramatic example is the Japanese cotton industry where the number of spindles fell from 12 million to 2 million. War damage accounted only for 7 per cent of this decline; the rest resulted from scrapping due to lack of access to cotton imports and to markets. But in those countries for which data are available, it appears that the total capital stock in 1945 was at about the prewar level (Table 2.1).

Bottlenecks

This productive capacity could not be fully exploited until certain strategic bottlenecks were overcome. Workers had to have food, factories required fuel, and the transport system had to permit the movement of materials and finished goods.

Inland transport was very seriously dislocated due to bombing, especially in Germany. Less than 10 per cent of the German railways – which prewar had carried two-thirds of all goods transported – was still operational: 2395 rail bridges (including every one over the Rhine), 10,000 locomotives and more than 100,000 goods wagons had been destroyed. Less than 40 per cent of the remaining locomotives were immediately operational. But total stocks of locos and wagons were actually greater than before the war. Large numbers had been looted from elsewhere in Europe. In France also the railways were badly hit. The stock of locomotives was about three-quarters of the prewar level and less than half of the track was operational: 7500 bridges had been destroyed – for example, none remained over the Seine between Paris and the Channel. Italy had lost 10 per cent of its locomotives and around one-fifth of the wagon stock. In Japan railway losses were relatively light because the Allies had not seriously tried to paralyse the system through bombing. In the United States the railways had been very profitable during the war and were in good shape, having received priority for materials.

The deliberate creation of bottlenecks – destruction of bridges being the clearest example – could, when peace came, be reversed rapidly by diverting resources towards clearing them. By the first quarter of 1946 European railway traffic had regained its prewar level. Even in Germany 90 per cent of the main lines were operating within a year. The hard winter of 1946–7 brought a renewed crisis as the poorly maintained locomotives and rolling stock creaked under the strain of loads transferred from the frozen canals. A crash programme of repairs, instituted after that winter, succeeded in eliminating the transport problem, demonstrating that it was not a fundamental brake on recovery.

Shipping was essential to bring in to Europe and Japan urgently needed supplies. Yet construction in Europe and Japan had made up for only a small part of wartime sinkings. European shipping tonnage had been reduced by nearly 40 per cent and the Japanese merchant fleet was cut by more than 80 per cent. However US shipping capacity had trebled, practically offsetting European and Japanese losses. So the bottleneck in international transport lay not in the size of the shipping stock but in its ownership. Thus the difficulty for Europe and Japan was to find the dollars to pay for the shipping space.

The second major bottleneck was fuel. In the first quarter of 1946 European coal production was only 70 per cent of the prewar level. Here the major problem was not direct war damage but the deterioration of equipment run at full stretch during the war, combined with exhaustion of the miners who in many countries were being required to work on inadequate rations. Imports from the United States were at a very low level, due to transport bottlenecks in American ports. Again, lack of fuel was no longer a constraint after the winter of 1946–7. Coal production improved in Europe as manpower was encouraged into the pits. The flow of imports was also increased. By 1947 coal consumption reached nearly 90 per cent of the prewar level, and less than three years after the war the UN could claim that the European coal shortage had largely been overcome. In Japan coal production in November 1945 fell to less than the amount required to run the railways. By the end of 1947 production was back to the prewar level though well below the wartime peak. Productivity (output per worker) was still only one-third of the peak level, reflecting in part the incapacity of the government to reorganize the industry.

Food shortage not only killed tens of thousands, it also threatened to undermine production more generally through reducing workers' capacity to work. In the 'crop year' June 1945 to June 1946 European food production was only 60 per cent of the average prewar level, reflecting the cumulative effect of insufficient use of fertilizers, scarcity of agricultural labour, loss of livestock, deterioration of equipment and the weather. But again, these problems were remedied quite quickly, and in northern and western Europe agricultural production exceeded the prewar level in 1947–8, with food imports from outside Europe running at a similar rate to prewar. In Japan the postwar years yielded 'bumper harvests'; it was the lack of imports – such as rice and sugar, which provided one-fifth of prewar calories – that caused the food shortages. The government's inability to organize collection and distribution of food meant that the towns suffered most. In Tokyo in May 1946 calorie consumption was only 1350, less than two-thirds of the prewar level.

Capital and labour

The basic physical requirements for production were therefore available. But the reconstruction of a viable capitalist system required more than adequate supplies of workers and factories and a desperate need for their products. Capitalism is not a system geared to production of goods simply because they are needed; it is geared to production for profit. For production to yield a profit, the employers must be in a position to compel the working class to produce a surplus for them: workers must be made to produce goods worth more than the capitalists are obliged to pay them in wages. To secure production of this surplus the employers must be able to hold wages down to a level which yields them a profit. They must also control activity on the factory floor so as to set the speed at which production takes place, and when and how new technology is introduced. As a class the capitalists must also exercise sufficient political control to ensure that such improvements in conditions – or reforms – as the working class secures through political action do not challenge the employers' right to own the means of production and deploy their profits to their best advantage. A factory only becomes part of *capital* if its owner is able to hire workers, control their work and invest the profits received without fear of confiscation.

The domination exercised by the capitalist class over the working class, both in the factories and in political life, is the fundamental *social relationship* underlying the capitalist system. This social relationship was far more deeply threatened by the ravages of the war than was the physical productive structure.

The United States and the United Kingdom

In the United States the wartime boom had consolidated the increased strength of the organized working class which a wave of unionization in the 1930s had effected. Four million workers joined unions, bringing total membership up to 14 million by the end of the war.

During the war the trade union leadership had cooperated in a no-strike policy with compulsory arbitration to limit wage increases. The mine workers constituted an important exception; they struck four times in 1943 to break through the wage freeze. Elsewhere in industry wildcat strikes took place. A study of the Detroit motor plants reported that most of the strikes were protests against discipline, against company policies or against the sacking of one or more workers. In 1944 more strikes took place than in any previous year; the auto workers' union leader bemoaned the fact that strikes were destroying the union.

The working class gained substantially from the wartime boom. Between 1941 and 1944 the increase in average earnings in manufacturing, adjusted for inflation ('real' earnings), was 19 per cent and family incomes were further boosted by average hours of work rising from 40½ to 45, as well as by more married women working. Consumption per head had been prevented from rising by a sharp increase in tax and by rationing; but higher real incomes were reflected in high savings. The end of the war saw these gains threatened. Through loss of overtime and downgrading of workers the weekly wages of non-war workers decreased 10 per cent between the spring of 1945 and the winter of 1946; war workers were estimated to have lost 31 per cent and their take-home pay was 11 per cent down on the 1941 level.

Days occupied in strikes rose from around 1 million a month during the latter months of the war to 7–8 million in the last three months of 1945 to 20 million in January 1946 and 23 million in February when 175,000 electrical workers and 800,000 steel workers joined the 225,000 General Motors (GM) workers and nearly a million others out on strike. In all, 116 million days were lost in 1946, prompting the Bureau of Labor Statistics to comment that it was the most concentrated strike wave in the country's history. Glass workers, machinists in California, New England textile workers and the GM workers, all struck for more than a hundred days. The government seized half the country's oil-refining capacity, the packing houses, the railways (where the workers only returned after being threatened with the draft) and the coal mines.

The key struggle took place at General Motors where the union demanded that the company 'open the books' to justify its assertion that it could not pay the 30 per cent claim – 'the 40-hour week at 48 hours' pay'. In the event the strikers secured a little over half the claim and fought off GM's attempt to secure union guarantees of no opposition to speedups and of absolutely no strikes. But the Ford management soon set the pattern, gaining the unrestricted right to hire and fire, promote and demote, fix production schedules, and discipline strikers and others charged with violating company rules.

Profits were high at the end of the war. In 1945 the share of profits in the value of output was 22 per cent. Since this measure will be used dozens of times in the course of this book it is important to make clear what it signifies. Out of every $100 of net output produced – that is, output after setting aside a sum to cover the wear and tear of fixed capital equipment – $22 went to the employers and $78 to the working class. Another way of visualizing this distribution of production is in terms of labour expended: out of every 100 days worked, 22 were devoted to producing the surplus for the employers (luxury goods, new investment goods) while the rest were producing the wage goods for the working class.

Even this is an oversimplification, and never more so than during wartime when the government bought nearly half of total production. To finance this spending, taxes had risen enormously: about 60 per cent of corporate profits were taken in taxation in 1945 as compared to 8 per cent in 1929. Thus, *after* taxation, the share of profits was actually 9 per cent in 1945 compared to 15 per cent in 1929, the peak prewar year for profits.

But employers are not primarily concerned with the share of profits in the value of output. Its main importance to them is as a determinant of the *rate of profit*, the percentage return on each $100 invested in plant and equipment, in stocks of materials and so forth. This rate of profit depends not only on the profit share, the ratio of profits to sales, but also on the value of output compared to the value of capital invested. In 1945 about $100 output was being produced for each $100 of capital invested; in 1929 around $66 of output was being produced for each $100 of capital invested. So, despite the fact that after taxation employers were receiving a smaller profit share on sales, the rate of profit on capital invested was boosted by the high level of sales and it was about the same level in 1945 as in 1929.

The high level of taxation of profits reflected the need to finance the war effort, and the fact that the employers had to be seen to be contributing a 'fair' share. The prospective ending of hostilities meant that this burden would certainly be lightened. But, as already pointed out, there was almost general agreement in the United States that the reduction of military spending would rapidly lead to a slump.

Despite these fears, US business strongly opposed an explicit government commitment to full employment, arguing that it would destroy private enterprise. A proposed Full Employment Bill was watered down to become the 1946 Employment Act. The right to 'useful, remunerative, regular and full-time employment' became the 'responsibility of the federal government to . . . promote free enterprise . . . under which there will be afforded useful employment for those who are willing and seeking to work'. One senator admitted that the bill simply 'promised anyone needing a job the right to go out and look for work' (quoted Apple, pp. 11, 12).

The level of share prices is an indication of the gloomy view taken of future profits – the value of a share depends on the stream of dividends expected to be paid on it. The level of share prices in 1945 was only a little over one-half that of 1929, and well below even that for 1930 when the Great Depression was well under- way. A strengthened working class determined to defend wartime gains, faced by a capitalist class anxious about preserving profits in difficult postwar circumstances, contained the possibility of serious confrontation. Months before the war ended, the mine workers had accepted a substantial pay offer only after the government had temporarily taken over the mines.

In the United Kingdom the challenge posed by organized labour was felt more on the political than the industrial plane. Not that industrial strength had declined: membership of unions had risen by about one-third during the war to bring it up to 8 million, around 45 per cent of the work force. The authority of the trade unions was officially recognized by their being heavily embroiled in the execution of wartime planning, paying out unemployment benefit for the Ministry of Labour, for example, and cooperating in the allocation of labour to individual firms. On the shop floor the power of workers was considerably increased by the strong demand for labour. In the Coventry munitions factories, man- agement frequently negotiated contracts with elected repre- sentatives of sections of workers to produce a certain amount of output. These sections would distribute the work and discipline workers collectively; removing these tasks from foremen and supervisors meant they became 'more concerned with coordination of production flows than with the maintenance of managerial authority' (Friedman, p. 213).

So long as production was high, and buoyant profits were guaranteed by the 'cost-plus' system of awarding munitions con- tracts (the share of profit in the value of output was at the same level as in 1938), enhanced shopfloor strength posed no particular threat to management. It was prepared to cede some measure of shopfloor control in return for a guaranteed high level of pro- duction. Average earnings in real terms were 24 per cent higher in 1944 than in 1938, but this was entirely due to extra overtime and bonuses. Weekly wage *rates* had no more than kept up with the increased cost of living. The trade union leadership had accepted the continuation of the wartime Order 1305 which made arbitration of wage disputes compulsory and virtually eliminated the right to strike. But if the much-feared postwar recession were to cut heavily into overtime and bonuses, there was no guarantee that the trade union leadership could hold back the shop floor. Such unease was clearly set out in a leader in the *Economist*:

'Whichever political party is proved, in a fortnight's time, to have won the general election, it is becoming clear that a period of labour unrest lies ahead. Strikes in transport undertakings and "go slow" movements at the docks are signs of a troubled mood. There is no need to be alarmist; nothing like the open industrial war of the uneasy post-Armistice months after the last war is to be expected. But at a time when the fullest effort is still demanded from skeleton staffs after the immediate incentive has passed, when manpower shortages are, for the moment, intensified rather than relaxed, when the first reductions from high wartime rates of pay are beginning to appear – this is hardly the time to expect serene and unbroken industrial peace. If the Conservative Government continues in office and gives an appearance of lack of sympathy with what the workers regard as their just grievances, there might be an epidemic of "grudge strikes". And if a Labour Government takes office, then – if all British and foreign precedents are followed – there is likely to be even more industrial unrest, not indeed to coerce the workers' government, but to assist in breaking down resistance to its policy' (14 July 1945).

In the event the election produced a landslide majority for a Labour government committed to a radical programme. This included:

- the restoration of trade union rights, lost in the Trade Disputes Act of 1927 (contracting 'out' rather than 'in' for payments of the political levy to the Labour Party and the right of civil service unions to affiliate to the Trades Union Congress);
- 'a tremendous overhaul, a programme of modernization, and the re-equipment of land, factories, machinery, schools and social services';
- 'drastic policies of replanning, keeping a firm constructive hand on the whole productive machinery';
- that 'Labour will not tolerate freedom to exploit others, to pay poor wages, or to push up prices for private profit';
- 'a firm public hand on industry in order to get jobs for all';
- public ownership of fuel and power, in land, transport, iron and steel;

- public supervision of monopolies and controls;
- land planning and a major housing programme;
- implementation of the 1944 Education Act and the raising of the school leaving age to sixteen as soon as possible;
- introduction of the national health service;
- extension of social insurance.

This series of reforms promised improved social conditions for the working class. But they would clearly be expensive. The effective taxation rate on company profits had risen during the war from around one-quarter to one-half. While business was calling for the immediate abolition of this extra tax as military spending was reduced, the chance of achieving it appeared seriously threatened by the need to finance social reforms.

Nationalization of some industries, and a wide-ranging series of controls over the rest, promised a much-diminished freedom to allocate capital where it was most profitable. The capitalist class had accepted many such restrictions during the war, as necessary to mobilize the resources for a project which it supported (fighting Hitler). In any case the wartime planning and controls, at the industry level, were carried out by representatives of the big firms. To accept similar restrictions from a Labour government in order to mobilize resources for a massive improvement in social welfare, under conditions in which it might not be possible to exclude trade unions from a say in the details of the planning, was a much more threatening proposition.

In the United Kingdom and United States, then, growth in the strength of organized labour flowed fundamentally from the full-employment conditions generated during wartime. It was reflected in demands for reforms in the fields of social welfare, employment and wages, and channelled through trade union or social-democratic party structures which did not pose any immediate threat to the continuation of capitalist domination of the economy. What was in doubt was the extent to which the boom conditions, necessary to satisfy these aspirations, could be maintained. If the economies faltered and slump conditions returned, demands for the economic controls proposed by Labour in the United Kingdom to be toughened could grow into a real threat to capitalism. And, in such a context, what could guarantee that the US labour movement would be immune to socialist contagion?

Japan and Germany

In these countries the threat was of a very different kind. With the regimes discredited after their catastrophic defeat, big business discredited for its support for those regimes, the people suffering terrible privations, and the old reformist leaderships in a weak position to reassert control, the situation apparently contained many of the ingredients for revolutionary changes. But there were formidable obstacles to such changes. The organized labour movement had been smashed years before, both politically and industrially. Workers' organizations and parties had to reconstitute themselves from scratch and establish their authority among workers. State power was in the hands of powerful occupying forces, committed to restoring bourgeois rule in one form or another. Initially, at least, they were regarded as much as liberators from fascist oppression as a foreign occupation. Besides, the terrible physical conditions in the aftermath of defeat demanded that all efforts be devoted to survival, focusing attention on immediate tasks rather than on broad political change. Such a complicated situation passed no straightforward death-sentence on capitalism. But even in Japan, where the historical basis for a challenge to capitalism seemed weakest, there was soon cause for alarm.

The Japanese labour movement had no lengthy tradition of broad organization. The trade unions, whose peak prewar membership was less than half a million, had been wiped out in the late 1930s. There are no reported cases of Japanese workers taking action against their employers or the regime before the surrender, or even in the interregnum before the occupying forces arrived, though in one or two cases Chinese or Korean forced labourers rose up in revolt. But as soon as the occupying powers made trade unions legal again, membership spread like wildfire. Within four months it reached double the prewar peak.

Within a few weeks of the ending of the war the first 'production control' struggle took place at the *Yomiuri* newspaper. Its militaristic president refused to accede to workers' demands for better conditions, democratization of the company's organization and acceptance of responsibility for militarism by senior officials. The workers, both editorial and printing staff, decided to produce the paper themselves: 'If we do that we don't have to worry about bankrupting the company. And if we gain the support of the readers by putting out an excellent newspaper, then we can reconstruct the *Yomiuri* as a democratic paper' (quoted Moore, p. 51). After publishing the paper for several weeks they won an agreement which included the resignation of the president, and formation of a management council on which they had equal representation. This latter position they used to continue the paper's exposure of government incompetence and business manipulations.

Workers were being laid off on a huge scale. In January 1946 sacked employees of the Itabashi Arsenal in Tokyo demanded the handing over of food and other goods stored there which were being effectively looted by businessmen to whom the government was selling them off at knockdown prices. Faced with a determined Communist Party leadership, and slogans such as 'People's control over the distribution of rationed food' and 'Kick out the military men: send them to the coal mines', the military commander was forced to hand over large quantities of food. From this springboard a regional Democratic Council on Food was formed with 300 organizations claiming 1½ million members. It was chaired by the *Yomiuri* union chairman. In the same month 50,000 demonstrated to welcome back from exile the communist leader Nosaka; 20,000 surrounded the prime minister's residence demanding the resignation of the Tokyo police chief and of the whole cabinet, which was composed of old right-wing politicians acting under the Occupation's orders.

Production control struggles were spreading rapidly at this time. They varied considerably in the extent to which the workers challenged management's rights. In the case of the Kanto electric power company, although workers elected by the union took over the jobs of senior management, 'actions which needed the decision of the president were all forwarded to the president and disposed of with the approval of the president' (Yamamoto, 1972, p. 69). On the Keisei railway in Tokyo, workers collected no fares for the first three days of their struggle. Management was at first intransigent in the face of union demands for a big pay increase, shorter hours, union recognition, equal union participation in a management council to run the firm and dismissal of corrupt supervisors. Management gave in, however, after a union decision to pay out very large wage bonuses from the fares now being collected. Workers at a Mitsui mine in Hokkaido decided to follow the *Yomiuri* and Keisei examples and engage in production control rather than a strike because 'the workers themselves must shoulder the burden of industrial reconstruction in Japan' (quoted Moore, p. 60). Despite reducing working hours from twelve to eight, output was doubled. At a Mitsubishi mine nearby, a 'People's Court' arraigned the management in a ten-hour 'People's Trial' where rank-and-file miners and their families denounced management for feeding their pets better than the workers. Improvements in pay and conditions, recognition of the union and formation of a management council were typical settlements. By March 1946 the number of production control struggles underway had built up to nearly forty.

These developments did not add up to an articulated challenge to the restoration of bourgeois rule in Japan. But they did suggest the possibility that the social relations underlying capitalism could come under severe strain.

As the Allied armies advanced through Germany they frequently found factories and mines in the hands of plant-based workers' committees. These had sometimes driven out SS units which had been ordered to destroy the plants. Work restarted within days and the provisional workers' committees procured food, clothing and housing and were the point of contact with the military authorities. Broader antifascist committees (antifas) sprang up in many towns. In Bremen the antifas circularized all the local plants calling for the formation of antifascist workers' councils where this had not already happened, their recognition by the management and the removal of all Nazis. On occasions antifas arrested notorious local Nazis, confiscated food hoards, and so forth.

The occupation authorities banned the antifas, depriving them of facilities, and refused requests for the open revival of the old political parties – a stance maintained until the autumn of 1945. The workers' factory councils were in most cases the only labour movement bodies allowed to operate. These works councils were frequently in effective control of the plants, the management having disappeared or been discredited. Their immediate tasks were practical: keeping the plants going and looking after the workers' welfare. In the disorganized conditions this required contact between the works councils within towns – one of the few reported attempts at cooperation beyond a local basis took place between works councils in four Ruhr towns in 1945, and was exclusively concerned with organizing barter transactions between the firms.

These practical, but extremely pressing, questions dominated their activity, but the councils also made widespread demands for nationalization, especially of war industries. In a conference held in November 1945 in the Ruhr, the foremen from the coal industry demanded the expropriation without compensation of the mine owners, and the transfer of the mines to the regional government. Krupp workers demanded in a memorandum to the military governor that Krupp's plants be expropriated and retooled for peaceful purposes. Similar demands were put forward by workers in other major plants.

Memories of the disastrous divisions in the trade union movement before the war led to strong demands for unity. Representatives of the old trade unions in Cologne, meeting before the US army arrived, called for the formation of one union, with industrial branches. This call was endorsed in September by a meeting of union representatives from all the Rhine towns. In the Hanover area a unified local union organization was actually formed soon after the war ended.

A parallel desire for unity existed on the political front. In Hamburg, in the summer of 1945, the military government's refusal to allow political parties to reconstitute themselves led to the setting up of a Socialist Free Union. It demanded full employment, state control of key industries, nationalization of the land, trade union control of labour exchanges, state control of foreign trade, extensive denazification and a new democratic constitution. Within five weeks it was reported to have attracted 50,000 workers. Social democratic leaders persuaded the military government that it was politically suspicious and it was dissolved. The *Economist* (19 January 1946) noted that the union 'had become too strongly political in character'.

In the early days after the defeat, the German Communist Party (KPD) was a major force, especially in the Ruhr where half the members of works councils in the mines also belonged to the KPD and where, by the end of 1945, its membership is said to have reached 50,000.

In fact the KPD's programme was less radical than contemporary Social Democratic Party (SPD) statements. It called for the expropriation of 'Nazi bosses' and war criminals, the breaking up of the nobility's and the Junkers' large estates and the nationalization of utilities such as electricity, gas and water. But reconstruction was to take place on the principle of 'completely unrestricted development of free trade and private entrepreneurial initiative on the basis of private ownership' (quoted Graf, p. 43). It was no more radical than the Christian Democrats' (CDU) programme which actually called for state ownership of natural resources and 'key monopoly industries', as well as for the elimination of large-scale capitalist enterprises. Such was the strength of the reaction against fascism that even the CDU contained a radical wing which was able to commit it to the abolition of capitalism because it had not been 'adequate for the vital national and social interests of the German people' (quoted Graf, p. 50).

Italy and France

On any scale of postwar dislocation Italy and France occupied an intermediate position between the Anglo-Saxon 'victors' and the main defeated powers. France had suffered its defeat five years earlier; and Italy ended the war fighting the Germans. But it was in these countries that the position of the capitalist class was most threatened. Both contained mass resistance movements. Their status as cobelligerents also made an extended period of Anglo-American occupation much more problematic.

In Italy the working class played a leading role in the resistance, first to Mussolini's government until its fall in August 1943, and then to the puppet regime in the north and its German masters. As early as March 1943 a strike wave began at Fiat in Turin and spread to Pirelli and other factories in Milan, gaining substantial wage increases. A general strike in Milan at the end of March saw workers' councils set up in the factories. In August Badoglio's government, which replaced Mussolini's, was forced under threat of further strikes to legalize these councils. In November-December 1943 a further strike wave started in Turin, halting production for nine days. On 1 March 1944, a mass general strike was called in the German-occupied areas. Perhaps as many as a million workers came out. In Milan, many industrialists agreed to pay workers for the days they struck, despite German orders to the contrary. 'Premature holidays' were declared in some places to circumvent the strike.

As the Allied armies moved up Italy the resistance in the north, directed by the multiparty Committees of National Liberation, struggled against the German occupation. More than 150,000 resistance fighters tied down as many as fourteen Axis divisions during 1944. Observers agreed that 'workers were in the forefront of the actual fighting' (*Economist*, 9 June 1945).

Striking workers played an important role in the liberation of Genoa, Milan and Turin. Factory liberation committees helped to preserve plant from destruction or removal by the Germans. The Committee for National Liberation issued a decree before the Milan insurrection calling for the organization of management councils for firms, composed equally of owners and workers. The councils each nominated a 'works commissar' and a technical manager. In Turin a general strike was in progress a week before the insurrection. On May Day of 1945 a Communist Party leader demanded that workers, clerks and technicians participate in the administration of production 'on a level of absolute equality with the owners' (quoted Dalzell, p. 557). Communists and socialists were in a majority in the resistance, and constituted an overwhelming majority among workers. The following quotation gives a flavour of how precarious and unstable the position appeared at the end of 1945:

'The Italian employer today has genuine grievances. He is forbidden to dismiss his workmen unless they were active Fascists, were taken on after June 30, 1943, or have other resources at their disposal – this at a time when Italian industry is working at about 25 per cent of its average peacetime capacity. Labour's output is poor because the workers are hungry and tired; they expect to be provided with cheap food and clothes by their factory for the good reason that food and clothing can only be purchased at quite fantastic prices. Finally, the employer resents the "councils of management" which have been appointed in every big factory by the local Committee of National Liberation. These councils are intended to ensure that the notions of anti-Fascist patriots of Resistance days shall not now be flouted by the captains of industry; but it is certain that they concern themselves with politics instead of confining themselves to technical considerations. . . .

'The wage crisis has been chronic in Italy ever since the liberation last spring. The employers are right when they say that further wage increases only accelerate the inflation of the currency, but the workers are right when they insist that the wages paid at present are less than half what the barest subsistence level would dictate' (*Economist*, 24 November 1945).

In France the communists were recognized even by non-sympathizers as the most dynamic part of the resistance. In Paris the liberation took the form of an insurrection, described by Albert Camus as follows:

'Four or five thousand men, with a few hundred firearms between them, came out in accordance with a well worked-out plan, in order to hold up the retreating remnants of the German 7th Army. After less than a week 50,000 Parisians were on the barricades, in the districts of the Revolution (i.e. the working-class areas), and were fighting with arms captured from the enemy' (quoted Werth, p. 218). The National Council of the Resistance published a Charter committing those active in the movement to secure a formidable programme of social reform. It demanded 'the removal from the management of France's economy of the great economic and financial feudal forces'; the intensification of production in accordance with a plan to be decided upon by the state, after consultation with all those concerned with this production; and the nationalization of 'all the great monopolized means of production which are a product of common labour; of the sources of power; of mineral wealth; of insurance companies; and of the big banks'; a share of responsibility for the workers in the economic direction of enterprises; a guaranteed wage to bring 'security, dignity and the possibility of a fully human existence'; a complete plan of social security; adequate old-age pensions; the fullest educational possibilities for all French children, in accordance with their ability and wholly independent of their parents' social or financial position (quoted Werth, pp. 222–3). In Marseilles the Commissaire de la République appointed from Paris began to implement these measures, applying a regional programme of nationalization. Many firms were being run by workers' committees which took over what they regarded as collaborationist property. The first election, in October 1945, saw the left win more than half the vote: the communists 26.1 per cent and the socialists 24.8 per cent.

It is hard at this distance to capture the real alarm that swept the capitalist class after Hitler's defeat. A quotation from the *Economist* expresses it well:

'The collapse of that New Order imparted a great revolutionary momentum to Europe. It stimulated all the vague and confused but nevertheless radical and socialist impulses of the masses. Significantly, every programme with which the various Resistance groups throughout Europe emerged from the Underground contained demands for nationalization of banks and large-scale industries; and these programmes bore the signatures of Christian Democrats as well as of Socialists and Communists. The maxim of

French Socialism in the nineteenth century was Proudhon's "La propriété c'est le vol". The corresponding maxim, during the resistance era, was "La propriété c'est la collaboration'" (1 December 1945).

International relations

The smooth functioning of the capitalist system depends fundamentally on the establishment of domination in work places by capital over labour. But since capitalist production takes place within a system of nation states, it also requires that the relations between countries assume a reasonably ordered and stable shape. Between capitalist countries this means a trade and payments system within which the international division of labour can develop. Because they depend upon worldwide imported materials, the advanced countries must also have a relationship with the rest of the world that allows access, under favourable terms, to these sources of supply. Finally, the existence since 1917 of a noncapitalist part of the world poses the problem of containing the latent antagonism between the capitalist and non-capitalist blocs. These two blocs represent the distorted image, on the international plane, of domestic antagonism between the classes. The war had profoundly dislocated all these dimensions of the international system.

Relations between the advanced countries

During the war the major capitalist powers had fought for markets with tanks rather than tariffs. World trade had shrunk and was concentrated in basic materials and munitions. In 1946, world exports were three-quarters of their prewar (1937) level, and less than 60 per cent if the United States is excluded. Trade within Europe was running at less than half the prewar rate. The pattern of production had been shifted towards armaments, leading to a gross overexpansion of engineering and a rundown of such consumer industries as textiles. This would make it difficult to establish a new international division of labour once the web of bilateral agreements under which trade took place by the end of the war had been dismantled.

The most important change, however, was in the relative economic strengths of the major capitalist powers. In the autumn of 1945 industrial production in Germany and Japan was less than one-fifth of the prewar level, whereas in the United States it was one-half greater. But appearances were deceptive to some extent, reflecting more the immediate postwar dislocations in the defeated countries than a longer-run reduction in their capacity to produce relative to that of the United States. Indeed, the total stock of means of production appears to have actually risen more in Germany than in the United States, although the stock of machine tools expanded more in the United States than in Germany, and much more than in Japan (Table 2.1).

But while the potential capacity to produce, after overcoming bottlenecks, was very high in Germany and Japan, it was unclear whether they would be permitted to use this capacity to produce for world markets. This decision rested in the hands of the Allies.

The United States' relative economic position among the Allies had enormously strengthened. Its capital stock, and especially the stock of machine tools, had expanded markedly as compared with the United Kingdom and France. The immediate position was of sharper contrast still. At the beginning of 1946 industrial production in Northern Europe (excluding Germany) varied from two-thirds of the prewar level to around the same as prewar, while in the United States it was 50 per cent higher. And even that level of European production was heavily dependent on imports from the United States. These had doubled as compared with prewar. Europe was running a payments deficit with the United States of $4 billion in 1946, eight times as much as in 1938. The increased imports were mainly of food and manufactures (especially vehicles); materials imports were only one-third greater than prewar.

European and Japanese dependence on US imports emphasizes the crucial role the United States would have to play in any new financial system. The United States had not piled up huge claims on its allies. The $35 billion aid it extended through Lend-Lease was in the form of grants rather than loans. But more than two-thirds of the world's gold reserves were held in Fort Knox, while the United States' prewar rival for financial dominance, the United Kingdom, was in a much-weakened position. It had disposed of many foreign assets and incurred large debts with its former colonies in the Sterling Area.

In the aftermath of the war, then, the United States was in a dominating economic position among the advanced capitalist countries. The immediate figures for production and trade reflected the chaos elsewhere and so exaggerated the extent of such dominance. But whether or not the other capitalist countries would recover rapidly and could use all their capacity depended to a very substantial extent on the policies pursued by the United States.

The colonies

The war had given a major impetus to the struggle for colonial freedom, especially in those countries invaded by the Japanese. Much the most important case was China which, although formally independent, had been dominated for decades by imperialism. The collapse of Japanese control over much of China made it likely that the fundamental antagonism between Chiang Kai-shek's nationalist forces and Mao's communists would erupt into civil war. External support was strongly in favour of Chiang. The Americans were backing him and the USSR also signed a treaty with him, agreeing to give aid only to his government and to hand over to him Chinese territory liberated from the Japanese by the Red Army. But China's future remained problematic.

Elsewhere in the Far East, the colonial powers (Britain, France and Holland) had to cope with the strengthening of the nationalist forces in Malaya, Indo-China and Indonesia which the Japanese had encouraged. Initially the Japanese had pretended to offer liberation from imperialism. When in retreat, they further fomented nationalist struggles in order to disrupt the reimposition of the old imperial order. The *Economist* warned: 'However spurious the present Japanese-sponsored uprisings may be, nationalism is a profound and deeply rooted force in the Far East and it must be satisfied' (6 October 1945).

At first, it seems, there was little anxiety that a change in colonial status would limit economic relations with the advanced countries. Unilever, heavily involved in India, where the move to independence was by then accepted as inevitable, 'appears to have had remarkably few fears about the effects of Indian independence and took appropriately few precautions' (Fieldhouse, p. 185). Its first internal report on the subject in 1944 waved aside calls for Indian ownership of basic industries and Indian access to foreign companies' technology as 'more irritating than harmful, and transitory than permanent' (quoted Fieldhouse, p. 185). It assumed that India would retain close commercial and trading links with Britain.

The United States believed that colonial powers should prepare their colonies for independence, which should be granted 'progressively' and at the first 'practicable' moment. This liberal approach was clearly aimed at securing for US business access to natural resources on the same terms as the old colonial countries. Such a policy of heading off the more radical nationalist movements by concessions, while pressing for the breakdown of the exclusivity of colonial economic relations, might well be the best strategy for the capitalist system as a whole. The old colonial powers, however, would suffer from the loss of economic control and would face the difficulty of placating white settlers and limiting the radicalism of the nationalist movements.

Relations with the USSR

'Somebody . . . made an awful mistake in bringing about a situation where Russia was permitted to come out of a war with the power she will have. . . . England should never have permitted Hitler to rise. . . . The German people under a democracy would have been a far superior ally than Russia. . . . There is too much difference in the ideologies of the United States and Russia to work out a long-term programme of cooperation' (quoted Yergin, p. 118). This remark, made in a private conversation by US secretary of state Byrnes in the summer of 1945, sums up the problems posed for the capitalist world by the enormously enhanced power of the USSR.

Truman, who became US president in 1945, had bluntly stated in 1941: 'If we see that Germany is winning the war we ought to help Russia, and if Russia is winning we ought to help Germany, and in that way let them kill as many as possible' (quoted Horowitz, p. 61). Although the United States had not followed this policy, the USSR had nevertheless borne the brunt of Hitler's onslaught for years.

From the beginning of 1941 most of Germany's forces were engaged in fighting the USSR. When the long-delayed second front was opened, and at the peak of Anglo-American military involvement, the Russians still confronted almost 60 per cent of German divisions. Even in early 1945 the British and Americans were desperately appealing for the USSR to launch its winter offensive in order to relieve the pressure on their forces from Germany's drive into the Ardennes.

Although the devastation suffered was vast, with perhaps 20 million killed, the USSR was not fought to a standstill. By 1945 industrial production was running at its prewar level and the Red Army had been transformed into an enormous fighting machine. It controlled much of Eastern Europe and substantial parts of what had been Japan's mainland empire. Stalin summed up the implications in a conversation with Yugoslav communist leaders in the summer of 1945: 'This war is not as in the past. Whoever occupies a territory also imposes on it his own social system. Everyone imposes his own system as far as his army can reach' (quoted Djilas, 1977, p. 437).

Churchill had indeed agreed a division of 'spheres of influence' with Stalin in Moscow in October 1944 – Romania: 90 per cent for the USSR; Greece: 90 per cent for Britain (in cooperation with the United States); Bulgaria: 75 per cent for the Russians; Hungary and Yugoslavia: 50 per cent for the Russians. Significantly, Stalin also agreed to Churchill's request that the Soviet Union should 'soft-pedal the Communists in Italy and not stir them up' (quoted Yergin, p. 60).

But this sphere of influence agreement left many questions unanswered. If Stalin was right about armies imposing their social systems, as his capitalist allies feared, where did this leave Yugoslavia over which the USSR and Britain were supposed to share influence 50:50? Were part-socialist, part-capitalist countries possible? Moreover, the United States was not a party to the carve-up between Churchill and Stalin. Churchill told Stalin that it was 'better to express these things in diplomatic terms and not to use the phrase "dividing into spheres" because the Americans might be shocked' (quoted Yergin, p. 60). Many in the US administration remained unreconciled to Soviet domination of Eastern Europe, and the US government argued with the Russians throughout the second half of 1945 about the future of the governments of Poland, Romania and Bulgaria, ignoring the fact that 'they had their own new spheres in Italy and Japan where the Soviets had agreed to give them a free hand' (Yergin, p. 124). The future of Germany, divided into zones of occupation, was also highly uncertain. The USSR immediately pressed for the implementation of an earlier agreement specifying $20 billions of reparations from Germany. In dealing with the USSR, the Americans' confidence was greatly boosted by the 'successful' use of the atomic bombs. This had not only ended the war in Japan, but also removed the need to involve the USSR in a frontal assault on Japan, which would have strengthened Russia's position in the area.

In summary, the prospect of a redivision of the world into relatively stable spheres of influence was clouded by uncertainties. Where would the dividing lines be drawn? How would the social system develop in the Soviet sphere (with important implications for capitalist access to its markets)? How would the USSR use its influence with the greatly strengthened Communist parties in Western Europe?

The United States would clearly play a decisive role in settling these questions. It was bound to be the dominating capitalist power for some years and to shape the new trade and payments system. US occupation policy would control the fate of Japan and dominate that of Germany. Its decisions over aid to Western Europe would strongly influence the pattern of recovery there. Its attitude to the USSR would dominate one side of whatever new relationship would emerge between capitalism and the Eastern bloc. US attitudes towards the old colonial powers would shape any new forms of economic domination of the old colonies by the advanced countries. Conversely, the attitude taken by the Soviet Union would, through its influence on the Communist parties in Europe and Japan, deeply affect what happened there. The next chapter outlines the basic policies pursued by the two great powers.

3. Great Power Policies

Uncle Sam out for himself

The fundamental interests of US capital were to secure the largest possible markets for US exports and freedom to invest abroad wherever was most profitable, particularly where that was necessary to ensure access to raw materials. This was the cornerstone of postwar US policy. The reasons why are clear: fear of postwar depression, the consequent need for export markets to maintain demand and profits, and the memory of the impact of trade restrictions in the 1930s. So in 1943 a US State Department report pointed out that, 'A great expansion in the volume of international trade after the war will be essential to the attainment of full and effective employment in the United States as elsewhere' (quoted Kolko, p. 252). Secretary to the treasury Morgenthau told a Senate Committee in 1945 that America required a world system 'in which international trade and international investment can be carried on by businessmen on business principles' (quoted Kolko and Kolko, p. 16). A year later, assistant secretary of state Clayton said: 'We need markets – big markets – around the world in which to buy and sell. We ask no special privileges in any of those markets' (quoted ibid., p. 13). 'Special privileges' were hardly needed, of course, given the productive and financial power of US capital.

Precisely what policy towards Western Europe and Japan flowed from these objectives was less obvious. At one extreme was the option of exploiting to the hilt the position of economic dominance achieved by the United States. This would be reflected in insistence on absolute freedom of penetration of US goods, with no attempt to help the reconstruction of production inside these countries. At the other extreme the United States could concentrate on the fastest possible recovery in these economies on the grounds that this would be the best guarantee of an expanding market for US trade and investment in the long term. Both options carried their own risks. If the economies of Western Europe and Japan failed to recover rapidly, the market for US goods would stagnate. More threatening still, popular demands for effective policies would strengthen the appeal of socialist measures leading perhaps to the abolition of capitalism itself in one or more of these countries. The USA might be left with little or nothing to dominate. On the other hand giving maximum aid in order to hasten recovery would be expensive. It would involve accepting limitations on access to foreign markets for US products which competed too strongly with domestic industry. In the longer run it would risk building up industrial rivals to the point where they posed a serious competitive threat to US industry.

That the United States would use its economic might to gain concessions was clear enough from its dealings with the United Kingdom early on in the war. In February 1942 the United States insisted that the proposal to give Lend-Lease aid to its allies included agreement on the 'elimination of all forms of discriminatory treatment in international commerce'. In other words, eventual free entry of US goods should be guaranteed. Moreover, the US government decided that the amount of aid given should be enough to keep the United Kingdom's gold and dollar balances above the $600 million mark, to ensure some stability, but not enough to push the reserves above the $1 billion mark which would leave the United Kingdom with too much independence.

In terms of the two extreme options for US policy described above, the thrust adopted during the final years of the war and the early years thereafter was definitely towards taking full advantage of US dominance to achieve the most advantageous immediate position for US capital. This was felt most quickly in Europe and Japan where US aid was limited largely to emergency relief, without systematic planning for rebuilding production. Wherever possible, conditions thought favourable to US business were imposed on recipient countries, including pressure to give up colonial markets. In Germany and Japan the occupation authorities made little or no attempt to stimulate the process of economic recovery. While this had a perfectly understandable long-term political and military justification (fear of the resurrection of militaristic regimes), there was a strong undercurrent of more immediate economic self-interest (fear of renewed economic competition). Finally, the plans for the postwar world monetary and trading system drawn up by the United States enshrined both the central role of the US dollar and the principles of reducing balance of payments and trade restrictions. These principles could hardly be put into effect immediately, given the disorganized state of Europe and Japan, but the plans still represented an important registration of what the USA regarded as its vital interests and the extent to which it was prepared to use its economic muscle to further them.

Aid to Europe and Japan

The original US proposals for the postwar economy, released early in 1943, had contained a plan for a 'Bank for Reconstruction of the United and Associated Nations'. It was to have capital of $10 billion – half paid in immediately by members in gold and local currencies – and it could borrow extensively so that its total resources would have been much more than this capital. Its main purpose was 'to supply the huge volume of capital to the United and Associated Nations that will be needed for reconstruction, for relief and for economic recovery'.

Conservatives in the US administration succeeded in restricting the scope of the plans for the Bank by the time they were circulated. The British were keen to downplay it as well, since they expected to be making contributions rather than receiving loans. As agreed at the conference on international payments held at Bretton Woods in 1944, the Bank was limited in its lending to its nominal capital of $10 billion. Only one-tenth of its capital was paid in, and only the US contribution and one-tenth of the rest was in gold or dollars. So the Bank was left with only $¾ billion of resources, which could be used to purchase US commodities, plus what it could persuade the New York money market to lend. By the middle of 1947 all it had lent out was $92 million out of a $250 million loan to France; it was not till 1953 that it had lent out $1 billion.

The other body which seemed likely, at its inception, to play a major role in providing reconstruction aid was the United Nations Relief and Rehabilitation Administration. However, before the end of the war Congress forced rehabilitation to be defined as equivalent to relief, so that UNRRA's role as a provider of medium-term reconstruction aid was ruled out.

In the event the United States made some $10½ billions available during 1946 and 1947 in the form of grants and long-term government loans. This involved a series of pragmatic arrangements including Lend-Lease settlement, UNRRA and the

Anglo-US and Franco-US loans. Only a fraction was in the form of grants. In 1946 these dollars financed nearly half of Europe's imports from the United States (Chart 5.1), and considerably more in 1947. More than two-thirds of total Japanese imports (mainly food) were covered by US aid. Harsh conditions were imposed, especially in the case of the Anglo-US loan of $3.75 billion negotiated at the end of 1945. This required that sterling be made fully convertible so that any overseas holders could cash their pounds in for dollars at the Bank of England in order to buy American goods. Moreover, the British were forced to agree that no discriminatory import quotas would be applied against the United States. The secretary to the treasury said: 'Its most important purpose from our point of view is to cause the removal of emergency controls exercised by the United Kingdom over its international transactions far more speedily' (quoted Kolko and Kolko, p. 66). According to a recent historian, generally rather sympathetic to US policy, 'the effect was to subordinate Britain to an American-dominated international economic order' (Yergin, p. 177).

Just after Lend-Lease was ended the *Economist* commented bitterly: 'To replace Lend-Lease by the offer of loans on commercial terms, and to forget about Bretton Woods, the commercial proposals, and the stimulation of American exports makes sense. Or to preach expansion and non-discrimination, and to offer assistance of the dimensions and/or the terms that would make it possible to dismantle the economic defences also makes sense. But to thrust Britain back on its own resources and, as the rations are cut, to talk of non-discrimination and expansion does not make sense' (1 September 1945).

The US government worked hard to replace British capital's domination over the Empire. One example was in the Middle East where Britain's control of oil production had already been diminished during the war. In 1946, with government backing, the US oil companies broke off the prewar production and marketing arrangements with Britain. The US share of Middle East oil output, which had risen from 16 per cent to 31 per cent between 1939 and 1946, leaped up to 60 per cent by 1953.

International money and trade systems

Planning the trade and monetary systems reached a far more advanced stage during the war than did planning for recon-

struction of the war-damaged economies. The main debate was
between the United States and United Kingdom. The United
Kingdom wanted the new international financial institution – the
International Monetary Fund (IMF) – to have very large resources
($26 billion), with contributing countries having automatic rights
to substantial overdraft facilities. There would obviously be tremendous hunger for dollars, for dollars were now the only currency
which could be turned into whatever goods were desired, that is
US goods. Under the British plan drawn up by Keynes, the United
States could have found itself contributing $23 billions of exports
in exchange for credit balances at the IMF which paid hardly any
interest. Such long-term aid to Europe was not the function the
United States envisaged for the IMF. It was scarcely surprising,
then, that the United States insisted on a much restricted plan.
The final agreement at the Bretton Woods Conference of 1944
specified that the fund would only have $9 billions of resources,
access would only be in order to 'shorten the duration and lessen
the degree of disequilibrium' in the balances of payments of
members. Exchange rates were to be pegged to the dollar, and to
be changed only when there was a 'fundamental disequilibrium'.

On trade both the United States and United Kingdom agreed on
the desirability of an international convention to draw up precise
rules and a trade organization to police quantitative restrictions
(fixing imports at certain levels). These were only to be employed
for balance of payments reasons and should be non-discriminatory
as between sources of the imports. The United States wanted the
abolition of the United Kingdom's system of proportionately low
tariffs for their goods in the Empire and for Empire goods in the
United Kingdom; the British were only prepared to consider the
abolition of this Imperial Preference in the context of a big general
reduction in tariffs (especially the USA's high tariffs). In the
event, when the General Agreement on Tariffs and Trade
(GATT) was finally ratified in the spring of 1947 the United States
made concessions (frequently 50 per cent cuts) on tariffs on items
making up $1¾ billion of prewar imports, receiving concessions on
$1¼ billion of exports. The United Kingdom eliminated some 5
per cent of preferenced trade. The GATT rules set up a forum and
machinery for future modifications of the agreements.

The monetary and trade agreements had comparatively little
effect in the short run. The desperate payments difficulties of
Europe and Japan meant that any attempts substantially to liberal-

ize trade and payments had inevitably to be postponed. In any case the dollar shortage meant that the hunger for US commodities hardly had to be stimulated by forcing down artificial barriers. US capital was able to sell abroad whatever it was prepared to finance. Even by the end of 1952 only one-tenth of European dollar imports were free of quantitative restriction, and the first move to liberalize intra-European trade had to wait until 1949 when 30 per cent of trade was freed from restrictions.

The United States' hopes of removing exchange controls rapidly were just as illusory. Slow progress was made towards freeing intra-European transactions beginning at the end of 1947 and culminating in 1950 with the European Payments Union which organized multilateral settlement of payments balances.

The United Kingdom was the only major country to maintain the value of its currency, in relation to the dollar, unchanged in the years before 1949. France and Italy devalued hugely, and Japan and Germany were without official rates for some time. But the rates at which foreign exchange transactions were made were at least pegged on a day-to-day basis and adjusted infrequently, in contrast to the experience after the First World War when rates fluctuated wildly. The rates fixed generally left European countries rather uncompetitive in relation to US industry. But over the period in which an excess of imports from the United States for reconstruction needs was inevitable, such an overvalued exchange rate was to the Europeans' advantage since it meant that US supplies cost less.

US occupation policy

US occupation policy was of central significance because it shaped the course of events in the most important capitalist economies of Europe and Asia. It also illustrates particularly sharply the United States' attitude towards the rebuilding of the other advanced capitalist countries. Japan, where the United States was in sole control, presents the purest case. US policies had to pay only the scantest regard to the attitude of the Soviet Union, Britain and France, which, rather than occupying zones, as in the case of Germany, were merely represented on a toothless Far Eastern Commission.

The Supreme Commander of the Armies of the Pacific, General MacArthur, received blunt instructions from the US government: 'You will not assume any responsibility for the economic rehabilitation of Japan or the strengthening of the Japanese economy. You will make it clear to the Japanese people that you assume no obligation to maintain any particular standard of living in Japan' (Basic Initial Post-Surrender Directive, quoted J. Cohen, p. 417).

The initial policy on reparations was, in the words of a US government report, that the Allied powers should 'take no action to assist Japan in maintaining a standard of living higher than that of neighbouring Asiatic countries injured by Japanese aggression' (quoted J. Cohen, p. 420). Bearing in mind that such 'neighbouring Asiatic countries' included China, huge reparations seemed indicated. The recommendation was that these should be in the form of removals of equipment. Reparations in the form of current production would require the building up of Japanese industry to the extent necessary to generate massive export surpluses, which would re-establish Japanese industrial predominance in the area. The removals contemplated were vast: 20 million tons of pig-iron, steel-making and rolling capacity, more than three-quarters of the machine tool stock, the entire aluminium and magnesium industries, and three-quarters of ship-building facilities. The United States rapidly back-pedalled away from the devastating implications of the report and only a handful of machine tools was actually handed over. The original reparations plan would have destroyed for decades Japan's capacity to be a serious industrial competitor. Whatever its attractions, such a course would have cut off a market as well as competition, and would have made Japan's internal affairs very difficult to control.

Although reparations plans were never carried through, important reforms were initiated to break up the highly concentrated industrial structure and to improve workers' rights and conditions. Why should the United States engage in an aggressive policy of trust-busting and encouraging trade unions?

The Trade Union Law of December 1945 was modelled on US legislation and 'guarantees the right to organize and bargain collectively and recognizes the right to strike; laws and regulations infringing on the activities of labour unions are made invalid, and employers are forbidden to discharge workers for union activities' (J. Cohen, p. 437). The subsequent course of trade unionism led to allegations of communist influence in the relevant departments of the Occupation in Japan, yet the development of unionism in Japan was perfectly rational from the point of view of US business.

Japanese industry would gain an 'unfair advantage' if it could avoid the costs and problems of trade unionism incurred by US firms.

The paper prepared to guide the occupation authorities on the 'Treatment of Japanese Workers' Organizations' was extremely explicit on this issue: 'As soon as conditions are favourable, the Japanese trade unions, both by day-to-day negotiation with the employers and by pressure for national legislation, will undoubtedly press for an increase in the general wage level and the elimination of sub-standard wages. The achievement of such an objective could have important results internationally. Prewar Japan's foreign trade policies and practices had aroused widespread resentment. With relatively high technical efficiency in many lines of production and extremely low labour costs due to low wages paid to even the really skilled among her workers, she was able to undersell her commercial rivals in a wide range of goods in many parts of the world. This low wage level, it should be understood, was a product of the peculiar political, social and economic forces existing in the country, among which should be listed the violent opposition by government to genuine labour organizations. . . . Higher labour costs, therefore, would not only move in the direction of eliminating the unfair advantage long enjoyed by Japanese manufacturing and exporting interests, an advantage maintained to the detriment of the labouring classes in that country as well as to the legitimate business and labour interests of other lands, but the redistribution of income resulting from it would be a step in the desired direction of turning Japanese productive energies towards meeting the long neglected demands of the domestic consumers' (quoted Moore, pp. 64–5).

The Occupation's breakup of the Zaibatsu – the giant holding companies that dominated industry – can also be explained by the fact that the competitive power of Japanese capital was concentrated in these enterprises. While the justification was always couched in terms of their role in Japanese militàrism, this militarism was in reality the most concentrated expression of the outward economic thrust of Japanese capital. Breaking down the giant enterprises, especially in the context of massive reparations and unions able to negotiate better wages and conditions, would obliterate the competitive threat posed by Japanese capital. The Edwards report on Japanese combines, written for the Occupation at the beginning of 1946, makes very clear the relevance of these considerations:

'Japan's industry has been under the control of a few great combines, supported and strengthened by the Japanese government. The concentration of control has encouraged the persistence of semi-feudal relations between employer and employee, held down wages, and blocked the development of labour unions. It has discouraged the launching of independent business ventures and thereby retarded the rise of a Japanese middle class. In the absence of such groups there has been no economic basis for independence in politics nor much development of the conflicting interests and democratic and humanitarian sentiments which elsewhere serve as counterweights to military designs. Moreover, the low wages and concentrated profits of the Zaibatsu system have limited the domestic market and intensified the importance of exports, and thus have given incentive to Japanese imperialism. The combines have been so dependent upon government favour that . . . they necessarily became instruments of their government in international politics. They necessarily served its purpose in order to be loyal not only to Japan but to their own profits' (quoted J. Halliday, p. 178).

The directive sent to MacArthur on the basis of this report called for a ferocious policy: 'The dissolution of all excessive concentrations of economic power' covering any enterprise 'if its asset value is very large . . . or if it controls substantial financial institutions and/or substantial industrial or commercial ones . . . or if it produces or sells or distributes a large proportion of the total supply of the products of a major industry' (quoted J. Halliday, pp. 179–80). In the event, although the major Zaibatsu groups were broken up through the dissolution of the holding companies and by removing the major families' controlling interests, the banks were not included in the final dismantling plans and were able to play a big role in the groups' later reformation. The great trading companies of Mitsui and Mitsubishi were fragmented, however; the Mitsui Company employed some 700,000 people and was split up into 170 companies. Breaking up the trading companies provided 'the chief ground for the Japanese conviction that the policy was aimed primarily at weakening their country's competitive power in foreign markets' (Allen, p. 133).

The British and American governments had originally favoured operating the occupation of Germany through a German government. The administration set up by Admiral Doenitz was in fact maintained for about three weeks after the surrender, but adverse press criticism in the United States led to its removal at the end of May 1945. The exercise of state power then fell directly on the occupation military government. Initially it was understaffed, of doubtful legitimacy in the eyes of most of the population, and faced problems even from the occupation forces themselves. US troops staged mass demonstrations in Germany, as in Italy, in the summer of 1945, demanding to be sent home immediately.

Supported at first by the French, US policy was designed to destroy German capitalism rather than to rehabilitate it. Before the surrender, Roosevelt had considered, and for a brief period apparently adopted, proposals from within his administration to de-industrialize Germany and turn it into a predominantly agricultural economy. One motive for supporting this scheme was to ensure that the USSR would find difficulty in seizing part of German output as reparations for war damage. The British moved quickly towards favouring the revival of German industry.

After considerable vacillation (different sections of the administration were pushing different lines) Truman eventually approved, on 10 May 1945, a Joint Chiefs of Staff directive (JCS 1067) which laid down basic policy: 'Except as may be necessary to carry out [your basic] objectives, you will take no steps (a) looking towards the economic rehabilitation of Germany or (b) designed to maintain or strengthen the German economy.'

Output was to be limited to a level sufficient to provide a minimum standard of material welfare. All plant over and above that required to produce such a level of output was to be dismantled and shipped abroad for reparations. Large industrial empires and cartels were to be broken up. These measures were originally justified in terms of preventing the possibility of future aggression. Thus deconcentration of the banks, for example, was argued on the grounds that a centralized banking structure had made it easier to finance war expenditure.

The level-of-industry plan of 1946 prohibited production in excess of half the 1938 level. Eighteen hundred plants were scheduled for dismantling in the Western zones. Contrary to the case of Japan, substantial reparations got underway. In 1946 plant comprising around 2 per cent of the capital stock was dismantled, one-quarter going to the USSR. The heads of the Krupp and IG Farben empires were arrested and the firms placed under the control of trustees. A 'liquidation commission' was set up to carry out deconcentration measures. Eventually the IG Farben concern was split into four separate companies (in 1953), the twelve major steel firms were divided into twenty-eight units, with limitations on their coal interests, and the three biggest banks were split temporarily into thirty-three regionally based banks.

The chief respect in which policy in Germany differed from that pursued by the Occupation in Japan concerned the labour movement. German labour posed a more immediate threat to the restoration of normally functioning capitalist relations. It had a long history and a capacity to organize rapidly, as the antifas and works councils showed. If the immediate practical goals of restoring production and distribution of basic necessities could not be realized then demands for the socialization of production, already widespread, would become more insistent. The basic policies in both the British and the American zones were suppression of the radical and broad-based antifas, refusal to allow immediate reorganization of unions or parties at a national level and, after this period of quarantine, slow buildup of an 'acceptable' structure.

The authorities' nightmare was that a single union covering all workers might develop, its centralization enhancing its power. The British Trades Union Congress (TUC) was sent to Germany to convince the SPD trade union leaders that unions should be organized industry by industry with only a loose national federation, on the grounds that this would limit the KPD's influence. Initially local unions were not even allowed to levy contributions or hire offices, and were only allowed to link up with others in the same industry after the leadership agreed in August 1946 to the industry-based structure.

Uncle Joe in control

Just as the US government's policies were to be decisive for the countries liberated by its armies, so the policies of the Soviet government were decisive where the Red Army held sway. History determined which considerations dominated policy. For the United States, where the Great Depression had threatened the very survival of capitalism, economic access to Europe and Japan and their colonies was the paramount consideration. For the Soviet Union, where Hitler's invasion had almost crushed the

Stalinist system, establishing a ring of allied 'buffer states' as a bulwark against future imperialist attack was the overriding necessity. These dominating concerns clearly had consequences for the type of social system which could be acceptable to each major power in its sphere of influence.

The socialist transformation of society in Western Europe or Japan was obviously inconsistent with the United States' economic ambitions. Similarly the restoration in Eastern Europe of the old regimes, which had collaborated with the Nazis and were implacably hostile to Russia, was quite unacceptable to Stalin. Both major powers had an interest in the failure in the designs of the other. The United States stood to lose access to the markets of Eastern Europe if those countries were fully integrated into the Stalinist system. The Soviet Union would have to deal with a more united powerful enemy if Western Europe and Japan were consolidated into a United States-dominated bloc. Each major power confronted internal opposition inside their zones of influence, which looked in turn towards the other. The United States faced a radicalized mass movement in Western Europe, generally led by Communist parties faithful to Moscow. In Eastern Europe Russia faced substantial sectors who were opposed to socialism, distrustful of the Soviet Union and oriented more to the United States. Of the two, the opposition faced by the Soviet Union was undoubtedly less of a threat, being on the defensive, fragmented, with its leadership discredited and generally disoriented by the outcome of the war. The left in Europe, with the partial exception of Germany, was on the offensive, cohesive, with a strong and tested leadership, and determined not to miss the opportunity for implementing important measures of social reform.

The Soviet Union, it seemed, was in a much better position than the United States to implement its own designs in its sphere, and to frustrate its opponent in the other. While the USA had the greater economic strength, which it could deploy to steer developments via aid and loans, the USSR had the military advantage of close proximity to its sphere of influence. Most importantly, socialist forces in both Eastern and Western Europe were much stronger than those favouring all-out capitalist restoration.

People's democracy

The crucial question was how Stalin proposed to take advantage of this apparently favourable position. The method devised was to oblige the Communist parties (CPs), in both Eastern and Western Europe, to follow the theory of 'People's Democracy'. The CPs were to enter 'national democratic' coalitions which would include all antifascists, from Communists through Socialists and Liberals to Christian Democrats. These coalition governments would carry out measures of national reconstruction which would include nationalization of industries and distribution of land owned by Nazis or collaborators and their purging from the army, police and civil service. According to Stalin, the building of socialism in the USSR together with Soviet victories in the war provided a framework, safe from intervention by imperialism, for a different road to socialism from the Russian one:

'Once the political power of the financial and landed oligarchy had been destroyed by the liberation, which cut it off from its economic basis by expropriation and nationalization, long-term cooperation became possible between the working class, small peasant proprietors and the middle bourgeoisie, industrial, commercial and agricultural, as part of a gradual transition to socialism. The nationalized sector would continue to grow and the capitalist sector to decline, and small peasants would gradually and voluntarily go over to cooperative forms of production, until the whole economy rested on a socialist basis. The class struggle would go on, but would take peaceful and evolutionary forms within the democratic parliamentary system' (Claudin, p. 461).

Stalin went so far as to tell Tito: 'Today Socialism is possible even under the British monarchy. Just recently a delegation of the British Labour Party was here, and we talked about this in particular. Yes, there is much that is new' (quoted Djilas, 1962, p. 104).

How these policies fared in Western Europe and Japan is the subject of the next chapter; but further light is thrown on the substance and motivation for the policies by briefly examining their implementation in Eastern Europe.

At first sight many of Stalin's actions seem incomprehensible. As Isaac Deutscher pointed out, much of what he did could hardly have been better designed to stir up the maximum of bitterness against Russia, thus discrediting the very idea of socialism for which the power and prestige of the Soviet Union should have been, and was elsewhere, a major asset. He refused to make concessions to the Poles over their Eastern frontiers, insisted on the expulsion of the whole of the German population from the provinces ceded to Poland, demanded reparations from Germany,

Austria, Hungary, Romania, Bulgaria and Finland, and even demanded that 80 per cent of German industry should be dismantled. Deutscher comments: 'He could not have been unaware that his scheme, as chimerical as ruthless, if it had been carried out, would have entailed the dispersal of the German working class, the main, if not the only, social force to which communism could have appealed and whose support it might have enlisted' (Deutscher, p. 537).

Everywhere the interests of building support for socialism seemed to be subordinated to Russia's short-term national interest (in striking parallel to the United States' short-sighted pursuit of immediate economic interest described earlier).

But then in Germany, as elsewhere, socialism was proclaimed by Stalin to be off the agenda. Wolfgang Leonhard, at the end of the war training to return to Germany with CP leaders exiled in Moscow, was instructed thus: 'Our political task was not to consist of establishing socialism in Germany or encouraging a socialist development. On the contrary, this must be condemned and resisted as a dangerous tendency. Germany was on the threshold of a bourgeois-democratic transformation, which in substance and content would be the completion of the bourgeois-democratic revolution of 1848. The policy was therefore to support this process and to repudiate every kind of socialist slogan which under present-day conditions could be nothing but pure demagogy' (Leonhard, pp. 281–2).

The CP leaderships in Eastern Europe took great pains to gain the confidence of their coalition partners and of the economic interests they represented. In discussions with Hungarian CP leaders in December 1944, Stalin was reported as saying, 'We ought to underline more strongly the defence of private property and the preservation and development of private enterprise. There must be nothing scary in our formulas' (quoted McCagg, pp. 315–16). Some years later the Hungarian CP leader Rakosi pointed out that many of the communist rank and file were 'surprised at such a broad coalition . . . and treated it with antagonism', arguing: 'Now the Red Army has come to liberate us. Let us profit by this opportunity to restore proletarian dictatorship.' But, he went on, 'Even a theoretical suggestion of a goal of proletarian dictatorship would have created upheaval in the ranks of our coalition partners' (quoted McCagg, pp. 35–6).

Once the most pressing task was no longer the defeat of fascism, the strain of maintaining coalitions between parties representing diametrically opposed interests was bound to become intolerable. Workers, middle-class people and antifascist elements of the bourgeoisie could perhaps agree on purging collaborators from economic, political and military positions and on basic democratic reforms. But the reconstruction of the economy, which was bound to be the priority, was also certain to involve fundamental conflict of interests. And this conflict provided a basis from which the discredited right-wing leaders could attempt to worm their way back by proclaiming their identity of interests with the middle classes who felt threatened by measures of socialist reconstruction.

Perhaps, as some supporters of the approach argued later, it was the best way of building up support for socialist measures – by demonstrating that of the coalition partners only the CP was capable of carrying through the necessary measures of reconstruction. Building up such support was definitely necessary in countries such as Hungary where the left was weak, securing only one-third of the votes in the 1945 election (the CP gaining 17 per cent). Alternatively, was the whole tactic a ruse to buy time in which the CPs could gain control of the state apparatus, a process begun while the countries were effectively under Soviet military occupation, in preparation for a coup and the destruction of opposition parties? Or was it a tactic to maintain the wartime alliance, with allies for whom parliamentary forms were important? None of these explanations is wholly convincing, despite their function in justifying the strategy. There was a further, more fundamental consideration. The Czech experience serves to reveal it.

The Czech case

The Communist Party in Czechoslovakia was not in such a strong position in 1945 as it was in Yugoslavia. There the CP was in effective sole control of the country, having led an enormous partisan struggle against the Germans. Nevertheless the Czechoslovak CP was extremely well placed. Founded on the most organized working class in Eastern Europe, it had participated actively in the final defeat of the Germans. The CP benefited enormously from the widespread acceptance, after the disastrous prewar experience, of the necessity for friendly relations with the USSR, and this was symbolized in 1943 by a treaty signed with

Russia by the Czech government in exile, to last twenty years and pledging 'permanent friendship and friendly postwar cooperation'.

As elsewhere in occupied Europe, the Czech resistance generated radical social demands. Early in 1945 the underground trade union organization wrote to the politicians in Moscow: 'The main demands of the working people at home [are] the nationalization of all large industrial, metal, chemical and foodstuffs factories, of banks, insurance and forests, as well as the public ownership of agricultural property over thirty hectares in area; this we consider the minimum economic programme of the first domestic government' (quoted Bloomfield, pp. 36–7).

Before the liberation the CP leadership was much more cautious on the question of nationalization than was its socialist partner in the coalition. Such caution was quite in tune with the general line of the CPs: 'The nationalization of the basic means of production was conspicuously absent from the programmes of the communist-led political fronts in 1944–5. Usually their references were restricted to nationalization in the sense of confiscation by the state of industrial and other assets belonging to the enemy (German, Italian or Hungarian, as the case might be) and to collaborators and war criminals' (Brus, p. 36). After the liberation of Czechoslovakia, works councils took over the running of industry, confiscated some firms and put many others under a system of temporary 'national administration' in which the works councils exerted considerable powers. The government allowed firms to be taken over where managements' 'antagonistic attitude' to employees was hampering production, and 'militant workers, headed by their works councils, were frequently ready to resort to strikes so that a particular firm could be included among the state-controlled ones' (Kovanda, p. 259). By the summer of 1945 this system covered 75 per cent of industrial employment.

The CP maintained its cautious attitude towards nationalization: 'The two most radical segments of the working class, the works councils and the Social Democratic Party, were the most emphatic in calling for nationalization. The policy of the Communist Party was, by contrast, for a relatively long time one of evasiveness and procrastination' (Kovanda, p. 262).

The CP only came out clearly for nationalization after many groups of workers, in mines and engineering, for example, had demanded it. The emphasis was still strongly nationalistic, focusing on foreign-owned companies. The CP leader Gottwald emphasized that the private sector would have plenty of room to operate alongside nationalized concerns and would be 'fully supported by the government' (quoted Bloomfield, p. 73). The announcement of the nationalizations led to an explosion of demands for their extension, coming from workers in every sector of industry, supported by sections of the central trade union organization and the Social Democratic Party. The CP took a much more cautious attitude, particularly in respect of demands for taking over trade and consumer goods industries. When the nationalization decrees were signed at the end of October 1945 they covered all industrial enterprises employing more than five hundred workers (which provided 60 per cent of industrial employment), banking and finance. This went well beyond foreign-owned companies but, with the support of the CP, Czech owners were fully compensated. Distribution, much of the food industry and other sectors, such as clothing, building and printing, were left mainly in private hands, and no limit was placed on the future size of private firms.

At each stage the CP was pressed by the trade union movement to support more decisive measures of socialist transformation. The CP, with 38 per cent of the vote, and Social Democratic Party together won 50 per cent of the votes in the May 1946 election which, in contrast to widespread allegations of malpractice elsewhere in Eastern Europe, was agreed even by the US ambassador to have been fair. So mass support was clearly there. It was manifest again in the autumn of 1946 when protest strikes greeted attempts by the right-wing parties to have the smaller foreign-owned firms, not covered by the nationalization measures, sold off to the private sector. In no way, then, could the CP explain its moderate and measured approach by lack of support for radical measures.

The most plausible explanation is that the course followed by the CPs in Czechoslovakia and elsewhere, especially where the mood of the people was at its most radical, was one designed to keep the process of social transformation firmly under control. The German CP leader, Walter Ulbricht, said of some administrative measures implemented in Berlin: 'It's quite clear – it's got to look democratic but we must have everything under our control' (quoted Leonhard, p. 303). This could have been a motto for the whole process in Eastern Europe. The crucial point, however, is that going through the parliamentary procedures of coalition governments was aimed more at subordinating any independent working-class activity to the control of the CPs than at pacifying the West or winning over wavering elements inside the countries concerned.

At every stage in the process the independent activity of the working class was hijacked into safe channels.

The Czech unions demanded that the armed detachments of workers, who had fought in the final risings against the Nazis, be given a role in internal security under trade union direction. They were disbanded, however, on the orders of the communist-controlled Ministry of the Interior. A similar fate befell the anti-fascist committees which had sprung up in East Germany. Leonhard describes the activities of one committee in Berlin:

'Immediately after the capitulation of the Wehrmacht in Berlin, this organization had set to work on the most pressing tasks without waiting for any directives, not even ours. Engineers, technicians and specialists were recruited to arrange for the provision of gas, water and electric current; clearing of rubble from the streets was organized; hospitals and schools were got going; in brief, everything was done which needed to be done at the time' (p. 321). Yet Ulbricht ordered such antifascist committees to be dissolved immediately, arguing variously that they were a front for Nazis and that they were diverting communists from establishing themselves in the administration.

In Czechoslovakia the works councils which had been running the factories and mines in the period before nationalization were given only a minor advisory role. Again, this was the general pattern: 'Factory committees (or councils) lost their importance (and even such statutory rights as they had achieved) as soon as proper state administration of industry was achieved. It seems safe to say that workers' self-management or control was used as a tool of nationalization (especially so in the ex-enemy countries where the process took more time) and was quickly suppressed afterwards' (Brus, p. 39).

In Czechoslovakia, indeed, the councils were a tool used by a working class on the offensive, and their power was wielded more aggressively than the Communist Party wished. The CP responded by subordinating the works councils to the central trade union movement which it controlled.

East and West

Stalin's remark about each side imposing its social system on the territories it liberated is highly relevant. The social system of the

Soviet Union did not allow for the working class to take independent initiatives and control society from the bottom. Mass
struggle for social change from the base would not spontaneously
fall into the bureaucratic and directed Soviet mould. A shift
towards democratic socialism within any of the East European
countries would have posed major problems for the continuation
of bureaucratic control in the rest of the area and even the Soviet
Union. So, in Czechoslovakia, where the possibilities for democratic workers' control of society were most favourable, the CP
used its authority to slow the movement down and divert it into
safe channels. The seizure of power by the CP, when it did take
place in February 1948, was tightly and rigidly directed.

The implications of all this for Western Europe and Japan were
profound. The 'Popular Front' tactic in Europe and elsewhere, in
which CPs participated in coalition governments with capitalist
parties, served Stalin's purposes admirably. It provided a way of
dousing revolutionary enthusiasm in Europe by channelling it into
parliamentary politics. At the same time it gave the labour
movement maximum leverage against possible aggressive moves
by the capitalist countries aimed at the Soviet Union. If Stalin was
not prepared to envisage independent working-class action to take
control of society in the areas he nearly controlled, why should he
encourage it in Western Europe where the labour movement had
in general much richer traditions of struggle, and where there was
no Red Army to help enforce the authority of the CP and see that
matters stayed in hand? As we shall see in the next chapter, the
influence Stalin wielded through his control over the Japanese and
Western European Communist parties played a vital role in determining how reconstruction proceeded.

4. The First Two Years

In the first two postwar years the pattern of recovery varied from country to country. The United States and United Kingdom reconverted industry to peacetime uses rapidly. France and Italy raised production steadily towards prewar levels. Germany and Japan made little progress.

Reconstruction required high investment to eliminate transport and fuel bottlenecks and to renovate consumer goods industries neglected during the war. This was achieved everywhere except Germany, where investment was still very low in 1947 (Table 4.1).

Table 4.1 Production and investment, 1937–47

| | Industrial production | | Non-residential investment[3] | | Share of total fixed investment in GDP[4] | |
| | 1938=100 | | 1937=100 | | Percentages | |
	1946	1947	1946	1947	1937	1947
USA	156[1]	175[1]	161	193	15.7	17.2
UK	106	115	85	102	16.1	13.1
France	84	99	119	132	16.1	21.2
Italy	61	92	81	113	21.4	29.3
Germany	29	34	35	46	19.6	n.a.
Japan	31[2]	37[2]	80	93	18.1	28.7

1. 1937=100.
2. 1934–6=100.
3. Total fixed investment less housing investment, except for Germany (manufacturing and mining investment) and Japan (total fixed investment).
4. At constant market prices. For Italy, includes stockbuilding.

Source: see Appendix.

Investment and wages

Under capitalism, high profits are normally a precondition for high investment since they provide the motive and much of the finance to invest. But in the immediate postwar years firms could finance investment by running down financial assets accumulated during the war. And fears about their future value could make building up machinery and stocks preferable to hanging on to financial assets. With production limited by shortages and uncertainties, high investment financed in this way would pull up prices and eat into real wages. So high profits would still tend to accompany high investment, but as effect rather than cause.

With production low, the working class could achieve tolerable real wages only by accepting widespread dismissals and speedup on remaining jobs. Successful resistance to dismissals would result in low productivity. Satisfactory profits for employers would then imply very low real wages.

Two other groups complicate the picture. One is middle-class savers or rentiers (people for whom a significant part of their income is returns on financial assets). Governments had financed much wartime spending by selling bonds to this group, which thereby accumulated enormous savings. If these savings were spent then prices would rise further, screwing down real wages and boosting profits. This could be avoided only by wiping out these savings. Monetary reform often sought to do exactly this, by replacing hoarded cash with smaller amounts of new currency. This was obviously unpopular with the middle classes (although attempts to spend their savings would have had similar effects since the resulting inflation would have severely devalued remaining savings).

The other main complication was the peasantry. Chronic food shortages raised the price of food relative to manufactured goods (especially on the black market). This meant higher real incomes for peasants. If they spent these on consumption (buying more manufactures or eating more) then this would squeeze workers' consumption further. But if they saved their extra incomes, say, then this would allow high investment without high profits. In effect, capitalists could finance investment by running down financial assets, which would finish up under peasants' mattresses.

The final squeeze on wages came from high government spending. There were pressures to repair dilapidated social capital, such as housing, and to improve social welfare programmes. If these were to be paid for from taxes then much of the burden would have to fall on workers so as not to jeopardize investment. Where taxation was limited by political considerations, governments would have to borrow more. Surplus profits and middle-class incomes would have to be that much higher to provide the funds. Government investment in nationalized industries also had to be financed, implying high profits in those industries or borrowing from other sectors. Resources would only be available if real wages were low enough.

These pressures would be eased only if available resources exceeded production by a substantial margin, that is, if imports ran well ahead of exports. Such a balance of payments deficit would imply borrowing from abroad. In effect, capitalists could then continue to invest heavily with low profits and high workers' consumption. But this possibility was severely limited. Dollar reserves were low and credit difficult to obtain. The interconnection of these various pressures and constraints is illustrated below:

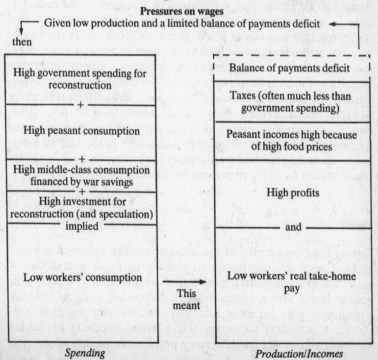

Pressures on wages

Given low production and a limited balance of payments deficit

then

Spending	Production/Incomes
High government spending for reconstruction	Balance of payments deficit
+	Taxes (often much less than government spending)
High peasant consumption	Peasant incomes high because of high food prices
+	
High middle-class consumption financed by war savings	
+	High profits
High investment for reconstruction (and speculation) implied	
	and
Low workers' consumption	Low workers' real take-home pay

This meant

One result was inflation. The excess of purchasing power over production pulled up prices. This helped to keep real wages down as money wage rises lagged behind prices (limiting workers' consumption). It reduced the value of cash hoards and financial assets (limiting middle-class consumption). It also made it hard for governments to sell more debt, since no one wants financial assets whose real value is falling. Governments were forced to pay for expenditure (finance deficits) by printing money. Inflation also meant that capitalists could often make more by hoarding commodities (investing in stocks) than by accumulating productive assets (investing in plant and equipment). So inflation twisted and distorted the whole pattern of reconstruction. Where it was repressed by price controls and rationing it both discouraged production and diverted much of it into black markets.

Whether or not workers would passively accept the severe hardships facing them in the aftermath of the war depended crucially on how far they felt – or could be persuaded to feel – that the reconstruction which their deprivations were underpinning was being carried out in their interests. The situation varied considerably in each country. In Germany and Japan, where no real reconstruction was taking place, demands arose within the labour movement for workers to intervene directly, gaining a real measure of power in government or the factories, or both. In France and Italy working-class parties were in coalition governments. Discontent accordingly centred on opposition to attempts to make workers redouble their efforts while black markets flourished, middle-class consumption was given more or less free rein, and speculative stockpiling proceeded unchecked. In the United Kingdom, where Labour had won a landslide victory in 1945, workers concentrated on trying to prevent backsliding by their party.

Japan

During the first months of the occupation, the Japanese government allowed big companies to plunder its funds and stocks of materials while industrial production stagnated at one-tenth the prewar level. The government then responded early in 1946 by launching a plan for more effective controls over the economy. Credit, agricultural deliveries and hoarded goods in particular were singled out. Six months later a new finance minister proposed massive subsidies to key sectors of industry to stimulate recovery. But successive governments, all solidly linked to big business, proved incapable of forceful reorganization. The Occupation became frustrated with the situation, which it euphemistically ascribed to 'government incompetence', and reversed its original policy of 'non-responsibility in the economic sphere' (J. Cohen, p. 419). From then onwards, any effective action flowed from its instructions.

By 1947 industrial production had only risen from one-tenth of prewar levels to a third. Petrol output was 6 per cent of its prewar peak, machine tool output 9 per cent, steel 12 per cent, cotton fabric 14 per cent and cement 20 per cent. One constraint was electricity. Demand outstripped supply despite the fact that electricity production (mainly hydroelectric) was running at almost double the prewar level. Demand was so high because coal production remained well below prewar levels even by 1947. Productivity in the mines was hardly one-third of the prewar level, partly because of union resistance to work speeds. Coal was also being used much less effectively on the railways, presumably due to lack of maintenance of the rolling stock. Imports of coking coal for steel production were no longer obtainable from prewar Asian sources.

Foreign exchange to buy imported raw materials was a crucial bottleneck. Cotton textiles, a major prewar export earner, is a good example. The Occupation considered the rehabilitation of this industry as a priority: 'Possibly the existence in the United States of large government held stocks of raw cotton influenced this determination' (J. Cohen, p. 484). Even though only one-sixth of prewar capacity remained, some spindles were still idle in 1947. The industry was in an impossible situation. It needed to export some 60 per cent of output to earn the dollars to buy the US cotton. Traditional markets, in the Sterling Area for example, were starved of dollars. Japanese textile exports to the United States were banned. The Americans were slow to release Japan from the double bind of having to buy cotton for dollars while being effectively prevented from earning them with textile exports.

Agriculture was much less dislocated than industry. Production was at about the prewar level, but the number of mouths to feed had risen by around one-tenth. Daily calorie consumption in Tokyo was 1350 in 1946. By mid-1947 it had risen only to 1700. Rapid inflation made peasants reluctant to sell rice to the government. Urban inhabitants made treks to the countryside to barter household goods for rice. In desperation the government followed suit in

1947; it began delivering fertilizers, textiles, cigarettes (8 for 72 litres of rice) and other goods, exchanging them for rice. Even the official figures show real farm incomes 20 per cent up on prewar.

The food problem was eased by around $300 million of food imports, paid for by US aid. But the relief was strictly limited. The balance of payments was in deficit to the tune of about 4 per cent of total output, or gross domestic product (GDP), in 1946 and 1947.

Inflation ran at a phenomenal 42 per cent a month in the six months after surrender. Production collapsed, while the huge stock of financial assets was further bloated by various handouts to big business ('compensation' payments for war damage and so forth). A currency reform instituted early in 1946 involved compulsory deposits of banknotes and limitation of withdrawals. Prices did decline at first, but by only half the increase of the immediately preceding weeks, when expectations of the reform had fuelled a spending spree. By the turn of the year the inflation was in full swing again. The government's borrowing requirement was some 9 per cent of GDP. Prices were three times as high in 1947 as in 1946. The basic inflationary mechanism is clearly explained by an American observer:

'Spiralling prices, due to an inadequate supply of raw materials and consumer goods, excess purchasing power, etc. tend to make the cost of living outrun the wage level at any time. The resultant pressure for higher wages, made possible by the new strength of the unions, the real economic basis for their demands and the weakness and disorganization of management, caused a higher wage level than the one upon which the government based its calculations in the prior fixing of official prices. . . . The increase in industrial costs in the face of fixed official prices forced a firm either to divert its output in whole or in part to the black market in order to realize a profit or, if it sold in legitimate markets at official prices, to incur a deficit which could only be made good by a government subsidy or a deficit-covering bank loan . . . in effect, government-related funds have been funnelled via the Reconstruction Finance Bank to finance industrial deficits' (J. Cohen, pp. 448–9).

Recorded profits were less than one-tenth of company output in 1947 (Table 4.2), less than one-quarter of the prewar level. With high overheads, and productivity so low, companies only managed to make any profits at all because real wages were hardly a third of the prewar level.

Table 4.2 Profits, wages and productivity: Japan, 1936–47

	Profit share[1]	Real wage[2]	Industrial production	Industrial employment	Industrial productivity
1936	38	100[3]	100[3]	100[3]	100[3]
1946	10	25[4]	31	86	36
1947	8	30	37	95	39

1. Net profits as percentage of net corporate product.
2. In terms of cost of living.
3. 1934–6=100.
4. Very rough estimate.

Source: see Appendix.

Recorded investment was high in relation to recorded profits. More houses were being built than in the 1930s. Government investment on infrastructure was twice the prewar level and comprised nearly half of total investment in 1946 and 1947. But private investment was also high. Investment in rebuilding stocks (of materials, food, goods, etc.) was estimated at an enormous 11 per cent of total production (reckoned at prewar prices). Private fixed investment (in plant and factories) was lower – a little over half the 1938 level (but was above that of the twenties and early thirties). The cotton textile industry invested heavily, increasing capacity by one-third in 1946 and 1947. Quite what the rest of the investment consisted of is unclear. Production of most investment goods appears to have been very low and imports non-existent.

A good deal of recorded investment may in fact have been in repairs or concealed stockbuilding. Clearly capitalists stood to gain from borrowing from banks to finance stock accumulation. And bigger and surer profits could often be made by hanging on to stocks rather than using them to raise output or invest in extra plant in a situation of heavy excess capacity. So fixed investment may not have been as high relative to profits as the figures indicate. To the extent that total investment really was high, it was financed by firms running down financial assets.

The inflation was catastrophic for rentiers. The proportion of the national income (itself a third lower than prewar) received as interest fell from 9 per cent in 1936 and 12 per cent in 1944 to 1 per cent in 1947. The share taken in rent fell from 4 per cent to 1 per cent. A capital levy was carried out, ostensibly to hit those with such 'real' assets as shares. But it was a farce, being based on prewar asset values when by 1947 the price level had risen a hundred times.

Inflation also kept real wages low. In 1947 they were only about 30 per cent of the prewar level even if calculated on the basis of official prices. The existence of an extensive and expensive black market means that the postwar figure exaggerates real purchasing power. The disparity in living standards was less than that in incomes since, in contrast to prewar, workers were making no savings (and spending such wartime savings as were still worth anything).

Roaring inflation and starvation wages made pay a major issue. By the end of 1946 membership of unions had rocketed to nearly 5 million, well over a third of the work force. The key wage agreement was negotiated in the electric power industry in autumn 1946. This 'Densan wage system', which embodied most union demands, linked wages to the cost of living. It was calculated after tax and included a basic wage, a strong age-related element (giving a single man of forty twice the pay of a twenty-year-old) and a substantial allowance based on family circumstances (giving a married man of thirty with three children double the basic wage of a man with no dependants). The principle was that wages should reflect living costs, with age and family circumstances regarded as relevant. But, an additional element (equivalent to the basic rate for a thirty- year-old) was to be determined by 'ability', judged on criteria of skill, experience and educational background. This element was apparently accepted as just by both workers and management, and its determination in individual cases not a matter of contention. The workshop supervisors who fixed it were in many cases elected by workshop meetings of union members. Other workers in less favourably placed industries struggled for comparable deals. Miners in Kyushu, lacking an effective regional organization, were defeated. But in Hokkaido a strong regional organization led an effective strike and forced the mine owners to concede.

Workers also resisted redundancies fiercely. Despite the low level of production, industrial employment was barely below its prewar level in 1947 (though a third less than its wartime peak). It also rose nearly as fast as production during 1947, even though productivity was less than 40 per cent of the prewar level (Table

4.2). Workers struck for more than 6 million days in 1946 and 'the Labour unions won all their strikes against discharges' (Okochi *et al.*, p. 319). Government plans to dismiss 43,000 seamen and 75,000 railway workers were beaten off by rank-and-file pressure, which forced the unions to call a ten-day seamen's strike and to fix a date for strike action by railwaymen. A quarter of a million workers engaged in 'production control' (Chapter 2). A few actions developed beyond struggles over union recognition and pay and conditions into battles for workers' control and planning. Workers in the Toyo Gosei chemical plant, faced with closure, excluded company executives, borrowed funds to expand capacity, bartered the ammonium sulphate they produced with a farmers' association, took on more workers and introduced a new wage system embodying a 50 per cent increase.

Massive numbers of workers took to the streets in the spring of 1946. In April, just before the first general election, 70,000 demonstrated in Tokyo, calling for the overthrow of the government. They disarmed police who fired warning shots. Order was restored only after American armoured cars appeared. On May Day half a million demonstrated in Tokyo, and some 1¼ million throughout the country, demanding a 'democratic government' and 'control of food by the people', and opposing suppression of workers' control. Two weeks later a quarter of a million, organized by trade unions and the Kanto District Council on Food, held a 'People's Rally to Secure Rice' (the average daily intake in Tokyo had reached a low of 1064 calories). The rally called for citizens' committees to control food distribution, for a 'democratic government with the Socialist and Communist parties as its nucleus and with trade unions, peasant organizations and democratically oriented cultural associations as its basis' (quoted Yamamoto, 1980–1, p. 26). The leaders sat in at the prime minister's residence, but left after MacArthur issued a statement denouncing these mass demonstrations as 'a menace not only to orderly government but to the basic purposes and security of the occupation itself' and said the occupation forces would take 'the necessary steps to control and remedy such a deplorable situation' (quoted Yamamoto, 1980–1, p. 30).

The Occupation intervened not only to threaten demonstrators; it also encouraged management at the *Yomiuri* newspaper to sack workers' leaders controlling the paper. The workers fought off company thugs who tried to prevent those sacked from entering the building. On 21 June 1946, 500 armed police forced their way in and made fifty arrests. Workers' leaders were charged with serious crimes. Both management and the Occupation threatened to close the paper. Faced with such powerful opposition the union retreated, abandoning control over the paper's operations. But it continued to demand recognition, initiating court action. Management then transferred union leaders outside Tokyo and organized a pro-management 'reconstruction council'. The union struck and reoccupied the paper. Management thugs threw them out while the police stood aside. Plans for a national press strike fizzled out. In October the union admitted defeat and dissolved itself. Workers taken back on the paper had to join the company union. This was an important defeat.

But struggles continued elsewhere. A mass rally of half a million in December 1946, called to coincide with a no-confidence vote in parliament, demanded the overthrow of the Yoshida cabinet. Following the motion's defeat, the 2½-million-strong government workers' union federation called for a general strike on 1 February 1947, defying a law passed the previous autumn denying their right to strike. Public sector workers were under particular pressure; their wages were lagging far behind inflation. They demanded wage rises, no dismissals, the conclusion of collective contracts and less authoritarian management. The Communist Party, announcing its support for the demands of the unions, called for the strike to aim at establishing a 'democratic people's government' – that is, a Socialist-led coalition cabinet. It also stated 'its confidence that SCAP [the occupation authorities] would not suppress a political strike of this nature and criticized the trend in the labour movement towards direct action and a frontal attack upon the rights of the capitalist owners of the means of production' (Moore, p. 234).

MacArthur initially pressed the government to concede to some of the strikers' economic demands, including a 50 per cent wage rise and a resumption of negotiations. But he then denounced 'the use of so deadly a social weapon in the present impoverished and emaciated state of Japan' (quoted Cole *et al.*, p. 15), prohibited the strike and told the union that defiance would 'provoke action of the most drastic nature against individual and organized labour interests' (quoted Moore, p. 239).

Even after this setback, the Socialist Party won 26 per cent of the vote in the April 1947 election on a programme including nationalization of the mines. The situation was highly unstable: 'The collapse of a Japanese cabinet as a result of a communist promoted general strike would indeed have greatly strengthened the communists and gained credit for their direct-action methods at the expense of constitutional processes. It is understandable that the American authorities should fear the development of a revolutionary situation which might have a sharp anti-American tendency' (*Economist*, 8 February 1947).

The Communist Party provided the leadership for the most militant workers. Although it secured only 4 per cent of the vote in the April 1946 and April 1947 elections, and had a membership of only 7500 in April 1946 (70,000 by the end of 1947), the CP led the mass demonstrations and campaign for a general strike. The union confederation Sanbetsu, founded in August 1946 with 1½ million members, was the most militant labour movement organization and under CP control.

Although there were divisions in the party and fluctuations in its pronouncements, the leadership was committed to a parliamentary road to socialism. Its demands for the downfall of an unpopular reactionary cabinet was not the first step towards insurrection. It even distanced itself from 'production control'. In December 1945 it called for 'workers' control over essential enterprise' as a prerequisite for restoring production. But by February 1946 it had amended this to a call for 'the heightening of the general efficiency of industry by employing a system of management councils' (quoted Moore, pp. 118, 124).

In sum, the situation in 1946 and 1947 did not provide a stable and healthy basis for capitalist reconstruction. High inflation, rampant speculation, high government and balance of payments deficits, were symptoms of instability (shared with Italy and France). Low production and profits represented further problems. Japanese workers, with only a minimal history of organization, were showing an extraordinary capacity for struggle. They had established strong shopfloor organizations. In a number of industries individual enterprise unions had welded themselves together into effective industry confederations. Moreover, the ruling class was unused to dealing with labour unrest.

Electorally, a 30 per cent vote for workers' parties posed something of a threat. But it proved easy to defuse. The peasants delivered a massive vote to conservative parties in the wake of a land reform, which increased the proportion of families owning more than half their land from 50 to 90 per cent. The Socialist Party was enticed into a coalition with one of the conservative parties and its programme shredded. Its plan for coal nationalization was reduced to a bill which 'signified that the obsolescent machinery in Japanese collieries would be modernized at the taxpayer's expense and soon returned, with the mines themselves, to private hands' (Cole *et al.*, p. 18). The crushing of workers' shopfloor strength, previewed at *Yomiuri*, was to prove a much tougher task.

Germany

The German economy's gradual emergence from the chaos of the summer of 1945 showed no more sense of direction than did the Japanese, but the problem was not the Japanese one of procrastination and vacillation by a weak national government. It was rather paralysis on the part of the occupying powers. They could not decide what they wanted a future Germany to look like. (From now on, when we refer to Germany we mean today's Federal Republic.) So long as the issue of eventual unification with the Soviet-occupied Eastern zone remained undecided, the Western occupation authorities did little more than maintain existing economic controls. They intervened decisively only on a few matters of particular interest to themselves, such as coal.

It is especially difficult to chart the exact course of recovery in Germany. Officially the wartime administrative system was used to control all prices, wages and the allocation of materials and consumer goods. But low production, inadequate rations and high stocks of liquid assets, amassed during the war, combined to produce tremendous excess demand for commodities. A black market flourished. According to one report, 'regular trade is the exception and exists only as a camouflage' (quoted Abelshauser, 1975, p. 5). In the autumn of 1946 it was suggested that only half of real production and stocks was being reported. Official estimates were that in 1947 at least one-tenth of production went to the black market. Obviously there is scope for a large margin of error. The best available estimates are that industrial production was growing rapidly by the middle of 1946. It fell back to little more than the level of the previous year during the winter of 1946–7 but then rebounded rapidly. By the end of 1947 it was around half the 1936 level.

As in Japan, fuel, materials and transport were the main bottlenecks. These constraints were often interconnected. At one stage there was a shortage of timber for shoring up mines. The foresters refused to work in the rain because they did not have good enough clothes and shoes. But the textile industries were dependent on coal to expand production, and so on.

Transport had been badly hit by bombing (Chapter 2). By the middle of 1946 the railways and canals were functioning effectively and there was apparently no transport shortage. But the exceptionally hard winter of 1946–7, combined with overuse of rolling stock, brought a major crisis. In January 1947 only two-thirds of transportation requirements could be met. A crash repair programme was launched and the system coped well next winter.

Coal was generally regarded as *the* key sector. Poor rations reduced output. The *Economist* noted: 'The situation in the Ruhr is becoming desperate. In the past week after the cut in rations a decrease in coal output by about 10 per cent was reported. By the end of March the decline in output was already nearly 20 per cent' (6 April 1946). By August 1946 miners' rations had risen to 4000 calories – about three times the average – and this, together with a 20 per cent wage increase, helped to boost the number of miners by nearly 40 per cent between 1945 and 1947.

But productivity per underground worker still stood at only about 60 per cent of prewar levels in 1947. In 1946 24 per cent of coal from the US and UK zones was exported. Although this was only slightly higher than the prewar share, the coal was bought at less than half the market price, leading to an estimated loss of foreign exchange earnings of some $200 milion by the end of 1947. Even more foreign exchange could have been earned by diverting coal, which made up three-quarters of exports in 1946, to domestic industry to permit production of other goods for export.

The iron and steel industry became a victim of attempts to demilitarize Germany. The initial industrial plan limited productive capacity to 5.8 million tons a year, less than one-third of prewar output. But the industry received such a low priority that even this level was nowhere near reached. Until early in 1948 the industry was forbidden to import Swedish iron ore, which had previously provided two-thirds of its supply. So it was forced to rely on inadequate amounts of poor-quality domestic ore. The British even shipped home half a million tons of scrap, bought at well below market prices.

Food production in the US and UK zones was only about 70 per cent of prewar levels in 1946–7; $660 million worth of food was imported in 1947, almost as much as in 1936. But it now consisted almost entirely of cereals whereas fat and meat imports had been important before the war. It was financed mainly by aid from the United States and Britain, totalling $470 million in 1946 and $600 million in 1947. Very little else was imported.

The United Nations calculated that in 1947 industrial employment in the Western zones stood at 89 per cent of the prewar level. Combining this with the production index suggests that average productivity was around one-half the prewar level. A figure of one-quarter was quoted for iron and steel in 1946, hit especially hard by low production. Hourly factory wages had typically fallen by one-quarter to one-third in money terms since the war had ended, and the forty-eight-hour week been reintroduced. The official cost of living index increased by 20 per cent between March 1945 and April 1946. But these figures under-estimate the decline in living standards. Rationing limited purchases and the black market inflated prices. Periodically the situation became desperate. The *Economist* reported (9 March 1946) that rations in the British zone had been reduced to 1014 calories.

An estimated two-fifths of a worker's income was spent on black market food, clothing and tobacco at five to ten times official prices. Uncontrolled commodities prices were reported in the summer of 1946 to be from three (shoe-polish) to sixteen (bootlaces) times the prewar level. In the spring of 1946 skilled workers were reported to be financing 40 per cent of expenditure out of savings.

The pressures on firms to operate on the black market were well described by the *Economist*: 'Several conditions make it inevitable that a large proportion of output should tend to go directly from the factory to some form of black market. The first is the low level of production in comparison with capacity; this means that enterprises work at a loss which can only be made good by selling – or more often bartering – some of their output on the black market. The second is the artificially low controlled prices. . . . The controlled rates of wages are also artificially low, which makes it necessary for the employer to supplement them in kind. The absence of any currency reform, coupled with the knowledge that a proportion of the existing note circulation will sooner or later be cancelled, makes for a plentiful supply of money on the black market. And finally, lack of food drives works managers to barter part of their production in exchange for canteen supplies' (26 April 1947).

It is impossible to calculate profits. At official wages and prices the low level of productivity probably implied losses. But with many sales at black market prices, the real purchasing power of wages was extremely low and savings were run down to boost family expenditure. While much production must have been consumed by the masses of the population, part of this consumption involved the transfer of financial assets from workers to black marketeers – profits of a sort. There was also, according to the available figures, some gross fixed investment in manufacturing and mining; although this did not cover depreciation (so that the capital stock fell even before taking account of reparations) it suggests some gross profits. There was probably also substantial stockbuilding on the expectation that prices would rise when controls were removed. As in Japan, this represented concealed profits.

The extreme hardship did not provoke major working-class unrest until the spring of 1947. The trade unions, permitted to develop during 1946, were led mainly by officials from the pre-1933 period, usually social democrats. These people were seldom foisted on the unions by the authorities. Their experience and anti-Nazi stance gave them some authority among the workers. But they nevertheless saw their task as checking workers' aspirations and assured the military authorities that they were doing their best to keep their members at work.

Elections for regional parliaments were held in 1946. The SPD received one-third of the votes in the US zone and, together with the KPD, around half in the more industrialized UK zone (the KPD averaged around 10 per cent, 14 per cent in North Rhine-Westphalia). In Hesse a referendum was included on the socialization of industry. US commander Clay insisted that it had to be voted on separately. When 71 per cent of the voters approved the proposal, he vetoed it. The trade union leadership tried to restrain such demands at the Bavarian Union Congress in 1947. One leader, Tarnow, produced an ingenious objection: 'The hour of the private capitalist system is passed, and therefore strikes which demand the handing over of concerns into common ownership are superfluous' (quoted Schmidt and Fichter, p. 29).

While nominally committed to socialization, SPD representatives combined with the right in the North Rhine-Westphalian regional parliament to vote down a motion put forward by 95 delegations, representing 100,000 workers, for the 'expropriation without compensation of the War-criminal coal barons of the Rhine and Ruhr'. The *Economist* described the situation in the Ruhr in the spring of 1947:

'If only the theoretical daily calorie level of 1550 for basic consumers could be maintained and honoured, then the miseries of cellar life and overcrowding and shortage of goods would matter much less. Only half this level is being met at the moment, and for the four weeks ahead the bread ration will be cut by two-fifths, from 92 ounces to 55. As nearly half the bread grain to be received in the next two months consists of maize – which makes a heavy and indigestible loaf – and as most families living in the towns can eat hardly anything but bread, there is great hardship ahead. To honour the official bread ration, 5000 tons of grain daily must be imported, and the deliveries planned for May fall far short of this figure.

'As for the rest of the diet, the fat ration nominally stands at seven ounces every four weeks; in fact, only two or three ounces were received on the last ration. Because of shortage of meat, fish and sugar have been substituted for two-thirds of the current meat ration. Families who were not lucky enough to lay in stocks of potatoes last autumn are now completely without them; even in the miners' canteens, which receive special issues, potatoes are often short. In these conditions it is not surprising that the mood of the people since the recent demonstrations has been explosive. A further strike of the miners to protest against the shortages is expected soon. If it comes, the effect on German exports and industry will be very serious' (26 April 1947).

Strikes swept through the Ruhr early in 1947. The demands initially concerned housing and food but soon spread to include nationalizations. Mass strikes over this issue took place in Düsseldorf and Essen. In February the factory councils organized ballots on nationalization without compensation. Voting in the mines was typically 90 per cent in favour. Strikes continued to spread: 85,000 workers came out in Wuppertal and 80,000 in Düsseldorf on 25 March. At the high point 350,000 workers were out and mass demonstrations held. Miners operated an effective 'go slow' when at work.

In a broadcast made during the strikes the US governor, Newman, said: 'In the US Congress there is a distinct inclination to oppose further shipment of food to Germany. This can be traced back to rumours of strikes, threats of strikes and a certain resistance in behaviour to the authorities. Strikes which endanger the policies of the occupying powers, or interfere with their plans, will not be tolerated . . . any person who behaves in such a manner will be punished, and do not forget, that under the laws of the military the guilty can be punished with the death sentence. Avoid agitators, and reject those who, out of selfish grounds, criticize the occupation. Be industrious! I have the power to cut the rations of anyone involved in work unrest . . . this would be drastic and extend for an indefinite period of time' (quoted Schmidt and Fichter, pp. 28, 29).

Troops clashed with demonstrators in Brunswick on 1 April and armoured patrols began to prowl the streets regularly.

The trade union leadership was once again obstructive. Boeckler, head of the trade union office in Cologne, threatened to expel anyone who participated in marches or strikes, and certain KPD leaders also urged workers back. A report on the founding conference of the German Union Federation stressed the decisive role for the trade union movement: 'Hitherto, the union officials have exerted a restraining influence over the workers, and have both preached and practised a policy of cooperation with the British authorities. The present mood of the populace is such, however, that checks and restraints can be of very little avail. Only an improvement in food supplies and the clearing up of the administrative confusion can bring any change' (*Economist*, 24 May 1947).

The Federation's constitution included the aim of 'ensuring for the workers an equal voice in the control of economic and social policy . . . and their participation on a basis of parity in all existing and future economic corporations' (ibid.).

Trade unions in the British zone drew up model works council constitutions covering matters affecting wages, welfare and working conditions and providing for regular reports from the management on production progress and programmes. They stipulated that the council should have access to the firm's books, and should be consulted on all questions of staffing and promotion. 'It is not surprising that some employers should have only agreed reluctantly to what some must have regarded as the signing away of their managerial rights. In some cases, their refusal to agree with the trade union terms has led to strikes' (ibid.). The conference also called for broader reconstruction measures, including the immediate socialization of basic industries (beginning with coal and steel), a halt to the dismantling of factories which could be put to peaceful purposes, land reform, a complete purge of the food administration and stricter measures to ensure deliveries from the farms.

Italy

In December 1945 the Christian democrats toppled the coalition government led by the radical resistance leader Parri by withdrawing their support. A series of coalitions led by the Christian democrat De Gasperi followed. De Gasperi's appointment prevented the radical aspirations of the liberation from being realized. It meant 'for the capitalist classes the end of the policy of factory works councils, the end of the fear of nationalization and of the equally dreaded changes in the currency, the end of state intervention in economic and social life to achieve greater social justice and the end of taxes on excess profits accrued from speculation and the war' (Catalano, p. 85). But the Communist Party stayed in the coalition in the name of 'national unity'. This line had been mapped out by CP leader Togliatti on his return from Moscow in March 1944.

Production reached 90 per cent of its prewar level in 1947. This rapid recovery flowed from high demand rather than effective government action, which, instead of using the much-expanded public sector as a motor for recovery, relied on private enterprise.

Basic public utilities – the railways, coal mining, telephones and part of the electricity supply – were already nationalized. The state had also acquired extremely important holdings in banking in the thirties. This gave it effective control over credit. Only 13 per cent of deposits were in private banks in 1945. The banks also owned strategic holdings in iron and steel, shipbuilding and engineering. IRI, the state company into which these holdings were concentrated, employed 233,000 workers in 1948 and undertook 5 per cent of investment. Although badly war-damaged, these firms had substantial excess capacity. Large state subsidies (about $30 million a year) were required to prevent wholesale redundancies. The government refused to use IRI as a 'pilot' of reconstruction as this would have been seen as an assault on private enterprise. Only the German Siemens interests and a few other engineering firms were taken over. On the other hand, privatization was impossible both politically and economically – as there were no private capitalists willing and able to buy the state holdings.

Nevertheless investment recovered strongly. By 1946 industrial fixed investment had nearly regained the prewar level. By 1947 it was 10 per cent higher. This suggests that profits must have recovered too; the fragmentary evidence available also supports this view. The law banning dismissals had, in the immediate postwar months, kept industrial employment above prewar levels. With production still very low in 1946, productivity cannot have been much over half the 1938 level. The major trade union confederation abandoned the ban on dismissals early in 1946, agreeing to reductions in employment of up to 20 per cent over four months. In return it received vague assurances of increased employment in healthy sectors. Industrial employment fell, and unemployment rose by ¾ million between March 1946 and March 1947. This, together with the recovery of production, allowed productivity to rise rapidly in 1947 (Table 4.3).

Table 4.3 Productivity and wages: Italy, 1938–47

Index numbers

	Industrial production	Industrial employment	Industrial productivity	Product wage[1]	Real wage[2]
1938	100	100	100	100	100
1946	61	115	53	58	60[3]
1947	92	105	88	86	88

1. In terms of prices of manufactures.
2. In terms of cost of living.
3. Very rough estimate.

Source: see Appendix.

Given productivity developments, real wages evolved favourably for the employers. They were around 60 per cent of the 1938 level in 1946 and still about 10 per cent less in 1947. But employers are not concerned with workers' incomes measured in terms of what they can buy. What matters to them is labour costs, measured in terms of the value of what their employees produce. However, these real labour costs (product wages) followed a very similar path to both real wages and to productivity (Table 4.3). So real product wages seem to have constituted a share of output in 1946–7 similar to that in 1938, at the height of fascist repression. Profitability also depends on the cost of other inputs. The prices of fuel and transport (mainly state-owned) had grown only one-third as fast as manufactured goods, and white-collar salaries had fallen by one-third or more relative to wages. Both developments worked to boost profitability. But the low level of capacity utilization, especially in 1946, substantially increased overheads, such as depreciation. Overall, the share of profits in industrial output in 1947 can hardly have been much below that in 1938.

Rapid inflation prevented the working class from increasing living standards faster. Price increases were running at nearly 100 per cent a year early in 1947, according to the official cost of living index, and rather more if the black market is taken into account. Rents were tightly controlled and bread rations subsidized. But food prices rose especially fast, transferring about 10 per cent of the national income into the hands of peasants and capitalist farmers. The sliding scale of wages negotiated early in 1946 provided only partial protection and was accompanied by a seven-month wage truce.

High demand and big government deficits fuelled inflation. The budget deficit was 9 per cent of GDP in 1947–8 (down from 29 per cent in 1944–5). Social expenditure had doubled as a percentage of GDP since before the war and huge subsidies were forthcoming to keep the prices of public sector services down while maintaining employment. These deficits added to hoards of financial assets which had already risen, in relation to GDP, by about one-half during the war. These were either spent directly or lent by banks to capitalists to spend. The middle-class lobby was powerful and effective. Plans for a capital levy and currency reform were shelved. Tax concessions for property income swelled the deficit further. So excess liquidity burnt itself out through inflation. By 1947 the ratio of liquid assets to GDP had fallen to less than half its wartime peak. Inflation encouraged speculation; stockbuilding was high in 1946 and reached 6 per cent of output in 1947. Share prices rose sixfold. The foreign exchanges were substantially freed, allowing exporters to make enormous profits by using their foreign currency to buy imports which could be resold at huge margins.

The pressure exerted by successful middle-class resistance to monetary reform and the consequent deficits and inflation was relieved somewhat by a substantial balance of payments deficit, which rose to 8½ per cent of GDP in 1947. US aid and credits were an important source of finance, covering a third of the deficit in 1947 (emigrants' remittances were also important). This permitted imports of essential fuel and food without corresponding exports. The resources released were available for investment. But inflation biased the pattern of accumulation towards stockbuilding. In 1947 the deficit was almost equal to stockpiling, so that much foreign borrowing was in effect squandered on speculation.

Despite the relief afforded by the payments deficit, the pressure on workers' living standards was enormous. In 1947 total output was 1000 billion lire (1954 prices) down on 1938, a fall of 11 per cent. Current public spending was 400 billion lire down (reflecting less military spending). But investment was 300 billion up. So 900 billion lire less domestic production was available for consumption, a fall of 15 per cent. The shift in the balance of payments provided an extra 400 billion lire, which reduced the decline in consumption to 9 per cent. But the population had grown. So consumption per head was 13 per cent less in 1947 than in 1938 (up from around 25 per cent less in 1946). Different groups were hit unevenly. Many peasants and small businesses faced much smaller cuts (if any) than working-class families. Salaried employees and those on fixed incomes fared worst.

Rising unemployment, cuts in consumption, accelerating inflation, rampant speculation and the lack of effective planning seems a recipe for working-class opposition. Reality had conspicuously failed to live up to the expectations held at the end of the war. But opposition was dampened and defused by the main workers' parties, particularly the Italian Communist Party (PCI).

From the moment that Togliatti collaborated with Marshal Badoglio's government after the fall of Mussolini in July 1943, the PCI followed a broad Popular Front policy. It maintained this line until it was expelled from De Gasperi's government in May 1947. Its conditions for participating in government were 'extremely moderate compared to the contemporary English labour party experience: a defence of the standard of living and employment and a few measures against war-time profiteering; it did not demand a radical redistribution of income, widespread nationalization or a welfare-state' (B. Salvati, p. 195). It even accepted postponement of the currency reform in order not to provoke a crisis before elections to the Constituent Assembly in spring 1946. The results disappointed the PCI. It secured only 19 per cent of the votes. Even combined with the Socialist Party's 21 per cent, the left vote was only marginally greater than the Christian Democrats' (DCs). After this setback, the PCI's attitude to the DCs became, if anything, even more conciliatory. The Communist-dominated union federation negotiated a wage truce.

Collaboration extended into the factories. Works councils were used to 'stimulate the rhythm of work, discipline and production'. In the Brida heavy engineering factory in Milan, a PCI stronghold, 'Stakhanov squads' of exemplary workers were formed to secure greater work effort: 'The militants collaborated because they were convinced they were working – not for the owner but for socialism' (B. Salvati, pp. 199–200).

In January 1947 Togliatti proudly affirmed in the Constituent Assembly that Italy had fewer strikes than other European countries: 'In the last years no political strike has taken place in Italy. . . . This is a country where the unions have signed a wage truce, a pact which is unique in the history of the working-class movement, because it determines a maximum wage, not a minimum one. This is really the striking and absurd feature of the economic situation in which we live: it is the working-class and the unions who are giving the best example and are taking all the necessary steps to preserve the discipline of production, order and social peace' (quoted B. Salvati, p. 197).

But the PCI found it difficult to sustain restraint. Although no national strikes took place, plenty of local walkouts occurred. In July 1946 a major strike wave among tanker drivers, printers, dock workers and hotel workers grew into a general strike lasting several days. Observers judged it to be a spontaneous reaction to the increasingly desperate economic situation.

The Communists' departure from the government was less dramatic in Italy than in France (see below). The three-party coalition had come under increasing strain. At the beginning of 1947 the Socialists split over increasingly close links with the communists. The right wing of the party withdrew from the government. This incident highlighted differences between the Christian Democrats and the Communists, whose leader Togliatti maintained that the only options were his party's programme or perpetual crisis. De Gasperi proposed to broaden his cabinet into a government of national unity. The left refused to support the move, fearing increased opposition from the right to such measures as a capital levy. De Gasperi resigned. After more manoeuvrings he formed a government composed entirely of Christian Democrats. The *Economist* warned: 'Beyond the political quarrel, there is the economic crisis, insoluble without strong government' (17 May 1947). It also noted: 'Without the support of the Communists Signor de Gasperi, or for that matter any Italian prime minister, would find the trade unions unmanageable' (ibid.). Since, according to one report, 'there was not a factory in the North and few in the centre in the period 1945–48 that was not armed' (quoted Allam and Sassoon, p. 177), it was clear that even a strong government faced formidable problems.

France

De Gaulle led the early postwar coalition governments in France. But he resigned early in 1946 over left-wing opposition to high military spending. No individual dominated the subsequent series of coalitions, which included conservatives as well as the socialists and the communists. The last was marginally the largest party. Its share of the vote peaked at 28.8 per cent in the November 1946 National Assembly election. The Socialist Party's vote fell from 24.6 per cent in October 1945 to 18.1 per cent in November 1946. The CP tried to persuade the socialists to join them in a Popular Front government, excluding the right. But they were rebuffed. As in Italy, the right-wing parties limited radical reforms and blocked action to check inflation by means of a capital levy, monetary reform and effective attacks on the black market. One journalist claimed early in 1947 that a fifth of the working population was engaged primarily in rackets: 'According to the authorities *everybody* today having anything to do with food or ration cards, or their control, at whatever stage of production or distribution, is certain to gain "illicit profits"' (quoted Werth, p. 321).

Despite the Socialist Party's unwillingness to exclude the conservatives from government, they, rather than the communists, 'most eagerly championed nationalization and most emphatically emphasized its socialist nature' (Kuisel, p. 50). The main union federation, the CGT, 'followed the communists closely when it portrayed nationalization as a continuation of patriotic resistance rather than the beginning of the destruction of capitalism. Trade union officials rejected the term "socialization" and said only provocateurs spoke of socialism and revolution in times of economic distress' (ibid., p. 51). Thorez, the CP leader, said that nationalizations were democratic and nothing to do with socialism or communism. In 1945, however, the communists did help secure the nationalization of those mines remaining in private hands, and of gas, electricity and the banking system. They then fought to dominate the tripartite boards – representing the government, workers and consumers – which had been established to run the industries.

The French government made a serious attempt after 1945 to plan the modernization of industry. The Monnet Plan, published early in 1947, contained ambitious schemes for investment in transport, energy, and iron and steel. In 1947 investment in these industries ran at between 1½ times (iron and steel) and five times (coal) the UK level. Most of this investment was in newly nationalized industries, and since their prices were held down substantial state loans were required to finance it. By 1947 industrial investment exceeded its prewar level, and public investment constituted around one-fifth of the total.

The state also provided grants to reconstruct war-damaged property. But to qualify for such a grant a recipient had to install an identical item in the same place, so there was no opportunity for modernization or relocation. Otherwise the state provided little finance for industry. The nationalization of the big four deposit banks and thirty-two major insurance companies provided a potential lever to influence investment through credit provision. In the early years this control could hardly have been very effective because firms were making high profits and possessed many financial assets accumulated during the war. The government nevertheless accused the banks of 'excessive caution in their credit policy, caution often amounting to downright sabotage and of deliberate attempts to bring pressure on the state' (quoted Werth, p. 278). Nationalization did not change very much, one observer noting how the banks 'continued to work hand in hand with big business' (ibid.).

Total production in 1947 was 1100 billion francs down on 1938 (in 1954 prices) – a fall of 9 per cent. Investment, including stockbuilding, was 800 billion higher than in 1938, and public current spending on goods and services 500 billion higher. So domestic production available for consumption was 25 per cent lower. The fall in actual consumption was held to 15 per cent by imports financed by borrowing from the United States and by running down reserves. Consumption per head was equally squeezed. Workers fared worst, while peasants and businessmen did best.

After the liberation, workers received wage rises which, according to the official price index, restored real wages to nearly 90 per cent of the prewar level. But the socialists abandoned a plan for monetary reform. Mendès-France, minister for the national economy, wanted to use the opportunity of a new banknote issue in March 1945 temporarily to block all bank accounts and limit individuals' expenditures to a level compatible with production. There was little parliamentary support for these proposals. As one commentator pointed out: 'In France the assault against the mountain of 600 millions of hoarded notes affects 18 million peasants – and that of course is a major political problem' (quoted Werth, p. 248). For electoral reasons, even the Communist Party opposed monetary reform. These cash holdings, built up during the war, boosted purchasing power enormously. Prices doubled between 1945 and 1946. According to official indices, real wages fell to only 60 per cent of prewar.

In fact, these figures considerably overestimate real purchasing power because of the black market. Between 1945 and 1947 real wages hardly exceeded half of the prewar level. Working hours had also risen to around forty-four hours, as compared with forty before the war. J.-P. Rioux graphically describes the situation in Paris:

'The very bareness of the official figure makes it clear that the parallel market is essential: scarcely 900 calories a day in August 1944 for adults in Paris, 1210 in September and 1515 in May 1945 (in the same official publication it is discretely revealed that even low grade civil servants in the National Statistical Office in sixteen large towns including Paris had between 1840 and 2540 calories a day in May-June 1944 and between 2050 and 2870 in September-October, thanks to "supplementary resources"). At the cost of waiting in endless queues when unexpected supplies of food arrived, of sometimes humiliating diplomacy towards the shopkeepers to whom the destiny of a family was linked by their ration cards, the rations are gathered and consumed without wasting a single gramme. Finally, to reach the 2000 calories necessary for survival, anything goes – exchange, food parcels from the family, gardens, allotments sometimes in the most unexpected places, discreet visits to the back of the shop, expeditions to farms of "friends", exchange with neighbours or workmates. These harsh days in this way had their lighter moments which fed the family conversation for a long time afterwards' (p. 40).

The process, already seen in Italy, whereby large amounts of money ended up in peasant hands is well illustrated by the French experience: 'How to make the peasants declare, and then sell their products at the official price, when the black market visits their home and makes a much more tempting offer. The producers have no interest in supplying food when they have no possibility of receiving the manufactured goods they need in return. The peasant table is, more often than not, well garnished and only the surplus is sold on the black market. . . . Savings are ample witness to the growth of deposits in the Crédit Agricole which grew from an index of 100 in 1938 to 743 in December 1944 and 1717 in December 1946. This reflects black market profits but also a transformation of part of their capital into money as it was impossible to replace fertilizers and depreciating machinery' (Rioux, p. 43).

Industrial productivity had fallen much less than real wages; it appears to have been 95 per cent of the prewar level in 1947 and nearly 90 per cent in 1946 (Table 4.4). The prices of materials and other inputs probably rose less than those of manufactures and, again as in Italy, salaries rose less rapidly than wages. Both developments worked to raise manufacturing profits. So by the end of 1946 the pressure of spending on investment and on consumption must have pushed industrial profits up to a very high

Table 4.4 Productivity and wages: France, 1938–47

Index numbers

	Industrial production	Industrial employment	Industrial productivity	Real wage[1]	Real wage[2]
1938	100	100	100	100	100
1946	84	96	87	58	40
1947	99	104	95	63	50

1. In terms of official cost of living.
2. In terms of actual cost of living.

Source: see Appendix.

level. No figures are available, but an official survey noted that the 'fortunes made in textiles and food for example are not a myth' (Closon, p. 24).

Nor did workers benefit from a radical restructuring of the tax system. 'Wage earners in particular, though their real income has risen considerably from the very low levels of the early postwar years, have certainly lost to farmers, industrialists and merchants' (UNECE, 1953, p. 80).

As in Italy, the Communist Party exerted a key influence on working-class reaction: 'Communist leadership can to a large extent determine the speed and the extent of the vicious spiral of wages and prices. Communist leadership can also make or mar the campaign for production, without which neither the immediate stabilization of prices nor the ultimate modernization of the French economy is possible' (*Economist*, 8 June 1946).

In the coal mines, for example, the CP used its influence to encourage more production for scarcely increased wages. Faced by staunch resistance by the miners to working for the old owners, the state first controlled, and then nationalized, the mines. Absenteeism remained high. In June 1945 Thorez said to northern miners: 'I say frankly that it is impossible to approve a strike by miners in the present period, especially when it starts outside the union . . . 20,000 to 30,000 tons have been lost in this way; it is a serious crime against the country, against the union and against the interest of the miners themselves' (quoted Lefranc, p. 30). At the beginning of 1946 he again informed miners that, 'To produce, is the highest form of class duty, of republican and patriotic duty' (ibid.).

De Gaulle said of Thorez: 'While still pushing forward the interests of communism, he acted in the public interest on many occasions. He never stopped giving the advice to work as much as possible whatever the cost. Was this simply a political tactic? That is not my affair; it is enough that France was served' (quoted Unir, p. 264). When the public sector workers threatened to strike at the end of 1945 Thorez blamed 'agitators'. Such action, he said, would 'be a crime against the fatherland'.

Workers were given no control in private enterprises in return for their restraint. The workers' committees which were set up 'were allowed to make suggestions about production processes, [but] nobody was obliged to take any notice' (Werth, pp. 278–9). The unions raised no objection to the key proviso in the Monnet

Plan that hours of work should be increased from forty-four to forty-eight.

In 1946 workers, dissatisfied with the slowness with which conditions improved, struck spontaneously, with particular impact in printing and the Post Office. The Communist Party denounced the disputes as the result of 'provocation'. Strikes were, it said, a 'tool of the trusts'.

The main strike wave occurred from April to July 1947. It began at Renault, nationalized because of its owner's collaboration. The communist-dominated union there had 'promoted the battle for production and de-emphasized wage demands more vigorously than anywhere else in the country' (Ross, p. 45). Wildcat strikes broke out on 25 April. Three days later 12,000 people had downed tools. The CGT denounced the strike leaders as 'Hitlero-Trotskyite provocateurs in the pay of de Gaulle'. But the workers forced it to call a one-hour strike, over which it lost control. All the 30,000-strong work force came out. Concessions the union had obtained from management were voted down. The union was forced to back the strike, which was rapidly spreading through the Paris metal-working industry, although it failed to take up all the demands of the strike committee. The Communist Party was obliged to follow suit to retain working-class support. Its ministers, who opposed the government's wage control policies, were dismissed by the prime minister.

The Communist Party felt obliged to leave the government once its working-class support was threatened. It still sought to use working-class discontent to pressurize the Socialist Party into joining it in a Popular Front government. But it was a socialist prime minister, Ramadier, who with strong US support had dismissed the communists. This signalled a decisive attempt to roll back working-class strength in the voting booths, and, most importantly, on the shop floor.

The United Kingdom

The United Kingdom faced no economic disruptions remotely comparable to those in continental Europe and Japan. Industrial production in 1946 was about equal to the 1938 level, with employment fractionally up and productivity down. There were three immediate economic problems: external payments, demobilization and the switch to peacetime production, and wartime accumulation of financial assets.

The current account deficit of the balance of payments was running at approximately 2 per cent of GDP. The basic problem was the massive turnaround on invisibles (income from services and from investment overseas). From the turn of the century to the Second World War the United Kingdom had run a deficit on visible trade (goods) of 5–6 per cent of GDP, more or less covered by a surplus on invisibles. By 1946, however, the invisibles account had run into deficit to the tune of 1 per cent of GDP. The turnaround was largely the result of a fall in interest, profits and dividends from abroad, from about 4 per cent of GDP in the 1920s and 1930s to 1 per cent in the late 1940s. Some £1000 million of external capital assets had been sold to help pay for the war, and £3000 million extra external liabilities contracted. The latter were mainly loans from the Sterling Area countries (mainly colonies whose currencies were tied to the pound). Another factor was the increase in the government deficit abroad (almost entirely military) which ran at over 3½ per cent of GDP in 1946 (falling to around 1½ per cent for the rest of the 1940s and 1 per cent for the 1950s). The overall deficit could also be expected to rise substantially once imports regained prewar levels, unless visible exports grew considerably. The problem of the external account became pressing when, on the surrender of Japan, US Lend-Lease aid ended.

Demobilization and the restructuring of production posed a problem on a vast scale. In 1944 and 1945 the armed forces employed about 20 per cent of the work force. Public authorities' current expenditure on goods and services had risen from 13.4 per cent of GDP in 1938 to an average of 43.0 per cent between 1939 and 1945. It remained 23.3 per cent in 1946.

More government expenditure had been financed by taxation than during the 1914–18 war (39 per cent in 1940 rising to 55 per cent in 1944). But with consumption limited by rationing, personal savings had risen massively, reaching a peak of 25 per cent of personal disposable income (up from less than 5 per cent before the war). The national debt had risen as fast, from £6½ billions in the 1930s to £21.4 billions at the end of 1945 (£25.6 billions by the end of 1947). By the end of the war it was approaching three years' GDP (twice the 1930s level). These financial assets posed a major (potential) inflationary threat.

The abrupt ending of US Lend-Lease coupled with the external payments situation made further US loans an urgent priority. The new government promptly despatched Keynes to Washington to negotiate one. The other economic priorities of the Labour government were rapid demobilization (and consequent reduction in government expenditure) and the restoration of peacetime production to provide resources for controlled expansion of private consumption, social reforms and, most urgently, increased exports (especially to the Dollar Area).

This last objective was made all the more urgent by the loan terms dictated by the United States. The $3.75 billion made available at the end of 1945 was conditional on the United Kingdom making sterling fully convertible within one year of ratification by Congress. Despite these pressures to open up the Empire the government exploited the colonies to the full. It required them to sell it their main export commodities at prices frequently well below world market levels. The government also accorded the colonies low priority for UK exports, preventing them from spending all their foreign exchange earnings. So the sterling balances grew in the late forties. Such high dollar earners as the Gold Coast (Ghana) and Malaysia were particularly ruthlessly exploited, being forced to add their dollars to the Sterling Area's common pool, much of which was used to buy UK imports. India, which had more political leverage, was treated more gently. An Indian historian has commented in response to Harold Wilson's statement that the dollar pool was a 'rough and ready way of allocating dollars amongst several major countries according to their needs', that 'it certainly was rough and ready – rough on the dollar surplus countries because the others were only too ready to spend the surplus' (Gupta, p. 111).

Demobilization proceeded fairly smoothly. 1946 was the only year in which unemployment exceeded 2 per cent (most of the unemployed were service personnel yet to be officially demobilized but released to seek work). Between 1945 and 1948 employment in the armed forces fell by 4,242,000. Civilian employment plus total unemployment rose by 3,375,000, so that nearly 900,000 people disappeared from the labour force. These were mostly women and old people brought into the labour force during the war. Absorption was facilitated by a marked drop in average weekly hours worked, down from 52.9 in 1943 to 46.5 in 1948 for male manual workers.

Housing posed the biggest problem. Destruction and deterioration of the housing stock during the war had led to a considerable shortage. Many demobbed soldiers and sailors took to squatting and often resisted eviction violently.

The problem of financial assets was dealt with by a combination of low interest rates to minimize debt servicing (interest payments were about 9 per cent of GDP in the 1920s, fell to 6 per cent in the 1930s and, despite rapid growth in the debt, remained at that level in 1947) and the maintenance of wartime controls. Materials controls directed investment and production into priority areas (especially exports) while rationing held down consumer demand, thereby staving off rapid inflation.

The government could only achieve all its objectives if production grew rapidly. In the long run this required high investment. But in the short term the government emphasized 'production drives' – propaganda exercises aimed at persuading people to work harder. It managed to mobilize an extremely wide range of political support for these drives, from capitalists to the CP.

Less immediately pressing, but ultimately more menacing, was the stagnation of pay. In 1946 and 1947 real earnings were slightly lower than in 1943 and 1944 (though a fifth higher than prewar). But take-home pay had risen much less. The average male manual worker now paid around 9 per cent of his wage in taxes and social security contributions, up from 2 per cent prewar. The government also rigged the retail price index by subsidizing items whose weight in the index was disproportionate to their true importance. Average consumption per head grew by more than 10 per cent in 1946, but by only a further 2 per cent in 1947, to reach a level only 2 per cent above that of 1938. The higher purchasing power of real wages and accumulated financial assets was bottled up by rationing.

Workers were not rewarded for restraining personal consumption by being provided with vastly expanded social services. The National Health Service, which was to involve a big injection of resources, was only in the planning stages. A smaller proportion of GDP was being spent on education than prewar (Table 4.5). Transfers absorbed a slightly higher share. Increased pensions and the family allowance cost more than was saved as a result of lower unemployment (in real terms the dole was no higher than prewar). Council housing was the only major area of public spending to leap ahead (doubling as compared to prewar), and even this should be judged against the wartime dilapidation of the housing stock. As late as 1947, military spending exceeded the 1938 level by more than did spending on the social services.

Table 4.5 The British welfare state, 1938–51

Spending as percentages of GDP

	Total transfers to persons	Health	Local current education	Local housing capital	Total[1]	Current military
1938	5.1	1.2	2.0	1.0	12.2	6.3
1946	6.8	n.a.	1.7	1.0	13.7	15.7
1947	6.4	n.a.	1.8	2.0	15.4	9.3
1948	6.0	2.0	1.9	2.3	16.8	6.3
1949	6.0	3.3	1.9	2.2	18.0	6.2
1950	5.9	3.5	1.9	2.1	17.6	6.3
1951	5.4	3.3	2.0	2.0	16.7	7.5

1. Current civil expenditure plus local authority housing.

Sources: Feinstein, Tables 2, 10; UK, *National Income and Expenditure 1946–51*, Tables 27, 30 and 31.

Nor were workers given effective industrial planning in exchange for wage restraint. Planning amounted to a maze of pragmatic controls inherited from the war. The official criterion for controlling prices was that they should guarantee a 'reasonable return' to high cost producers. So efficient firms earned very high profits while the inefficient remained in business. Most of the top personnel administering the controls were employers often seconded from major firms in the industry on an unpaid basis. Unilever employees filled ninety posts in the Ministry of Food, twelve of them senior; the director of the Iron and Steel Federation headed the steel rearmament panel; the match controller worked for Bryant and May – his office was on the firm's premises; and so on.

The Labour government also encouraged the formation and amalgamation of trade associations, often delegating the administration of controls to them (e.g. newsprint, imported meat, war surplus stocks, confectionery). Sometimes the task was entrusted to a single large firm (e.g. the Mond Nickel Company).

Allocations were normally determined by production shares. Trade associations expelled firms selling below government maximum prices. Harold Wilson, at the time president of the Board of Trade, summed it up well: '[This system] perpetuates the pattern of a particular industry or trade, featherbeds the inefficient and unenterprising, freezes out the newcomers and penalizes the efficient, growing firm. It has, in fact, many of the vices of the old, prewar type of control, dividing out whole markets between producers on the basis of arbitrary quotas, and doing this with all the statutory sanction of the state behind it' (quoted Rogow, p. 67).

But Labour did believe that direct control of resources in the nationalized industries was crucial to economic development. Since the major nationalized industries began to operate as such in 1947, this is a convenient place to discuss the role that nationalization played in Labour's strategy.

The Labour Party had long argued for nationalization, on both ideological and pragmatic grounds. In 1934 it had drawn up a radical programme to nationalize banking, land and those 'basic industries' (fuel and power, transport, iron and steel) which had 'failed the nation'. Between 1945 and 1951 the Labour government implemented the whole of this programme, with the important exceptions of banking and land. Nationalization seemed to the government to offer a solution to many economic problems – indeed, to be a substitute for comprehensive economic planning. First, it could end strategic shortages hampering private sector industrial growth, hence the concentration on 'basic' industries. Second, control of basic industries could ensure that supplies went to high-priority activities.

This conception of nationalization satisfied to a large extent the needs of the capitalist class. Most of the industries taken over – coal and railways, for example – had been unprofitable for a long time. Their prospects under fragmented private ownership were poor, as a string of official reports since the First World War had made clear. The 1944 Reid report on the coal industry had said that the mines needed vast investment and comprehensive reorganization, and that a public authority empowered to force through mergers and rationalization should be created.

Capitalists in the industries concerned received fairly generous compensation on nationalization. Others hoped to benefit from the rationalized services and lower prices which, interwar experience suggested, would not have happened under private ownership. They felt that industrial relations – exceptionally bitter, especially in mining – might improve. So resistance to the early nationalizations was muted.

Initial plans for workers' participation, via trade union representatives on boards, were watered down to a system of 'worker directors' not responsible to the workers. But nationalization probably did reduce industrial unrest (although more days were devoted to strikes in the mines in the year following nationalization than in that preceding it). Prices were held down; the nationalized industries' share of total profits fell from 31.5 per cent in 1930–8 to 14.2 per cent in 1948–9. Productivity improved. In 1951 the British coal industry was the only one in Europe with a higher output per man shift than prewar. This reflected reorganization, and perhaps speedup, as well as modernization. Investment in the nationalized industries was lower than prewar, suggesting that benefits to private industry from cheaper inputs would be limited.

Nor, indeed, did private industry invest much more than prewar. The ratio of fixed investment to GDP was a little higher in current prices terms, but this was more than offset by the fact that investment goods prices had risen nearly 30 per cent more than the average during the war. So in real terms the share of investment actually fell by 3 per cent of GDP to a level well below that of continental rivals (Table 4.1). While the volume of manufacturing investment was some 50 per cent higher than prewar, the ratio of manufacturing investment to manufacturing output was hardly higher at all (at around 9 per cent). Engineering – crucial for the production of investment goods for domestic modernization and for export – was investing less of its output than prewar (7 per cent in 1947, down from 7½ per cent in 1937).

Profits slipped back a little in 1947, but the profit share was hardly below the prewar level, and high capacity utilization will have boosted the profit rate. In comparison, returns from investing in financial assets were very low. Around 40 per cent of company income went in tax compared to 15 per cent prewar. The proportion of income paid out as dividends and interest fell further, as a result of dividend control (from 60 per cent in 1937 to 28 per cent in 1948). So company savings were high and firms spent less than their current savings on fixed investment, despite large stocks of liquid assets accumulated during the war. Although new shares issues were controlled, it is hard to believe that lack of finance was the reason for relatively sluggish investment.

But finance was not the only aspect of government control. Building was under tight rein until the mid-1950s, and investment in plant and machinery was limited by export targets for the engineering industries and import controls. The UK *Economic Survey* for 1947 explained: 'Import is permitted if the machine is of essential significance and cannot be supplied in comparable conditions from UK production' (p. 17). 'The provision of new equipment and maintenance . . . cannot all be done at once. There is not enough manpower, steel and building and engineering capacity, especially as a large part of the latter must be used for export. The government must therefore retain close control' (p. 25).

If controls did limit accumulation, this resulted from working-class pressure on government to improve living standards. Physical constraints on construction and engineering could have been avoided by cutting housebuilding further and reducing home consumption of engineering products. Alternatively, cuts in consumer good imports would have permitted higher imports (or lower exports) of machine tools. Also, if the controls really were holding back a huge pent-up demand for investment then their relaxation in the early fifties should have seen an investment boom. It did not.

It is impossible to establish how far low (by international standards) UK investment was due to working-class pressure (reflected in shopfloor resistance to the effects of modernization or in high taxation to pay for social services, or physical controls on investment to free resources to allow consumer imports). But the complacent attitude of UK management was probably the more important factor. This was encouraged by the continuing wartime practice of amicably sharing out markets, both at home and in the colonies (which absorbed 50 per cent of exports).

The 1947 position was both unsatisfactory and unsustainable. The balance of payments deficit of 4 per cent of GDP had to be cut. Unless the government could increase production rapidly, it would have to divert resources from either public services or investment (which was in any case too low to generate rapid productivity growth) or consumption (already growing too slowly to satisfy Labour's supporters).

Industrial struggle had been more muted than expected in the immediate postwar years. In 1945 less than 3 million days were occupied in strikes, half of which was accounted for by a dock strike, and there were a number of short strikes in the mines. In 1946 the number of days involved actually declined to just over 2 million, the motor industry accounting for half. Compared with the average number of days spent in strikes in 1919–20 (30 million) the situation appeared calm. But pressure was building up for continued reforms at just the time the government was facing equally compelling pressures to cut back. The *Economist* stated very clearly the disquiet which employers were feeling:

'When Parliament reassembled after the summer recess, the Government had just overcome the squatters' crisis. It meets again next week, after a short Christmas break, against the background of a strikers' crisis. To call in troops to safeguard London's food supply was undoubtedly the only course open to the Cabinet, although its immediate effect was not to stop the strike, but to spread it to the provinces and to the provision market workers and dockers.

'. . . 1947 has started badly, with the token strike of ship-builders in support of their claim for a five-day week, the "work to rule" movement of LNER [railway] shopmen, and now the trans-port strike. It would be prudent to bear in mind the possibility that the usual postwar industrial troubles have merely been postponed and not avoided. The present depressed standard of living in this country cannot be raised – or at least not raised quickly – unless there is a sharp increase in output per worker. Without this, the standard of living will soon fall since the country is still, in effect, living on Lend-Lease. . . . Though they are not averse to any increases in wages, what the workers really want, as shown by what they will strike for, is more leisure – the only thing that is quite certainly disastrous to the country. . . . It is painfully apparent that the workers will not follow their chairborne leaders; they prefer to follow the shopsteward in the street. It is true that there was the same irresponsibility and turbulence – indeed, far worse – after the war of 1914–18 and that it then disappeared. But it did not disappear before full employment also disappeared. Every time there is one of these unofficial strikes, the conclusion seems to be reinforced that it is only when there is some un-employment that organized labour will behave responsibly enough to make full employment possible' (18 January 1947).

The extent of successful capitalist reconstruction achieved in Europe and Japan by early 1947 cannot be read off from indices for production or investment. Even where output and accumulation had grown rapidly, balance of payments deficits, government deficits and rapid inflation were the economic manifestation of powerful, and as yet unresolved, conflicts as the various classes struggled to maintain or improve their position. The working class posed the biggest threat. Workers' demands had so far been checked by the trade union and party leaderships, but patience was wearing thin. The working class might deploy its formidably increased industrial power at any time. Such an offensive would almost inevitably transcend simple wage demands since the economy still was manifestly incapable of granting big rises. The obvious alternative to continued self-restraint was to press for workers' governments to take effective control over the economy. Even in Britain, where the situation was much less severe, Labour was finding it difficult to satisfy its supporters' aspirations.

In Germany and Japan, where effective recovery had hardly begun, workers suffered more severe hardships. If the occupying powers continued with their dismal failure to launch a determined assault on the obstacles to recovery then workers might attempt the task themselves, by methods, and along lines, quite inimical to capitalism. The deep crisis which had gripped the system in the immediate aftermath of the war had yet to be resolved. In the spring of 1947 the capitalist class still faced enormous difficulties. But help was at hand.

5. Marshall Aid: the United States Changes Tack

People who recall the immediate postwar years usually think first of the Marshall Plan and the beginning of the cold war. President Truman formally launched the cold war in a speech to Congress on 12 March 1947. He called for economic and military aid to Greece and Turkey and outlined what came to be known as the Truman Doctrine: 'It must be the policy of the United States to support free peoples who are resisting attempted subjugation by armed minorities or by outside pressure' (quoted Yergin, p. 283).

On 5 June secretary of state Marshall proposed a European Recovery Programme. The United States should help to draft it and provide support 'so far as it may be practicable for us to do so'. A week or so later he suggested that $5 or $6 billions a year might be required from the United States for several years. While the Marshall Plan was confined to Europe, a similar shift of policy towards Japan soon followed, with the US government calling, in November 1947, for the Japanese government to formulate a plan for economic recovery to ensure that 'the Japanese economy will be balanced at the earliest possible time' (quoted J. Halliday, p. 187).

These shifts in US thinking were to decisively influence reconstruction. They were also interlinked. One White House aide called the Marshall Plan 'a Truman Doctrine in action' (quoted Yergin, p. 321).

Europe's crisis?

Historians disagree about precisely why the United States decided to commit itself to participate more actively in European reconstruction. What is not in dispute is that reconstruction required continued American aid at existing levels. The crucial point is that before Marshall the United States had no plans to provide such aid. During 1946 food aid was channelled through UNRRA. But the United States decided in the autumn to terminate UNRRA, apparently justifying the move on the grounds of the extent of industrial recovery in Western Europe.

Although food and materials were now readily available on world markets, Western Europe lacked the dollars to buy them. It was running a huge deficit with the United States. In 1946 exports covered no more than one-quarter of imports, and the balance had not improved by 1947. Europe's deficit with the rest of the world

Chart 5.1 Europe's trade with the United States, 1946–50

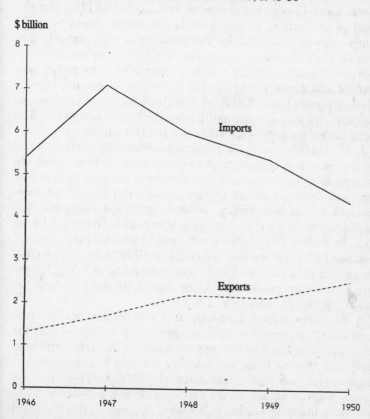

Source: US, *Balance of Payments*.

rose from $5.8 billion in 1946 to $7.5 billion in 1947. Much was
financed by US loans (Chart 5.1). Stringent conditions were often
attached (for example to the British loan). Gold and dollar reserves were running down rapidly. In the two years before
Marshall Aid was agreed, they had fallen by one-third. New
sources of finance were essential to maintain vital imports.

Neither Europe nor Japan was collapsing (contrary to many
later accounts). The terrible winter of 1946–7 had set back recovery. But this was a far cry from economic collapse. Even in the
first quarter of 1947 – badly hit by the weather – European industrial production was 16 per cent up on the same quarter of the
previous year. It also recovered rapidly: by the last quarter of 1947
it was some 12 per cent above the last quarter of 1946. But this
level of production, let alone further increases, could be maintained only if dollar aid for the purchase of vital imports continued. The European crisis was *potential* rather than actual.

It is obviously difficult – if not impossible – to decide how
Europe and Japan would have fared without continued US aid.
The apparently simpler issue of what Washington believed would
happen, and why it regarded the prospect as unacceptable, also
turns out to be a minefield of different interpretations.

J. M. Jones, a senior US diplomatic officer, privately summed
up the prospects in Europe at the time thus: 'If these areas are
allowed to spiral downwards into economic anarchy, then at best
they will drop out of the United States' orbit and try an independent nationalistic policy; at worst they will swing into the
Russian orbit. We will then face the world alone. What will be the
cost, in dollars and cents of our armaments and our economic
isolation? I do not see how we could possibly avoid a depression
far greater than that of 1929–32 and crushing taxes to pay for the
direct commitments we should be forced to make around the
world' (quoted Horowitz, pp. 126–7).

It has been argued forcefully that independent nationalistic
capitalist development in Europe was a real possibility – that 'the
real issue at stake was less the condition of Western European
capitalism than its form, and whether it would be cooperative or
competitive', and that 'Washington correctly perceived that recovery without United States participation was a basic threat to
American interests' (Kolko and Kolko, pp. 337–8). But the claim
that America was being shut out of European markets cannot be
sustained.

The European economies were far from developing into an insulated unit, trading mainly between themselves. In 1947 they exported to each other only just over half as much in real terms as in 1938. Imports from the rest of the world (excluding the United States) ran at only three-quarters of the prewar level. However, Europe bought 90 per cent more from the United States than prewar. Its exports accounted for 27 per cent of European imports in 1947, as compared with 10 per cent in 1938. Every available dollar was being spent on US food, raw materials and capital goods. The European capitalist class was in far too precarious a position, both economically and politically, to cut an independent path of development. Such an approach would be a desperate last resort, to be adopted only if American help was not forthcoming.

Britain might be seen as an exception. Its economic and political position was far less unstable than that of the main continental countries or of Japan. Indeed the British Treasury had examined the implications first of failure to secure a US loan and then of failure to secure substantial Marshall Aid. Early in 1946 a section of the Treasury floated a plan for a 'multilateral system based on sterling, excluding the USA'. The basic idea was a widened Sterling Area – including the French, Belgian and Dutch empires – within which dollars would be strictly pooled and imports controlled. But the paper admitted that the support of the European countries would be 'rather worthless economically' and that 'our policy would have to be based upon the fact that in a world of bankrupts the half-solvent is king' (quoted Clarke, p. 141). Keynes had poured scorn on the idea, asking rhetorically, 'What motive have [the other European countries] to rupture trade relations with the USA in order to lend us money they have not got?' (ibid., p. 135).

By mid-1947, when discussing the implications of 'inadequate Marshall Aid', the same Treasury officials had become far more pessimistic about going it alone. Talk of a general European dollar pool had given way to a more modest proposal for a series of bilateral arrangements 'primarily with the stronger countries (e.g. Australia, New Zealand, Eire, Denmark) rather than with countries which would be likely to be a drain on our resources and which would raise difficult questions of allocation of scarce supplies' (ibid., p. 178). While recognizing that the United Kingdom would be unable to fulfil its obligations to free trade and payments, the new paper had abandoned talk of 'walking out' of the IMF and the International Trade Organization, and of setting up parallel organizations centred around the Sterling Area.

It acknowledged that the import programme would have to be trimmed, although 'radical cuts in this programme will be extremely difficult to make, and if made, confront us with the prospect of a decay of industrial activity – a downward spiral towards the plight of Germany today' (ibid., p. 177). It also foresaw the need for 'drastic action, equivalent to national mobilization; to expand export production (e.g. coal and textiles), stimulate import-saving production (e.g. agriculture) and stop long-term capital projects . . . the building and investment programmes generally should be drastically cut down, to save timber, steel and manpower. We should not have resources for satisfying our elementary consumption needs plus exports plus investment' (ibid., pp. 175, 180).

So even the best placed potential recipient of Marshall Aid was in too feeble a position to envisage a future without such aid as anything other than desperate. In the Treasury's words, it would be a 'backs to the wall' situation. Marshall Aid was no bribe to lure Europe away from an emerging viable capitalist road of mutual cooperation, and independence from the United States.

Nor was it a bribe to keep Europe from toppling immediately into the Russian orbit. The European Communist parties were hardly poised to launch a Moscow-inspired insurrection. Only in Greece did the CP make a serious bid for state power, and in so doing broke with the Kremlin line. Stalin had ceded Greece to the Western sphere of influence in his discussions with Churchill. Early in 1946 the influential US foreign policy adviser, George Kennan, had admitted that the Soviet leaders envisaged 'revolutionary upheavals within the various capitalist countries' only after another inter-imperialist war. In the meantime, 'Democratic-progressive elements abroad are to be utilized to bring pressure to bear on capitalist governments along lines agreeable to Soviet interests' (Kennan, p. 548). He had added that the CPs would be used to 'increase social and industrial unrest', urging those with economic or national grievances 'to seek redress not in mediation and compromise, but in defiant violent struggle for destruction of other elements of society' (ibid., p. 555). But the Communist parties' behaviour during 1946 had proved him wrong on this score (Chapter 4).

Despite later rhetoric, the US administration clearly did not 'see communist activities as the *root* of the present difficulties in

Western Europe' (emphasis added). Kennan's background paper to Marshall argued that 'American effort in aid to Europe should be directed not to the combating of communism as such but to the restoration of the economic health and vigour of European society' (quoted Kolko and Kolko, p. 376). But it also observed that 'the Communists are exploiting the European crisis' and that US aid 'should aim, in other words, not to combat communism but the economic maladjustment which makes European society vulnerable to exploitation by any and all totalitarian movements and which Russian communism is now exploiting' (Kennan, p. 336).

So the United States did perceive a communist threat in Europe even though this existed despite, rather than because of, the policies pursued by the CPs. The fundamental point was that if working-class conditions did not improve – let alone if they deteriorated further – then mass struggles would inevitably erupt. The Communist parties, which had so far done their best to defuse such a response, might then be forced by rank-and-file pressure to lead the struggles. To do otherwise would jeopardize their influence within the working class. Where the CPs were less powerful, Socialist parties would experience the same pressures. The 'Communist Threat' was real. But the danger was that deteriorating economic conditions would breed demands for socialization, planning and workers' control, despite the policies of the CPs.

The capitalist class in Europe and Japan was in no state to deal with such pressures on its own. Speculation on what form of socialism, if any, might have emerged in Western Europe, had the United States washed its hands of the class struggle there, would probably be fruitless. President Truman was oversimplifying when he told a group of Congressmen in September 1947 that 'we'll have to provide a program of interim aid relief until the Marshall program gets going, or the governments of France and Italy will fall, Austria too, and for all practical purposes Europe will be Communist' (quoted Yergin, p. 328). But it was not an absurd scenario.

A US official put the essential point more clearly at a businessmen's meeting in February 1947: 'If the American program for world trade were to fail, its failure would hasten the spread of nationalization among the other countries of the world. . . . We cannot insulate ourselves against the movements that sweep around the globe. If every other major nation were to go Socialist, it would be extremely difficult, if not impossible, to preserve real private enterprise in the United States' (quoted Kolko and Kolko, p. 338).

So the fundamental task for the United States was to restructure provision of the resources necessary for European recovery – to replace existing pragmatic arrangements with ones designed to ensure the restoration of effective capitalist control. Kennan, a leading foreign affairs adviser, discussing the situation in France and Japan in early 1947, summarized the problem succinctly. It was, he said, a matter of imposing 'stringent measures of financial and social discipline' (p. 330). J. M. Jones later wrote: 'There was no confidence to spare. *World Report* published on January 21 [1947] a survey of the state of European recovery. It concluded that industrial recovery was beginning to stall. Lack of confidence and shortage of productive labour were partly responsible, but even more so was the feeling of helplessness and frustration which reduced and undermined government authority' (p. 83).

Economic problems in the United States

The United States adopted the Marshall plan mainly because it was concerned about the future of Europe (and Japan), with all that that implied for American interests. But economic problems at home also played a role.

As we have seen (Chapter 2), in early 1946 profits in the United States were high. But unprecedented numbers of workers were striking for improved living standards. The US Department of Commerce's *Survey of Current Business* echoed widespread fears of economic instability: 'The existing volume of cash deposits and liquid securities is often described as providing the seeds for a reflationary boom and collapse such as was associated with previous postwar periods. A disruptive inflation is of course a real possibility' (February 1946, p. 31).

In the event the shift to peacetime production proceeded more smoothly than had been feared. Output fell by $82 billion (1972 prices) between 1945 and 1946, with practically all of this fall accounted for by government payments to the forces. Private sector production fell by only $12 billion or 3 per cent, despite a $102 billion cut in government purchases from the private sector (largely munitions). The shortfall was made up by a rise in consumption and housebuilding ($30 billion and $13 billion respectively), a sharp rise in business fixed investment and restocking ($15 billion and $16 billion respectively), and an $18 billion increase in net exports (largely to Europe and Japan). Private spending was buoyed up by the release of pent-up demand when controls were abolished.

Liquid assets had grown considerably during the war. Personal savings had exceeded 20 per cent of personal income. Although upper income groups held most of these savings, there was nevertheless a widespread hunger for consumer goods. The real post-tax profit share fell from around 9 per cent in 1945 to 7 per cent in 1946. But this probably went unobserved, being masked by rapid inflation. Profits seemed higher because increases in the value of stocks, resulting solely from rising prices, were wrongly considered as profit, and because depreciation provision was insufficient, being based on the price paid for the machinery rather than on the current cost of replacing it. Calculated in this incorrect way, profits appeared to be both high and rising rapidly. Firms also had plenty of liquid assets and little debt. Demand for new capital goods was strong.

High spending allowed a fairly smooth reabsorption of ex-service personnel. Between 1945 and 1946 employment in the forces fell by 8 million, while the number of civilian jobs rose by nearly 4 million. Unemployment rose from a low point of 0.8 million at the end of the war to 2.7 million in March 1946 (down to 2.1 million by the end of the year). So around 2 million people apparently disappeared from the labour force. Numbers in higher education rose and some older war-workers retired. Most importantly, 2¼ million women workers left their jobs.

The film *Rosie the Riveter* provides a fascinating insight into the ways in which many women, who only a few years before had been pulled into the wartime factories, were suddenly despatched back home to rear children. The rise in private sector employment was almost exactly offset by a decline in hours worked – down from 45.4 in January 1945 to 40.4 in 1946 – as overtime wound down, especially in war-based industries. So total civilian hours changed little from those worked at the end of the war.

Marshall Aid affected the US economy most directly in the export field. The rise in net exports in 1946 had accounted for nearly one-fifth of the total rise in non-government spending. This rise prevented the fall in military expenditures from generating a major recession. Net exports (exports minus imports) of goods and services constituted 3.7 per cent of GDP in 1946. In the second quarter of 1947, when discussions over the Marshall Plan were most intense, net exports were running at an annual rate of $12.4 billion, or 5.4 per cent of GDP. And their importance was even greater than this figure suggests. Nearly 70 per cent of GDP was realized by consumption expenditures, most of which depended on workers keeping their jobs. Had exports fallen, workers producing them would have been put out of work. In 1946 16 per cent of agricultural machinery, 20 per cent of freight cars and motor trucks, 10 per cent of steel products and 40 per cent of wheat production were exported. If workers producing goods for export had lost their jobs then their spending would have fallen. Demand for consumer goods in the United States would have been hit, leading to job losses there. The likely extent of these 'multiplier' effects is difficult to calculate. But the importance of exports to overall employment was certainly far greater than their percentage of GDP. So spending in the United States was vulnerable to European countries' ability to buy US exports. Senior US officials were well aware of the changes. *The Economic Report of The President* (1948) said: 'The rate at which foreign countries were utilizing United States credits and their own gold and dollar assets was depleting these resources rapidly and the ability of some countries to import from the United States was being exhausted. Many of these countries were forced to put more rigid restrictions on their purchases from the United States' (p. 26).

In a speech in the spring of 1947, delivered some weeks before Marshall's, Dean Acheson had stressed graphically the importance of US exports: 'It is difficult to imagine $16 billion worth of commodities. This represents one month's work for each man and woman in the United States . . . when the process of reconversion at home is completed, we are going to find ourselves more dependent upon exports, than before the war, to maintain the levels of business activity to which our economy has become accustomed . . . continued political instability and "Acts of God" are retarding recovery to a greater degree than had been anticipated. The extreme need of foreign countries for American products is likely, therefore, to continue undiminished in 1948, while the capacity of foreign countries to pay in commodities will only be slightly increased. Under existing authorizations considerable sums will be available to offset next year's deficit. But these funds will taper off rapidly during the latter part of 1948 . . . we must push ahead with the reconstruction of these two great workshops of Europe and Asia – Germany and Japan – upon which the ultimate recovery of the two continents largely depends' (quoted Jones, pp. 277–8).

Jones says that 'the President's Council of Economic Advisers expected a slight business recession within twelve months; if the expected export decline, due to foreign inability to pay, coincided with weakness in the domestic economy, the effect on production, prices and employment in the United States, might be most serious' (p. 207).

US labour

In the month that Marshall announced his Plan, Congress passed the Taft-Hartley Bill, radically curtailing trade union rights. Four months later, Marshall addressed one of the two major union confederations, the Congress of Industrial Organizations (CIO), representing nearly half the organized working class. He warned against the 'enemies of democracy' who would 'undermine the confidence of the labour element in the stability of our institutions and the soundness of our tradition' (quoted Preis, p. 340).

While the Truman Doctrine and Marshall Plan were intended primarily to help re-establish 'social discipline' in Europe and Japan, they also had a domestic component. The 1945–6 strike wave (Chapter 2) had shown up weaknesses in domestic social discipline. The new initiatives were to help create the climate for an assault on organized labour at home to parallel those the United States was underwriting abroad.

The great strikes of early 1946 were contained only by wage increases of 15 per cent or more. The government sought to offset the effects on employers by easing price controls. Thus the steel settlement, in February 1946, of an extra 18½ cents a hour followed government authorization of a $5 dollar per ton increase in steel prices. This settlement, the first made by the giant US Steel in the face of a strike, set the pattern for the mass-production industries.

Truman responded to the May 1946 rail strike by pressing Congress to pass a law granting 'emergency powers to break strikes in any industry held by the government'. Strikers and union officials could be 'inducted into the Army . . . at such time, in such manner . . . and on such terms as may be prescribed by the President' (Preis, p. 290). The strike was called off just before the bill would have become law. At the end of May the mine workers struck, even though the government had taken nominal control of the mines. They won a substantial wage increase and, more importantly, a five-cent levy on each ton of coal to finance a health and welfare fund to be administered jointly by the union and the government. In the autumn the mine workers' leader, John Lewis, called for a renegotiation of the contract. The government responded with an injunction instructing Lewis to withdraw his announcement terminating the contract: 400,000 miners struck in protest. The judge fined the union $3½ million and Lewis $10,000. The strike was called off pending an appeal to the Supreme Court. On 12 December (well over a year after the end of wartime hostilities), Truman said that 'the recent soft coal strike makes it impossible to declare war formally at an end now' (quoted Preis, p. 299).

In March 1947 the Supreme Court reduced the fine to $700,000 provided the union withdrew its cancellation of the contract, which it did. In April the miners came out for six days' mourning after 111 of their members had been killed in a pit disaster. Most refused to re-enter mines which violated the safety code. Lewis instructed them to go back as soon as each mine was certified as conforming to the federal mining safety code, and they did so. When the contract finally ended in June, the employers conceded a 44 cents per hour wage increase, a doubling of the welfare royalty and acceptance of the federal mining safety code. Most other major unions accepted considerably smaller increases (between 7½ and 15 cents per hour) without strikes.

Business organized a massive campaign for the abolition of price controls, arguing that they were responsible for meat and bread shortages in the spring of 1946 – shortages which it may have partially contrived. Consumer prices rose 28 per cent and the wholesale price index by 25 per cent (faster than after the First World War). A worker with three dependants had seen real earnings rise by some 4½ per cent between September 1945 and April 1946. With the ending of price controls they began to fall. By 1947 they were around 15 per cent below January 1945. Profits also climbed sharply in 1947, to around 9 per cent of the value of production.

Business also pressed Congress to move beyond such crisis measures as seizing industries, obtaining injunctions and so forth, and to launch a more fundamental attack on the union movement. It did so with the Taft-Hartley Act of June 1947. This:

- outlawed the closed shop and permitted states to pass laws banning union shops;
- made illegal secondary strikes or boycotts to force management to recognize a non-certified union;
- required a sixty-day cooling-off period before a contract was ended;
- allowed employers to sue unions for breach of contract or for illegal strikes or boycotts;
- prohibited strikes by federal employees;
- allowed the president to seek an injunction to postpone for eighty days any strike deemed to affect 'national health and safety', pending conciliation, and to require a ballot before the strike could proceed;
- required union officers to swear they were neither members of the Communist Party nor supporters of any organization advocating 'unconstitutional' means of overthrowing the government;
- forbade union contributions to candidates in federal elections.

Truman opposed the bill but used its provisions twelve times during its first year on the statute books. The miners and Ford workers secured contracts which expressly protected them from damage suits under the act. But most union leaders, other than Lewis, signed the Taft-Hartley affidavit.

The common thread linking foreign policy initiatives and the offensive against labour was a stress on the 'Communist Threat'. Surprising as it may now seem, the Communist Party had built up a powerful position in the US labour movement. In 1946 it controlled unions making up roughly one-third of the CIO's membership. Its main bastions were in the half-million-strong United Electrical Workers (UEW), the food and tobacco, non-rail transport and agricultural machinery unions, and in local union coalitions in major industrial cities. It was also influential in the Union of Autoworkers (UAW).

The attack on the CP was not in response to any recent industrial militancy on its part. During the war it had helped moderate industrial conflict. *Business Week* commented astutely: 'Since Russia's involvement in the war, the leadership in these unions has moved from the extreme left wing to the extreme right wing. Today they have perhaps the best no-strike record of any section of organized labour; they are the most vigorous proponents of labour management cooperation; they are the only serious advocates of incentive wages. . . . In general, employers with whom they deal now have the most peaceful labour relations in industry' (quoted Brecher, p. 221).

Nor did the end of hostilities produce a shift to militant class struggle. In the General Motors strike in early 1946 the electrical workers, in the CP-controlled UEW, settled before the UAW did. As the UAW president explained, this 'put us in an awful spot since GM now will come to us insisting that we settle on the same terms' (quoted Preis, p. 279). When Walter Reuther won the presidency of the UAW in the convention which followed the strike, he was opposed by the CP, despite support from the most militant sections.

The attack on the CP in the unions began in earnest at the November 1946 CIO convention, which passed a policy statement containing the words: 'We resent and reject efforts of the Communist Party or other political parties and their adherents to interfere in the affairs of the CIO' (ibid., p. 332). This opened the way for unions to ban communists from holding office. The witch-hunt helped to defuse the strike wave, ease the implementation of Taft-Hartley and consolidate the position of union leaders prepared to reach an accommodation with business. Union organizations in the electrical and farm machinery industries were split. Within a year of its launch, Reuther had used a 'Get the Commies' campaign to win undisputed control of the crucial UAW and to suppress all opposition.

The adoption of the Truman Doctrine and Marshall Plan obviously helped the attack on the United States CP, which could now be presented as an enemy fifth column. But the emphasis on the Communist Party as such was mainly a device to link industrial militancy with political subversion. This allowed a far wider ranging assault directed at all left-wingers and union militants. Again, the foreign policy parallels are clear.

How the Marshall Plan worked

As soon as the Marshall Plan – or European Recovery Programme (ERP) – was announced, the IMF eased its tough lending conditions. Together with the World Bank, it lent more than $1 billion to Europe in the next twelve months. In December 1947 Truman persuaded Congress to agree $600 million in emergency aid for France, Italy and Austria to tide them over until Marshall Aid came on tap. Congress finally sanctioned $13 billion Marshall Aid, to be spread over four years. This was less than half the amount the Europeans had asked for. But they, and especially the United Kingdom, nevertheless responded quickly and enthusiastically, establishing a Committee of European Economic Cooperation (later converted into the OEEC) to devise a recovery programme. Much to the relief of the United States, the USSR declined to participate on the grounds that the sovereignty of individual countries in making their own reconstruction plans would be violated and that German reparations would be set aside.

The European governments sat down to draw up these plans in a relatively relaxed economic climate. Prospects had improved considerably since the first half of 1947. Industrial production had regained its prewar level (and was well above if Germany is excluded). Agricultural production was improving after the bad winter of 1946–7, though more slowly than industry. Despite worsening terms of trade (import prices rising faster than export prices) worth $1500 million, the trade deficit with the United States had been cut by almost a third (and the overall deficit by only slightly less).

Table 5.1 Receipts of US non-military grants and government long-term capital, 1946–50

$ million per year

	UK	France	Germany	Italy	Japan
1946–47	1722	948	371	474	419
1948–50	857	668	847	378	373

Source: US, *Balance of Payments*, Table 46.

Only Germany received a major increase in US assistance after 1947 (Table 5.1). The United States insisted on recipients drawing up four-year reconstruction plans to help it systematize and monitor aid flows (and see a clear end to them). William Clayton, US under-secretary for economic affairs, wrote to his government from Paris at the end of August: 'In determining requirements of coal and steel, account should be taken of relative efficiencies of available plants and other related matters . . . attention must be given to an initial selective utilization of productive capacity, without regard to national boundaries' (quoted Balfour, p. 84). Such international planning to secure maximum production and to distribute the output was both unacceptable to the European governments concerned, and, as Clayton and the United States ambassadors in Paris and London admitted a couple of weeks later, was not in the United States' interests anyway: 'Such a procedure and organization would result in a planned economy to a dangerous degree. It is almost certain to lead to international cartels which would stimulate nationalism and frustrate the ultimate restoration of natural economic forces' (ibid.). The 'nationalism' they referred to was not the nationalism that was preventing European-wide planning, but the assertion of European interests against the United States and the 'natural economic forces' of free trade and capitalist competition. Accordingly, the United States accepted that the overall plan should be based on separate four-year plans submitted to the OEEC by each country.

In fact many of the national plans were mutually incompatible. For example, the continental countries aimed at a surplus of £50 million on trade with the United Kingdom, while Britain envisaged no equivalent deficit.

European output was expected to reach 120 per cent of the 1938 level by the end of the plan period (a 35 per cent increase over 1947). Exports were to rise from $6 to $10.6 billion (leaving a dollar deficit of $1.4 billion). But the OEEC was sceptical about this figure – derived from individual national plan targets. It argued that unless imports were held down to 75 per cent of national plan targets a deficit of $3 billion would result. US aid was expected to total a sum equivalent to around 5 per cent of European production.

Marshall Aid brought a clear shift in the form of US aid. From 1947 loans repayable with interest dropped sharply. Non-military grants rose correspondingly (Chart 5.2). In line with this commitment to greater support for European governments, the Americans also relaxed pressure on them to open up their economies to US capital.

Chart 5.2 US aid to Europe, 1946–50

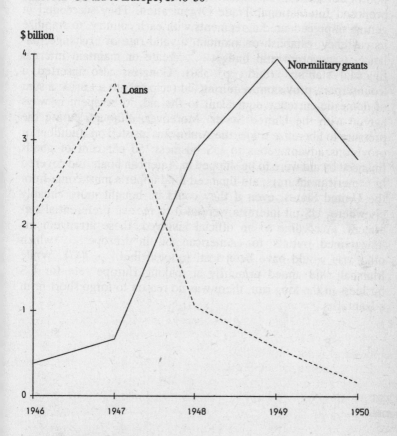

Source: US, *Balance of Payments*.

Free trade hawks had wanted to use Marshall Aid as a lever to break open the Sterling Area. One had written: 'We have in our hands bargaining weapons we may never possess again. . . . If we cannot now obtain the liquidation of the Ottawa System [Sterling Area controls against dollar imports] we shall never do so' (quoted Kolko and Kolko, p. 366). But the US government rejected this approach, recognizing a prior need to support the British and other European economies. Even so, the Americans tried to persuade the Europeans to accept IMF consultation as a precondition of devaluation, and a binding assent to the principles of the proposed International Trade Organization. They succeeded in getting unprecedented agreements with each country 'to stabilize its currency, establish or maintain a valid rate of exchange, balance its governmental budget . . . create or maintain internal financial stability' (ibid., p. 380). Congress also inserted a 'counterpart' provision, requiring aid recipients to set aside a sum of domestic currency equivalent to the aid, to be spent in ways agreed with the United States. Moreover, although easing the pressure to liberalize trade, the Americans insisted on a number of provisions advantageous to US business: 50 per cent of goods financed by aid were to be shipped in American boats and covered by American insurers; aid-financed food imports must come from the United States, even if they could be bought more cheaply elsewhere; US oil interests were also to receive preferential treatment. According to an official involved, these arrangements 'maintained outlets for American oil in Europe . . . which otherwise would have been lost' (quoted ibid., p. 447). While Marshall Aid aimed primarily at making Europe safe for US business in the long run, there was no reason to forgo short-term advantages.

6. The New Turn in Europe and Japan

The years after 1947 saw no marked acceleration in the pace of expansion, other than in Germany. Total European production

Chart 6.1 Gross domestic product, 1947–51

Index numbers
1938 = 100

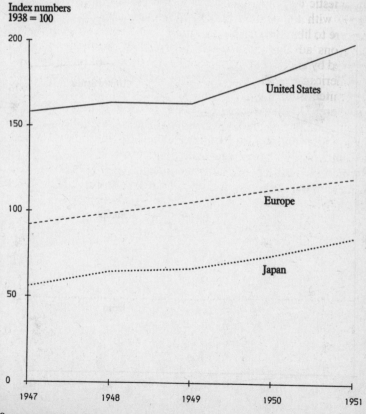

Source: see Appendix.

grew at a rather steady 7 per cent or so a year, and industrial production at around 10 per cent (Chart 6.1). In most countries of Western Europe prewar output levels were exceeded in 1948 (1951 in Germany). Japan did not find the impetus to escape the stagnation which set in during 1949 until the Korean war (Chapter 7). In 1951 output was still well below the prewar level.

European investment grew no faster than production as a whole (Chart 6.2). In Japan it stagnated. Accumulation rates showed no great upward spurt. In Germany, where the capital stock fell in

Chart 6.2 Gross fixed investment, 1947–51

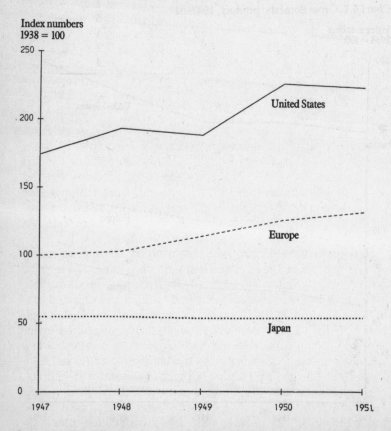

Source: see Appendix.

1947, the subsequent strong rise in investment drove the accumulation rate only to some 4 per cent in 1950 – similar to elsewhere but hardly remarkable when compared to subsequent experience. Accumulation was generally maintained at around the rather moderate rate established by 1947 (Table 6.1).

Table 6.1 Accumulation: growth of the business capital stock, 1947–51

Annual percentage growth rates

	USA	UK	France	Italy	Japan	Germany
1947	3.9	1.7	3.9	1.5	4.2	−1.9
1948	3.9	1.8	3.9	0.6	4.6	−0.5
1949	2.9	2.0	3.8	0.2	4.4	3.9
1950	3.6	2.7	3.6	0.6	4.7	4.1
1951	3.6	2.1	3.2	1.5	5.3	5.2

Source: see Appendix.

Neither European nor Japanese expansion was markedly faster than that in the United States. In 1951 the United States was still producing at double the 1938 rate, whereas European output had only grown by one-fifth. In 1950 the rate of US accumulation was comparable to that of France, Japan and Germany, and well above that of the United Kingdom and Italy. No one was yet 'catching up' the United States.

Nor was continued European expansion based on massive import growth from the United States or elsewhere (Table 6.2). Indeed, imports fell in 1948 and only regained 1947 levels in 1951. Meanwhile exports steamed ahead and by 1950 had regained pre-war levels, with imports still some 10 per cent below. So although Marshall Aid allowed the flow of necessary imports to be maintained, it did no more. The increase in exports was reflected in a reduction in Europe's deficit with the United States (Chart 5.1). Indeed, the Marshall Aid was not all used to finance extra imports. Having dropped from $10.5 billion in 1945 to $7.3 billion in June 1948, the reserves of ERP recipients actually increased by $2 billion by 1950. So growth after 1947 was neither especially spectacular nor based on a massive increase in Marshall Aid

Table 6.2 Volume of trade, 1947–51

Index numbers
1938=100

	USA		Europe (with outside Europe)		Japan	
	Imports	*Exports*	*Imports*	*Exports*	*Imports*	*Exports*
1947	130	227	98	60	11	5
1948	150	182	88	78	15	8
1949	147	182	89	90	24	16
1950	174	163	88	105	26	35
1951	180	195	97	119	35	47

Source: see Appendix.

financed imports. Nevertheless, substantial productivity gains were achieved. European industrial productivity rose by 42 per cent in the four years after 1947. In Japan it practically trebled (Chart 6.3). These rises ran well ahead of those to be expected from accumulation.

Much labour must have been underutilized in 1947. Throughout most of Europe and Japan industry was producing less than pre-war, with more workers. Where materials shortages limited output, workers were often kept on. Even where there was acute overall labour shortage, as in France and Britain, it was difficult for employers to reduce employment levels. The common thread in this bewildering tapestry is the employment of workers surplus to management requirements. In other words, many more workers were employed than would have been required to produce the same output at maximum productivity levels. Productivity was held down by effective worker opposition to dismissals and to the implied speeding-up and intensification of production.

The most important feature of the three or four years after 1947 was a general attempt, particularly in continental Europe and Japan, to reimpose managerial control by dismissing workers, especially trade union militants, and by attacking trade unions. This assault on the labour movement was backed up by deflationary financial policies and had the effect of pushing up productivity dramatically. While the resulting unemployment

Chart 6.3 Industrial productivity, 1947–51

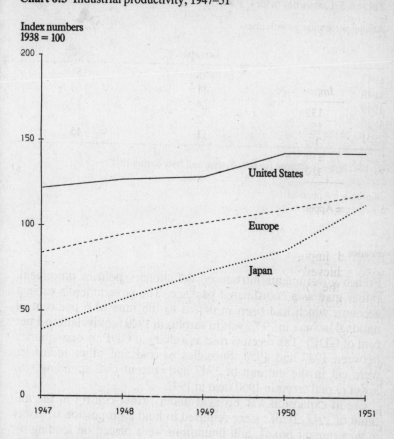

Index numbers
1938 = 100

Source: see Appendix.

weakened labour, the reduced inflation rate in Europe and Japan in 1949 and 1950 respectively (Table 6.3) was very popular with middle-class savers. This restoration of 'financial and social discipline' was the period's outstanding contribution towards the foundations of the great boom of the fifties and sixties. It deserves, therefore, to be discussed in some detail.

Table 6.3 Consumer prices, 1947–51

Annual percentage growth rates

	Europe	Japan
1947	25[1]	151
1948	11	68
1949	4	17
1950	2	−2
1951	11	15

1. 1947 figure is average for UK, France and Italy during 1947.

Source: see Appendix.

France

French governments introduced deflationary policies piecemeal, rather than as a coordinated package. The government's current account, which had been in deficit to the tune of 6 per cent of national income in 1947, was in surplus in 1949 (equivalent to 1 per cent of GDP). Tax receipts rose as a share of GDP by one-quarter between 1947 and 1950. Subsidies to coal and other industries were cut in the autumn of 1947 and current civil spending was lower in real terms in 1950 than in 1947.

Credit expansion was brought under firmer control in the autumn of 1948. Banks were required to hold a proportion of assets in government bonds, and limitations were placed on lending by the Bank of France to the commercial banks. The rate of increase of wholesale prices declined from 70 per cent during 1947 to 33 per cent during 1948; wholesale prices fell in the first half of 1949. Industrial production fell during 1949, and although unemployment only reached an estimated 50,000 (as compared with 10,000 in 1947), applicants per vacancy rose nearly threefold between 1948 and 1949.

Profits shot up, as production grew with little or no employment increase, boosting productivity (Table 6.4). Real wages stagnated after 1948 at well below the prewar level.

The communist union leadership had disciplined workers well enough to guarantee profitable production up till 1947. But

Table 6.4 Productivity and wages: France, 1947–50

Index numbers
1938=100

	Industrial production	Industrial employment	Industrial productivity	Real wage[1]
1947	99	104	95	63
1948	113	108	105	78
1949	122	109	112	77
1950	128	110	116	78

1. In terms of the official cost of living index. From 1948 product wages appear to be a few per cent lower.

Source: see Appendix.

rank-and-file resistance had increasingly undermined its effectiveness. From 1947 the employers increasingly took on the job themselves. Shortly after the expulsion of the CP from the government, the *Economist* described the situation as follows:

'The dream of the Resistance has faded and French society is back in the impasse which destroyed the Popular Front in 1936. The bourgeoisie are not reconciled to the passing of a large measure of political and even economic power to the organized working class, and their response today, as in 1936, is a sort of concealed strike. Then it took the form of a flight from the franc to foreign currency. Today exchange control restricts this possibility. The answer is therefore hoarding, tax-evasion, failure to invest and luxurious spending. The Government lacking sufficient revenue from taxation, and unable to induce saving, cannot balance the budget and has resorted to inflation. But the workers, pinched by rising prices and conscious of their greater political influence, resort to the weapon of the open strike for higher wages, and thus the inflationary spiral spins the faster' (26 July 1947).

This stalemate was broken over the next eighteen months.

In the autumn of 1947 the CGT launched a campaign for a general wage rise, although the socialist minority denounced calls for a general strike as 'excessive'. Higher fuel and transport prices triggered a general strike.

'On November 12, police, acting on orders from the new Gaullist mayor of Marseilles, broke up a CGT-organized protest against a rise in trolley fares. The arrest of several demonstrators prompted the CGT to call another protest in front of the Marseilles Palais de Justice. The police were called in again, and this time one protester was killed. By November 14 Marseilles was shut down by a general strike. Simultaneously the situation exploded in the North of France when Léon Delfosse, the PCF [Communist Party] miners' leader, was fired from the Coal Board, leading to a miners' strike. The occasion was seized by the CGT to begin its strike offensive. The Marseilles railroad strike became the core of a national railroad shut-down, spreading from railroad centre to railroad centre. Next, PCF-dominated federations and departmental unions went out in force. On November 14 the Paris metals sector shut down (beginning at Renault), then the building trades, then gas and electricity, the Post Office and the docks. In very short order 2 million workers were out' (Ross, pp. 52–3).

The CP employed exceptionally vigorous tactics to spread the strike. CGT members in the mines refused to hand out safety equipment and used the Coal Board's motor pool to transport flying pickets. The government responded ferociously: it introduced legislation carrying severe penalties for 'interfering with the right to work', and called up 80,000 army reservists. Police broke up picket lines and occupied Paris's power stations. Soldiers were used to break the railway strike. Police and army intervention then became general. Hundreds of workers were arrested and imprisoned. The number on strike fell to a third of the peak of 3 million, and on 9 December the strike was called off. None of the demands had been won.

In the aftermath of the strike the socialist minority in the CGT split to form the Force Ouvrière (FO), taking around one-third of the membership. (It was especially strong among civil servants.) A few years later, George Meaney of the American Federation of Labor boasted that 'it was thanks to the money of American workers – the workers of Detroit and elsewhere – that we were able to create a split, important to us all, in the French CGT, by creating the Force Ouvrière Fédération' (quoted Werth, p. 385).

In the autumn of 1948 the government issued a series of decrees to reduce employment in the nationalized industries by 10 per cent, and to implement a tougher system of work discipline. The CGT organized a referendum among the miners, who voted overwhelmingly to strike. But other workers were not persuaded to come out in support.

The CGT next called a twenty-four-hour strike of mine safety crews in response to alleged police brutalities. The government then conscripted the crews, obliging them to stay on the job. The CGT responded by calling them out on indefinite strike, threatening pit safety. The government then despatched troops to mining areas, to remove strikers from the pit-heads. CGT officials were fired from the Coal Board and family allowances to striking miners reduced. The strikers began to drift back to work at the end of October. By mid-November, when the strike was six weeks old, over a thousand workers had been arrested, and nearly five hundred policemen injured. The CGT called off the strike on 30 November, having won none of their demands. At least three thousand militants were sacked and the CGT's influence was seriously weakened. The miners were not to strike for another fifteen years.

A contributory factor to the defeat of the strike was the division in the trade union movement which followed the strikes of the previous year. Attempts were made to replace local workers' representatives who belonged to the CGT, by FO supporters. In the middle of the strike a certain François Mitterrand was reported as offering, on behalf of the cabinet, negotiations 'notably with trade union organizations that have displayed in this period of crisis, a republican and patriotic attitude' (*Economist*, 30 October 1948). Socialist ministers were responsible both for the decrees which sparked off the strike and for the measures which broke it.

Labour movement divisions presented the employers with a golden opportunity to use divide-and-rule tactics. They had no effective organizations at all until the middle of 1946; by 1949 their organization covered 90 per cent of capital employed. They could settle disputes with non-CGT unions quickly and then use police to intimidate the now-isolated strikers. The FO's virulently anti-communist leadership opposed any unity of action with the CGT. The employers took every advantage of the weakness that these divisions brought. Their federation came out against the conclusion of any major collective bargaining agreements which were allowed under a law passed early in 1950. None was signed. George Ross, on whose account the foregoing is based, concludes: 'After 1944 the French labour movement had been more powerful than at any point in the history of French capitalism. During the cold war the whole atmosphere of French industrial relations changed, to the labour movement's detriment' (p. 67).

Italy

The Italian government began to deflate the economy soon after ejecting the PCI from the ruling coalition in May 1947. It tightened monetary policy sharply in the autumn, requiring banks to deposit substantial assets with the central bank rather than lending to the private sector. Over the next year bank lending rose less than one-third as fast as in the previous one. Share prices halved. Many goods prices fell too, especially on the black market, as speculators unloaded stocks. Between 1947 and 1949 the share of tax receipts in national income rose from 15 to 22 per cent, while subsidies were cut from 5 to 1 per cent. The volume of current civil public expenditure fell by one-quarter between 1948 and 1949, but military spending was maintained. Investment in public works fell by one-quarter between 1947 and 1949.

Industrial production slowed down during 1948. Deflationary pressure also held prices down and caused a big jump in the real cost of employing labour (the product wage (Table 6.5)). Fuel and transport costs rose, too, as nationalized industry deficits were reduced, intensifying the squeeze on private sector profits.

Table 6.5 Productivity and wages: Italy, 1947–51

Index numbers
1938=100

	Industrial production	Industrial employment	Industrial productivity	Product wage[1]	Real wage[2]
1947	92	105	88	86	88
1948	96	105	91	109	108
1949	105	104	101	117	109
1950	122	102	120	125	113
1951	138	104	133	124	114

1. In terms of prices of manufactures.
2. In terms of cost of living.

Source: see Appendix.

Bankruptcies doubled from one-third of the prewar level in 1947 to two-thirds in 1949.

Over 2 million had been unemployed before the deflation, which seems to have boosted the number only marginally. But employers took advantage of the squeeze to launch an assault on the power of the unions, at shopfloor level, to resist redundancies and rationalization. The government refused to subsidize firms to keep on workers; although the ban on dismissals had been lifted, workers had previously successfully resisted redundancies. The *Economist* (13 December 1947) had written of the 'symbolic figure' of the 'workman whom his employer fears to lay off but refuses to pay', quoting press reports that thousands of engineering workers were in this position. An *Economist* report a year later (6 November 1948) symbolized the shift in conditions in its title:

Cold War in Italian Industry

Italian employers are now making serious efforts to reduce their staffs to reasonable proportions for the work in hand. This action has long been hanging over the already strained relations which exist in many parts of industry between employer and employee. But it is essential if excessive Italian production costs are to be reduced. The feeling is growing among employers that they are now in a stronger position to try their hand than a few weeks ago.

Workers, however, are putting up a stiff running fight. Last week the Fiat motor company's Mirafiore factory in Turin, the largest in Italy, employing 50,000 people, and of prime importance in the country's export drive, was reduced to operating on what has become known as a 'non-collaboration' basis, because seven workers were dismissed. 'Non-collaboration' means that a worker refuses to go one iota out of his prescribed routine. If so much as a screwdriver is needed, he will stop work until it is brought to him; he deliberately does nothing at all about getting it himself. When this system was first introduced for a week last December, production in Italian industry was estimated to have fallen by 60 per cent. The Fiat management has now retorted with a statement that the proportional loss of takings will be debited to wage-checks.

Many other big works are also suffering from resistance in this and other forms. Daily one-hour strikes are staged or planned over a period. Last week the Snia Viscosa management of the company's Pignotte works in Florence was completely frustrated by a stay-in strike of redundant workers who had been dismissed. It remains to be seen what the upshot of all this will be, but one thing seems clear. The present cold war in Italian industry will concentrate growing attention on the battle between the Communist and non-Communist trade unions.

This important union split took place in the summer of 1948. Expelled from government, the PCI had used its controlling influence to make the main union confederation (CGIL) adopt a more aggressive posture. At the beginning of December 1947 the 'big strike of the week' took place in Milan against the government's attempt to remove the mayor. A 'citizens' committee' took over the town hall for twenty-four hours. The government began moving troops northwards. Further general strikes were planned in Genoa, Turin and Venice. Fears grew that an 'occupation of the Northern Plain' by striking workers would cut 'Italy off from Western Europe' (*Economist*, 6 December 1947). But a general strike in Rome against unemployment and in support of public works was met by 'an effective deployment of the police forces'. It was called off on the second day (20 December 1947) as it was fizzling out. The left's weakness was shown in the April 1948 election when the Christian Democrats won 48 per cent of the votes, more than half as much again as the PCI and Left Socialists combined.

The biggest industrial upsurge occurred after an assassination attempt on Togliatti in July. The *Economist* (24 July 1948) described the reaction: 'In Genoa almost immediately, about 50,000 workmen, pouring in from the industrial suburbs to the centre of the town, disarmed the police en route, seized four armoured cars and established road blocks with machine guns. . . . In Milan, the local Chamber of Labour ordered all workers to stand at their factory posts, suspending all work. Later two factories, the Motta Confectionery Works and the Bezzi Engineering Works, both of which have been cleared by police of sit-down strikers, were entered by force . . . there was extensive sabotage to railway lines in Northern Italy.'

There were allegations that the dreaded insurrectionary 'Plan K' (or 'Z': no one was sure which) had been launched. The CGIL proclaimed a general strike, but called it off after three days. Nevertheless, the decision by the Communist and Socialist majority to call the strike provided the excuse for the Christian Democrat section of the CGIL to split off. It formed the CISL. As with the Force Ouvrière in France, money from US unions helped in its formation. By 1950 the CGIL had lost around 1 million members. The employers systematically favoured the CISL, both in the few national agreements signed in following years and in local agreements, which were 'often granted by firms rather than having been exacted by the workers and made with national "non-communist" unions or the black-leg unions encouraged by many firms' (B. Salvati, p. 208).

The benefits of deflation and the employers' offensive showed up when production grew rapidly after 1949 (Table 6.5). Production shot up without an increase in industrial employment; productivity was forced up to a level one-third higher than prewar. Since the industrial accumulation rate was low (Table 6.1), work intensification must have accounted for much of the productivity gain. The temporarily unfavourable effects of deflation on profits were soon reversed. By 1951 the balance between what workers produced for their employers (productivity) and the cost of employing them (product wage) was more favourable to employers than under Mussolini in 1938.

In going for deflation, the government apparently opted to waste Marshall Aid. During the years 1948–50 ERP donations ran at $250–300 million a year but, rather than being spent on imports to reconstruct and expand capacity, all of this and more was simply hoarded as gold. The reserves rose from $70 million in September 1947 to $885 million in December 1949. Nor did the government strive vigorously to secure as much Marshall Aid as possible; the $1.3 billion received by the end of 1951 was little over half the sum acquired by France.

These deflationary policies provided strong criticism. The mission administering Marshall Aid was particularly vehement. The Bank of Italy responded unconvincingly with long lists of state aids to industry (allegedly equivalent to 10–15 per cent of industrial investment over the years 1945–51, and one-third financed by 'counterpart' funds). Later commentators have presented the deflation as a triumph for the middle classes and peasants, whose salaries and savings were hit particularly hard by the inflation. These groups did swing behind the government in the 1948 election. But deflation also played another, more fundamental role. It created an economic climate in which a degree of capitalist control adequate for future accumulation could be reimposed.

This was the fundamental task achieved in the years after 1947. Italy is the clearest example of how the need for social and financial discipline took precedence over physical reconstruction in these years. Marshall Aid was primarily symbolic of wholehearted US support for this project.

Japan

By successfully banning the proposed February 1947 general strike (Chapter 4), the US Occupation had shown itself capable of intervening effectively against any major labour movement offensive. In July 1948 MacArthur greeted a threatened strike by government employees with a directive to the government declaring that public sector workers had no right to strike or engage in disruptive tactics. Again the response was ineffective. A planned postal workers' protest was called off because of lack of support.

However, the situation was one of stalemate rather than of consolidated capitalist control. The public sector workers had proposed the strike because their pay had lagged behind both inflation and private sector incomes. As the *Economist* explained at the time: 'Japanese private capitalism . . . has proved very adaptable to the new order of things; in order to avoid trouble many industrialists have not only granted substantial wage increases, but have maintained full-time union officials on their pay-rolls and provided them with office space and printing equipment. As a result, rates of pay and union privileges in private industry have risen well above those in state employment' (28 August 1948).

Such 'adaptability' was a sign of weakness rather than strength. Productivity remained low, reflecting the employers' inability to prune the labour force. In 1948 only one major company succeeded in imposing sackings, and then only after it was surrounded by 'four American army tanks, one cavalry squadron, three airplanes and 1800 armed police' (Okochi *et al.*, p. 336). Company profits hardly rose at all. In 1948 they were hardly higher as a share of production than in 1947 (Table 6.6). Retained profits (after depreciation) were non-existent.

Table 6.6 Profits, wages and productivity: Japan, 1947–51

	Profit share[1]	Real wage[2,3]	Industrial production[3]	Industrial employment[3]	Industrial productivity[3]
1947	8	30	37	95	39
1948	9	49	55	96	57
1949	15	66	71	97	73
1950	22	85	84	98	86
1951	26	92	114	101	113

1. Net profits as percentage of corporate product.
2. In terms of cost of living.
3. Index numbers: 1934–6=100.

Source: see Appendix.

The government was carrying out more than half of investment, and providing much of the finance for the rest. The Reconstruction Finance Bank was an important channel for funds. During 1947 and 1948 it made loans equivalent to more than 40 per cent of private investment. The United States provided grants of around $400 million to finance essential imports. The government then, in effect, lent back the yen counterpart of these dollars to finance private capital accumulation (the payments deficit was equivalent to some 55 per cent of private fixed investments during 1947–8). Private fixed investment is recorded as 80 per cent of its prewar level, presumably because the inflation (80 per cent or so in 1948) made it cheap to borrow; but in 1948 more than half the total amount accumulated was in the form of stocks – an estimated 9 per cent of GDP. Such stockbuilding both reflected and exacerbated the inflation. Food shortages were a further problem. The peasant, unable to secure in exchange for rice either enough consumer goods or money which would maintain purchasing power, tended to 'consume more of his produce within his family, or to direct as much as he can to the black market, where prices fluctuate between 10 and 100 times the official rates' (*Economist*, 17 January 1948).

So the position was deadlocked. The labour movement was not powerful enough to bulldoze away the block to decisive action imposed by the Occupation. Private capital was too weak to reassert control in the factories, and the government unable to act decisively to stabilize the financial system and promote accumulation.

During 1947 and 1948 the United States came round to the view that it should intervene to break the stalemate and revitalize the Japanese economy to strengthen the world capitalist system. In early 1948 George Kennan recommended ending deconcentration purges, promoting economic recovery and expanding police numbers in cities where 'the problem of Communist activity would be most acute' (Kennan, p. 390). At the end of 1948 the Occupation, advised by a prominent banker, proposed a nine-point stabilization programme including a balanced budget, wage and price controls, longer hours of work and mass lay-offs. Another banker, Joseph Dodge, was sent to Japan in early 1949 to oversee the programme. Government expenditures – especially pay-rolls, subsidies and unemployment pay – were to be cut to balance the budget. State handouts were to be restricted to 'those projects contributing to the economic stability of Japan' (quoted Tsuru, p. 9). Wage increases were to be granted only as a reward for productivity gains.

Some 700,000 workers were sacked 'as a direct result of the retrenchment measures' (Levine, p. 73). Dodge was quite clear about what he was doing. He noted that 'the standard of living has probably been permitted to go too high' and that higher unemployment 'will in turn lead to increased efficiency of labour and a greater production' (quoted Kolko and Kolko, pp. 522–4). The private sector's response to this government lead was clearly set out by the *Economist*'s correspondent:

'With hoarse democratic shouts of "Down with Communism!" Japanese employers are rushing in to hold down working conditions and wage scales and to knock out the tottering Japanese trade union movement. They have been swift to scent advantages in the current labour retrenchment programme, imposed by the belated "austerity" orders of Mr Joseph M. Dodge, the Detroit banker whom Washington dispatched to Tokyo to enforce the economic reforms. . . . Unemployment in Japan is expected to reach the four million mark as the public services and big industries shed their tens of thousands of surplus employees, and the government fumbles apologetically the task of unemployment relief and reabsorption. . . .

'The Communists threatened "a summer revolution", "an August labour offensive" (which has now been shifted to September, or it may be October) and a programme of strikes from one end of Japan to the other. But only words were violent as the dismissal notices were issued. And then even the words lost their violence when an elderly, inoffensive railway executive, charged with the technical responsibility of sacking surplus railwaymen, was found, cut to pieces, on a Tokyo railway track. . . . The public revulsion against the Communists in general, and dismissed railwaymen in particular, was bitter and spontaneous. That was seven weeks ago. There has been no arrest. The railwaymen, like other dismissed workers, wilted under horrified public opinion. . . .

'Now employers, in common with the government, are exploiting the situation with Oriental expedience and mock-humble opportunism. This week the Japanese League of Employers' Associations in a long report full of pious phrases and unashamed hypocrisy, has drawn up recommendations for nation-wide adoption by all employers who are hampered by the existence of unions, whether Communist-infiltrated or not. They said among other things:

> It was for a time regarded as a legal issue whether or not an employer could dismiss his employees on the ground that they lacked the sincerity to cooperate with him. However, the latest mass discharge of railway employees has furnished a decisive precedent. We are authorized to dismiss all those who either have committed acts interfering with the normal management of enterprises or who have assisted others in the commission of such acts. . . .

> When a second union is organized for the purpose of improving the condition of the enterprise by means of adequate labour-management collaboration in harmony with the actual state of affairs, the employer should give priority to this second union, regardless of the number of its members.

'Other useful suggestions are made for reducing retirement allowances "in view of the present social and economic condition of the nation", for revising labour contracts, for restricting union membership and for "otherwise democratizing labour unions". The moral effect of including union officials among the first batch of discharged employees is gently referred to in passing. Finally, the League pays warm tribute to the remarkable legislation, proposed by the government, which will empower the police to arrest and punish equally all the leaders of any union of which an obscure member has committed a crime of violence' (24 September 1949).

There were also 'some successful efforts by employers to produce internal splits often by excluding middle-aged workers from displacement lists and providing them with augmented wage increases' (ibid.).

In 1950 the Occupation instigated a 'red purge': 12,000 communists were sacked, 11,000 from private sector jobs, including 2500 union officials. Sanbetsu, the CP-dominated union confederation, was destroyed. A new federation, initially based on anticommunist 'democratization leagues', was set up. Days devoted to strikes fell by one-half, three-quarters of which were in mining, where employers managed to cut jobs by 10 per cent.

Production stagnated during 1949 as credit expansion halted. Recorded sackings rose from less than 20,000 a month in early 1949 to 85,000 per month in March 1950. Nevertheless, business fixed investment held steady, though stockbuilding fell sharply. Profits rose in 1949. But the real benefit was felt in 1950 and 1951 when production leaped ahead with virtually no increase in employment. By 1951 industrial productivity was well above prewar levels, while real wages were well below. The profit share was extremely high (Table 6.6).

Germany

Germany seems the obvious case of a floundering economy rescued by Marshall Aid. In 1947 industrial production was only one-third or so of prewar; by 1951 it had overtaken the 1938 figure. But the recovery was only symbolically based on US dollars. The Allies' decision to work to restore German capitalism fully in the zones they controlled was the real key. Other consequences flowed from this. One was partition. Any system for integrating the Russian zone into the new Germany would have had somehow to incorporate the substantial state ownership and planning established in Eastern Europe. However the labour movement in the Western zones had to be disabused of notions of the socialization of industry. This implied strengthening the market economy in the West. The maze of controls, black market deals and barter must be swept away and money restored to its role of prime arbiter of economic life. Most obviously, wages must be paid in cash, and spent on goods in the shops. But they should also be held down to a 'realistic' level in relation to workers' output. In other words, profits must be restored to a level sufficient to revive German capitalists' shattered confidence and restore adequate accumulation. Marshall's dollars, as in Italy, symbolized wholehearted American support for this project. But their direct economic contribution was secondary.

The June 1948 monetary reform was decisive. The year's gap between Marshall's speech and the implementation of effective measures to restore the German economy resulted from the need to secure French acceptance of a strong capitalist Germany, manoeuvres to blame the Russians for partition, and so forth.

The situation remained chaotic in early 1948. The *Economist* reported: 'For the third year in succession, a food crisis has reduced the Ruhr to rebellion and despair. The authorities' persistent failure in recent weeks to honour the fat ration has led to strike action in various towns, factories and mines. Had it not been for the remarkable restraint and responsibility shown by the leaders of the German trade unions, there might well have been a general stoppage of work' (24 January 1948). In fact, communist calls for strike action at the Ruhr trade union conference at the end of the month were defeated. SPD trade union leader Boeckler said that 'it would not bring a single grain or a single loaf of bread more' (quoted Schmidt, p. 141). The same *Economist* report explained why monetary reform was crucial:

'The story is told in Frankfurt of a German businessman in Hamburg who found the work of his factory held up for want of cement. So he set off in his car, and drove, on black market petrol, from Hamburg to Frankfurt. There he bought in the black market some packets of chocolate, such as are sold to GIs in their stores for $1.05 a box, and to Germans illegally for 250 marks. With these he drove to Munich, where he bartered the chocolate for silk stockings, smuggled in from the Soviet zone. He then went on to the Bavarian Alps, where he bartered the stockings to a peasant for butter. With the butter on board he drove all the way back to Hamburg. There he bartered his butter for cement.

'The tale might be continued further. The Hamburg manufacturer would produce in his factory just enough to enable him to secure by barter sufficient food and goods to keep his workmen and his family, and to offset the losses which he had incurred through selling a part of his output legally at the prewar fixed price. Then, bearing in mind that currency reform is planned for the spring, and that a large proportion of his cash and bank account will be cancelled, he would store his remaining goods and raw materials as far away from the eyes of authority as possible.'

The Christian Democrats, who controlled the Bizonal Executive Council, had earlier claimed to support nationalization. But when it came to the crunch they refused to act, preferring to allow the chaos to discredit planning and pave the way for unhampered free enterprise. They found excuses to prevent Council meetings, claiming on one occasion that the building had been booked for amateur dramatics. A law requiring householders to declare stocks of goods was simply ignored: of 350,000 questionnaires issued in Frankfurt only 14 were returned. Some SPD leaders favoured 'postponing' (i.e. abandoning) demands for socialization and entering a coalition with the CDU. But the leadership opted to stay in opposition, fearing that a coalition might allow the communists to accuse the SPD of betraying workers' interests.

Although Boeckler had said in September 1947 that, whatever the implications of the Marshall Plan, 'the unions would continue the struggle for socialization with more energy' (quoted Schmidt, p. 116), the party did little to encourage such action. The trade union leadership forced through support for the Marshall Plan at a special conference held in June 1948, despite the fact that the leadership 'saw correctly that Marshall credits were conditional on abandonment or postponement of trade union plans for the socialization of key industries' (Graf, p. 59). The military authorities had indeed made their stance abundantly clear. They had continued to block all local attempts to pass laws to socialize industry or to extend radically the power of works councils. In the spring of 1948 the British authorities refused, under American pressure, to accept a law, passed in the region covering the Ruhr and North Rhine-Westphalia, to socialize industry (significantly, the Christian Democrats then withdrew their previous support for the measure). The US commander Clay also blocked a law passed by the Hesse government, supported by the CDU, giving works councils decision-making rights over such issues as production methods.

Economic stalemate prevailed. The market was not allowed to function freely to promote revival on its own terms. The monetary reform broke the deadlock. All individuals and institutions were obliged to register holdings in cash or bank deposits. These were then converted into Deutschmarks (DMs) at what transpired to be a rate of 6½ DMs for 100 Reichmarks. All individuals were given 60 DMs in two instalments, and businesses 60 DMs per employee (roughly the weekly wage). The national debt was simply cancelled. Private debts were converted at a rate of 1 for 10. This harsh discrimination against holders of government debt was supposed to be offset by a scheme for 'equalization of war burdens' involving taxation of those holding assets whose real worth was not touched by the reform (such as shares). Almost all manufactures were freed from price and physical controls (clothing and shoes remained rationed but their prices were decontrolled). Price controls were retained for food, utilities, transport and rents (though often perfunctorily administered). Wages were decontrolled shortly after the monetary reform.

Money in circulation compared to production at existing prices fell to about one-third of its prewar level. Firms, initially short of cash, began unloading stocks. Barter disappeared. Black market prices tumbled. 'Housewives strolled down the streets gazing in astonishment at shop windows – at shoes, leather handbags, tools, perambulators, bicycles, cherries in baskets' (*Economist*, 3 July 1948). As the same report explained, absenteeism fell dramatically, from 18 to 20 per cent to 2 or 3, according to Nuremburg manufacturers, and 'makers of heavy engineering products, which could not be used for payment of wages in kind and were difficult things to barter with, had been starved of labour in the days of cigarette currency; within the first week of the new money a manufacturer of heavy transformers and electric motors was getting a steady trickle of applicants for jobs'.

But the collapse of the black market did not signify a collapse of prices. Consumers, starved of commodities and fearing further cuts in the value of financial assets in the wake of the reform, spent cash holdings pell mell. Firms borrowed from banks, which had been allocated surplus reserves. Prices rose 15 per cent in the first six months after the reform. The British military government hardly boosted confidence in the currency by remarking in November that 'the future of the D-Mark was a matter for considerable alarm'. The same report continued: 'Dr Erhard's hope that the removal of price controls would permit a normal competitive price structure to be found has been brought to nothing by the activities of the business people in whom he put his confidence. Rather than face price competition they have banded together to enforce "price discipline" – in other words, to ensure that profits are not reduced by outsiders who cut production costs' (*Economist*, 27 November 1948).

Profits were high. The balance between the cost of employing labour (product wage) and productivity seems to have been similar in the second half of 1948 to 1938 – both variables stood at around 60 per cent of the prewar level. This balance was to persist through the following couple of years of expansion, and then to become even more favourable to profits in 1951 (Table 6.7).

Table 6.7 Productivity and wages: Germany, 1948–51

Index numbers
1938=100

	Industrial production	Industrial employment	Industrial productivity	Product wage[1]	Real wage[2]
1948 (second half)	61	103	59	64	75
1949	75	108	69	74	85
1950	94	114	82	84	101
1951	113	124	91	80	105

1. In terms of prices of manufactures.
2. In terms of cost of living.

Source: see Appendix.

In 1948 lower costs of materials and other inputs relative to output prices also helped maintain profits. Capitalists who had accumulated stocks also made vast windfall profits. The UN Economic Commission for Europe (UNECE) reported that during 'the first year after the monetary reform, profits were already higher in relation to wages and salaries than they had been before the war' (1953, p. 74). The central bank's report for 1948–9 also acknowledged that 'price increases in many branches of production soon went beyond mere adjustment to the higher costs, so that in many cases large profits resulted' (1948–9, p. 5).

Given high profits, it is not surprising that investment more than doubled in 1948, with the increase concentrated in the second half of the year. Much of the investment was in 'palatial hotels, restaurants, movies and shops' (Balogh, p. 84). The UNECE noted that low wages 'permitted for a small class, a degree of luxury consumption unheard of in most other European countries and contrasting sharply with the low living standards of the wage earners' (1953, p. 75).

Living costs rose less than the prices of industrial output (rents, for example, increased by much less). So the purchasing power of the pre-tax wages in 1948 stood at three-quarters of prewar. But taxes had risen sharply, reducing net disposable pay by significantly more. By the end of the year the black market had reappeared in food and other controlled items, rendering the official cost of living index increasingly misleading. In August workers held demonstrations against profiteering, and purchasing strikes took place in the Ruhr. In Stuttgart feelings ran particularly high, and a total curfew was imposed for several days. On 12 November some 9 million workers took part in a twenty-four-hour general strike against price rises and shortages.

The situation increasingly threatened economic recovery. The SPD and the labour movement favoured circumscribing the market with state ownership, workers' control, physical planning of production and price controls. Such a solution would at the very least have postponed restoration of untrammelled German capitalism. To achieve such a restoration, capitalist methods of 'social and financial discipline' were required. The authorities, aware of this, responded to the inflation by a monetary squeeze. Bank lending was restricted by increasing by one-half the reserves banks were obliged to hold and by an embargo on further credits. Production slowed down. Prices stabilized and then slid back; the cost of living fell by 7 per cent during 1949. Bankruptcies rose and unemployment soared.

Numbers out of work had already officially risen from half a million in June 1948 to three-quarters in December (employment had continued to rise but many more workers had sought official jobs now that they would be paid in cash of real value); during 1949, waged employment fell by one-quarter of a million, and official unemployment doubled, reaching 11 per cent of wage and salary earners. Unemployment levels were three times as high in the agricultural regions as in the industrial areas. But it rose faster in the latter, reaching 6 per cent. The rate for refugees was around three times as high as that for the indigenous population.

Employment did not fall because of a fall in output. Output merely stagnated for a period in the middle of 1949. Employers took advantage of the credit squeeze and slackening demand to reorganize: 'The process of rationalization of industry – involving re-equipment, adoption of labour-saving processes and machinery and substitution of more for less efficient labour – is going on apace, not only releasing labour but inhibiting reabsorption of those released' (Heller, p. 534). By the end of 1949 industry was producing one-quarter more output than a year earlier, with no more workers. Spare capacity abounded. The UNECE estimated in 1949 that industry could employ a million more workers, since it was operating at only 75 per cent capacity. An import liberalization policy, introduced in the summer of 1949, put employers under further pressure to rationalize. Half of Germany's imports from Europe were freed from controls, even during 1949 and 1950.

The jump in unemployment further weakened the unions, whose funds had been nearly wiped out by the monetary reform. Since only one-quarter of workers had secured the 15 per cent increase in wages authorized by the military government in April 1948, the abolition of wage controls in October – when unemployment was already rising – posed no threat. The position of militants in the unions was weakened by organizational measures against communists: for example, the metal workers' union, IG Metall, changed its basis of organization from work place to geographical area or industry; at the end of 1948 all KPD members were voted off the Ruhr miners' executive.

Low wages permitted high profits, which encouraged investment, production was increasing rapidly after the end of 1949, and the increases in productivity permitted increases in real wages without profitability being threatened. The weakened state of the trade unions and slow growth of real pay ensured that money wage claims did not challenge these high profits. Business investment more than doubled in 1949 and brought the rate of accumulation up to about 4 per cent a year. Although Germany devalued less in 1949 against the dollar than did the UK and most other European economies (Chapter 7), the very low level of real wages permitted a rapid expansion of exports in the boom conditions of the Korean war. The volume of exports increased by about six times between

1948 and 1951 to regain the prewar level, and this helped to maintain the expansion and ensure that the rising profits were invested. Exceptionally favourable tax concessions for investment and the wiping out of the burden of interest payments by the monetary reform also encouraged the ploughing back of expanding profits into increased investment; in the two and a half years after currency reform 70 per cent of investment was financed from firms' retained profits. By 1952 the rate of accumulation had been levered up to 6 per cent (Table 6.1) – three times the rate in Germany's European rivals and twice that in the United States.

Marshall Aid played only a limited role. Foreign aid peaked in 1948, at just over $1 billion (little actually contributed under the Marshall Plan). This level was maintained in 1949 when Marshall Aid was in full swing. Aid in these two years was around 5 per cent of GDP, representing two-thirds of total imports in 1948, but by 1949 the proportion was less than one-half. By 1951 it was less than one-tenth. The dollars did finance imported raw materials, vital to the expansion of production in 1948 and 1949. But the real extent of aid was less than the gross figures suggest. Significant foreign exchange losses resulted from the underpricing of German coal exports (put at $100 million in 1950 and 1951). There were requirements to use more expensive Dutch and Belgian ports, and limitations on how Marshall Aid could be spent (Chapter 5). By 1951 exports were quite adequate to meet the import bill.

The 'counterpart funds' played some role in financing investment. Given the authorities' extreme distaste for deficit financing, the availability of these DMs – the 'counterpart' of dollar imports – to the government may have made 'respectable' the financing of some investment in basic industries – fuel, transport and iron and steel. But even in 1950, when the use of these funds was at a maximum, they constituted only 9 per cent of total investment. Over the five and a half years after monetary reform they represented only 3 per cent of total investment. In any case the availability of these counterpart funds for investment was enormously outweighed by the occupation costs paid (in DMs) by the German authorities; these amounted to about 5 per cent of GDP over the years 1949–52, twelve times the value of the counterpart funds available for investment. Of course, Germany was thereby provided with 'defence' which cost a smaller percentage of GDP than was the case for the occupying powers, but this cannot disguise the fact that the costs were obligatory charges levied to pay for armies of occupation and far outweighed the counterpart funds available for investment.

So the dollars provided by Marshall Aid were only of temporary importance in 1948–9. Far more significant was the wholehearted commitment they signified on the part of the United States to the restoration of untrammelled (West) German capitalism. The first elections for the parliament, in August 1949, registered the success of this restoration. The SPD and KPD combined secured only one-third of the votes, compared to 44 per cent in state elections during 1946–8.

The socialization of industry, especially the basic industries of the Ruhr, was effectively ruled out after 1947. Despite IG Metall's threat in 1950 that it would bring business to a standstill if the old owners were restored, they did indeed regain control. The old shareholders were allocated shares in the new companies, though multiple holdings were restricted. So the ownership of Ruhr steel and coal merely became slightly more dispersed. But the workers clung stubbornly to the issue of codetermination in industry. The *Economist* reported: 'In Germany the trade unions, which have made a valiant effort to prune their ranks of communists, find themselves pushed into the background, and advised by the American military government to concentrate their efforts on questions of hours and wages; . . . the trade union leaders fear that industrial workers if they receive no satisfaction from the Western powers on codetermination, may drift in the direction of communism' (14 May 1949).

In 1950 IG Metall secured 96 per cent of the vote in the steel mills for strike action if their demands were not met; 93 per cent of miners voted to support the struggle. After intervention by Chancellor Adenauer, the employers conceded parity on supervisory boards. This was a tactical retreat. As the head of the Iron and Steel Control Board put it, works councils were 'claiming rights of interference in the conduct of the works without assuming corresponding responsibilities. Giving the workers and the trade unions a share in these responsibilities should go a long way towards forestalling labour trouble in industry' (quoted Spiro, p. 33). The authority of the boards was confined to local works and personnel matters. The key demands of 1946–7 had been parity with employers on issues of the type, methods and layout of production, investment, sales, price setting and mergers. None was conceded (Chapter 9). These demands were inconsistent with the full restoration of capitalism. When they were laid to rest with the acceptance of the watered-down system of codetermination, the postwar challenge to the system had been definitely contained.

The United Kingdom

In the United Kingdom the shift in policy after the announcement of the Marshall plan was milder than in continental Europe and Japan because the political and economic situation was less threatening. The government sought to divert resources away from consumption (private and social service) towards exports and investment (Chapter 4), although workers' consumption was growing very slowly. By 1948 it was barely higher than before the war (Table 6.8).

The first moves came in the autumn of 1947 when the attempt to make sterling convertible into other currencies, which the United States had made a condition of the dollar loan, collapsed after a few weeks. The government introduced a deflationary budget to hold back consumption at home. It also cast around for ways of earning dollars.

Having previously limited the colonies' ability to borrow in London to finance capital projects, the government succumbed to a wave of enthusiasm for aiding colonial developments specifically geared to helping the British balance of payments. The schemes were more or less disastrous. The most spectacular was the Groundnut Scheme in Tanganyika (Tanzania). This cost some £40 million and yielded less groundnuts than had been bought for planting.

Vague calls for wage restraint were replaced in February 1948 by an altogether firmer statement on *Personal Incomes, Costs and Prices*. This proposed that manufacturers should not be allowed to justify price increases by wage rises. In practice this sanction was a less effective means of enforcing wage restraint than the strong support of the right-wing trade union leaderships.

At the time of the 1949 devaluation the call for restraint was replaced by a wage freeze, again supported by the union leaders. The TUC asked for various concessions in exchange for maintaining the wage freeze, including the continuation of food subsidies, rent control and expenditure on social services. Most

Table 6.8 Profits and wages: Britain, 1938–51

	Profit shares as percentage of net domestic product			Index numbers of living standards	
	Before tax[1]	*After tax*[2]	*Undistributed profits*[3]	*Real wage*	*Real personal consumption per head of population*
1938	12.5	9.8	7.7	100	100
1945	12.3	n.a.	n.a.	121	90
1946	13.0	6.2	6.5	120	100
1947	11.8	3.9	5.5	122	102
1948	14.0	6.1	7.7	124	102
1949	13.7	6.4	7.7	126	103
1950	13.2	5.0	7.9	128	105
1951	14.5	4.5	7.3	128	105

1. Corporate profits net of capital consumption and stock appreciation.
2. As (1) but net of taxes (UK) on company income.
3. Undistributed profits net of stock appreciation, gross of capital consumption.

Source: see Appendix.

were partially eroded over the final three years of the Labour government. But the wage freeze had a major impact. Real wage rates fell continuously from 1946 to 1951, though earnings rose slowly through overtime and local agreements. Consumption per head crept up. The policy was finally undermined by rank-and-file pressure. In September 1950 the Trades Union Congress annual conference rejected wage restraint against the advice of its General Council.

The continuation of Order 1305 (Chapter 2) provided the backdrop to the wages policy. Its antistrike provisions were first used in 1949 when gas maintenance workers were prosecuted and sentenced to one year's imprisonment. The other strikers returned to work and the sentences were reduced to £50 fines on appeal. In the following year an attempt to use the Order against London dockers failed because of spontaneous working-class resistance, and it was finally repealed.

As well as the clampdown on wages, 1948 also saw the beginnings of the erosion of Labour's social programmes. The housebuilding target was reduced, as were the plans for future expenditure on education and health. The principle of free medical services on which the health service had been founded was also abandoned: the budget introduced a one-shilling (5p) prescription charge. After the devaluation in the autumn of 1949, government spending was cut by a further 8½ per cent. Health expenditure increased as a proportion of GDP up to 1949 (Table 4.5), but then stabilized.

In a White Paper published in December of 1948 the government attempted to make explicit the planning of priorities in the shares of national expenditure. This was done over a four-year period, in line with the requirements of the OEEC as part of the run-in to Marshall Aid. It calculated the extent to which the rate of growth of consumption would have to be limited if the investment (public and private) and current state spending objectives were to be reached. A 12 per cent growth of GDP was projected. Consumption was to increase by 5 per cent. The investment share was to be 20 per cent.

The document had little or no practical effect. But it did reflect the fact that consumption was the main area of expenditure amenable to control, so that other expenditure objectives could be met. Hence the importance of wage control.

The Labour government made no attempt to institute economic planning, even of the indicative kind. It explicitly rejected real economic planning as being inherently antidemocratic: 'It is not possible to establish firm and definite plans. . . . No other method of progressing is possible in a democratic community. For . . . policies can be fulfilled only if they gain the voluntary cooperation of people as groups and individuals. The means of control which can be effectively used within a democracy are limited' (1948 White Paper, quoted Pritt, p. 283).

In September 1949 the pound was devalued from $4.03 to $2.80 after sterling export earnings (particularly raw materials exports from the Empire) were hit by the US recession (Chapter 7). This, together with the accompanying wage freeze and spending cuts, paved the way for a substantial improvement in the payments position. Profits rose sharply in 1948 and remained high during the rest of the Labour government's term of office.

Alongside the Labour government's retreat towards pro-business policies, a witch-hunt was launched against communists in the trade unions. The CP moved into a position of opposing the Labour government in the autumn of 1947, following the more aggressive line adopted by the Cominform, the newly formed international organization of Communist parties. At the end of 1947, the Labour Party national executive committee issued a circular which in effect invited trade unions to dismiss officials who were CP members: 'We can expect a campaign of sabotage by Communists and their fellow travellers . . . we can expect inspired attempts to promote discontent in the factories . . . we can expect intensified attempts to undermine and destroy the Labour Movement' (quoted Pritt, p. 160). In the spring of 1948 the government announced a purge of communists in the civil service. The *Economist* reported (23 October 1948): 'The question of communist influence and leadership in the British trade union movement has now become an issue of first-class importance. What has happened in France could happen here if communist influence was sufficiently strong.' It pointed out that the miners had a communist secretary, who had just described the Marshall Plan as 'the American pattern for the reconstruction of Europe at the expense of the working class', and communist leaders in Wales and Scotland. In the engineers' union two out of the national committee of seven, and three out of four national organizers, were communists. The electricians had just elected communists as president and secretary. Eight out of thirty-eight members of the transport workers' executive were communists, as was the president of the builders' union. The *Economist* urged the TUC to intervene 'to end the equivocal position of communist union officials'. In July 1949 the transport workers took the lead by debarring communists from holding office, in line with the letter and the spirit of the TUC's anticommunist circular. This signalled an important weakening of the left. It was noted that 'while the conference was passing a resolution banning Communists from holding office in the union, and while their general secretary was making a highly responsible speech about the necessity for wage stabilization, many of the union's members in the London docks were stubbornly resisting all exhortations to return to work' (*Economist*, 16 July 1949).

The same issue reported that 'among trade union officials there would be support for a legal prohibition of unofficial strikes' in essential industries, but that, given the mood of the dockers, legal threats would not work. 'No section of workers has had its conditions of work more radically improved at the community's expense

Chart 6.4a Profitability, 1945–51[1]

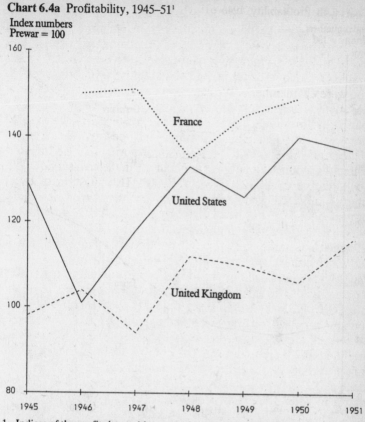

Index numbers
Prewar = 100

France

United States

United Kingdom

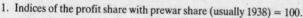

1. Indices of the profit share with prewar share (usually 1938) = 100.

Source: see Appendix.

than the dockers. Yet what is the result? A most marked decline in both efficiency and responsibility.' Despite the anticommunist witch-hunt, and the control exerted by the right-wing leadership, employers in Britain never launched a frontal assault on the labour movement comparable to those in France, Italy, Japan or even the USA. This may actually have weakened the employers in the long run. Complacent, with their markets carved up at home and in the Empire, they failed to launch the kind of 'rationalization' drive against the labour movement that was a precondition for the investment booms of the fifties in continental Europe and Japan.

Chart 6.4b Profitability, 1946–51[1]

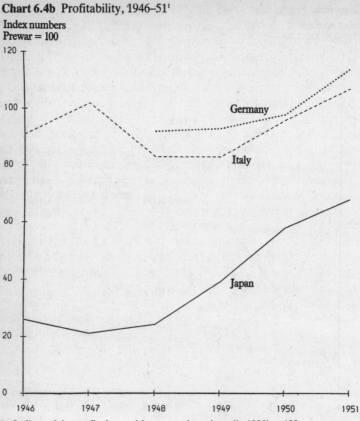

Index numbers
Prewar = 100

1. Indices of the profit share with prewar share (usually 1938) = 100.

Source: see Appendix.

Summary

Much had happened in the few years following the launch of the
Marshall Plan. The United States had recognized that the reconstruction of an effective world capitalist system required its
wholehearted support for the restoration of 'social and financial
discipline' elsewhere, and had been prepared to delay prising open
foreign markets to US business to this end. The USSR had been
safely contained within its Eastern European bunker. While the
USSR's sphere of influence had been more firmly consolidated

than the United States had initially hoped, it was also more limited than the USA had subsequently feared. And hostility to the USSR was to prove a useful weapon against the labour movement. While the colonial revolution had achieved a great victory in China, imperialism had elsewhere begun successfully to combine moves towards political freedom with continued economic domination.

The continental European and Japanese labour movements had suffered crushing defeats. They had been forced to retreat enormously from the apparently commanding positions they had held in 1945 – both on the shop floor and politically. The balance between wages and productivity was extremely favourable to the employers. Profits were comparable to prewar levels, even in the countries then under the yoke of fascism (Chart 6.4). In the United Kingdom developments had been less dramatic, but, nevertheless, decisive. In 1945 many people had believed that the Tories would never govern again. In fact, the first ever majority Labour government was to be followed by thirteen years of unbroken Tory rule and an erosion of socialist ideas. The US labour movement's postwar offensive was contained in a climate of virulent anticommunism.

So the basic conditions for renewed capitalist expansion had been established, and the basis laid for the great boom of the 1950s and 1960s. But it was to take a few more years to get really going.

7. Towards the Boom

The great postwar boom did not emerge easily from the stabilization in the late 1940s. Indeed, prospects initially appeared gloomy. Industrial production in OEEC Europe (excluding Germany) slowed down, its growth rate declining from 12 per cent between 1947 and 1948 to 5 per cent between the first halves of 1949 and 1950. Possibilities for rapid growth were far from physically exhausted. Unemployment rose in several countries and subsequent events were to show the existence of spare capacity which could be taken up rapidly to permit much faster growth. The slowdown rather resulted from deflation (Chapter 6) and the onset of recession in the United States.

The US recession

Pent-up consumer demand in the United States had largely disappeared by the end of 1947. Low-income families had exhausted wartime savings. The 1948 *Economic Report of The President* noted that 'more than a quarter of all spending units and almost half of those with income under $2000 a year held no liquid assets in 1947' (p. 20). In 1948 the average proportion of income saved rose from 3.1 per cent to 5.9 per cent (a level roughly maintained for the next two decades). So consumption decelerated sharply. In 1947 investment was high in 'utilities, transportation and those lines of manufacturing, such as textiles, which had not undergone a normal rate of expansion or modernization of factories during the war period' (p. 22). But investment in many mass-production industries peaked in 1947. Total business investment stagnated from early 1948. Profits peaked then too. By mid-1948 exports were 20 per cent down on the previous year, despite emergency aid to Europe – a grim reminder of what would have happened without the Marshall Plan. Expansion was maintained, only because the government raised its spending by nearly one-half, boosting civil projects in particular (the budget surplus fell from $15 billion in 1947 to $3 billion in 1948).

This stimulus was not maintained in 1949 and production began to fall. Business investment led the way down, declining by about 4 per cent of GDP, of which nearly two-thirds consisted of destocking. Unemployment doubled to 7.6 per cent.

The recession seemed to confirm the universal prognostications of doom (Chapter 1). In fact, a major slump was not in the offing. But the United States was probably only saved from a bout of stagnation by the outbreak of the Korean war in the middle of 1950. Meanwhile the improvement in Europe was registered and consolidated by a substantial round of successful devaluations.

The 1949 devaluations

Europe and Japan could reduce their massive deficits with the United States only by improving their competitiveness. Otherwise increases in production would inevitably be choked off by payments constraints and the United States would see no end to the need for dollar aid. Improved European competitiveness would have a further advantage for US exporters: the elimination of the deficit would make it possible to resume pressure to eliminate European barriers to their exports, since the argument that they were necessary to reduce the deficit would no longer hold.

Devaluations can succeed only if workers in the devaluing countries pay the necessary price. Devaluation increases import costs, and hence the cost of living. If workers gain compensatory pay rises then the competitive benefit of the devaluation is soon eroded. The increase in export profits (as UK goods sold for dollars in the United States, for example, bring in more pounds) makes it even harder to persuade workers to accept a cut in living standards. 1949, with the labour movement in retreat throughout Europe and Japan, was an auspicious year for successful devaluation.

Aware of these considerations, the US Treasury began applying pressure for devaluations, especially of sterling, in that year. The US recession led to a sharp deterioration in the Sterling Area's balance of payments. Between January and mid-September of 1949 the United Kingdom lost half a billion dollars – more than one-quarter of its reserves. The government then carried out a 30 per cent devaluation. Amidst French cries of 'trade war', most European countries followed suit with more modest devaluations (a little over 20 per cent for France and for Germany, a little under 10 per cent for Italy; Japan had only established an official rate in April 1949 and it was not readjusted). Rough estimates suggest that (with the exception of France) the devaluations improved European competitiveness considerably compared to prewar (Table 7.1).

Table 7.1 Prices and exchange rates, end of 1949

Index numbers
Prewar=100

	(1) Wholesale prices	(2) Dollar value of currency as percentage of prewar value	Dollar wholesale prices $\frac{(1) \times (2)}{100}$
USA	200	100	200
UK	246	57	140
France	1,944	11	213
Germany	195	59	127
Italy	4,747	3	142
Japan	21,886	1	219

Source: Bank for International Settlements, *Annual Report 1949–50*, pp. 95, 104, 154.

Wholesale prices in dollars had risen by less than 50 per cent in the United Kingdom, Germany and Italy while doubling in the United States. The establishment of competitive exchange rates was further evidence that real wage rates could be held down, and profitability jacked up, to the level necessary for sustained accumulation. The immediate impact of the devaluations, however, was swamped by that of the Korean war.

The Korean upswing

The US economy revived on the expectation of hostilities in Korea. Stockbuilding took off at the beginning of 1950, reaching a massive rate by the end of the year. Business fixed investment recovered: by the middle of 1950 it had reached a level, above the 1948 peak, which was to be maintained for the next five years. Government spending on goods and services – this time military – began to shoot up at the end of 1950. By the end of 1951 it absorbed a phenomenal 7½ per cent more of GDP than in the middle of 1950. Taxes were increased rapidly so that the deficit only reached $5½ billion a year during 1952–4, 1½ per cent of GDP. Consumption hardly grew and post-tax profits did not exceed their 1948 peak since profits tax rose sharply. But the enormous increase in military spending boosted production considerably, simply by absorbing so many resources.

The Korean war generated a dramatic commodities boom. Wool, rubber, tin, cotton and other basic commodities more or less trebled in price. The terms of trade for raw materials against manufactures improved by 30 per cent between the first halves of 1950 and 1951. Raw material imports took off before hostilities began in June 1950. Between the first halves of 1949 and 1950 manufacturing production in the United States, Japan and the OEEC rose by 8 per cent and imports of raw materials by 20 per cent. 'Normal' restocking as output rose was boosted by speculation, encouraged by a doubling of US stockpile contracts in the first half of 1950. When the boom in production got underway materials supplies were limited and prices soared. Between the first halves of 1950 and 1951 manufacturing production rose by 17 per cent and raw material imports by 4 per cent. In the first quarter of 1951 stockpile contracts ran at ten times the 1949 level. In 1951 the rise in military spending accounted for half of the 7½ per cent expansion of production in the capitalist countries.

The raw materials boom subsided towards the middle of 1951. Commercial stocks reached saturation levels and consumer spending fell behind consumer goods production. Demand for raw materials for both consumer goods and military production fell off, while supply continued to grow. Prices fell sharply.

In 1952 the rate of stockbuilding halved, as did the growth rate of total production, which fell to 3½ per cent. Military spending accounted directly for three-quarters of the total expansion (the United States' share on its own accounting for 60 per cent). Unemployment continued to fall in North America (to 3.2 per cent in 1952, compared to 6.1 per cent in 1950); in Western Europe it rose a little as industrial production stagnated (to 6.2 per cent compared to 5.7 per cent in 1950). Inflation, which had been running at around 10 per cent in 1951, subsided very rapidly as the deterioration in the terms of trade (about 7 per cent in 1951) was reversed in 1952. In North America inflation was down to 1½ per cent in 1952. The decline took a little longer in Europe but by 1953 inflation on both sides of the Atlantic was a mere ½ per cent. The inflationary surge ebbed rapidly because trade unions put in only moderate wage claims. Real wages were maintained or slightly increased in 1951, but high inflation rate did not lead to further rapid pay rises. With the fallback in materials prices after 1951, this moderate bargaining yielded real wage increases of 3 to 5 per cent in 1952 and 1953.

The jump in inflation did boost profits in 1950 and 1951 (Chart 6.4). But company reports exaggerated the increase by including inflated stock values. In France, for example, the share of profits in national income appeared to rise by nearly one-half between 1949 and 1951, whereas after adjusting for inflation the rise was less than one-tenth. In the United States and United Kingdom stiff tax increases on profits, levied to help finance military spending, actually pushed down the after-tax profit share (Table 6.8).

Investment and the boom

In retrospect it might seem that the Korean war boom and sub-sequent rearmament should have provided the ideal impetus for a sustained boom. The deflations and assaults on the labour movement after 1947 had restored the conditions for profitable production. The expansionary effect of the war could have pro-vided the prospect of expanding markets necessary to justify a major increase in investment, which in turn would have pushed production to greater heights.

In fact, the Korean boom generated only a small increase in investment which soon petered out. Investment in plant and machinery rose by just 5 per cent in 1951. Only in Germany, where reconstruction had been so delayed, was the rate of accumulation substantially higher in 1951 than two or three years earlier (Table 6.1). Business investment actually fell a little in 1952 and its growth rate between 1950 and 1954 was less than 3 per cent a year, not much more than a third of the rate which was to be achieved over the following decade. For the advanced countries as a whole the rate of accumulation during 1954 was no higher than in 1951. The beginnings of an investment boom in Europe were apparent, but accumulation had yet to take off in Japan, and in the United States it was slipping back from the 1951 peak.

The main explanation for the sluggishness of investment, despite the high profits and booming markets in the early 1950s, must lie in a lack of confidence on the part of employers. While the most dangerous legacies of the previous decade had been dismantled or contained by 1950, further years of tranquillity and relative prosperity were needed to erase its memory. Stock markets are an indication of expectations about future profits. In 1951 the level of 'real' share prices (that is, adjusted for inflation) was everywhere below prewar, and far below in Europe and Japan. Even by 1954 stock markets outside the United States remained more gloomy than prewar (Table 7.2).

Table 7.2 Real share prices, 1929–59[1]

Index numbers

	1929	1937	1951	1954	1959
USA	122	100	90	114	206
UK	88	100	72	80	108
France	300	100	63	112	178
Italy	150	100	38	53	114
Japan	n.a.	100	16	25	95

1. Share indices adjusted by consumer price index. Data for Germany are not available.

Source: UN, *Statistical Yearbook*, 1960 and earlier issues.

The columns of the *Economist* reflected unease about the extent to which real stability had yet been achieved: 'In the third year of the Marshall Plan, which has succeeded beyond expectation in rebuilding European economies, in conditions of prosperity and restored standards of living – in short, in what ought to be a good year – a quarter of both the French and Italian electorates voted communist. . . . There is almost nowhere a positive faith in the possibilities of progress, such as the Russians and Americans in their different ways, both have' (7 July 1951).

Optimistic assessments of the situation in Japan were also discounted: 'The true picture is of the Japanese nation, facing a grim struggle for existence on the basis of somewhat artificial and distorted economic conditions, and of a Japanese people dazed and strained after all their chequered experiences in the last ten years' (10 November 1951). A couple of years later the problems of potential conflicts in Japan remained. 'Fundamentally Japan's difficulties are simple and backbreaking: costs are too high, hungry mouths are too many, markets are too few . . . costs, however, can be cut only if equipment is modernized, with consequent incitement – never very necessary in Japan – to staff retrenchment, which in turn must provoke industrial unrest, already strong and mounting' (6 June 1953).

Early in 1951 a report headlined 'Strike Pressure in France' reported that 'France was hit by a new wave of strikes the most serious since the big coal strike of October and November 1948. . . . It is a revealing fact that when the Communists tried to mobilize the workers behind political slogans – for instance, against General Eisenhower – they met with failure; but with a rapid rise in the cost of living they found it easy enough to start a strike about wages' (March 24 1951).

Some two and a half years later another strike wave involved '2 million strikers paralysing the public services of France and the movement spreading to private industry . . . unable to topple a centre-right government in the Assembly, they are trying to register the vote of no confidence outside the Chamber. It is a near revolutionary situation' (15 August 1953).

Italy was 'by no means in a state of boom. And the relative stability has been obtained at a level far too low to give every Italian an adequate standard of living' (19 June 1952). In the autumn of 1953 a major strike took place in support of a 10 to 15 per cent pay rise. 'The twenty-four-hour token strike of September 24th is regarded by many observers in Rome as the most imposing trade union demonstration since the war. Over 5 million workers of all three union organizations (Communist, Catholic and Social Democrat) came out. In the North the strike was almost 100 per cent effective in the bigger factories' (3 October 1953).

Germany seemed the outstanding success story in terms of political stability. In 1953 the *Economist* confidently wrote of the

Christian Democrats' electoral success: 'For Germany's neighbours the outstanding fact of last Sunday's elections is that Dr Adenauer is estabished as the most powerful statesman on the continent. The disparity between his position and that of the politicians who temporarily govern France and Italy is startling. So, too, is the German vote that eliminated the Communists and the Communist success in the Italian elections; or between the stable labour conditions in Germany and the strikes in France' (12 September 1953). Within a year, however, it was reporting that widespread strikes involving public sector workers in Hamburg and metal workers in Bavaria were shattering such complacency: 'Peace in the labour world has lasted so long that everyone had come to feel that "Germans don't strike"' (14 August 1954). A fortnight later its correspondent wrote: 'On the whole West Germany's economy can now bear increased wages, but its political structure would be shaken by class struggle. It is likely that extremism on the part of the unions is less to be feared than a stubborn attitude amongst a section of the employers.'

All these movements were successfully contained, but the essential point is that 'informed' opinion was still jittery. This bred poor business confidence and hesitancy over long-term investment plans. The UN Economic Commission for Europe, writing early in 1953, stressed clearly the link between economic confidence and political stability: 'At the beginning of 1953 there was stagnation in production and shrinking trade in Western Europe, in sharp contrast to the one-and-a-half-year-old resolve of the OEEC countries to secure an increase in production of 25 per cent in five years. It would be rash to attempt a forecast about cyclical movements in the near future: the developments over the seven post-war years . . . serve to stress the influence which political changes in Europe and elsewhere exert on Western Europe's economy' (UNECE, 1953, p. 52). A year later the UN, with rather a rosy memory, reported a substantial decline in private investment, and commented: 'There was in general no return to the climate of confident expectations which had characterized the years up to 1950' (UNECE, 1954, p. 1).

Contrary to the UNECE's expectations, however, a general upswing started in Europe in 1954: 'The general impression was that, after the Korean boom, Western Europe – with the notable exception of West Germany – had entered a period, not of outright downturn, but rather of protracted stagnation. On top of this came, in the latter half of 1953 and the beginning of 1954, two new factors which added to apprehensiveness. One was the onset of American recession and the other was a pronounced weakening in European markets for coal and steel' (UNECE, 1955, p. 3). But the US recession proved less severe and protracted than had been anticipated (the *Economist* had feared a 'medium-sized slump'). It also had less impact than had been expected, since US military expenditures in Europe (running at about \$2 billion per year) still more than covered Europe's increased trade deficit with the United States. So, paradoxically, the US recession may have boosted confidence in Europe by showing that stagnation in the United States did not necessarily imply stagnation in Europe.

Moreover, in longer-term perspective, Europe was proceeding in the United States' footsteps. 'One of the most notable features of the present upswing in Western Europe is the great increase in purchases of consumer durable goods. The expansion of the West European motor-car industry was largely destined for European markets, and concurrently there has been a growing sale of furniture, electrical appliances and other durable household goods which, when added to the increase in purchases of motor-cars constitutes a veritable wave of consumer buying. Much of this expanding demand has been financed by means of consumer credit' (UNECE, 1955, p. 21).

Most fundamentally, the struggles of the early 1950s had shown that the challenge posed by the labour movement, already severely weakened by the onslaught of the late 1940s, could be contained by affordable improvements in living standards. Amidst widespread reports of the 'Investment Boom of 1955', the rate of accumulation climbed steadily in Europe to reach a rate of over 4½ per cent by 1956 – half as much again as five years before. Japan was to prove to be close behind (Chapter 8). The great boom was on its way.

Part II

The Great Boom
1950–74

8. The Golden Years

> The wealth of those societies in which the capitalist mode of production prevails presents itself as an 'immense accumulation of commodities'.

Those opening words from Marx's *Capital* could have been written about the long postwar boom, the most striking feature of which was a quite breathtaking growth in production.

By 1973 output in the advanced capitalist countries (ACCs) was 180 per cent higher than in 1950 – almost three times as great. More was produced in that quarter century than in the previous three quarters, and many times more than in any comparable period in human history (Table 8.1).

Table 8.1 Long-term growth, 1820–1973

Average annual percentage growth rates[1]

	Output	Output per head of population	Stock of fixed capital	Exports
1820–1870	2.2	1.0	n.a.	4.0
1870–1913	2.5	1.4	2.9	3.9
1913–1950	1.9	1.2	1.7	1.0
1950–1973	4.9	3.8	5.5	8.6

1. Arithmetic averages of individual country figures.

Source: Maddison, 1982, p. 91.

With growth on that scale, output doubles every sixteen years. If these rates were maintained then, with population growing at the rate of 1 per cent a year, each generation could expect to be roughly twice as well off as its parents and four times as well off as its grandparents.

Moreover, figures of this sort understate the pace of development. Being purely quantitative measures, they fail to illuminate qualitative advances. People not only had more than their forebears; they also had revolutionary new products. By 1969 millions of people were able to watch on colour TV as the first human set foot on the moon.

The fifties and sixties were capitalism's golden age. As a British prime minister remarked at the time, people had never had it so good.

Workers and means of production

The increase in output was out of all proportion to the growth of employment. The number of people classified as in civilian employment rose by only 29 per cent between 1952 and 1973. So most of the extra production represented an increase in output per worker. Annual productivity doubled, a growth rate of 3.3 per cent a year.

Longer working hours do not account for the increase, because on the whole the 'normal' working week was reduced and holidays grew longer. The number of married women employed on a part-time basis also grew rapidly. The Organization for Economic Cooperation and Development (OECD, expanded from the OEEC) has suggested that hours of work decreased by about 0.3 per cent a year during the 1950s, and by 0.8 per cent a year during the 1960s. Overall, therefore, hourly productivity probably rose significantly faster than yearly productivity, though measuring hours of work is difficult, especially in the self-employed sector.

The main cause of spiralling productivity was a phenomenal increase in the quantity and quality of means of production. The stock of these means of production was 2½ times as great in 1973 as it was in 1952. Since employment growth was relatively modest, the mass of means of production per worker more than doubled over the period. It was as though each worker was confronted by two machines where one had stood before.

The machines changed as well, however. Technological advances meant that the new generations of machinery embodied important innovations. By the end of the boom the machines

Chart 8.1 ACC production, capital stock, productivity and employment, 1952–70

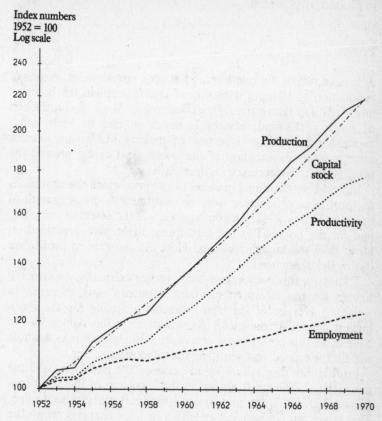

Index numbers
1952 = 100
Log scale

Source: see Appendix.

confronting the average worker not only were more numerous than before but also bore little resemblance to those in use two decades previously.

These developments were accompanied by changes in work practices, shaped partly by the nature of the new machinery and partly by struggle on the factory floor. Since such changes are inherently unquantifiable, it is impossible to say whether or not people were generally working harder by the end of the boom. But there is no doubt that most were working differently, and that changes in the labour process were part and parcel of the explosion in productive potential.

Profits

A breakdown of the relationship between employment, means of production and output does not, of course, explain the boom in any way other than a purely statistical sense. Since the production of more goods and services is never an end in itself under capitalism but always a means to making profit, any serious attempt at an explanation of the boom must centre around the returns capitalists received on their outlays.

In Part I we examined in detail the ways in which the conditions for profitable production were reconstituted in the aftermath of the war. This process of reconstruction was the essential launching pad for the boom. But the subsequent flight path depended on more than the launch facilities. How did the rate of profit fare during the boom itself?

To answer this question we have, rather unusually, constructed figures for the advanced capitalist countries' rate of profit (a weighted average of the best estimates available for the seven biggest capitalist countries). As described in the Appendix, we have done this both for the corporate business sector as a whole and for the crucial, and sensitive, manufacturing sector.

Profitability displays no trend between the mid-fifties and the mid-sixties, although it dipped in the recession of the late fifties (Chart 8.2). From the mid-sixties onwards it moves into decline. This latter fall is discussed at length in later chapters. Here the focus is on how profitability was maintained up till then.

Profit shares and rates

We shall examine the development of the rate of profit in terms of two statistical components. One is the share of profits in the value of output. The other is the ratio of output to capital.

Changes in the profit share register relative changes in the costs of employing labour (wages inclusive of all taxes on labour incomes and employment) and the value of output produced. If

Chart 8.2 ACC profit rates, 1955–68

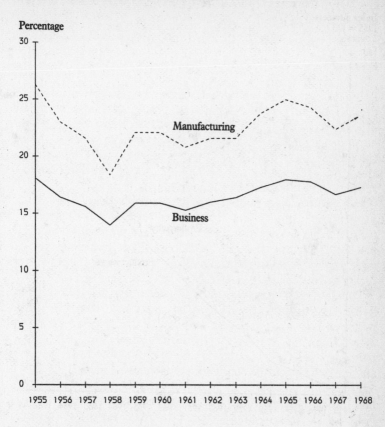

Percentage

Source: see Appendix.

real product wages rise more slowly than productivity then the profit share rises. If the growth of labour costs exceeds that of productivity, the profit share is squeezed. There was virtually no change in the profit share between the mid-fifties and mid-sixties. In other words, the real cost of employing labour rose at the same rate as productivity – about 3½ per cent a year (Chart 8.3).

Since the rate of profit is the percentage return on capital employed, a constant profit share maintains a constant profit rate only if the ratio of output to capital remains constant. This ratio in

Chart 8.3 ACC business productivity and product wages, 1955–68

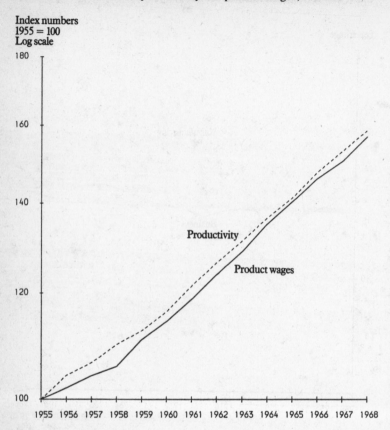

Index numbers
1955 = 100
Log scale

Source: see Appendix.

turn depends on the relative rate of growth of capital employed and of output produced.

We have already seen that both the quantity of means of production in use and the output produced by their operation grew enormously. In manufacturing and business, the two grew very closely in parallel until the mid-sixties, so that the ratio of output to capital remained fairly constant (Chart 8.4).

Chart 8.4 ACC business mechanization and output-capital ratio, 1955–70

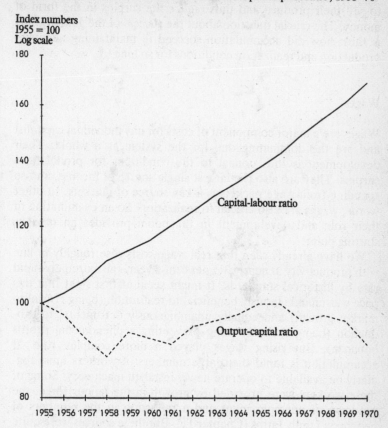

Index numbers
1955 = 100
Log scale

Capital-labour ratio

Output-capital ratio

Source: see Appendix.

Production and realization

Thus far, the account remains a statistical description of certain features of the boom. To get beyond this, and to try and understand the processes involved, we return to the basic requirements for profitable production. We have already argued that a period of sustained, profitable expansion can occur only if healthy conditions for producing surplus can be maintained, that is, if an adequate balance between productivity and real wages can be sustained. But capitalists also need expanding markets if they are to sell their produce and thus *realize* the surplus in the form of money. The crucial question about the success of the golden years is thus: how did accumulation succeed in maintaining adequate production and realization conditions for so long?

Wages

Wages are a major component of costs for any individual capitalist and are the dominating one for the system as a whole. Their development is thus crucial to the conditions for producing a surplus. They are also the largest single source of income, and so spending from wage packets is a key source of markets. In other words, wages are also crucial to realization. So an examination of their role and development in the boom provides an obvious starting point.

We have already seen that real wage costs rose roughly in line with productivity at nearly 3½ per cent a year – an extremely rapid rate by historical standards. It might seem at first sight that this pace was unambiguously beneficial to realization (being crucial to market growth) and equally unambiguously detrimental to production (being the only thing preventing a phenomenal profits bonanza). But rising wages played a more complex role. If accumulation is rapid then large numbers of workers must regularly be available to operate newly installed machinery. Some of these workers were provided by growth in the labour force, the rundown of unemployment and a reduction in the numbers of people on family farms (Chapter 11). But these sources were quite inadequate. The boom would have run out of steam very quickly indeed if capitalists had been forced to find extra employees to operate all the new machines. Much more important was the transfer of workers from old machines to new ones. If means of production remain in use for twenty years (a reasonable figure) then the scrapping of old ones releases some 5 per cent of the work force to work with new equipment every year. This figure exceeds the annual growth in the labour force during the boom by a factor of more than four.

Wage rises are the main immediate cause of scrapping. The criterion for capitalists to scrap old equipment is not whether the machine is physically serviceable – most machinery is withdrawn from use well before it has worn out – but whether it can any longer be operated profitably. And the key factor which renders unprofitable the operation of older vintages of machinery is a rise in wage costs.

Thus, paradoxical as it may seem, the rapid growth of means of production during the boom depended upon much scrapping of means of production. If this scrapping had not occurred then capitalists would have been unable to find workers to operate new machines and would have been forced to cut back accumulation sharply.

The rise in wages was therefore not basically damaging to production conditions. Given labour constraints, it was essential to the pace of accumulation and hence to the rate of growth of productivity. The growth in average productivity resulted from a combination of two processes: the rapid installation of new, high-productivity machinery and the fast scrapping of old, low-productivity machines. If wages had not risen, most of this scrapping would not have happened and productivity would have grown much less quickly than it did.

Rising wages were important for markets primarily because workers' additional spending accounted for the bulk of the growth in consumption expenditure. Rising spending on consumer goods in turn allowed the industries producing them to grow more or less in line with those producing means of production. Indeed, an important element of the boom was the mass production of durable goods and the improvement of the technologies required to produce them. This growth of consumption was essential to stability. If real wages had remained constant between 1955 and 1970, with productivity growth unaffected, then the share of profits would have increased from 15 to 20 per cent of the value of output to around one-half. If accumulation could have risen in parallel then it would have reached a rate of 15 per cent a year. With consumption growing at only about 1 per cent a year (the rate of growth of the labour force), the system would have become one in which machines were being installed at hectic rates in order to produce other machines.

The example is absurd because, apart from anything else, workers would not have been available to operate the new machines. The process could never have gone that far. But that is precisely the point: the boom would have been pulled up sharply if consumption had not grown fast enough, and rising wages were essential to that growth. The phenomenal Japanese expansion of the late 1950s, in which production outstripped consumption and accumulation accelerated enormously, was altogether exceptional and only temporarily sustainable.

In the advanced capitalist countries as a whole the share of consumption declined far less than it did in Japan in those exceptional years – between 1952 and 1973 it only slid down from 62.9 per cent of GDP to 59.5 per cent. The part financed out of wages (and the incomes of the self-employed corresponding to the

Chart 8.5 ACC consumption, 1952–70

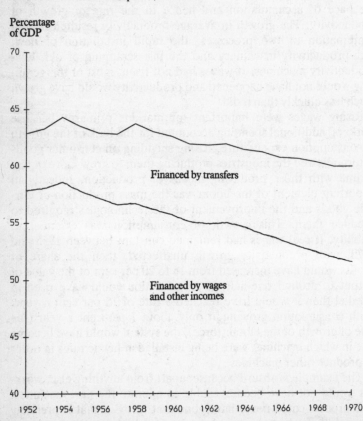

Percentage of GDP

Financed by transfers

Financed by wages and other incomes

Source: see Appendix.

average wage) fell by rather more than this (Chart 8.5). Consumption financed from government transfers (pensions etc.) rose from 5 per cent of GDP in 1952 to 10 per cent in 1973, and it was partly to pay for this that the average proportion of incomes taken by direct taxation rose from 16 per cent in 1952 to 22 per cent in 1973.

Despite this increased taxation, despite a rise in the proportion of incomes saved from 6 per cent to 11 per cent and despite a probable slight rise in the share of total incomes in the form of rent, dividends and interest and high self-employment earnings, consumption out of wages still constituted some 45 per cent of GDP in 1970. If wages per head had not increased, the share of GDP accounted for by consumption out of wage earnings would have fallen from 52 per cent in 1952 to 31 per cent in 1970; this would have required an inconceivable rise in other types of spending (by capitalists and government) if the increase in production was to be sold.

Regardless of their importance in sustaining accumulation by providing a growing market for consumer goods, wages must be regarded as a basically passive element in the process of realization. The development of wages is largely a product of the process of accumulation itself.

A capitalist boom requires *surplus* to be realized. Workers' spending as a whole provides the demand which realizes the profits of capitalists producing consumer goods. But the pay of their employees is an expense which reduces profits, not a source of demand which realizes them. Only the spending of workers employed elsewhere realizes profits in the consumer goods industries. These workers will only be employed if there is demand for the products they make – for export, from the government or from the employers themselves. So the realization of all the surplus ultimately depends on sufficient spending by the employers (on investment or consumption), the government or by those purchasing exports.

Why wages rose

It is one thing to describe the key role played by rising labour costs and another to explain why they rose. But the functions provide clues to the mechanisms. On the production side, labour constraints in the context of rapid accumulation will tend to pull up wages as capitalists compete for workers. Those with new, more productive equipment are prepared to pay higher wages to attract labour than are those with older machinery because the former can operate profitably at higher wage levels than the latter. And they may need to pay more if enough workers are to be available – unless sufficient old machines are forced out of operation there will be a shortage of workers to operate the new.

On the realization side, firms with new capacity will tend to cut prices in an attempt to win markets from their rivals with older equipment. Productivity gains on the new equipment allow such cuts without a fall in profits. The effect is for labour costs to rise relative to the price of the product. Real wage rises were thus a product of the competitive process whereby more efficient firms drove out weaker rivals to obtain both labour and markets, which less efficient producers would otherwise have hung on to.

A question which arises from this analysis is whether competition for labour or for markets was the more fundamental in pulling up wages. Real wages vary according to the net outcome of competition in the labour market, which determines changes in money wages, and competition in the product markets, which determines price changes. At any point in time a shortage of either labour or markets is likely to be the dominant factor constraining accumulation at the existing real wage level. It then makes sense to ascribe the subsequent rise in real wages primarily to whichever of the two markets sees the more intense competition.

In a number of countries a distinct shift took place during the course of the boom. Labour markets tightened noticeably as reserves of unemployed labour and underemployment on family farms were progressively exhausted (this development is discussed in later chapters). As a broad generalization, it is thus reasonable to say that the role of tight labour markets in driving up real wages eclipsed that of competition in product markets as the boom progressed. But that is a generalization. There was considerable variation between countries and between industries.

Emphasizing the role of competition between firms in raising real wages may appear to fly in the face of the everyday reality of pay negotiations. The image conjured up is certainly nearer to a North African bazaar than to trade unionists and employers sitting round a table. But the contrast is less sharp than appears. In the golden years institutionalized pay bargaining constituted one of the transmission mechanisms through which the requirements of accumulation, and the competitive struggles bred by them, generated the necessary real wage increases.

Negotiations over pay are about changes in money wages. What happens to real wages depends on changes in both money wages and prices. Unions do not negotiate with employers about the prices of the products they produce. So they can only raise real wages if product markets are tight enough to prevent the employers from passing all money wage increases on in higher prices. And the tightness of product markets is out of union control.

The need for a certain amount of scrapping if accumulation is to proceed smoothly determines a necessary rise in product wages. If collective bargaining yields less than the required rise then firms will not be able to find enough workers to operate all newly installed machines and will have to pay above the settlement. This will result in a further rise in wages. If negotiations yield more than the required rise then too much scrapping may result, generating unemployment. This did not happen significantly during the boom; the trend was for unemployment to fall. Alternatively, firms will pass on the 'excess' component of the settlement in higher prices, and real wages will rise by less than expected. This was a factor in the development of inflation from around the mid-1960s. If collective bargaining 'gets it right' then the process is simplified but not altered fundamentally.

Exports

If wages cannot realize the surplus, this leaves sales of exports, and spending by the government or the employers themselves as sources of demand. The advanced capitalist bloc could have realized surplus by running a positive trade balance with the rest of the world (i.e., the less developed countries and the Eastern bloc). By selling more outside the advanced bloc than was bought in, capitalists could have increased their assets (in the form of third world factories, gold or financial assets) without accumulating means of production at home.

Exports to less developed countries rose from $20 billion in 1958 (the earliest year for which data are available) to $42 billion in 1970 and those to centrally planned economies from $2 billion to

$8 billion. The 1970 total represents only 2½ per cent of OECD GDP, a slightly smaller proportion than in 1958. And most of the money coming in was offset by spending on imports into the bloc. The export surplus of the industrial countries in 1970, for example, was only $9 billion. This represented less than ½ per cent of OECD output, or 3 per cent of investment. So it was of trivial significance as a means of realizing surplus.

Chart 8.6 ACC components of government spending, 1952–70

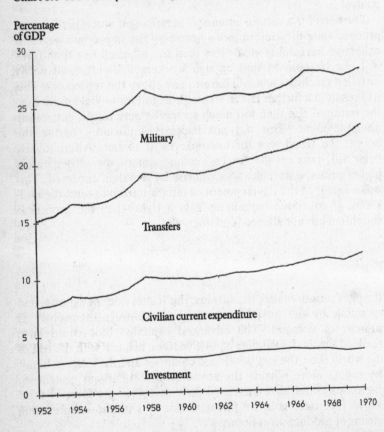

Percentage of GDP

Military

Transfers

Civilian current expenditure

Investment

Source: see Appendix.

Government spending

Civil spending on goods and services (health, education and so on) increased by 50 per cent more than total output, and grants to persons (e.g. pensions) grew twice as fast. Both róse by some 4 per cent of GDP. More than half of this increase was offset by a declining share of military expenditure. The share of government investment was fairly steady (Chart 8.6). The effect was a more rapid rise in government spending than in output.

The impact of an increased share of government expenditure depends on the way it is financed. If the money is borrowed, then capitalists can get richer without investing in means of production. They stock up on financial assets such as government bonds, and the government realizes surplus by spending its borrowings on buying commodities. Demand rises and, providing higher real wages do not cut into profits, the economy expands, justifying higher investment. This Keynesian process of governments pumping up demand for commodities has disadvantages: government interest payments grow and attempts to finance them by taxation tend eventually to reduce profits. But these problems are not immediately apparent, and so need not inhibit accumulation for some time.

In any case, this was not, by and large, the way state spending was financed in the boom. Total government deficits fluctuated between 1 per cent of output in the recession years of 1958 and 1967 and minus 1 per cent in the boom years of 1955, 1960 and 1969. Despite rising interest rates, debt interest rose only from 2¼ per cent of personal income in 1952 to 2½ per cent in 1973. So, contrary to those who ascribe great importance to Keynesian policies, the boom was in no sense based on government deficits.

The overwhelming bulk of state spending, then, was financed by taxation. So increases in state spending were largely offset by corresponding reductions by taxpayers. With workers' real gross incomes determined primarily by accumulation, higher taxes bit into take-home pay. But the balanced-budget method of financing extra expenditure by higher taxation is still expansionary to the extent that tax bills are met by reduced saving rather than by cutbacks in spending. So increased state spending probably did aid realization. Without it, even higher investment would have been needed to achieve the same growth of demand.

Investment ›

Investment constitutes demand for the surplus product in the form of means of production. Since the level of investment measures the level of such demand, the growth in the investment level measures the direct contribution of accumulation to the growth in markets. (Clearly there is also an indirect contribution via the resulting growth in wages.)

1958 was the only year in which the level of investment fell, and the average growth rate over any five-year period was always at least 4 per cent per annum. So a growing level of investment encouraged more production by realizing an increasing absolute amount of surplus.

It also prevented a fall in the rate of growth of output despite a tendency in the decade from the mid-fifties for the share of workers' savings to rise – a development which restrained consumption growth. Output would have slowed had the investment share not risen. As it was, improved profitability and fulfilled expectations of rising sales led to an expansion of investment. The rate of accumulation increased, rather than the growth of output slackening.

The rise in the investment share resulted partly from an increase in the weight of the high accumulators – Germany and especially Japan. Most of the rise was in the form of manufacturing and other business investment (Chart 8.7).

In 1961, 78 per cent of corporate business investment was financed by retained earnings. The remainder, equivalent to 2.8 per cent of GDP, was paid for by borrowing from the personal sector (i.e., workers' savings and rentier incomes). By 1973 this self-financing ratio had fallen to 64 per cent, and 5.6 per cent of GDP was borrowed by firms to cover the shortfall. This offset the tendency towards stagnation generated by increased workers' savings.

So accumulation played the decisive role in maintaining favourable realization conditions. The boom in accumulation was essentially self-sustaining. It simultaneously increased the surplus produced by the working class and ensured that this surplus found a market, generating steadily rising profits for the employers.

Chart 8.7 ACC components of investment, 1952–70

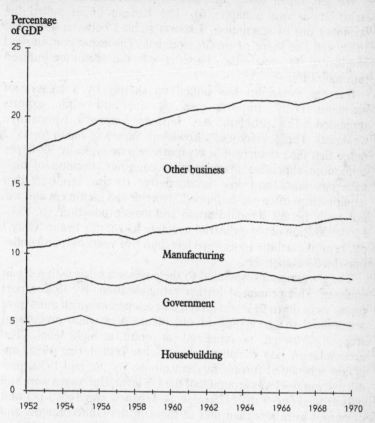

Source: see Appendix.

The Japanese economic miracle

The boom was most powerful in Japan, and the period 1955–61 was decisive. Over those years accumulation built up the phenomenal momentum which it was to sustain through the sixties. This period – the most gleaming episode of the golden years – illustrates the fundamental dynamics of the boom particularly well because it shows them in operation in top gear and with enormous effect.

We left Japan under the screws of the deflationary Dodge stabilization plan (Chapter 6). The Korean boom pulled the economy out of stagnation. Exports trebled between 1949 and 1952, and the share of profits doubled. The expansion allowed employers to reap the benefits of the deflation-induced rationalization.

But the expansion was pulled up sharply by a balance of payments crisis. Imports rose by one-third while exports stagnated. The problem was Japanese capital's competitive weakness. The government's *Economic Survey of Japan* for 1952 noted that the products of heavy industry were typically 30–40 per cent more expensive than in other countries, because of high materials costs and low productivity. It also reported that 'equipment is often old-fashioned, decrepit and inefficient and will not easily permit standardization and mass production' (p. 114). Modernization of the industrial structure had hardly begun. Only 7 per cent of machine tools were less than five years old, and under one-third less than ten.

The government responded to the payments crisis with a credit squeeze. This prompted further rationalization. By 1955 export prices were down to world levels, a development which must have accelerated the scrapping of old plant. And while investment stopped growing, it remained at quite a high level. The accumulation rate remained about 4 per cent during 1955, implying substantial further modernization. By the mid-1950s productivity in steel was around half the US level. But wages were still only around one-fifth of US rates. So Japanese wage costs per unit of output were less than half of those in the United States, and below European levels. Productivity in cotton-spinning was almost equal to the US level, and much higher than that in Europe. Without this productivity increase exports could not have expanded fast enough to balance the additional imports required to sustain the 1955–61 expansion.

Over those six years real business investment shot up by 170 per cent, boosting the rate of accumulation from around 4 per cent a year to 12 per cent. Business investment grew to absorb about one-quarter of GDP. Production of investment goods trebled, while consumption (public and private) rose by less than 50 per cent. The rate of accumulation in those branches most closely tied to investment (machinery, metals, construction) reached 25–35 per cent per year, implying a doubling of the capital stock every three years or less. No industrialized country had ever achieved such a burst of accumulation before.

Myth has it that the accumulation was financed by frugal Japanese workers. Their savings were indeed high by Western standards (largely because of poor government welfare provision and high and escalating housing costs), and they rose over the period from 9 to 16 per cent of their income. But as a share of GDP, workers' savings rose by only 3 per cent while investment leaped up by 13 per cent. The rise in the share of fixed investment, from 19 per cent of GDP in 1955 to 33 per cent in 1961, was paralleled by one in the share of (pre-tax) gross profit incomes, up from 31 to 39 per cent. This latter rise generated much of the necessary finance.

The share of profits was able to rise quickly because real wages did not need to grow in line with productivity. Rapid accumulation maintained expanding markets – much extra output consisted of means of production bought by capitalists – so that demand shortage did not pull down prices and hence push up real wages. Since labour reserves were adequate, there was no need, either, for an acceleration of wages and faster scrapping in order to release workers for employment on new machines.

Employment rose by about one-tenth. Employment in industry and services, which gained 2½ million workers from agriculture, grew by only around one-quarter, which seems modest in relation to the increase in the capital stock. But the extra workers imparted a decisive flexibility to accumulation. Employment in construction rose by two-thirds over the six years, increasing its share of non-agricultural employment by more than half a million. Employment in electrical machinery trebled, again increasing its share by half a million. Such employment leaps in particular industries could not have occurred in a tight labour market with slow labour-force growth.

The labour market tightened considerably over six years. The unemployment rate and the ratio of job-seekers to vacancies both fell precipitately. By 1961 they had reached levels which were to persist, with minor ups and downs, for the remainder of the decade. Labour turnover rose, as did voluntary quits. Annual money wage increases rose to about twice those of the mid-fifties. The most significant development, signalling a decisive shift in labour market conditions, was an acceleration of *product* wages (real wages in terms of the product) in line with money wages. In manufacturing, average product wage growth rose from 6 per cent a year in the mid-fifties to 12 per cent in the early sixties. A similar acceleration occurred elsewhere. The upswing of accumulation partially absorbed the huge pool of labour in backward sectors (including ex-agricultural workers drawn into service industries in the early fifties). As the labour market tightened, faster product wage growth limited the expansion of the backward sector, and thereby ensured an elastic labour supply for the dynamic modern sectors. This effect was accentuated by a squeezing of differentials, especially in large manufacturing firms. Product wages probably accelerated only about half as much in the largest firms as in the smallest, thus facilitating the expansion of the former at the expense of the latter.

These developments prevented newly accumulated means of production from being starved of labour. They ensured that few of the extra workers entering the market were trapped in small-scale operations and provided an elasticity of labour supply essential to very rapid accumulation in advanced sectors. In 1955 one-third of manufacturing workers were employed in enterprises with less than twenty workers. By 1961 the proportion had fallen to one-quarter. The number of manufacturing plants with more than thirty workers had risen by two-thirds. Small-scale industry constituted a huge 'tail' of ancient means of production which could be scrapped without jeopardizing profits in modern enterprises. So the rise in product wages was both the clearest expression of tightening labour markets and the mechanism which prevented it from inhibiting accumulation.

New techniques of production were introduced at an accelerating rate. Between the end of 1955 and 1961 the volume of capital per worker rose by almost one-half. In the chemicals industry it more than doubled. The rate of introduction of new techniques from overseas trebled in 1960. By the next year more than half of manufacturing production used foreign technology. The proportion was higher in the fastest growing sectors, such as electrical machinery, transport equipment and iron and steel. By the end of the six years Japan possessed a younger stock of machine tools than the United Kingdom or the United States: 40 per cent was less than five years old. Productivity had more than doubled in the chemicals, transport equipment and electrical machinery industries.

Fast productivity growth in the sectors producing means of production ensured a rapid reduction in the real cost of capital goods. This offset the effect of rising mechanization on capital costs, and, combined with a rise in capacity utilization, pushed the output-capital ratio up. So the profit rate rose faster than the share. The pre-tax rate of profit for business rose from about 19 per cent in 1955 to 27 per cent in 1961.

In sum, accelerating accumulation pushed up employment quite rapidly, but not as fast as the stock of capital rose since mechanization proceeded apace (Chart 8.8).

Chart 8.8 Japanese business capital stock, mechanization, output-capital ratio, 1955–61

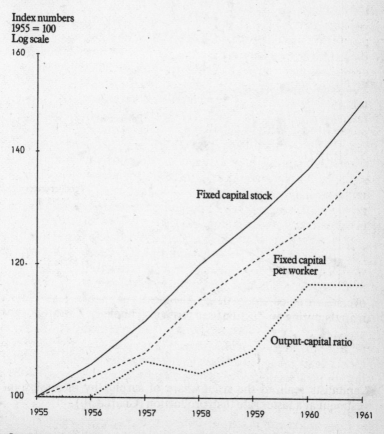

Index numbers
1955 = 100
Log scale

Source: see Appendix.

Ample labour supplies permitted the operation of new machines without the need for product wages to rise as fast as productivity. The situation was also eased by rapid mechanization (Chart 8.9).

Chart 8.9 Japanese business productivity and product wages, 1955–61

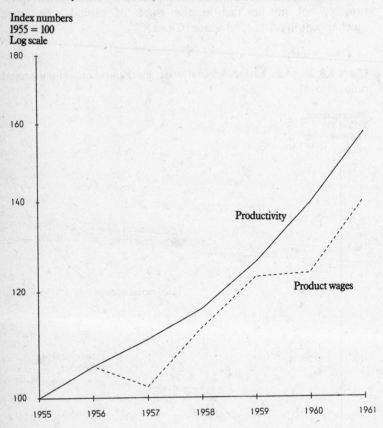

Index numbers
1955 = 100
Log scale

Source: see Appendix.

Capitalists realized the rising share of surplus by increasing investment at a faster rate than production (Chart 8.10).

Chart 8.10 Japanese business investment and profits, 1955–61

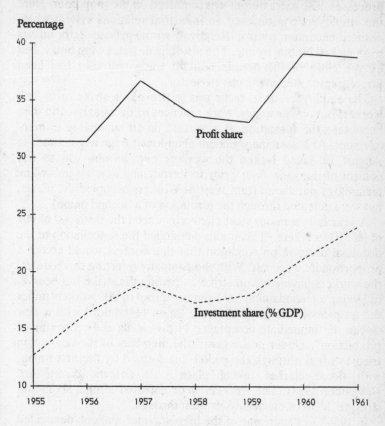

Source: see Appendix.

Since productivity rose faster than mechanization, the output-capital ratio rose, boosting the profit rate still further. By the end of the period, however, the tighter labour market forced product wages to rise as fast as productivity to ensure sufficient scrapping to provide labour to operate newly installed equipment. The share and rate of profit and the accumulation rate more or less stabilized at the very high levels established over the previous six years.

The speed and economic mechanics of this burst of accumulation were dazzling. But it is important not to become so mesmerized by them as to lose sight of the underlying social processes. The extra output was produced on the shop floor. Here the employers consolidated an industrial relations system which ensured maximum control. Relatively strong private sector unions were picked off one by one. The resulting disputes were bitter. But by the close of the decade militant trade unionism had been literally eradicated in the private sector.

The employers' usual tactic was to provoke a strike or to lock workers out – over wages, work practices or dismissals – and then encourage the formation of a 'second union' amenable to management. At Nissan management abandoned wage negotiations in August 1953 and locked the workers out. Its aim was to win control of the shop floor prior to introducing new assembly-line technology purchased from Austin. Workers occupied the plants, but were defeated through the formation of a 'second union'.

A year later a major steel plant announced the dismissal of 901 of its 3700 workers: 'The unions demanded the cancellation of the dismissal decision on condition that the workers would accept a proportionate wage cut. With the company rejecting this request, the workers have gone on strike . . . while the strike has been in full swing a second union has been organized by 800 workers under the auspices of Zenro [right-wing union federation] with a new slogan of "immediate acceptance of dismissals and reopening of production". Under police guard the members of the new union tried to break through the picket line formed by the first union, with fierce clashes taking place . . .' (*Oriental Economist*, November 1954). The workers were defeated after a six-month struggle. Most of the dismissals went through.

In 1958 Oji Paper, one of the biggest paper-makers, demanded an end to the closed shop. Oji workers were among the highest paid in Japan. They had previously won compensation of 1 million yen each for eight former employees dismissed in the 'red purge' and had set them up in business near the company's housing projects. After a 145-day strike, with much violence on the picket line, a settlement was reached. Leaders of the 'first' union were subsequently sacked for alleged harassment of members of the newly formed 'second union'. Workers deserted the first union in droves.

These struggles culminated in a dispute at the Miike Coal Mines, owned by Mitsui Mining, the biggest mining firm in Japan. The company tried to sack 1300 workers, including 300 union leaders, for 'sabotage'. The *Oriental Economist* – whose sympathies mirror those of its occidental namesake – explained the situation: 'The mechanization of the mine has already been carried to an admirable point. . . . Nevertheless the per worker per month production of the mine is a lowly 14 tons in comparison with the usual 20 tons. Why? The answer is too obvious to miss. The majority of the workers there work only two or three hours a day. . . . The union's control of its workers is literally fabulous. . . . No one can break into the miners' housing area without "security clearance" at the gate by the union guards . . . the orders from management are completely disregarded and the directions from union leaders are kept to the letter . . .' (January 1960).

The union took selective strike action. Management responded with a lockout. Picketing was violent. At its peak, 100,000 policemen confronted an equal number of union supporters, mobilized by the militant federation Sohyo. One striker was killed and 1000 were injured. But, with unions in all other coal companies, and in Mitsui's other mines, accepting management plans, the Miike workers were isolated. Finally they had to accept the dismissals. The struggle was seen as a trial of strength, and the employers' victory as decisive. No major strike has occurred in large-scale private industry since.

Aggressive tactics by management and state support are not the only explanation for the employers' victory. The trade union movement was immature. Its roots among workers were shallow and the tactics of its leadership weak. The ease with which management could organize 'second unions' cannot be explained simply by intimidation, important though that was.

The wages system furnished employers with an important weapon. Once the unions were in retreat, management increasingly used those elements of the pay packet based on age and ability to undermine them further. Workers feared that opposition to the employer would lose them the ability bonus, which was increasingly determined by cooperativeness rather than skill. If they were sacked they stood to lose old-age and long-service premiums. These features of the wages system were strengthened ('lifetime employment', 'seniority wages') as the anti-union offensive gathered strength through the fifties. By 1955, 39 per cent of pay was determined by 'ability' (up from 26 per cent in 1947). The wages system also helped to create a climate favourable for introducing 'second unions' through weakening worker solidarity. An American observer noted in 1957: 'In some cases companies introduced job classification and revised their wage structures based on job evaluations. . . . However in many cases it is doubtful whether these are anything other than the traditional wage system in a new disguise – for "merit", "loyalty" and "co-operation", which are often tied to length of service have been used as major criteria for wage increases granted in this fashion . . . managements have not proceeded hastily towards full-blown wage rationalization because of their own concern with preserving worker identification with the enterprise. . . . Management has not been insistent on displacing the permanent/temporary worker system with job seniority procedures (i.e. first in/first out) because of its own sense of paternalistic responsibility and because of the flexibility of operations afforded by the employment of temporary workers' (Levine, pp. 117–19).

In 1958 workers aged twenty to twenty-five earned less than half as much as those between forty and fifty years old, as compared with around 60 per cent in the interwar period and in 1948. Older workers, anxious to protect their ability bonuses, often supported the 'second union' bureaucrats. The successful introduction of these pro-management 'second unions' was as fundamental to Japan's subsequent economic success as the phenomenal accumulation rate. The two went hand in hand.

9. A New, Managed Capitalism?

The astonishing economic achievements of the golden years led many to conclude that capitalism had undergone a qualitative transformation – that the bad old days of slumps and class antagonisms had been transcended for ever. The most important expression of this view was the development in many countries of a broad political consensus, embracing the major parties of both left and right, and subscribed to by trade unions and employers' associations.

Its central feature was acceptance of the so-called mixed economy – that is, a capitalist framework within which state enterprise was tolerated and the government held responsible for managing the economy. Broadly speaking, workers obtained certain rights and material benefits. The most important rights were those to free trade unions and certain forms of representation. The most important benefits were adequate job provision, regular pay rises and state welfare services. In return, they did not question capitalist ownership or control. Capitalists were prepared to tolerate these rights and provisions in return for a profitable economic environment.

Acceptance by the left of the basic parameters of the mixed economy was exemplified by Antony Crosland's book *The Future of Socialism*, published in 1956. He argued: 'Traditionally, or at least since Marx, socialist thought has been dominated by the economic problems posed by capitalism, poverty, mass unemployment, squalor, instability and even the possibility of the collapse of the whole system. . . . Capitalism has been reformed almost out of all recognition. Despite occasional minor recessions and balance of payments crises, full employment and at least a tolerable degree of stability are likely to be maintained. Automation can be expected steadily to solve any remaining problems of under production. Looking ahead our present rate of growth will give us a national output three times as high in fifty years' (p. 5l7). He also predicted that 'any government which tampered with the basic framework of the full-employment welfare state would meet with a sharp reversal at the polls' (p. 61). Three years earlier, Churchill had signalled a similar acceptance on the part of the Tories when he said, 'Party differences are now in practice mainly those of emphasis' (quoted Gilmour, p. 20).

The necessary analytic underpinning for the consensus was the belief that the state could manipulate the economy to achieve these goals, most importantly that it could always manipulate spending to ensure full employment. In later chapters we argue that this was always unrealistic as a long-term perspective – that the processes which maintained the boom inevitably also undermined it. Here we look at some examples of attempts to reshape features of the economy within the parameters of the consensus.

The welfare state

The ultimate principle of the welfare state is well summarized by a French resistance declaration demanding 'a complete plan of social security, designed to secure the means of existence for all French men and women wherever they are incapable of providing such means for themselves by working' (quoted Saint-Jours, p. 122). The United Kingdom Beveridge report echoed the theme in more prosaic language: 'Social insurance should aim at guaranteeing the minimum income needed for subsistence' (quoted Rimlinger, p. 149).

The principle is no invention of the 1940s, and the practice no innovation of the 1950s. Large-scale social insurance – covering sickness, accidents and old-age pensions – was introduced in Germany in the 1880s following the Kaiser's announcement, inspired by Bismarck, that 'the cure of social ills must be sought not exclusively in the repression of Social Democratic excess, but simultaneously in the positive advancement of the welfare of the working masses' (quoted Rimlinger, p. 114).

The first state-run programme of unemployment insurance was introduced in the United Kingdom by the Liberal government in 1911, with flat rates of benefit and contributions by employers, employees and the state. A small non-contributory pension came in 1908 and health insurance in 1911. After the First World War the coverage of unemployment insurance was extended and a contributory pension scheme introduced. In 1930 a scheme for social insurance was implemented in France, covering pensions, sickness and a system of family allowances.

Although not new, the welfare state did expand enormously in the postwar period. The share of gross domestic product absorbed by government civil spending (a rather broader category than welfare spending, though debt interest and subsidies have been omitted) rose from 15 per cent in 1952 to 24 per cent in 1973.

This huge expansion was by no means carried out solely by governments of the left. In the seven major countries the only periods of majority left governments between 1950 and 1973 were those of Wilson in the United Kingdom (1964–70) and Brandt in Germany (1970–3), yet spending on welfare rose under Macmillan, Adenauer, de Gaulle, under both Nixon and Kennedy, as well as under a succession of Italian and to some extent even Japanese prime ministers of the right. The expansion of welfare spending was noticeably faster in the sixties than the fifties – especially in Europe. But, although this undoubtedly reflected increased working-class pressure as full employment was achieved or approached (Chapters 11 and 12), such pressure drew a response from right-wing governments as well as from those of the left elected as a direct result of it.

The welfare systems introduced in the immediate postwar years built on previous achievements. Existing prewar schemes were generally restored or consolidated. Even the United Kingdom Beveridge scheme had only a minor effect on unemployment insurance. In the United States unemployment insurance, accident compensation and public assistance underwent no major changes.

The continuity with prewar schemes created important international diversities. Thus the British scheme was based on flat-rate contributions and benefits, while the European and American ones varied with earnings. But gaps in previous schemes were often plugged by incorporating innovations from abroad. Family allowances, introduced in Britain in the Beveridge scheme, had been in operation in France since 1932. (They were not reintroduced into Germany until 1954 because of their associations with Nazi population policy.)

Coverage was often broadened. Schemes which had been confined to industrial workers before the war were typically extended to include the self-employed, farm workers and domestic servants. In many cases, reduced contributions qualifications meant that more people became eligible for benefit. (In the United States in the late 1940s, only one-fifth of the over-sixty-fives were insured or receiving pensions.)

Unemployment insurance in Europe has generally become both more generous and easier to obtain. Comparing the situation in 1975 with the year of introduction (generally prewar), on average the ratio of benefits to earnings had risen slightly, the duration of benefits had doubled to nearly a year, the delay before eligibility to benefit had halved (to two days), and the period of disqualification (on account of dismissal for misconduct, for example) had halved to about three weeks.

The one really radical innovation was the replacement in Britain of sickness insurance by the National Health Service (NHS), free as of right without means test or contribution (although prescription charges were introduced in 1950). But this was unique in terms of universal supply based on need. Elsewhere, earnings-related insurance, plus 'social aid' at a distinctly lower level for those not covered, continued prewar traditions.

An important development in the fifties was the linking of benefits to rising living standards. This was most explicitly promulgated in the German pension reform of 1957, which Adenauer forced through to great electoral benefit, in the teeth of strong opposition from the central bank and the employers. But benefits were regularly revised upwards to similar effect elsewhere.

The same German reform reinforced the 'insurance' principle behind pensions, by tying them more closely to past contributions. This eliminated the minimum pension level which had survived since Bismarck, and substantially widened differentials. The British Labour Party also proposed replacing flat-rate contributions and benefits by a scheme aimed at raising pensions to a level equivalent to half of earnings. A scheme of this sort was finally implemented in the seventies. There was also a trend towards adding an earnings-related supplement to previously flat-rate unemployment benefits (for example, the United Kingdom) or moving to entirely earnings-related payments (Germany).

Pensions give some indication of the level of benefits by the early seventies. For a married couple they were reckoned to be between 50 and 60 per cent of post-tax earnings in France, Germany and the United States, about one-third in Britain and Italy, and probably barely one-fifth in Japan. For unemployment pay and sickness benefit the ratio averaged one-half higher (varying from three times as high in Japan to one-half in Italy).

Did the postwar development of the welfare state remould capitalism to give it a more human face, or were the changes largely cosmetic? The answer is complex.

The new measures did bring about a large flow of resources to the disadvantaged. By the early 1970s a typical continental European country was devoting a little over 20 per cent of GDP to social expenditure, the United States and United Kingdom 17–18 per cent, and Japan 10 per cent. The extension of coverage, plugging of gaps, index-linking and softening of contribution eligibility criteria, brought enormous gains to many people.

Wider coverage accounts for well over half of the increase in the proportion of output devoted to welfare provision during the 1960s. Cash benefits also rose faster than inflation, growing in line with average incomes (Table 9.1).

Table 9.1 Growth of ACC welfare spending in the 1960s

	As percentage of GDP	due to	Demographic changes[1]	Coverage[2]	Real costs and benefits per recipient
Education	1.1		0.0	0.6	0.5
Income maintenance	2.0		0.8	1.2	0.0[3]
Health	1.9		0.1	1.1	0.8
Total	5.0		0.9	2.9	1.3

1. The effect on spending of the changing age-structure of the population (old people, children).
2. The effect on spending of welfare schemes covering an increasing proportion of the population.
3. No change relative to average income levels.

Source: OECD, *Public Expenditure Trends*, Table 7.

But there were also important limitations. The welfare state never came close to eliminating poverty. On the basis of standardized poverty figures (a percentage of national earnings based on the average of national official poverty standards), in the early 1970s 3 per cent of the German population lived in poverty, 7½ per cent of the British, 13 per cent of the US, and 16 per cent of the French.

A crucial question about the growth of the welfare state is whether it undermined employers' control over labour by reducing the compulsion to work. Two cases should be distinguished. The one dear to the heart of the popular press is the possibility of individuals opting out of the labour market altogether to 'sponge' off the state. By depriving employers of potential labour, this could force up wages. The rise in real levels of social assistance which occurred in the boom could have made such opting out more feasible, even if the social assistance rates did not rise relative to earnings (which they generally did not – child benefit in particular fell substantially relative to average incomes). Relaxation in eligibility criteria would also reduce the pressure on able-bodied recipients to look for work. However, the rise in pensions relative to incomes which occurred in most countries also increased the cost of not working – for the farsighted, at least – since pensions were generally linked to contributions from pay. In fact, 'social aid' (transfers to people not eligible for pensions, unemployment benefit and so forth) constituted only 5 per cent of all money spent on transfers in the early 1970s. In the two countries where it was more important, the United States and United Kingdom, the proportion of transfers going to social aid hardly increased during the 1960s. The low level of social assistance and the stigma attached to receiving it make it implausible that significant 'scrounging' took place.

However, the development of welfare benefits may well have reduced dependence on any particular employer. Unemployment benefits on average rose in line with pre-tax incomes during the sixties. But since the tax burden on earnings rose, there was probably some small rise in the net amount received while out of work, relative to pay received while working. The benefits sometimes received by strikers' families also rose in absolute terms. Health expenses were covered for those not in work. So the financial hardships imposed by temporary unemployment or strikes fell. This helped give workers the confidence to stand up to their employers – to quit or strike or be sacked seemed less daunting.

These developments should not be seen in isolation. They reinforced others. The most important factor reducing fear of the sack was the reduction in unemployment, which increased the chances of getting another job quickly. Higher living standards enabled many workers to save a little, providing additional insurance against the financial costs of the sack, of quitting or of striking. The important rise in some countries in the proportion of families with two adults working acted in the same direction.

The tax burden imposed on workers to pay for welfare services opened up a gap between the cost of labour to the employer (the wage gross of employers and employees' social security contributions and of income tax) and what the worker received (the wage net of all these deductions). As the tax burden edged up, so did the gap widen between the sum that a pay settlement gave workers and what it cost employers. Unions bargaining with individual employers, or at industry level, sought to maximize the return to their members for working, welfare benefits being unaffected by the negotiations. So the rising tax 'wedge' heightened conflict over wages.

So, while growth of the welfare state hardly loosened the compulsion on workers to work, it did undermine dependence on any particular employer and provided an additional source of conflict, in the course of which such greater independence could be exercised.

German codetermination

The right of workers to organized representation was another important feature of the consensus. This usually took the form of institutionalized collective bargaining between trade unions and employers. But in Germany it also involved the apparently more advanced form of 'codetermination', which has aroused considerable interest.

This interest stems in part from Germany's outstanding economic record in the boom. Did codetermination contribute to its 'economic miracle'? But there is also another reason for the interest. From the mid-1970s, left parties came increasingly to adopt a more radical approach to the consensus (Chapter 19). One feature of this shift was an emphasis on industrial democracy, which drew heavily on principles of codetermination.

Codetermination – the right of workers to help direct the firms they work in – was a major preoccupation of German trade unions in the years after the war (Chapter 6). At first they regarded it as a prerequisite for the socialization of large-scale heavy industry. Then, as the German economy was firmly steered towards a reconstructed capitalism, codetermination was presented as a substitute for socialization – an alternative way of assuring that big business would never again play the political role it had in the thirties. Codetermination received enormous support. In 1950 and 1951 well over 90 per cent of metal workers and miners voted in favour of strike action to secure a special codetermination law for their industries.

The system involved workers electing half of the members of supervisory boards, with the shareholders electing the rest and appointing a 'neutral' chair. The workers could also veto (in effect, nominate) the labour director, responsible broadly for personnel questions. Outside the steel and coal industries, workers could elect one-third of the supervisory board. In all industries works councils, elected by the employees, had the right to 'codetermine' some issues (working hours, holidays, implementation of pay scales), to veto others (hirings, job classification, transfers), to be consulted over yet others (mass redundancies, individual dismissals) and to receive economic information (profits, production, investment).

But workers' influence has been more constrained than these provisions might suggest. The labour director in steel and coal firms is a member of the management board which controls the day-to-day operations of the firm (the other members being the production and business managers). His or her mandate generally covers most of the issues over which the works council has codetermination rights but excludes questions of incentives and job evaluation. These labour directors may well have initiated enlightened personnel policies, but that is a long way from real worker representation in the overall direction of the firm: 'The labour director is charged in law with carrying out his function in the best interests of the firm as a whole. Since he is chosen by workers he is theoretically subject to extensive loyalty conflict. Most labour directors have resolved this conflict by operating as responsible managers rather than as worker agents *per se*. They have been most successful when they have been able to win the trust and acceptance of the other management board members. When they have not been able to do so they have been isolated and their influence has been drastically reduced' (Adams and Rummel, p. 12).

The worker members of the supervisory board are elected partly by the works council and partly by the trade unions. Outside steel and coal, minority representation means that the committees are usually balanced to favour the employer, and information is restricted. The general consensus is that worker influence on these boards has been limited. Furthermore, minimal communication between the board members and the workers seems to take place, with board members legally bound to secrecy over 'sensitive' company matters. So it would be hard, if not impossible, for worker representatives to mobilize the work force against the employers. Nor can the works councils do so. Failure to agree over 'social matters' in which they have codetermination rights, such as holiday schedules or welfare provision, results in arbitration. Disagreements over the important personnel issues of hiring, firing, classification or redeployment are resolved in the Labour Court. Works councils have to be consulted over mass lay-offs but have no right to call strikes.

Certain weaknesses are clear. Workers' representatives are often removed from the shop floor, which cannot mandate them. Their access to information is limited and their right to use it even more so, as are their areas of influence and the sanctions they can use.

Nor does codetermination appear to have done much to improve work conditions. 'Exhausting physical effort, excessive heat, hazardous safety and health conditions have been far less points of attention (and redress) than in the American steel industry, and at least straight-time workers endure a high measure of personal . . . coercion (speed-up in one word) by supervision' (Herding, pp. 329–30). This despite the fact that, as the same author notes, in codetermination plants 'work crews in the key operations enjoy a high degree of autonomy in setting their own pace, breaks, etc.' (p. 330). One survey reported that workers regard works councils as a part of management. But workers participate heavily in elections. Turnouts of 80 per cent are typical. Pressure for increased influence resulted in a 1972 Act which extended codetermination rights in a number of personnel matters, such as employment contracts and training. A 1976 Act extended a weakened form of parity codetermination to all firms with more than 2000 employees. It is weaker than in steel and coal because one of the worker nominees must be a senior executive and the chair, a shareholder nominee, has two votes.

The employers, too, clearly have strong reservations. They went to court and tried, unsuccessfully, to have the 1976 Act declared unconstitutional. However weak today, codetermination does serve to remind employers both of the days when their prerogatives were generally and seriously challenged and of the fact that such a situation could recur.

The limitations of codetermination in Germany and the reactions of the employers towards it are of general relevance to any struggle for industrial democracy (Chapter 19).

French economic planning

> The characteristic attitude in large-scale economic management, both inside government and in the private sector, which has made itself increasingly felt during the post-war period, is the pursuit of intellectual coherence. Its most obvious manifestation is in long-range national planning. . . . Economic planning is the most characteristic expression of the new capitalism (Shonfield, pp. 67, 121).

This view in 1965 of the author of *Modern Capitalism* – at the time probably the most influential interpretation of postwar trends in the advanced countries – was fully in line with the consensus. If governments were to manage the new capitalism then economic planning was clearly of the essence.

Shonfield singled out France as the innovator in the field. So what was French planning? Most governments manipulated tax rates and government expenditure to influence the overall level of spending in the economy. But this Keynesian demand management could not dispel much of the economic uncertainty faced by business. Keynes himself had argued for 'the collection and dissemination on a great scale of data relating to the business situation including full publicity, by law if necessary, of all business facts which it is useful to know. These measures would involve society in exercising directive intelligence through some appropriate organ of action over many of the intricacies of private business, yet it would leave private initiative and enterprise unhindered' (quoted Estrin and Holmes, p. 8). Precisely this kind of 'generalized market research' lay at the heart of French planning. Its consistency and coherence were supposed to encourage a common view about the future to which firms would respond with bold investment plans – nudged, if necessary, by government tax and credit policies.

The process evolved from the Monnet Plan for the reconstruction of six basic sectors, formulated at the end of 1945 to persuade the US government that the French were sufficiently serious about modernization to justify a loan (Chapter 4). Modernization Commissions, the basic planning units, brought together civil servants and managers (the trade unionists involved have never played a major role) to thrash out targets for output and investment.

This process continued to form the basis for planning. But hit-and-miss targets were increasingly replaced by sophisticated forecasts for individual industries' markets based on aims for the overall growth of the economy and its division into private consumption, government spending and so forth.

The Monnet Plan itself undoubtedly facilitated the reconstruction of the basic sectors. The Americans were persuaded to allow the 'counterpart funds' to Marshall Aid to be used for these purposes, and their backing helped Monnet to protect the investment targets from the deflationary policies of the time. The fact that three of the six sectors were nationalized – coal, electricity and railways – helped. Their own programmes were incorporated in the plan, which must have reduced scepticism and helped in obtaining priority finance. The impact on the private sector – the real test – is harder to assess. Proposals for 'state contracts with trade associations, groups of concerns or, in exceptional cases, individual enterprises' (Kuisel, p. 234) or even the nationalization of recalcitrant firms were never implemented. Nor could they have been after business regained its initiative in 1947. Controls over foreign exchange, credits and scarce materials could hardly force anybody to expand. Yet, one member of Monnet's team remembered that plan as having 'ably manoeuvred a reluctant steel industry to modernize' (ibid., p. 245).

Jacques Delors, later to be minister of finance in Mitterrand's socialist government, records that when Monnet first gathered the steel masters together and demanded the reconstitution of prewar production capacity within four years, 'Two or more cases of heart seizure reportedly ensued' (Delors, p. 15). Nevertheless, the target was reached only a year late. When in 1951 he demanded another 40 per cent expansion, 'that did not work at all, since these steel masters had been so nourished on Malthusianism that their dominant fear was over-production. In this case, the planning response was not simply financial incentives, but direct intervention to change the steel cartel itself. . . . If you reproduce this anecdote some ten or twenty times in different industries, you begin to explain the role of the Plan during this first period' (ibid.).

Judging the effect of subsequent plans on the private sector becomes even harder as the number of commissions, and the equations in the planning models, grow.

The evidence shows that firms took notice of the plan, at least by the 1960s. In 1967 79 per cent of firms knew the plan's forecasts for the economy as a whole and 50 per cent (85 per cent of those with more than 5000 employees) knew of the production and investment forecasts for their industry group; 24 per cent (51 per cent of the biggest) said that the plan forecasts affected their investment decisions.

There seems to be a consensus that the plan did encourage accumulation, at least up to the late sixties. 'According to the witnesses we have consulted, it seems likely that the growth expectations set forth in the Second National Plan (1954–57) were in contradiction to the conventional wisdom at the beginning of the 1950s, which expected that only low rates of growth were possible. . . . The picture of a growing economy provided by the Plan, in which production was sure of finding sales, probably played a significant part in the resumption of growth after 1952' (Carré *et al.*, p. 471).

A sophisticated statistical evaluation suggested that in the late fifties and early sixties the plan provided better pictures of the evolution of the economy than would have been derived simply by extrapolating past trends. But it seems likely that the importance of the plan in creating a 'growth climate' diminished as the experience of rapid growth meant that business came to expect it anyway. This in itself, however, would be success of a sort.

Even if the Plan's effect on the *level* of accumulation was bound to diminish, it could still have significantly influenced its *pattern*. At least until the early 1970s, however, the government made no systematic attempt to shape the pattern of industry. The Fifth National Plan's objective of greater concentration to achieve two or three dominant firms – 'National Champions' – in each sector, for example, was *entirely* non-selective. The government did not choose the firms; it simply changed legal and tax rules to help mergers.

Mechanisms for selective intervention were available. The planners could determine the availability of finance: 'Every single externally financed project was therefore meant to be scrutinized for conformity with the targets and if the projects passed this test the Commission would see to it that sufficient tax and credit incentives would be made available' (Estrin and Holmes, p. 179). But, since there was no overall industrial strategy, it is hardly surprising that the finance tended to be granted almost automatically.

What of the pattern of investment within each industry? According to one observer: 'There is in general no noticeable discrepancy between the target of the branch and the sum of the targets of the individual companies' (quoted S. Cohen, p. 68). This means that 'The French system of detailed target planning involves . . . the toleration of agreements between firms to fix the share each will take of the planned expansion' (ibid., pp. 71–2).

During the 1950s and 1960s Plan forecasts for business investment were always well below the outcome. Between 1965 and 1970, for example, business investment grew by 8.5 per cent a year, while only 5.8 per cent a year had been expected. The discrepancy was systematically much larger than that for production growth. This suggests that firms may have formally agreed to share out capacity growth, but then invested to increase their share. Such investment over and above plan targets may in fact have speeded up modernization.

All in all, planning may have temporarily acted as a catalyst in launching French capital on its dynamic growth path. It certainly did not create the potential for that path, which was provided by the backward state of French industry, the strong position of the employers and favourable external circumstances (Chapters 2, 4 and 6). It probably played only a small role in maintaining accumulation once that got going. And planning certainly proved incapable of maintaining accumulation once conditions became unfavourable. In the seventies, growth faltered in France as elsewhere. The credibility of the plan was undermined by its increasing unrealism, the clear political motivation behind its projections and the resort by governments to orthodox deflationary policies. By 1979 only 9 per cent of employers regarded the Plan as very important. Even recession-hit industries wanted less planning rather than more. In France, as elsewhere, capital preferred to ditch the consensus in favour of more traditional capitalist virtues (Chapter 17).

But the trade unions strongly criticized the erosion of planning and 'regretted the lack of any attempt to articulate real priorities other than the need to submit to world market forces' (Estrin and Holmes, p. 116). This survey reported a 'nostalgia' among socialists for the Fourth National Plan of the early sixties. When elected in 1981, the Mitterrand government harked back to the legacy of planning in the first postwar decades (Chapter 19).

Japanese industrial policy

The lack of an industrial policy is generally regarded as a weakness of French planning. Japan is often cited as the prime example of a successful industrial policy playing a key role in the dynamism of accumulation. Was Japan's industrial structure successfully orchestrated by the bureaucrats of its Ministry of International Trade and Industry (MITI)?

General measures to stimulate accumulation in Japan differed little in kind or degree from those employed elsewhere. The government provided investment finance directly through such institutions as the Japan Development Bank. But even at their early fifties peak, these funds constituted only 7 per cent of industrial finance (12 per cent of that raised outside the firm). By the second half of the fifties the proportion had declined to 4 per cent. The government also provided a multitude of tax concessions which at their 1955 peak probably reduced average corporation-tax liability by one-fifth, falling to around 12 per cent in the early sixties. Many were fairly standard provisions for bad debts, and so forth. The more innovative included: accelerated depreciation on 'special machinery', 'special repairs' (to heavy plant), research and development, exemption from tax on income from sales of 'important new products', exemption from customs duty on 'important equipment' and exemption of certain exports from income tax. But they reduced tax payments by only 6 per cent during the years 1959 to 1963.

Such aggregate figures could be misleading, however. Both government lending and tax concessions were highly selective, being steered towards particular industries. Government favour also helped firms secure loans from private banks. Tariffs and prohibition of foreign firms from setting up in Japan were further important weapons.

The Japanese government decided on a number of occasions to foster particular industries, using a large armoury of policies. A few case studies illustrate the process.

It was clear after the war that Japan could no longer rely on textile exports for most of its foreign exchange earnings (Chapter 2). So it adopted a policy of fostering basic 'heavy industries' (steel, chemicals, shipbuilding). After 1947 a policy of 'planned shipbuilding' operated. Every year the government announced the total tonnage to be built of each type of ship and selected which shipbuilders and (domestic) owners should be involved. A high percentage of the funds required (80 per cent or more in the early fifties) was supplied cheaply by the Japan Development Bank. The interest rate subsidy sometimes involved deferral of repayment for fifteen years. Cheap loans to finance exports were 'perhaps the most significant assistance to shipbuilding' (Magaziner and Hout, p. 69). The companies also profited from a bizarre system whereby shipbuilders who exported were given import quotas for raw sugar, which could be sold at a hefty profit. The result was Japan's first 'miracle' industry. By the early seventies Japanese yards were launching over half the world's ships.

Steel, also designated as a key recovery sector immediately after the war, was a key input into major export industries such as ships (and in turn the development of huge ore-carrying ships allowed the Japanese steel industry to overcome a major disadvantage in transport costs for materials). In the 1950s the industry developed under two five-year 'rationalization plans' developed by the industry together with MITI. Steel benefited from major government loans, accounting for half its borrowing during the first five-year plan. Ten per cent of its finances still came from government sources in the early sixties. It also received a host of tax concessions.

The government has been continuously involved in the process of capacity expansion: 'Representatives of the privately owned steel producing firms gather under the umbrella of the Japan Iron and Steel Federation to present and discuss tentative investment plans for the coming year. (Often these representatives, usually managing directors, are MITI alumni.) The producers' plans are evaluated in relation to the demand outlook for the industry and the existing pattern of market shares. After these meetings and informal discussions among these managers and the officials of the Iron and Steel Section of MITI's Heavy Industries Bureau, the presidents of the steel companies try to reach a consensus on the rate and timing of the major investments of individual producers. MITI participates *ex officio* in these meetings. . . .

'After consensus has been reached, MITI issues a report recommending a course of action to the industry. . . .

'It has been said that no application from a major firm for a capacity increment has ever been flatly rejected, although some have been delayed. This, of course, is the mechanism of the consensus process: the expanding firm is persuaded either to delay its application or to accept a delayed approval. When this persuasion fails, consensus is frustrated' (Magaziner and Hout, p. 48).

Strikingly, MITI frequently tried to *slow down* the rate of accumulation to avoid overcapacity, a problem exacerbated by the increasing size of new plants which reduced the number to be built each year. In 1965 Sumimoto, which has tried to remain independent of MITI's 'administrative guidance', broke with an industry decision to delay all new investment in rolling facilities. MITI disciplined it by limiting its allocation of imported coking coal. In 1967 'eight steel makers sought approval to begin building new furnaces, but according to MITI's projections only two were needed. Five received approval, one with a year's delay' (Kaplan, p. 148). This prompted MITI to seek mergers. But the resultant creation of Japan Steel 'only served to consolidate two conservative producers. The impact on the other producers, at least Sumimoto and Kawasaka, who did not oppose the merger, may have been counter-productive in stimulating continued aggressive expansion' (p. 151).

'The value of government support to the industry cannot be measured in terms of cash expenditures. By the judicious application of support in the areas where it could be most effective, government has done a great deal for the industry. Selective measures – help through the insurance of debt for building greenfield plants, assistance in procuring raw materials and forming anti-recession cartels – have provided support without extinguishing competition or stifling initiative in individual companies. Even capacity expansion co-operation has been carried out in such a way as to allow substantial continued internal competition and even greater market share changes than occurred in the United States. The actual flow of funds from government to the industry represented by loans, grants and tax allowances has been minimal, at least since the late 1950s. Per ton of steel, such assistance has been substantially less than that supplied by many European governments (often to subsidize the losses of uncompetitive plants)' (Magaziner and Hout, p. 54).

Steel was certainly another Japanese success story. By 1977 Japan had twenty-five blast-furnaces in operation with a capacity of over 2 million tons. The EEC had seven and the United States none.

In the early 1950s the Japanese motor industry consisted of a handful of clapped-out truck producers, rescued from bankruptcy by the Korean war. The Japanese central bank originally favoured car imports. But MITI argued that a domestic industry should be nurtured because of its critical importance, and won. The government's key role in the early days was to protect the industry. Foreign investment was more or less prohibited (it had to contribute to the development of the domestic industry). Quotas at first restricted imports to $½ million a year. In the mid-1960s quotas were replaced by prohibitively high tariffs. Import of foreign technology was encouraged, with the stipulation that 90 per cent of licensed parts be produced domestically within five years. Nissan was the only major producer to enter into a licensing agreement (with Austin). Toyota and Prince (later to merge with Nissan) used domestic technology. The industry benefited from access to Japan Development Bank loans, and various tax concessions. But MITI 'played little or no role in the investment policies or technological development activities of the producers' (Kaplan, p. 116).

MITI helped to promote streamlining in the parts industries over the years 1956 to 1966, aimed at modernization and rationalization of the number of suppliers. But it failed comprehensively to push through various plans for mergers between the assemblers. Instead of merging with each other, or one of the bigger concerns, in the early seventies three of the smaller firms signed affiliation agreements with the American Big Three as MITI opposition was overcome by political pressure for foreign capital liberalization.

Today Japan is the biggest car exporter in the world.

Finally, the computer industry which 'MITI has unequivocally dominated' (Kaplan, p. 78). IBM was granted the right to manufacture in Japan in 1960 in return for licensing basic patents to Japanese manufacturers, and most major Japanese companies entered technical assistance agreements with big American manufacturers. By the mid-1960s MITI recognized the importance of the industry by increasing loans and subsidies and embarking on a series of attempts to rationalize the industry and/or organize cooperative ventures. The culmination was the Very Large-Scale Integration project involving MITI's electronics research institute, the state and telecommunications laboratory and five major computer manufacturers. MITI's attempts at consolidation failed to overcome the firms' competitive attitude (indicating limitations to MITI's 'dominance'). As well as assisting technology development, MITI organized a leasing corporation to lease only Japanese computers on competitive terms to those available abroad. The industry was protected until the early 1970s by the rule that foreign machines (including IBM machines produced in Japan) could only be purchased if a suitable Japanese model was not available. While Japanese computers were hardly a factor in the boom years, they were to become a major force in the 1980s.

It is difficult to draw a neat conclusion. MITI clearly pushed strongly to develop certain key industries. It provided finance, ensured protection and, on occasion, encouraged technological development. In a few cases, such as steel, it effectively coordinated expansion plans.

On the other hand MITI seems to have been rather unsuccessful in securing rationalization through mergers. MITI sometimes held back accumulation in the steel industry. In the other cases it played a facilitating rather than a decisive role. Moreover the case studies reported, where MITI was highly influential, were not entirely typical:

'Some of the rapidly expanding "new" industries, the products of which have been increasingly exported all over the world – such as motor cycles, bearings (especially miniature bearings), transistor radios, TV sets, tape recorders, pianos and zippers – received relatively little government assistance even in their infancy periods. By and large these industries were able to stand up by themselves, with little government protection or planning' (Komiya, 1975, pp. 219–20).

Clearly, industrial policy cannot fully explain the extraordinary dynamism of Japanese accumulation. Other factors were at work (Chapter 8).

Conclusions

The boom saw the generalization and expansion of state welfare provisions, unprecedented attempts by governments to plan for economic growth and shape industrial structures, and some experiments in worker involvement in the direction of enterprises. The most important point to recognize, however, is that these developments did not substantially undermine the essential relationships underpinning capitalist economies. Despite the increased strength of labour, as reflected in welfare provisions and moves towards 'industrial democracy', workers were still obliged to sell their labour power to employers whose freedom of action they might be able to limit, but certainly not control. Despite the growing importance of state intervention through macroeconomic planning and industrial policies, the essential decisions about investment were still taken by the controllers of private capital, on the basis of private profitability.

Perhaps the most important aspect of attempts to manage the 'mixed economy' during the golden years was that people believed they could work. This helped maintain confidence, which in turn helped maintain accumulation. Accumulation generated jobs, regular increases in living standards, resources for welfare and profits. These in turn reproduced the consensus.

When the boom conditions began to disintegrate, the economic logic of capitalist production reasserted itself in a very brutal fashion (Chapter 14). But the development of state intervention in the course of the boom had an important effect on reactions to growing economic difficulties. Many on the right blamed the breakdown of the boom precisely on government interference (Chapter 18). The left, by contrast, saw the greater worker and state involvement in the economy as a pointer to how the crisis could be resolved in the interests of working people (Chapter 19). In this way the patterns set in the boom left their imprint firmly on the years of mass unemployment which followed.

10. The Eclipse of US Domination

Our discussion of the dynamics of the boom in Chapter 8 focused on the advanced capitalist countries as a group. Of course the boom was very uneven as between countries; the wave of accumulation in Japan was more powerful than elsewhere. By far the most important aspect of this uneven development was the undermining of the economic dominance of the United States.

Table 10.1 Weight of the US economy, 1950–70

Percentages

	1950	1970
US share of ACC output	58[1]	47
US share of ACC capital stock	52[1]	45
US output per head of population in relation to		
United Kingdom	182	166
France	217	133
Germany	270	133
Italy	400	217
US manufacturing productivity in relation to		
United Kingdom	279	285
Germany	367	232
Japan	n.a.	272[3]
US share of manufacturing output (big 10)	62[2]	44[4]
US share of manufacturing exports (world)	33	16

1. 1952.   2. 1953.   3. Using Roy's estimates of Japanese productivity relative to Germany.   4. 1971.

Sources: Kravis, Table 1; Prais, 1981, Table A1; Branson, Tables 3.8, 3.13; Roy, Table 3.

This chapter discusses some aspects and implications of this process.

At the beginning of the boom the economic might of the United States was overwhelming (Table 10.1). In 1952 nearly 60 per cent of the production of the ACCs was located there, produced by around 33 per cent of the total number of workers operating over half of the business capital stock. Careful studies of the total level of output per head of the population in 1950 suggested that, taking the United States as 100, the United Kingdom scored 55, France

Chart 10.1 Shares of ACC production, 1952–70

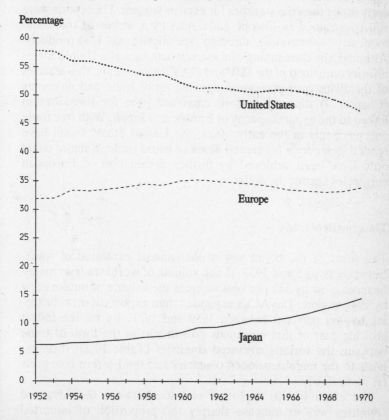

Source: see Appendix.

46, Germany 37 and Italy 25. In coal mining US productivity was somewhere between four and five times greater than that in either the United Kingdom or Germany and about seven times as great as in France. In manufacturing the USA was nearly three times as productive per worker as Britain, nearly four times as productive as Germany and the differential was considerably greater in relation to Japan. In 1950 the USA produced six times as many manufactures as Germany and thirty times as many as Japan; in 1953 it exported five times as many manufactures as Germany and seventeen times as many as Japan. In 1957 only seven non-US firms were in the biggest fifty in the world.

The dominance of US business was more overwhelming in the early fifties than the statistics for exports suggest. US exports were still constrained in Europe and Japan by a welter of trade and monetary restrictions, directed specifically at US products. Although the dismantling of these restrictions was a United States priority enshrined in the IMF and GATT agreements, the debacles of the 1940s over premature opening up of trade and payments (Chapter 4) dictated a more measured pace for liberalization linked to the export capacity of Europe and Japan. With free trade and payments in the early fifties, the United States would have tended to secure a far greater share of world trade. Balance could only have been achieved by further devaluation of European currencies against the dollar.

The growth of trade

The years of the boom saw a phenomenal explosion of trade. Between 1951–3 and 1969–71 the volume of world trade in manufactures grew by 349 per cent whereas the volume of output grew by 194 per cent. The ACCs expanded their exports of manufacturing by 480 per cent between 1950 and 1971. By far the fastest growing part of that enormous growth was in the form of trade between the various advanced countries (Table 10.2); their exports to the underdeveloped countries and the Eastern bloc grew far more slowly.

The effect of this explosion of trade between the advanced countries was to increase sharply the proportion of imported manufactured goods consumed inside these countries. Within Europe in particular, 'import penetration' rose far above

Table 10.2 Exports of manufactures, 1950–71

$ billion, 1955 prices

	1950	1971
Within Europe	4.6	46.7
Within North America	2.5	11.7
Europe to and from North America	2.6	15.6
Japan to and from Europe and North America	0.3	13.7
Total	10.0	87.8
To rest of world	14.3	53.2
TOTAL	24.3	141.0

Source: Batchelor *et al.*, Table 2.4.

the levels of the early fifties, which in turn were similar to the very low levels of the interwar period (Table 10.3). The levels reached by 1971 exceeded even the considerable levels achieved before the First World War. In the United States, however, the rise in import penetration, all of which occurred in the 1960s, represented the first serious incursion this century by imported manufactured goods. Only Japan, of the major exporters, remained virtually impervious to import penetration – all the phenomenal growth of manufactured exports being devoted to paying for the soaring import bill for materials (Chapter 12).

Table 10.3 Import penetration by manufactures, 1913–71[1]

Percentages

	1913	1937	1950	1963	1971
Europe[2]	13	6	6	11	17
USA	3	2	2	3	8
Japan	34	11	3	4	5

1. Imports as a percentage of production of manufactures plus imports.
2. Unweighted average of UK, France, Germany, Italy.

Sources: Maizels, Table 6.4; Batchelor *et al.*, Table 3.3.

For the industrial countries as a whole, around half the increase in imported manufactures between the years 1950 and 1963 represented greater import penetration of the domestic market and half reflected a larger market; between 1963 and 1971, when trade between the advanced countries grew by 156 per cent, almost two-thirds of the increase represented imports taking a greater share of the domestic market.

A major development encouraging trade between the advanced countries was tariff cuts. The reduction of tariff barriers after the formation of the EEC in 1958 increased trade by the order of 25–35 per cent. Within EFTA (the free trade zone formed by seven of the non-EEC European countries, including at that time the United Kingdom) lower barriers resulted in extra imports of around 10–15 per cent for the countries concerned. The Kennedy round of cuts in the later sixties saw the average level of tariffs on manufactures falling by one-third, and by half on machinery and vehicles. Very high rates of tariff covering about 7 per cent of goods in the United States and United Kingdom almost disappeared, and the proportion of trade (excluding agriculture and fuels) which attracted tariffs of 15 per cent or less rose from 54 per cent to 85 per cent in the USA, from 37 per cent to 85 per cent in the United Kingdom and from 71 per cent to 97 per cent for the EEC. Additional imports generated may have been around 15 per cent for the United Kingdom, rather less for the EEC but a good deal larger for the United States.

Some of the rise in import penetration would undoubtedly have occurred anyway, especially in the fifties when non-tariff restrictions were dismantled and firms took advantage of falling transport costs and rapid growth of demand to break into new markets. But still tariff cuts in the sixties were certainly an important influence on trade during the period. Only the Japanese market remained more or less impenetrable.

International oligopoly

This great expansion of trade and competition between the advanced capitalist countries outweighed the trend within each country or bloc towards more monopolization. The data are patchy, but indicate a steady, if unspectacular, rise in concentration. Data for the USA, EEC and Japan all point to an increase in the share of manufacturing output accounted for by the largest firms (Chart 10.2).

Chart 10.2 Share of manufacturing output produced by top firms, 1960, 1970

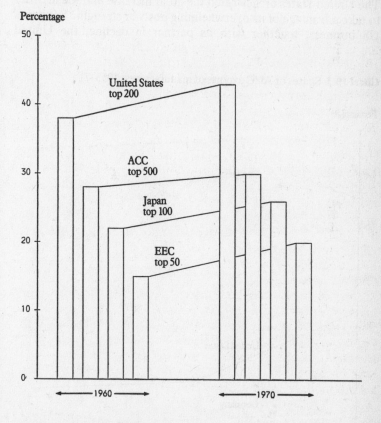

Percentage

United States
top 200

ACC
top 500

Japan
top 100

EEC
top 50

1960   1970

Sources: Caves, pp. 511–12; Dunning and Pearce, Tables 3.6, 4.28; Japan, *Census of Manufactures*; Locksley and Ward, p. 96.

Whatever impact this increased monopolization had in reducing the degree of competition in domestic markets was swamped in most instances by the greater challenge from imports. Indeed, much of the merger movement within countries was a reaction to the strengthening of overseas competition.

US business slips back

The United States orchestrated the great increase in trade in order to take advantage of its overwhelming postwar strength. Yet it was US business, together with its partner in decline, the United

Chart 10.3 Shares of ACC exports of manufactures, 1953–71

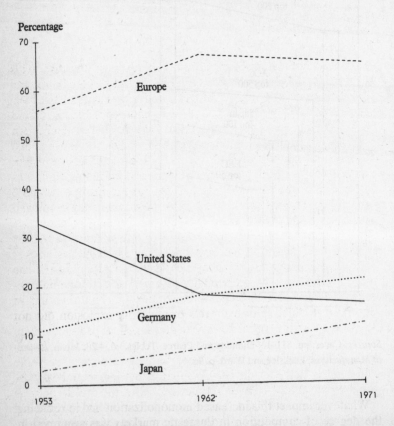

Source: Branson, Table 13.3.

Kingdom, which of all the major ACCs gained least from the boom in trade (Chart 10.3, Table 10.4).

Table 10.4 Growth of export volumes, 1953–71

Average annual percentage growth rates

	1953–59	1959–71
USA	0.2	6.3
Germany	16.9	9.2
Japan	19.0	15.9

Source: Branson, Table 3.14.

The fundamental problem faced by US business was that rivals in Europe and Japan were accumulating capital at a far faster rate (Chart 10.4) and were doing so on the basis of far lower wage costs (Table 10.5). Between 1955 and 1970 the capital stock in US manufacturing rose by 57 per cent; in the major European countries the rise was 116 per cent, and in Japan it was some 500 per cent. Taking into account the rise in employment, the rise in capital stock per head (an index of increased mechanization) was 38 per cent in the United States, 87 per cent in Europe, and 203 per cent in Japan (Chart 10.5). New investment per employed worker in US manufacturing in 1955 was running at about 1.6 times the European level, and nearly five times that of Japan; by 1970 US manufacturing was investing about the same per worker as European industry and one-third less than Japanese. In the United States average productivity rose by less than one-half between 1954 and 1970, in Japan it rose three and a half times and in Europe it doubled. But even this productivity explosion did not bring the average level of European and Japanese productivity up to that of the United States (Chart 10.6). The data are exceptionally complicated to evaluate, but the estimates in Table 10.1 suggest that even in 1970 US manufacturing retained a productivity advantage of over 100 per cent. But the crucial point is that old plants in the USA, and in some industries not only the old plants, were increasingly faced with the challenge of new plants in Europe and Japan with techniques and labour productivity approaching US levels, but with far lower wage costs. In 1960 hourly manufacturing labour costs, including social security contributions, were around three times as high in the USA as in Europe, and ten times as high as in Japan. Even the far faster growth of money wages outside the USA in the years up to 1970 left capital in Europe and Japan with a huge advantage in terms of labour costs (Table 10.5).

Chart 10.4 Business capital stock, 1952–70

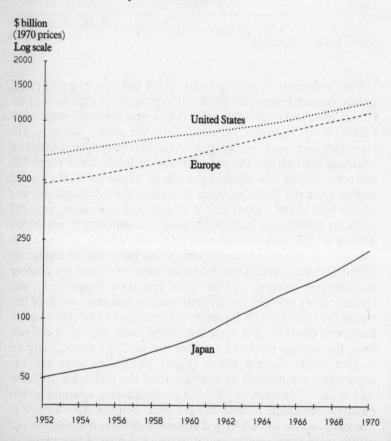

Source: see Appendix.

Table 10.5 Hourly labour costs in manufacturing, 1960–70

Index numbers
USA=100

	1960	*1970*
Germany	33	57
UK	34	40
Japan	10	23

Sources: Ray, 1972, Table 1; 1976, Table 1.

Chart 10.5 Mechanization: manufacturing capital-labour ratio, 1955–70

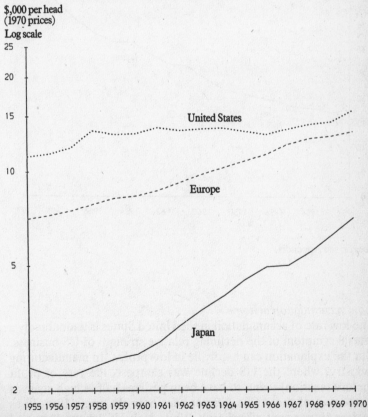

$,000 per head
(1970 prices)
Log scale

Source: see Appendix.

Chart 10.6 Ratios to US business productivity, 1952–70

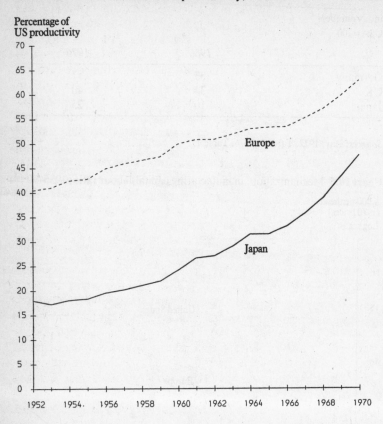

Source: see Appendix.

Low accumulation at home

The low rate of accumulation in the United States is undoubtedly a crucial symptom of the declining relative strength of US business. But the explanation can hardly lie in low profits. In manufacturing industry, where the US decline was sharpest, the rate of profit (before taxation) seems to have been perhaps half as high again as in the rest of the ACCs (28 per cent over the years 1955–70 as against 19 per cent elsewhere). While high US labour costs and productivity appear to have had roughly offsetting effects, leaving the share of profits similar in the United States to elsewhere, the output-capital ratio was much higher in the USA, suggesting very efficient organization of production (including shift-working).

Taxation appears to have taken a slightly higher fraction of gross profits in the United States than in some other countries (around one-third in the USA in the mid-fifties as against about one-fifth in Japan). This did not reflect higher state spending. Over the period 1952–70 government spending on civil and military programmes comprised 26 per cent of GDP in both the United States and the rest of the major ACCs. Certainly the weight of military spending was much greater (9.4 per cent of GDP as against 3.9 per cent), but this was balanced by lower spending on civil programmes, especially social security transfers which took 8.6 per cent of GDP in other countries and only 5.1 per cent in the USA. Whatever disadvantages US capital faced in terms of policing the 'free world' were more or less offset by lower state spending on the working class.

In any case, shortage of profits is quite implausible as an explanatory factor. Companies in the countries which were accumulating rapidly were investing much more than their retained profits – borrowing the rest from the banks or money market. Thus Japanese companies in the early sixties were financing more than 40 per cent of their investment by tapping external sources of funds; French firms borrowed one-third of the funds they needed and German firms probably did the same. But US companies only ploughed back into new investment a sum equal to their profits. They undoubtedly could have borrowed more and expanded their capital stock faster. If they had done so, the economy would have retained a much fuller utilization of capacity, which in turn would have increased the companies' profits (from 1957 to 1963 the capacity utilization rate in manufacturing averaged only 80.5 per cent, nearly 12 per cent less than the peak achieved in 1966).

So why did US companies fail to invest at a higher rate? Perhaps part of the answer lies in the fact that much of the new technology which had been developed before and during the war had already been incorporated into the capital stock. The existing technology may not have offered sufficient new opportunities, in contrast to Europe and Japan where the combination of backward technology and low wages offered great scope for profitable modernization.

But even if the relative lack of profitable investment opportunities goes some way to explaining the poor investment rate, then if US business had felt itself under more pressure, it might have made greater efforts to improve technology. In the early sixties, the United States was spending roughly 2¾ per cent of GDP on research and development (R and D) as compared with 1½–2 per cent in continental Europe and Japan. But about half of US R and D was financed by the federal government, 80 per cent of which went for space and military purposes. Indeed it was precisely the industries which most benefited from this R and D (aerospace, electronics) which maintained their world lead most effectively. Other sectors such as steel and cars were more complacent.

All this suggests that lack of competitive pressure felt by US business played an important role in the loss of its pre-eminent position. The structure of domestic industry was probably dominated by fewer firms than in Japan or the EEC taken as a whole. But this is a crude indicator, at best, for how business behaves. Industries dominated by very few giant firms may be ferociously competitive; these few firms may invest at very high rates, as in Japan. The comparative stability of the oligopolistic structure in the United States may well have bred a complacency which Japanese and German capitalists, faced with rebuilding their position on world markets almost from scratch, could never afford.

Once launched on a path of low accumulation, there was a strong tendency to stick there. Wages were only pulled up slowly, implying weak pressure to scrap old plant and replace it with new. By contrast, rapid accumulation, such as occurred in Japan, forces its logic on each individual firm. In that situation failure to accumulate in the face of rapidly rising real wage costs spells disaster. US business appears to have been locked into a pattern of low accumulation from which it proved difficult to escape even when the rising tide of competition began, in the sixties, to have a noticeable effect in the domestic US market.

Investment abroad

However sluggish in its domestic investment, US business did respond to the possibilities for profitable investment in Europe by a wave of overseas investment. The total book value of US direct investment overseas rose from $12 billion in 1950 to $78 billion in 1970. Manufacturing investment in Europe, to gain access to the cheaper labour and to escape the external tariff after the formation of the EEC in 1958, grew fastest, rising from $1 billion in 1950 to $14 billion in 1970.

Three aspects of this 'American Challenge', as it was called, need emphasizing. First, it never represented a major investment outlet for US business as a whole. Taking the years 1956–70, if all (net) US direct investment overseas had instead been invested in the United States, gross private investment there would have increased only by around 4 per cent. Second, this investment abroad was not financed out of domestic profits; over the same period US business received profits from its past investment overseas equivalent to around 1¼ times as much as it was sending overseas. While switching towards Europe (where 31 per cent of US direct investment was located in 1970 as compared to 15 per cent in 1955) from Latin America (where the share fell from 38 per cent to 19 per cent) and from mining and petroleum to manufacturing (32 per cent in 1950, 41 per cent in 1970), on average US overseas investment more than financed itself.

Third, while of modest significance for US business as a whole, overseas investment was much more important for the giant multinational enterprises. Over the period 1957–65 for US manufacturing, extra sales by overseas subsidiaries counted for an estimated 13 per cent of the total increase in production (additional exports counted for only a trivial 2 per cent). For a sample of giant US firms, increased production by their subsidiaries overseas represented 29 per cent of additional sales. By 1966 20 per cent of their total sales was accounted for by overseas subsidiaries. In 1972 an estimated 22.5 per cent of US multinationals' production took place overseas. In that year petroleum, office and photographic equipment multinationals (mainly American) reported overseas production ratios of 58 per cent, 41 per cent and 37 per cent respectively.

The fact that they tapped in to the rapidly expanding European market undoubtedly helped the giant US firms to offset some of the effects of slow domestic growth. Nevertheless they still grew substantially more slowly than their rivals from the EEC and Japan, even in the crucial high-research-intensity sectors (Table 10.6). This eroded the extent to which the giant US firms towered over the rest. In 1957 74 out of the top 100 firms were from the

United States; in 1972 the figure was 53. The sales of the largest 100 US firms were nearly double the sales of the largest 100 non-US firms in 1962; in 1972 they were only 40 per cent more. Since the US firms were usually the largest, their slower growth of sales led to a reduced concentration in the industries concerned – measured by the sales of the top 3 firms as a proportion of the top 20. In eleven out of sixteen industries the concentration ratio declined, reflecting the greater degree of competition as European and Japanese firms began to match US firms for size. To take the case of cars, in 1962 the big 3 US producers accounted for 67.5 per cent of the sales of the top 20 producers; in 1972 the share was 58.1 per cent. In 1957 the biggest 3 US car firms sold 11.6 times as much as their three biggest rivals; in 1972 the difference was 4.2 times. In iron and steel the ratio fell from 4.7 times to 0.9.

As the case of cars suggests, the giant US firms, although squeezed, were by no means throttled. As late as 1977 the biggest 5 firms in aerospace, office equipment (including computers), scientific and photographic equipment were still American, as were the biggest 4 in paper and wood, the biggest 3 in vehicles, the biggest 2 in electronics and rubber, and 3 out of the biggest 5 in petroleum, industrial equipment and food.

Table 10.6 Growth of sales of giant firms, 1962–72
Percentage by which growth
of EEC and Japanese firms
exceeded that of US

	EEC	Japan
High Research Intensity	29	71
e.g. electronics	19	50
Medium Research Intensity	27	158
e.g. motor vehicles	51	218
Low Research Intensity	7	68
e.g. textiles	11	57
All giant firms	26	106

Source: Dunning and Pearce, Table 5.5.

The boom, Bretton Woods and the dollar

The decline of the position of US capital was one of the most important developments of the boom. Just as the enthronement of the dollar at the centre of the world's monetary system symbolized US dominance at the end of the war, so the weakening of the dollar was to symbolize the erosion of that power.

The international financial system established, essentially by the United States, at Bretton Woods in 1944 (Chapter 3) was not fully implemented immediately. Indeed, it was not until the late 1950s that full convertibility for trade purposes of most European currencies was achieved. Only then were businesses in Europe entirely free to use their domestic currencies to buy dollars in order to pay for imports; and controls on capital movements remained widespread. Nevertheless the progressively more complete operation of the system of pegged exchange rates between convertible currencies undoubtedly assisted the massive expansion of trade which occurred. The heyday of the Bretton Woods system was short-lived, however. As the 1960s rolled on, fundamental weaknesses of the system were revealed, centring on the contradictory role of the dollar. Various attempts to patch up the system failed, and the final crisis phase of the boom (Chapter 13) saw enormous financial turbulence and the abandonment of the Bretton Woods framework.

The general interest of US business and finance in the postwar period, perceived as such from 1947 onwards at least, was that the capitalist world as a whole should expand rapidly, with as open access as possible for US commodities and capital. Inasmuch as the Bretton Woods system contributed both as a framework for the expansion of the other capitalist countries and as a mechanism for granting US exports and capital access as soon as practicable, it can only be counted as a success. But a more subtle question concerns the terms on which the United States gained this access. The very operation of the system, while putting the dollar in a privileged position in certain respects, made it progressively more difficult for US business to take full advantage of the opportunities on offer.

The dollar was the lynchpin of the Bretton Woods system. Not only were the values of other currencies effectively pegged to the dollar (formally speaking, to gold) but dollars had to make up the greater part of the other countries' official holdings of reserves.

This is because production of gold, at the fixed price of $35 an ounce, was insufficient to provide for both its industrial and monetary uses. But perhaps more importantly, other countries found dollars not just as good as gold, but better than gold since they could earn interest on their dollar holdings. In the 1950s about three-fifths of total gold production found its way into official reserves. But this represented an increase in the stock of gold held as reserves of only 17 per cent. Over the same period the value of trade in goods and services, which these reserves were supposed to support, more than doubled. In the 1960s, out of a higher total level of gold production (which peaked in 1965) much less than 10 per cent reached the reserves, constituting an increase of a mere 3 per cent. In the 1950s most of the additional reserves which countries accumulated to support their burgeoning trade had to consist of dollars; in the 1960s gold's contribution was negligible.

US gains

This situation, in which other countries were relying on the United States to provide them with the dollars needed to boost their reserves, seemed to leave the USA in a highly privileged position, for the only way that other countries could accumulate reserves was if the USA provided them, by spending abroad more than it received. This is just what the United States did.

Its overall deficit was not the result of a trade deficit (merchandise trade showed a surplus of $70 billion over the years 1950–67). Receipts of interest and dividends netted a further $60 billion. But government expenditure abroad (on loans, grants and for military purposes) together with the outflow of capital exceeded these credit items and resulted in $30 billion of gold or dollars flowing into foreign central banks. Up to the late 1950s this inflow of dollars was generally welcome as it relieved the earlier shortages. However the combination of rising amounts of dollars held abroad (dollar liabilities) and falling US gold stocks ($7½ billion over the eight years) meant that by 1968 the US gold stock could hardly have repaid 40 per cent of the dollars held abroad in reserves. As this ratio fell, the convertibility of dollars into gold became more and more fragile until it finally snapped (Table 10.7).

Before considering how events developed, it is important to clarify in whose interests the system had been operating. At first sight, it seems clear that the United States was gaining. Could it

Table 10.7 US balance of payments, 1950–67

$ billion

	1950–59	1960–67
Merchandise trade	29.3	39.6
Services and remittances	− 5.3	− 8.5
Net military transactions	−23.1	−20.5
US government grants (ex. military)	−20.5	−14.8
Net interest and dividends received	25.5	36.5
Current account balance	6.0	32.3
Direct investment (net)	−17.2	−27.9
Investment in shares and bonds (net)	− 3.7	− 6.4
Government loans	− 4.1	−10.6
Long-term capital	−25.0	−44.9
Balance on current and long-term capital	−19.0	−12.6
Dollars held abroad by private sector[1]	1.5[2]	− 2.8
Financed by		
Dollars held abroad in official reserves	13.0[3]	8.1
Reduction in US reserves	4.5	6.7
(of which gold)	(5.1)	(7.4)

1. Includes net short-term capital.
2. US liquid liabilities to private foreigners are not included.
3. Includes US liquid liabilities to private foreigners.

Source: US, *Survey of Current Business*, June 1975, October 1972.

not buy up businesses abroad ($45 billion over the whole period 1950–67), make loans and grants to foreign governments ($50 billion) or finance military expenditure abroad ($44 billion) simply by printing money? Was it not buying businesses and influence abroad with worthless pieces of paper?

Such a description, attractive to critics of the United States from de Gaulle leftwards, is an oversimplification. First of all, the US deficit was not financed literally with paper dollars; foreign central banks which received dollars invested in the New York money market at the going rate of interest. This meant that the USA was actually borrowing overseas, though admittedly paying rather a low rate of interest in *real* terms (after allowing for inflation, the real rate of interest on US Treasury bills was 1½ per cent over the years 1960–6). The United States, or to be more precise, US capital, was clearly gaining if it could borrow at 1½ per cent and invest in setting up or buying businesses in Europe, which would earn a much greater rate of profit. But the reason that US business was investing so much in Europe and elsewhere was not that the United States could run a balance of payments deficit financed by borrowing from central banks overseas. Their investments were based on their monopolistic position in world markets, their competitive edge in terms of know-how, manufacturing techniques and products, which made investment to capture overseas markets attractive. If the United States had not been able to run a deficit to finance the investment abroad, one response could have been a lower value of the dollar, more competitive exports and a sufficient trade surplus to finance the overseas investment. As their resistance to a dollar devaluation against their currencies showed, European and Japanese capital stood to lose more if the United States financed its capital outflow through a trade surplus. The real objection to the United States was in relation to US activities abroad rather than to their financing. In short, claims that the United States was abusing its financial position were a way of claiming that US competition was 'unfair' rather than just effective.

The real European complaint was that US financial power attracted funds to New York and that US industrial power was strong enough to allow it to organize successfully a large volume of production overseas. What prevented French or German firms borrowing on similar terms in Europe or the United States to those faced by US firms, and using the money to buy up firms in Europe or indeed the United States, was their financial and industrial weakness, not the state of Europe's balance of payments. The charge that the USA was abusing, rather than simply using, its position, only had weight to the extent that the United States was putting pressure on central banks abroad *not* to convert more of their dollars into gold. Such pressure began in a mild way in 1960 after some speculative activity in the gold market occurred, based on dawning fears that the dollar might not for ever be 'as good as gold' (i.e., fixed in terms of gold). The United States responded by informally requesting her partners to use restraint in exercising their right to convert dollars into gold. In the next year the United States and other major countries founded the 'Gold Pool' under which they would all, not just the USA, supply gold to stabilize the private gold market.

As the gold backing for the dollar crumbled in the 1960s, the United States increased its pressure on central banks not to join private speculators in demanding gold; in 1967 West Germany issued a formal declaration undertaking not to 'cash in' its dollars for gold, and most other countries, with the notable exception of France, apparently made unofficial statements to the same effect. Finally in 1968, as the private speculative pressure mounted, the Gold Pool was dissolved (in reality it had been drained). The private market for gold was allowed to find its own level. Formally the United States still maintained the myth that it would convert official holdings of dollars into gold at the old price of $35, while informing other central banks that if they attempted to take advantage of this offer at all it would instantly be withdrawn.

Despite all this pressure to sustain the position of the dollar, it seems that the extent to which the USA was gaining by its ability to finance a deficit was limited. Such gains should show up in receipts of profits from the investments made abroad. But between 1960 and 1967 the amount of interest, profits and dividends received from abroad (net of payments) increased only from $3.4 to $5.3 billion. Most of this increase in any case represented the returns on the investments which the United States had 'earned' by investing the surplus earned from exports exceeding imports. The part of the increase due to its 'privileged' position of being able to borrow cheaply and invest profitably abroad must have been rather small, let alone the part which could be in any way attributed to direct pressure on foreign central banks to provide this finance.

Costs of maintaining the dollar

Furthermore, there were very considerable costs to the USA involved in maintaining the value of the dollar, not against gold, but against other currencies. In the 1960s the US balance on merchandise trade failed to grow, and then sank to virtually nothing in 1968, while the amount US business was investing abroad was rising steadily. In terms of relative costs, US competitiveness hardly changed over the sixties. But as European and Japanese business turned their attention to the US market their relatively low wage costs allowed them to make substantial inroads. At the same time these low wage costs and the expanding European market encouraged a growing level of US foreign investment. The United States began to buy more consumer goods from abroad than it exported in 1959; by 1969 the deficit was $4 billion; in 1968 the balance on cars became negative. Only in capital goods and chemicals was there a growing balance – the combined surplus rising from $5 to $11 billion between 1959 and 1969. A lower exchange rate would have tended to enhance the competitiveness and profitability of US exports and import substitutes. Workers' real wages would have been reduced, provided money wages did not rise. The billion-dollar question was whether a devaluation of the dollar would jeopardize New York's position as a financial centre. Certainly it was regarded as worthwhile to protect the dollar by limiting capital outflows. In 1963 an interest equalization tax was imposed to reduce purchases of foreign bonds and shares; in 1965 US bank lending to foreigners was curtailed. In 1968 US multinationals were required to raise the funds abroad to finance their overseas investments. How long the dollar could be defended and to what extent it was actually in the interests of US capital to do so were resolved by the crisis which followed. This radically changed both the function of the US dollar in the international monetary system, and its relationship with other currencies.

International monetary reform

Some rather fundamental reform of the international monetary system would have been inevitable even without the deterioration in the US balance of payments at the end of the 1960s. The basic contradiction was that the very process by which the rest of the world obtained international liquidity (piling up dollars) undermined the status of that liquidity (by reducing the gold backing of the dollar). Barring central banks from cashing in dollars for gold prevented the stocks in Fort Knox from declining, but left growing dollar liabilities. All the ingenious forms of longer-term borrowing undertaken by the United States from overseas monetary authorities merely changed the form of these liabilities, and could only be a stop-gap. The only way that the gold backing of the dollar could be increased would be by an increase in the price of gold. At a stroke the gold reserves in Fort Knox would be worth more dollars, thus improving backing for the dollar; gold reserves for other central banks would be worth more, encouraging them to accumulate further interest-earning dollar reserves; gold production would be stimulated and private demand reduced (as industry tried to economize and speculators took their profits), allowing countries to absorb additional gold into their reserves.

The immediate costs to the United States would have been political, the main gainers being the major gold producers – South Africa and the USSR – and those who had previously speculated against the dollar by demanding gold. More fundamentally there was no guarantee that a once-and-for-all increase in the price of gold (a doubling was frequently suggested) would suffice. If the only problem was that the price of gold, fixed prewar at \$35 an ounce, had to be adjusted for the wartime inflation in order to secure an adequate supply, then perhaps doubling the gold price would do the trick. Certainly US inflation subsequently had been extremely low; between 1952 and 1967 the US wholesale price index rose at only 0.8 per cent a year. With other currencies fixed to the dollar, this limited the inflation rates elsewhere, the average price of the exports of OECD countries rising by only 0.9 per cent a year. So the insufficiency of gold reserves resulted from higher volume of trade, not higher prices. But by the end of the sixties, the US boom, associated first with Keynesian measures and then with the Vietnam war, was seriously threatening US price stability. Between 1967 and 1970 US wholesale prices rose by 3.3 per cent a year. Continuation of inflation at this kind of rate would cause the whole problem to recur in that the value of gold stocks, at the new fixed price, would be regarded as insufficient in relation to the rising value of trade, and speculation on a further gold price rise, against the dollar, would redouble (as it would have been proved so profitable the first time). Only a return to US price stability would allow a once-and-for-all rise in the gold price to work, and there was nothing in the act of raising the price of gold which would make that more likely (indeed, the improved gold backing for the dollar would relax such pressure as there was on the US government to maintain price stability in order to defend the dollar). Otherwise an increase in the price of gold seemed to guarantee a continued subservience for the position of the dollar in the international monetary system: always under threat of further humiliation by falling in value in relation to gold. It was for these reasons that the United States in the late 1960s consistently opposed an increase in the official price of gold.

It is highly likely that there was no possible adjustment to the gold price in the 1960s which would have ensured an adequate flow of gold into the reserves of the USA and other countries. The balance between industrial demand, speculation and monetary needs could probably never have been achieved in the inflationary context of the time. At the other extreme from attempting to stabilize the monetary system by an appropriate use of the price mechanism (the price of gold) there arose a multitude of plans for the conscious creation of international money which would certainly supplement, and perhaps do away with, the role of gold and even dollars as part of international reserves. The US government began to look favourably on such plans in the mid-sixties, presumably out of a realization that something more permanent than arm-twisting had to be done to protect the gold in Fort Knox. The system of special drawing rights (SDRs), agreed in 1968 and implemented in 1970, gave countries credits in the books of the IMF, fixed in value to gold and earning an interest rate of 1½ per cent, which they could use to settle balance of payments deficits. This 'paper gold' was intended to take the heat off the dollar by increasing what was in effect the gold content of reserves. The supply of SDRs to be made available would not be disturbed by the vagaries of industrial demand, Russian gold sales or speculation. The initial allocations ($9½ billion spread over three years) were expected to provide for a reasonable growth of reserves in the context of a staunching of the flow of dollars. It seemed to be a triumph for international cooperation and reason. As we shall see, this triumph was short-lived (Chapter 12). In the turmoil that ensued, it became apparent that US capital, while weakened, was by no means incapable of defending its interests.

11. Overaccumulation

The decline of the United States was not the only problem generated by the boom. The sheer pace of accumulation was itself a mixed blessing. It propelled capitalism up the longest and steepest economic incline in history, but at a cost. Towards the end, the engine of growth was overheating badly and the ride was increasingly bumpy. *Overaccumulation* had set in.

The basic idea of overaccumulation is that capitalism sometimes generates a higher rate of accumulation than can be sustained, and thus the rate of accumulation has eventually to fall. Towards the end of the postwar boom, an imbalance between accumulation and the labour supply led to increasingly severe labour shortage. The excess demand for labour generated a faster scrapping of old equipment. Real wages were pulled up and older machines rendered unprofitable, allowing a faster transfer of workers to the new machines. This could in principle have occurred smoothly: as profitability slid down, accumulation could have declined gently to a sustainable rate. But the capitalist system has no mechanism guaranteeing a smooth transition in such circumstances. In the late sixties the initial effect of overaccumulation was a period of feverish growth, with rapidly rising wages and prices and an enthusiasm for get-rich-quick schemes. These temporarily masked, but could not suppress, the deterioration in profitability. Capitalist confidence was undermined, investment collapsed and a spectacular crash occurred. Overaccumulation gave rise, not to a mild decline in the growth rate, but to a classic capitalist crisis.

This chapter and the following two examine this process. This one focuses on underlying developments in accumulation. The next two give a more blow-by-blow account of mounting economic difficulties.

Development of the working class

One way in which rapid accumulation undermines the conditions for its own existence is by creating a mass proletariat. Capitalism's hunger for additional workers creates a larger and larger class of waged workers. Their economic conditions are essentially similar – in that they are deprived of the wherewithal to produce on their own account and so must work under others for wages – and their interests are ultimately antagonistic to those of their employers.

Total employment rose, in line with population growth, by 30 per cent between 1950 and 1970. In the absence of any bizarre large-scale shift out of waged into other forms of employment, this would in itself have increased the size of the working class by almost a third. As it was, the proletariat grew considerably faster than total employment. While civilian employment in the ACCs rose by 46 million, the number of self-employed and 'family workers' fell by 20 million. In 1954, 31 per cent of those officially classified as in work were in this category. By 1973 the proportion had fallen to 17 per cent.

Outside agriculture the number of self-employed actually grew by 1 million, while falling substantially as a proportion of total employment. The growth of services, with many opportunities for small businesses, was the main reason for the growth in absolute numbers. In industry the self-employed were generally slowly squeezed by the superior performance of big business, although 15 per cent of those engaged in manufacturing in Italy and Japan were still self-employed in 1970.

So the story behind the statistical shift from self-employment to wage labour is one of an exodus from the land. For the individuals concerned the trek was often one away from the dreary world of the family farm towards the bright lights of the big city. For society as a whole it was a process of massive proletarianization.

A number of factors made this development possible. One was underemployment in the countryside. Many farms had more family workers than could be fully employed, and so migration to the cities could occur without loss of food output. In Japan, the United States, France and Germany the number of unpaid family workers fell by nearly 12 million, or 70 per cent. Mechanization in the countryside also reduced labour requirements. This was achieved partly through capitalist agriculture driving out family farms. The number of self-employed farmers in the United States, Japan, France and Germany fell about 6 million, or 50 per cent.

Reduced underemployment, mechanization (spurred on in part by the exodus of family workers) and improved methods of cultivation allowed agricultural output to grow significantly and employment to fall substantially. Productivity grew faster in agriculture than in industry, both overall (Table 11.1) and within every major country except Japan.

Table 11.1 ACC sector growth rates, 1955–68

Average annual percentage growth rates

	Output	*Productivity*
Agriculture	1.8	5.6
Industry	5.7	4.2
Services	4.9	3.0

Sources: OECD, *The Growth of Output 1960–80*, Tables 3 and 7; Ohkawa and Rosovsky, Table 2.5.

These developments within agriculture reflected the growth in demand for labour in other sectors. This proceeded at a faster pace in services than in industry (Table 11.2).

Table 11.2 ACC growth of employment, 1955–68

Average annual percentage growth rates

Total	*Agriculture*	*Industry*	*Services*
1.0	−3.8	1.5	2.0

Source: OECD, *The Growth of Output 1960–80*, Tables 4 and 5.

The pattern of demand – including the rise in the share of investment (Chapter 8) – ensured that industrial production rose more quickly than the output of services. Nevertheless, employment grew faster in services as productivity rose more slowly (though the measurement of output and hence productivity in many services is difficult).

Some of the growth in service employment was in state provision outside the market, notably in the form of the welfare state (Chapter 9). State employment rose from some 11½ per cent of total employment in 1960 to some 14½ per cent in 1974. (Nationalized industry employees are excluded; they produce commodities for the market and contribute directly to the pool of surplus.) Some privately employed labour also works for non-profit-making bodies. In Japan, where state welfare provision is poor, this constitutes some 2 per cent of employment. None of these jobs is strictly capitalist. But they are wage labour, and those performing them are a part of the working class.

The proletarianization of previously independent producers also increased union membership. In the ACCs membership grew from about 49 million in 1952 to 62 million in 1970. But the proportion of wage and salary earners in unions declined from 37 per cent in 1952 to 31 per cent in the late sixties. Much of the explanation for this lies in two interrelated trends: towards more white-collar jobs and towards more service jobs, both traditionally weakly organized. In both Britain and Germany the number of manual workers stayed virtually constant over the boom while white-collar employment rose by 50 per cent in the United Kingdom and doubled in Germany. Since unionization levels among white-collar workers are about half those for blue-collar in both countries, this shift worked to pull down the average level of unionization even though more white-collar workers started to join unions.

Overall membership figures are crude indicators of the development of unionization. They lump together the British miners, the American teamsters and Japanese 'company' unions. But, for Europe at least, certain generalizations can be made. They include the increasing importance of white-collar and public sector unions and the cementing, in the context of continuous growth in living standards, of the power of national trade union bureaucracies. These developments were to influence the form of workers' struggles once full employment was achieved (Chapter 12).

The late 1960s: the problem of full employment

By the mid-sixties the enormous growth of waged jobs had
effectively created full employment. The measured unemployment
rate for the advanced capitalist countries had fallen below 3 per
cent. It then fluctuated around that level until 1973, although
rising quite sharply in the 1971–2 recession (Chapter 12).

In full employment lay both the historic achievement of the
boom and its undoing. The difficulties raised by full employment
manifested themselves most obviously in accelerating inflation. A
less noticeable but ultimately more crucial problem was a general
decline in profitability. But perhaps the most fundamental
difficulty was a threat to capitalist control on the shop floor. The
Polish economist Kalecki, a quarter of a century before, had
predicted just such a development: 'The *maintenance* of full
employment would cause social and political changes which would
give a new impetus to the opposition of the business leaders.
Under a régime of permanent full employment, "the sack" would
cease to play its role as a disciplinary measure . . . "discipline in
the factories" and "political stability" are more appreciated by
business leaders than profits. Their class instinct tells them that
lasting full employment is unsound from their point of view and
that unemployment is an integral part of the normal capitalist
system' (Kalecki, pp. 140–1).

Tight labour markets

Measured in terms of unemployment rates, the intensity of demand for labour appears to have subsided a little by 1970 (Chart
11.1a). But unemployment can be an unreliable indicator of the
tightness of labour markets. Patterns of registration shift as regulations change, or as previously 'marginalized' groups, such as
married women, become consolidated into the labour force. Rapid
changes in the pattern of demand for labour (across regions or
industries) can also leave a residual of 'structural' unemployment
in a context of intense labour shortage. The speed of the upswing
in 1972–3 generated bottlenecks and labour market 'mismatches'.

Chart 11.1a Unemployment rates, 1965–75

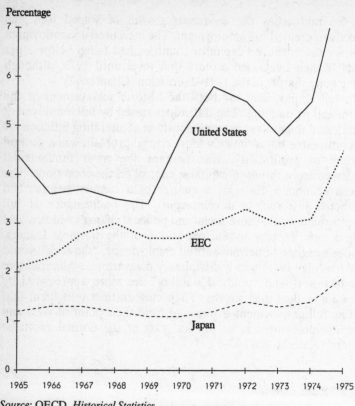

Source: OECD, *Historical Statistics*.

An alternative indicator of demand for labour is employers' notification of vacancies. Although open to misinterpretation, this at least in principle shows the extent to which employers were hunting for workers. Vacancy figures show intensity of demand reaching a peak in Germany in 1970 and in Japan in 1973 (Chart 11.1b). In the United Kingdom and United States as well, vacancy figures show extremely tight labour markets in the early seventies.

Chart 11.1b Job vacancies, 1965–75

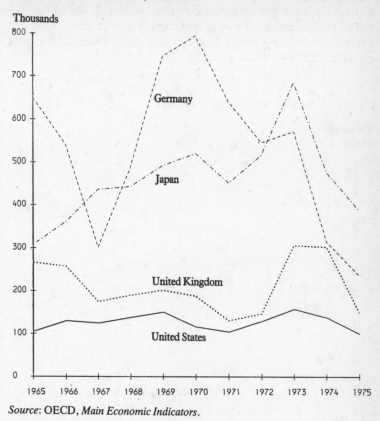

Source: OECD, *Main Economic Indicators*.

Accumulation and the demand for labour

The very high level of demand for labour was maintained
throughout the late sixties and early seventies by the trend of
capital accumulation. The accumulation rate for the ACCs peaked
in 1970 at just over 5½ per cent – an increase of over 1 percentage
point relative to the early sixties. In Europe the rate of
accumulation peaked first in the early 1960s, then a decade later at
a slightly lower level. In the United States it peaked around 1966,

but was still much higher in the early seventies than in the early sixties. In Japan the accumulation rate peaked at the end of the sixties and the increasing weight of the Japanese capital stock also contributes to the upward trend in the ACC accumulation rate over the 1960s as a whole (Chart 11.2).

Chart 11.2 Business accumulation, 1960–73[1]

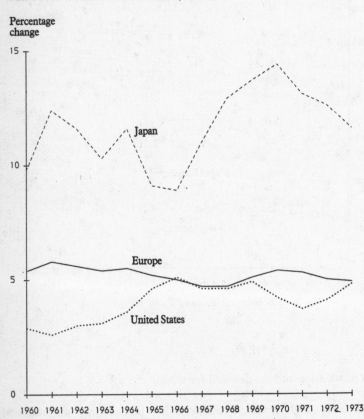

1. Growth rates of gross fixed capital stock.

Source: see Appendix.

The impact of accumulation on demand for labour depends on its form as well as its extent. If accumulation in the boom had been based on an unchanged mass of machinery per worker then an extension of the capital stock would have required an equivalent increase in workers employed. But new means of production systematically embodied a higher degree of mechanization than

Chart 11.3 ACC business accumulation and employment, 1962–71[1]

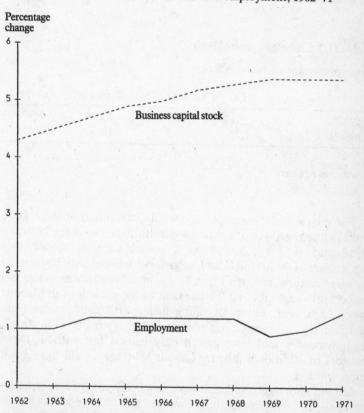

1. Percentage growth rate of five-year moving average centred on year specified (so that figures for 1962 include changes in 1960 and 1961, and figures for 1971 include changes in 1972 and 1973).

Source: see Appendix.

their predecessors (Chapter 8). So the rate of growth of employment was much less than the rate of accumulation (Chart 11.3). But in the absence of an increase in the speed of mechanization in the early seventies, the peak rates of accumulation achieved at that time generated peak intensities of demand for labour. Since labour supply did not increase to meet this demand, the growth of civilian employment was only marginally higher in the late sixties and early seventies than in the first half of the sixties (Table 11.3).

Table 11.3 Civil employment, 1960–73

Average annual percentage growth rates

	ACC	USA	Japan	Europe
1960–66	1.1	1.7	1.4	0.3
1966–73	1.2	2.2	1.2	0.2

Source: see Appendix.

For the capitalist countries as a whole, about half of the 1.7 per cent per year growth of the non-agricultural labour force between 1968 and 1973 resulted from a combination of a declining agricultural labour force and increasing female participation in non-agricultural labour (Table 11.4). Immigration was much less important – contributing 0.1 per cent to the growth of the labour force each year. Given declining male participation rates (due particularly to earlier retirement and extended education), employment would have grown only half as fast without these sources of additional labour. Labour shortage would have been more intense.

Labour shortage could also have been relieved by longer hours of work. In fact, average hours worked per year generally fell in the late 1960s and early 1970s, according to rather sketchy data available. This continued the trend of the early 1960s, as workers used their stronger bargaining position in tight labour markets to reduce time spent at work. However, it also reflected the growth of part-time work as more married women entered the labour force.

Table 11.4 Sources of labour, 1968–73

Average annual percentage growth rates

	ACC	USA	Japan	Europe
Growth of 'home' population of working age	1.0	1.5	1.2	0.4
Effect of net migration	0.1	0.2	0	0.1
Growth of total population of working age	1.1	1.7	1.2	0.5
Effect of change in participation rates	0.2	0.3	0.3	0.1
Growth of labour force	1.3	2.0	1.5	0.6
Effect of decline in agricultural labour force	0.4	0.2	0.7	0.5
Growth of non-agricultural labour force	1.7	2.2	2.2	1.1
of which women	2.4	3.1	2.2	1.8

Sources: OECD, *Labour Force Statistics*; McCracken, Table A11.

The profits squeeze

An increasing imbalance between accumulation and supplies of additional labour requires the faster scrapping of old plants to speed up the transfer of workers to new means of production. With little additional labour available, employers compete fiercely for labour to operate newly installed machinery. A faster increase in money wages results. Inflation may accelerate as well, but, if faster scrapping is to occur, not as fast as money wages. For it is the increase in product wages (the real cost to the employer of hiring workers) which makes the old machinery unprofitable and permits labour to be transferred to the new. This faster scrapping, and the faster growth of product wages which causes it, are signs that the rate of accumulation is excessive in relation to the available labour supply. A further sign of overaccumulation is a squeeze of profits.

Between 1968 and 1973 the share of profits in business output fell by about 15 per cent (Table 11.5). All the blocs experienced the squeeze, though with varying intensity. In Europe the profit share fell in the early sixties and again in the early seventies. A sharp decline began in the United States after 1966. In Japan profitability plummeted after 1970. Although the squeeze on profits occurred during very different time periods, the falls were quite similar: profit shares declined to around 75 per cent of peak levels almost everywhere. 1969 marks the onset of decline for the ACCs as a whole because that is the first year in which a rising share in Japan no longer outweighed declines elsewhere (Charts 11.4, 11.5).

Table 11.5 Profit shares, 1960–73

Percentages

	ACC	USA	Europe	Japan
Business				
Peak year[1]	23.5[2]	22.5[3]	25.4[4]	36.1[5]
1973	19.9	16.7	19.5	28.1
1973/peak year	0.85	0.74	0.77	0.78
Manufacturing				
Peak year[1]	23.7[2]	22.8[3]	25.9[4]	40.7[5]
1973	20.6	17.8	17.9	32.9
1973/peak year	0.87	0.78	0.69	0.81

1. Year before sustained decline in profitability. 2. 1968. 3. 1966. 4. 1960.
5. 1970.

Source: see Appendix.

In each bloc the decline in profit shares started at about the time that the accumulation rate peaked. This is no coincidence: accelerated accumulation, combined with labour shortage, was the basic cause of the profits squeeze.

It was not the only influence at work, however. The behaviour of both productivity and product wages do not conform precisely

Chart 11.4 Business profit shares, 1960–73

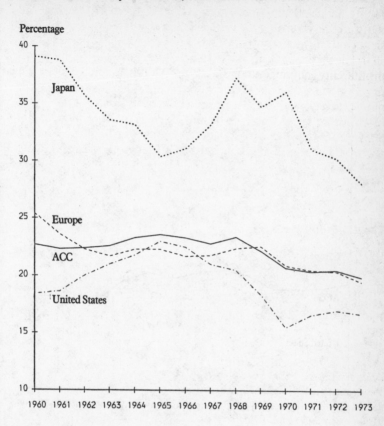

Source: see Appendix.

to the simplest description of overaccumulation. Productivity and product wages determine the course of the profit share and an account of their movements is given in the next two sections. Tracing the course of the profits squeeze is inevitably rather complicated and speculative because the various influences cannot be quantified.

Chart 11.5 Manufacturing profit shares, 1960–73

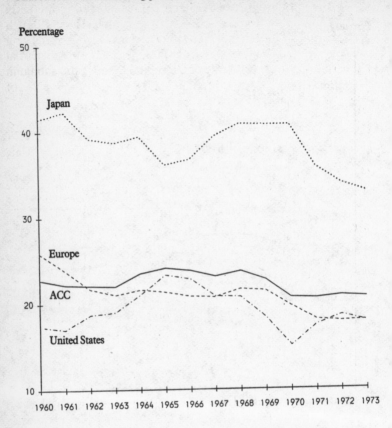

Source: see Appendix.

Productivity growth

Faster scrapping of old plant as a result of insufficient labour should increase the rate of growth of labour productivity. With a faster rate of transfer of workers from old machines to new ones, the proportion of more modern, higher-productivity machines in use rises. Yet faster productivity growth did not occur in the early seventies. Despite a faster rate of accumulation in relation to the labour force (reflected in the capital-labour ratio growing nearly

½ per cent per year faster), the growth of productivity was around ½ per cent slower between 1968 and 1973 compared to the early 1960s (Table 11.6). The decline took place in all the blocs, though most sharply in the United States and Japan. In manufacturing industry, productivity growth was maintained, but the substantial acceleration in the growth rate of the capital-labour ratio should in theory have led to faster productivity growth as the pace of mechanization rose.

Table 11.6 Productivity and mechanization, 1960–73

Average annual percentage growth rates

	ACC	USA	Japan	Europe
Business				
Productivity(per worker)				
1960–68	4.0	2.6	8.9	4.4
1968–73	3.4	1.3	7.7	4.2
Capital-labour ratio				
1960–68	3.7	1.7	8.9	5.2
1968–73	4.0	2.2	12.2	4.6
Manufacturing				
Productivity (per hour)				
1960–68	5.0	3.3	10.0	5.8
1968–73	5.2	3.6	11.2	5.6
Capital-labour ratio				
1960–68	3.2	0.7	9.7	5.3
1968–73	4.6	2.8	12.5	4.4

Sources: Appendix; US Bureau of Labor Statistics, *Underlying Data*.

Three factors probably contributed to the decline in productivity growth. The argument that faster scrapping leads to a faster growth of productivity assumes that mechanization – the installation of new machines – continues to yield the same increases in productivity. If mechanization was to yield less productivity gains, however, then average productivity growth would slip back despite faster scrapping.

It is plausible to suppose that the most productive increases in mechanization in Europe and Japan occurred in the fifties and sixties. A laggard in the technological race may take shortcuts to 'catch up'. Productivity growth would then decline as the frontier set by the United States was approached. But this cannot fully explain the slowdown. Europe and Japan still lagged far behind in the late sixties and seventies. In 1970 Germany remained a poor second, with manufacturing productivity less than half that of the United States (Table 10.1). Moreover, 'catching up' cannot explain the slowdown in US productivity. If mechanization was yielding less productivity gains there, as is suggested by the failure of manufacturing productivity to accelerate, it must have been because the technical frontier was being pushed forward less rapidly, due perhaps to the exhaustion of certain particularly important technological advances.

Productivity growth does not depend solely on equipment – whether or not new, high-productivity machines replace old, low-productivity ones. Productivity on the whole range of plant, old and new, may be improved as experience in operating it breeds better methods of organization. Conceivably such gains were tailing off by the late sixties. Productivity is also affected by the extent to which the employers can maintain or increase the intensity of labour – the proportion of the working day during which the worker is literally working – and the speed of that work. Faster production lines and increased labour 'flexibility' (so that workers carry out a wider range of tasks) raise productivity on the whole range of plant. Tight labour markets and increased union strength at the end of the sixties may well have made it more difficult for employers to increase work intensity and carry out schemes of reorganization. This probably contributed to the slower growth in labour productivity at that time.

One special factor which had contributed to higher productivity growth in the United States in the early 1960s was the strong boom then happening: capacity utilization in manufacturing rose from around 80 per cent to 91 per cent in 1966, boosting productivity. By contrast, capacity utilization was roughly the same in 1973 as in 1968 (around 87 per cent), so that productivity growth over that period was not inflated in the same way.

Product wages

As we have seen, a faster increase in product wages is the basic factor which forces a faster rate of scrapping when there is a growing discrepancy between accumulation and the available labour supply. The growth rate of product wages did peak in 1969, just when accumulation was reaching its peak, and it grew a little faster (about ½ per cent per year) between 1968 and 1973 than over the period 1960–8. This fairly small increase in product wage growth underestimates the increased pressures to scrap (and thus the extent of overaccumulation) for two reasons. A slowdown in the productivity gains on all plants (old and new) – gains which could be obtained from reorganization and more intensive work – meant that a given growth of product wages already implied faster scrapping. Some old plants which would otherwise have remained profitable as a result of faster or more effective working would have become unprofitable as a result of these productivity gains not being achieved. Secondly, the rising cost of raw materials (Chapter 12) tended to increase scrapping by making old plants unprofitable even in the absence of a faster growth of product wages. The case of the United States illustrates this. Between 1960 and 1968 materials prices rose about ½ per cent per year and final goods prices by about 1 per cent. Between 1968 and 1973, by contrast, final goods prices rose by 4½ per cent per year while materials prices shot up by 11½ per cent per year. The effect of this rapid increase in the cost of materials, relative to the price at which final output was sold, was to make some old plants less profitable. Overaccumulation meant there was insufficient labour to keep old plants going, so they had to be scrapped. Faster materials price increases meant that this required only a small acceleration in product wage growth (Chart 11.6).

International competition

As if all these factors, and their relationships, were not complex enough, there is another influence on the profit share which must be mentioned. Increased international competition almost certainly contributed to holding down profit margins. More trade and investment flows, based on the tendency towards an equalization of productivity levels, must have decreased the extent

Chart 11.6 ACC business productivity and product wages, 1962–71[1]

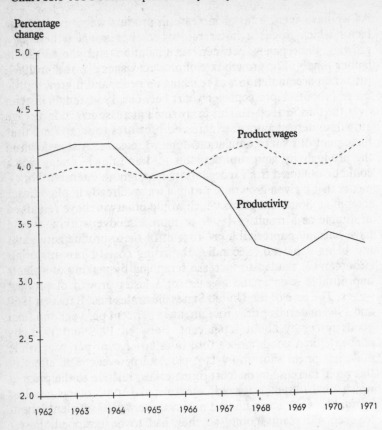

1. Percentage growth rate of five-year moving average centred on year specified (see note to Chart 11.3).

Source: see Appendix.

of monopoly power exercised by domestic producers. It certainly contributed to holding down inflation, so that the money wages generated by the high demand for labour were easily translated into product wage increases and the necessary scrapping rates achieved. The increased general level of international competition, which may have eroded profit margins in all the countries concerned, must be distinguished from sudden shifts in the relative competitiveness of individual countries. Such shifts may drastically worsen the profitability of the country suffering reduced competitiveness. An extreme example was the sharp decline in competitiveness of Japanese industry between 1970 and 1973 when a rising yen pushed up Japanese relative labour costs by one-third. This may have played some role in the big decline in the profitability of Japanese industry over the same period as Japanese exporters were forced to accept lower profit margins, but there will have been some compensating improvement in the profitability of import-competing industries in the United States and Europe as Japanese exporters found themselves obliged to raise their prices to recoup some of the cost increases.

Even in this period in Japan, however, it is highly unlikely that the exchange rate movement was the dominating factor in declining profitability. For profitability appears to have fallen just as fast outside manufacturing where the pressure of international competition must have been negligible. Forces working to equalize profit rates could hardly have transmitted the effects of international competition to these insulated sectors in such a short space of time. Labour shortage, by contrast, affected all sectors and is a much more plausible explanation for the profits squeeze.

Falling output-capital ratio

The rate of profit depends on the output-capital ratio as well as on the share of profits (Chapter 8). A faster rate of scrapping would tend to reduce the measured output-capital ratio. Some part of the scrapped capital stock would still count in the statistics, since these are based on the assumption of a constant scrapping rate (a constant economic life). During the periods when the profit share declined, a definite fall in the output-capital ratio occurred. The fall in the output-capital ratio was around 5–10 per cent in both business and manufacturing for the ACCs as a whole (Table 11.7). For the individual blocs the falling output-capital ratios were rather greater (10–20 per cent) and thus contributed significantly to falls in profitability.

If faster scrapping was properly taken into account in the capital stock statistics it would show up in a higher figure for depreciation (and thus a lower profit share) rather than a falling output-capital ratio. But it seems likely that influences other than faster scrap-

Table 11.7 Output-capital ratios, 1960–73

	ACC	USA	Europe	Japan
Business				
Peak year[1]	0.73[2]	0.99[3]	0.64[4]	0.89[5]
1973	0.69	0.89	0.58	0.70
1973/peak year	0.94	0.90	0.91	0.79
Manufacturing				
Peak year[1]	0.99[2]	1.53[3]	0.77[4]	1.14[5]
1973	0.94	1.27	0.68	1.02
1973/peak year	0.95	0.83	0.88	0.89

1. Year before sustained decline in profitability.
2. 1968. 3. 1966. 4. 1960. 5. 1970.

Source: see Appendix.

ping also contributed to the decline in the measured ratio of output to capital. All the factors discussed above which reduced the growth rate of labour productivity contributed to the fall. In addition, the relative price of capital goods stopped declining. In the early 1970s the price of investment goods rose slightly faster than the price of output, whereas in the 1960s the price of output had risen about 1 per cent faster than the price of investment goods. The explanation for the changed pattern of relative prices is not clear. Possibly the productivity slowdown was particularly marked in investment goods sectors (the US construction industry is an example frequently cited). In addition, the very high demand in the early seventies may well have pushed up investment goods prices especially fast. It is certainly the case that the rapid increase in materials prices would tend to push up investment goods prices (which include an imported materials element) faster than output prices (which are defined to exclude the impact of import prices). Finally, some part of the fall in the output-capital ratio in the United States after 1966 must have reflected the decreasing capacity utilization. While it is impossible to measure precisely the influence of these factors, they all probably contributed to the falling output-capital ratio and the consequent decline in the profit rate.

Falling rate of profit

Declining profit shares and falling output-capital ratios combined to push down the rate of profit (Charts 11.7, 11.8). Between 1968 and 1973 the profit rate for the ACCs as a whole fell in the business and manufacturing sectors by one-fifth. By 1973 the profit rate in business and manufacturing had fallen from its previous peak in each major bloc by about one-third. The fall began in Europe in 1960, in the United States in the mid-1960s, and in Japan in 1970 (Table 11.8).

Chart 11.7 Business profit rates, 1960–73

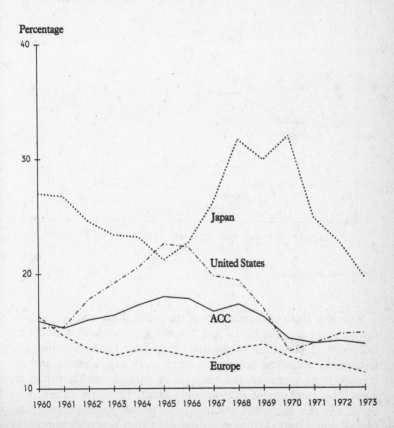

Chart 11.8 Manufacturing profit rates, 1960–73

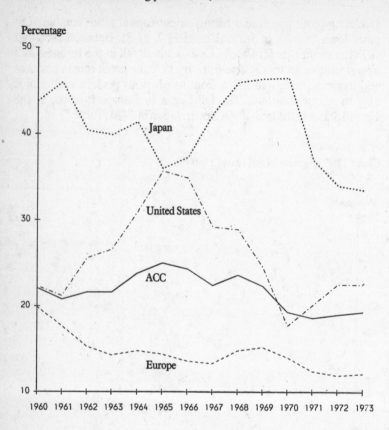

Source: see Appendix.

It is clear from our discussion of the profit share and the output-capital ratio that the profit rate was subject to a large number of influences. Decreasing productivity gains from mechanization, difficulties in obtaining more productive work organization and increased work intensity, the pressure of rising materials prices on costs, the pressure of international competition on prices, and especially fast increases in investment goods prices probably all played some part. Lower capacity utilization was also important for explaining the fall in the profit rate in the United States,

Table 11.8 Profit rates, 1960–73

Percentages

	ACC	USA	Europe	Japan
Business				
Peak year[1]	17.2[2]	22.3[3]	16.3[4]	32.0[5]
1973	13.6	14.8	11.3	19.6
1973/peak year	0.79	0.66	0.69	0.61
Manufacturing				
Peak year[1]	23.6[2]	34.9[3]	19.9[4]	46.5[5]
1973	19.3	22.5	12.1	33.5
1973/peak year	0.82	0.64	0.61	0.72

1. Year before sustained decline in profitability.
2. 1968. 3. 1966. 4. 1960. 5. 1970.

Source: see Appendix.

though this is only a partial explanation.

Despite the complex set of influences, we would emphasize the high rate of accumulation as the most fundamental factor behind the decline in profitability. The intense demand for labour which it generated both tended to depress the profit rate directly by dragging up product wages and provided the backdrop to other contributory factors such as difficulties of work organization and wages explosions (Chapter 12). It was also partly in response to the effects of overaccumulation that deflationary policies led to decreased capacity utilization in the United States. Finally, the uneven pattern of accumulation between sectors (investment goods and consumer goods), between commodities (basic materials and others) and between countries (leading to heightened international competition) also helped depress profitability. Whatever weight one attaches to each of these factors, the extent and pattern of accumulation undeniably drove down the rate of profit in the years before 1973.

Post-tax profits

Although it is the profit rate before taxation which reflects the underlying economic forces of capital accumulation, labour supply and competitiveness, it is the profit rate *after* taxation which is of most direct concern to employers. Governments could have offset declining profitability by cutting taxes on profits, either by cutting rates of corporation tax or by increasing the generosity of tax allowances given for capital investment. Data on post-tax profitability is sketchy, but figures from various sources for the effective rate of taxation – that is, the proportion of profits taken by tax – give some indication of the trend (Table 11.9).

Table 11.9 Effective tax rates on profits, 1960–73[1]

Percentages

	USA	UK	Japan	France
1960	47	38	n.a.	28
1965	37	36	n.a.	27
1970	39	40	16	26
1973	39	11	19	29

1. Different taxation systems and methods of estimation make the figures for different countries not readily comparable.

Sources: Grimm, Table 5; Bank of England, *Quarterly Bulletin*, June 1981, June 1976; Japan, *Annual Report on National Accounts*, 1982, p. 36; Mairesse and Delestre, Table 1.

In the United States the substantial cut in the burden of corporate taxation occurred before the fall-off in profitability in the mid-1960s, so the fall from then on is similar pre-tax and post-tax. Only in the United Kingdom were there major tax concessions which radically affected the falling profit rate. The Conservative government of 1970–4 substantially increased tax allowances for investment. The Labour government of 1974–9 retrospectively removed tax from inflationary increases in stock values. The effect was to reduce the tax burden sharply. The post-tax rate of profit was actually higher than the pre-tax rate in some years in the mid-

and late 1970s, implying that the government was providing more of the finance for investment, via tax concessions and grants, than it was taking from profits in taxation. The post-tax rate estimated for the early seventies was only a little below that of the early sixties. In the United Kingdom, then, the impact of declining profitability was cushioned by tax concessions for companies. This meant a shift in the burden of taxation towards workers, reducing the extent to which they benefited from their increased bargaining strength.

Did workers gain?

At first glance it might seem that workers clearly gained from the onset of overaccumulation. Full employment meant a more or less guaranteed job, shorter hours, and perhaps reduced labour intensity and improved working conditions. Finally, the faster growth of product wages would seem to imply faster growth of living standards.

But the issue is more complex. Whether or not accelerated product wages lead to a faster increase in living standards depends on how the prices of the goods that workers consume move relative to those of the goods they produce, and on any changes in the proportion of their incomes that workers pay in taxation which are not reflected in increased benefits or social services.

For the advanced capitalist countries as a whole, real take-home pay rose nearly 1 per cent a year faster in the early seventies than in the sixties. The slowdown in yearly productivity growth was offset by a substantially slower rise in the prices of consumer goods than in the prices of domestic production as a whole, with the result that growth of wages in terms of the purchasing power of consumer goods exceeded that relative to output as a whole – the product wage (Table 11.10). This was not because import prices rose markedly slower than those of home products: the 'external terms of trade' – the ratio between export and import prices – had a negligible effect on domestic purchasing power. Although import prices accelerated, so did export prices (they rose practically as fast as domestic production in the early seventies rather than much slower, as had been the case in the sixties).

Table 11.10 Productivity, real wages and the profits squeeze, 1960–73

Average annual percentage growth rates

		(1) Productivity	(2) External terms of trade	(3) Internal terms of trade	(4) Tax	(5) Warranted post-tax real wage	(6) Actual post-tax real wage	(7) Share of wages
ACC	1960–68	4.0	0	0.2	-0.4	3.8	3.7	-0.1
	1968–73	3.4	0	0.6	-0.4	3.6	4.5	0.9
Europe	1960–68	4.4	0.1	0.2	-1.0	3.7	4.3	0.6
	1968–73	4.2	0	0.8	-0.3	4.7	5.4	0.7
USA	1960–66	3.0	0	0.2	-0.1	3.1	2.2	-0.9
	1966–73	1.3	0	0.5	-0.6	1.2	2.2	1.0
Japan	1960–70	9.1	0	-0.6	0	8.5	9.0	0.5
	1970–73	6.3	-0.2	0	-0.7	5.4	9.4	4.0

(1) GDP per person employed.

(2) External terms of trade measures effect of relative rise of import prices on purchasing power of domestic incomes.

(3) Internal terms of trade measures effect of rise of consumer prices relative to prices of total output on purchasing power of domestic incomes.

(4) Tax measures effect of burden of tax (direct and indirect) on take-home incomes.

(5) Warranted post-tax wages is increase which will leave share of profits constant given productivity, terms of trade effects and tax, i.e. the sum of columns (1) to (4).

(6)

(7) The share of wages in total incomes rises to the extent that actual post-tax real wages rise faster than 'warranted', i.e. column (6) less (5).

Sources: see Appendix; OECD, *National Accounts*, 1952–78, Vols. I and II; OECD, *Economic Outlook*, Reference Statistics, December 1981.

Instead, there was a marked slowing down in the growth of consumer prices relative to those of the other categories of total production. The prices of government expenditures on goods and services and of investment goods both rose 1 percentage point or so a year faster, relative to consumer goods (Table 11.11).

Table 11.11 ACC price changes, 1961–73

Average annual percentage growth rates

	Domestic production	Imports	Exports	Private consumption	Public consumption	Invest-ment
1961–68	3.4	1.3	1.5	3.2	4.8	2.6
1968–73	5.9	5.1	5.0	5.4	8.2	6.2

Source: OECD, *National Accounts*, 1950–79, Vol. I, pp. 82–3.

Possible contributory factors include relatively rapid increases in pay for government employees, slow productivity growth in investment goods industries and very high demand for certain investment goods.

These apparently obscure developments make a real difference to the picture. The relative deceleration of the prices of the goods that workers bought offset the adverse effect of the productivity slowdown on their living standards. So the growth of the share of wages did imply a faster growth of living standards, rather than simply offsetting slower productivity growth.

But taxation must also be taken into account. Throughout the 1960s the share of total incomes taken in tax (a rough indicator of the tax burden on workers) had risen steadily. This reduced the growth of take-home pay by around ½ a percentage point a year. If this trend had intensified in the early seventies then workers' consumption would have been held back despite the rising wage share. In fact, for the ACCs as a whole, the burden of taxation continued to grow at the same rate, so that the rise in the share of pre-tax wages was translated into higher take-home pay.

In Europe the tax rate grew considerably more slowly, so take-home pay grew much faster. In Japan and the United States the increase in the wage share was sufficiently strong to keep up the

Table 11.12 Public expenditure, 1960–73

Percentage of GDP

	1960	1968	1973
ACC			
Civil[1]	19.2	21.9	24.2
Military	6.6	5.8	4.1
USA			
Civil[1]	16.8	19.4	22.5
Military	9.1	8.8	5.7
Europe			
Civil[1]	23.1	27.4	28.8
Military	4.4	3.7	3.4
Japan			
Civil[1]	15.2	16.0	18.7
Military	0.9	0.7	0.7

1. *Civil* spending refers to 'programmes'; i.e., it excludes debt interest and subsidies (the effect of the latter is included in the discussion of taxation).

Source: see Appendix.

earlier momentum of take-home pay increases, despite both slow productivity growth and a rising tax take. So, while the overall picture results from a combination of rather diverse trends in the major blocs, the net outcome is that workers undoubtedly benefited in terms of take-home pay (Table 11.10).

Workers' living standards also depend on government services. Spending on these rose steadily in the sixties. There was a sharp twist towards civil spending. Military spending was drastically reduced in the United States, allowing a very rapid rise in civil expenditure. In Japan civil spending also increased sharply. In Europe, where the share of civil spending had risen steadily throughout the sixties, the pace was not maintained (Table 11.12).

Of the 2½ percentage points increase in the share of civil spending in total production about half is accounted for by services (health and education) and half by transfers. Practically all the higher share of spending is accounted for by increases in the relative cost of providing them. So the 'quantity' of services provided (measured, for example, by the number of workers employed in providing them) rose no faster than output as a whole. The rise in the share of transfers (pensions, dole, etc.) also probably took the form (as it did over the period as a whole, see Chapter 9) of an extension of coverage of schemes rather than of a growth in real value in excess of productivity. But the substantial cut in military spending which allowed accelerated expansion of welfare services without a correspondingly faster rise in the burden of taxation represented a gain for workers. It was another product of pressure for improved conditions.

Therefore, in the early 1970s the working class made substantial gains in take-home pay and public services, as well as in high employment, cuts in hours and probably improved conditions of work. For the moment, capital was bearing the costs of overaccumulation.

Inflation

Thus far the discussion has been conducted entirely in 'real' terms: the shares of incomes going to profits and wages, productivity, hours of work, and so on. The only prices discussed have been *relative*: investment goods in relation to consumer goods, imports relative to exports and so forth. Changes in the overall price level have been ignored.

Adjustment to full employment could in principle occur without any tendency towards inflation. Competition for labour would pull up money wages more rapidly. Higher inflation would enable old capital to stay competitive, but profitable capacity would then exceed market demand. So competition for markets from the cheaper products made on newly installed machinery would hold price increases down to the existing rate. The faster growth of money wages would mean a faster growth of product wages. Older vintages would be scrapped more quickly, making space for the new in both labour and product markets. Faster growth of product wages would mean faster growth of real wages. Consumption would rise as a share of production, and profits and investment decline. Steady extension of credit would allow the expanded production to be sold without any change in the rate of inflation.

But this is not what happened in the early seventies. Inflation rose steadily from the mid-1960s. In 1965 consumer prices rose on average by 3 per cent a year in the ACCs. By 1973 the average annual inflation rate had risen to 7.8 per cent. Prices accelerated for a number of interrelated reasons. Trade unions, strengthened by high demand for labour, secured money wage increases which, given the existing inflation rate, exceeded those required to generate sufficient extra scrapping. On occasions, wage pressure exploded in very sharp increases, especially where it had previously been compressed by incomes policies. Such wage increases tended to reduce profitability. This happened directly when employers were unable to raise prices sufficiently to offset 'excessive' wage increases because of growing international competition and fixed exchange rates. But international competition was not always binding. Governments sometimes responded by promptly devaluing the currency to offset the cost disadvantage of the wage increases.

Even where prices could be raised to offset the wage increases, aggregate profits would still fall eventually if credit was not extended fast enough to allow the sale of the same volume of commodities at the higher price level. So governments faced strong pressure to offset the adverse effects of wage explosions on profitability by facilitating a rapid expansion of credit. When they acquiesced, the result was higher inflation. Capitalists were also unwilling to accept the decline in accumulation implied by the falling rate of profit. Access to credit enabled capitalists to maintain the rate of accumulation by increasing the proportion of funds borrowed (largely workers' savings). In Germany and the United States in particular, business borrowing was higher in the early seventies than in the early and mid-sixties. Business borrowing in Japan and France also peaked in 1973 (Table 11.13).

This additional borrowing, being routed in part through the banking system, ensured a faster growth of the money supply. The investment financed by this borrowing stoked up demand for commodities, permitting sales to be maintained at higher and higher prices.

Governments were not responsible for this expansion of credit in the sense of running larger deficits and printing money to finance them. There was no upward trend in government borrowing (Table 11.14). On average the advanced countries were in rough budget balance. But governments failed to prevent the expansion of credit. They allowed the banking system to respond

Table 11.13 Business borrowing[1] as a percentage of fixed investment, 1962–73

	USA	Japan	France	Germany[2]	UK
1962–67	15.4	n.a.	32.3	31.9	n.a.
1968–72	27.2	29.4[3]	31.8	33.8	5.2
1973	36.1	39.2	40.8	41.2	8.3

1. Business borrowing is the difference between saving (including transfers) and fixed investment. Refers to non-financial corporate and quasi-corporate sector.
2. Includes unincorporated enterprises.
3. 1970–2.

Source: OECD, *National Accounts*, 1981, Vol. II.

to demands from capitalists for credit at rates of interest which failed to keep up with inflation (that is, at declining 'real' interest rates). This helped to maintain the return on shareholders' investment. Even though investments earned less overall, by financing an increasing proportion through borrowing at declining real interest rates, capitalists helped maintain the profitability of shareholders' funds. In the United Kingdom, for example, between 1965 and 1973, the fall in the pre-tax rate of profit to shareholders was one-seventh, while the return on all capital employed fell by more than one-quarter.

Table 11.14 Government surpluses, 1965–73

Percentages of GDP

	ACC	USA	Europe	Japan
1965–67	−0.4	−0.2	−1.2	0.8
1968–70	0.3	0.4	−0.6	1.8
1971–73	−0.3	0.0	−1.5	1.3

Source: see Appendix.

With inflation eroding the purchasing power of accumulated savings, workers were obliged to save more of their incomes if they were to rebuild the value of past savings. So the extra credit funnelled through the banks was ultimately provided by workers.

In the fifties and early sixties the cost of imports had risen much more slowly than prices inside the advanced countries. But in the early seventies the cost of imported raw materials accelerated rapidly (Chapter 12).

With workers attempting to increase their real incomes by militant wage bargaining, and capitalists attempting to maintain accumulation through extended borrowing, these higher materials costs could not be absorbed without a struggle. Employers passed the burden on to workers via higher prices. Workers responded with higher wage demands. Governments permitted the credit expansion required to finance the higher price level. Part of the burden was thereby eventually eliminated as the prices of advanced countries' exports to the primary producers rose – reducing the deterioration in the terms of trade. The rest was shunted back and forth between capitalists and workers as wages chased prices and vice versa. The net result was further inflation.

Governments' credit policies were not constrained by international monetary considerations. The relative decline of US capital (Chapter 10) was reflected in large balance of payments deficits as US goods became less and less competitive and war expenditures in Vietnam climbed. These deficits, combined with substantial outflows of capital, provided the other advanced countries with additional dollar reserves. So their credit policies were not generally held back by balance of payments considerations. And when the external account did pose a problem, governments often devalued rather than pursue deflationary policies to the extent that would have been necessary. The floating of the pound in 1972 symbolized this turnaround in favour of sustaining expansion regardless of the inflationary cost.

The acceleration of US inflation relaxed the constraint on price rises, previously provided by the linking of other currencies to the dollar. And where internal inflationary pressures were stronger than in the United States, devaluation was used to push the constraint aside. Countries with lower inflation rates resisted revaluation as this would reduce export profitability. The net result was a tendency to chronic balance of payments surpluses, which stoked up inflationary pressure by maintaining high demand for

Overaccumulation

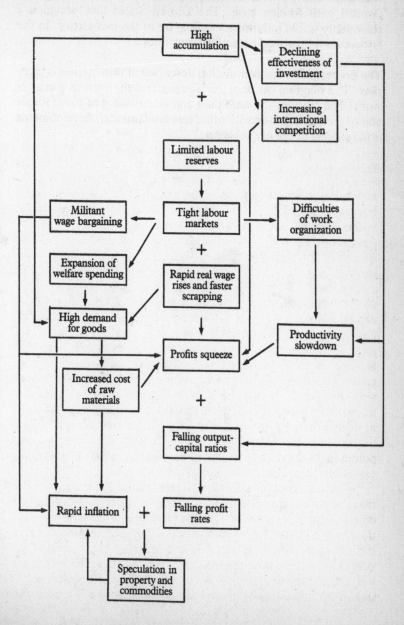

goods. This came both from abroad and from borrowers at home, who could easily obtain credit from the banking system which was flooded with foreign cash. The United States had provided a reasonably stable inflationary ceiling up to the mid-sixties. In the late sixties it furnished a steadily rising floor.

The process of overaccumulation described in this chapter is complex. The diagram on page 267 summarizes the various forces at work. The story of the unfolding and intertwining of these forces and of their interaction with other less fundamental, developments is the subject of the next chapter.

12. Overheating

In the late 1960s most economic commentators believed that the long boom was permanent. Keynesianism seemed to have banished mass unemployment for ever and wage rises seemed as natural and regular as the tides. Since the mid-1970s, by contrast, the mood has been one of gloom and despondency. This chapter and the next tell the story of how things turned sour.

Overaccumulation sets in

The rate of accumulation for the advanced capitalist countries as a whole began to rise significantly in the early sixties and continued upwards until 1970. The rise was from a trend rate of some 4 per cent a year in 1960 to a little over 5½ per cent in 1970. Employment growth remained fairly constant at somewhere between 1 per cent and 1.5 per cent a year, and the level of capacity utilization began to rise. The manufacturing rate of profit began to fall after 1968, as did that for total business. Inflation averaged 3.8 per cent a year between 1965 and 1969, over twice the rate of the first half of the decade. By the end of the sixties it had reached 5 per cent a year. For the system as a whole the picture is a 'classic' one of overaccumulation and consequent 'overheating'.

But these aggregate developments are the net outcome of differing experiences in the major blocs. The United States entered a long period of expansion in 1961. This was already proceeding strongly by 1965, having been further reinforced by a round of tax cuts in 1964 and the failure of the administration to finance by additional taxation the growing expenditures associated with the buildup of the Vietnam war and the social programmes initiated in response to civil rights demands (notably Johnson's 'Great Society' programmes).

Despite burgeoning expenditures, the administration did not apply for a temporary tax surcharge until 1967, and it was not enacted until June 1968 – a result of unwillingness to tax people further to pay for an increasingly unpopular war. Monetary policy was expansionary from 1966 to late 1968. Attempts at incomes policy, the 'wage-price guideposts', were ineffective.

Expenditure became excessive in the second half of 1965 and remained high until 1969. Official unemployment fell below 4 per cent (traditionally thought of as the 'full employment' level) in 1966 and fell to 3.5 per cent in 1969. The rate of profit for both manufacturing and business as a whole began to fall after 1966. The rate of increase of the consumer price index rose from around 2 per cent a year in the early 1960s to 5½ per cent in 1969.

In Europe cyclical developments were fairly divergent in the mid-sixties, but came increasingly to follow the German pattern towards the end of the decade. Germany was in a boom phase in 1964–5 which was extended by election-motivated tax cuts in 1965. The introduction of restrictive monetary policies then contributed to Germany's first significant recessionary interlude – in 1966–7 – in the long boom. A major expansionary budget – Germany's first recourse in the long boom to deficit financing – then led to an extremely powerful upswing, beginning in 1968 and continuing to 1970. This generated a general European upswing beginning in the middle of 1967 and continuing until 1970. Many of the smaller countries which had strong trading links with Germany, such as the Netherlands, were simply pulled along. Strongly expansionary policies were pursued in France after the 1968 general strike. Italy had been in a state of relative stagnation since the 1962–3 boom, but a further expansion got underway in 1968. Britain, on the other hand, pursued contractionary policies after the 1967 sterling devaluation.

This synchronized European upturn brought an acceleration of prices. This occurred later than in the United States. It is hard to disentangle the effects on inflation of the upturn from those of the wage explosions and devaluations (see below). Profits had begun to fall for Europe as a whole as early as 1961.

Japan had experienced a 'stop-go' pattern in the early 1960s, with expansionary phases generating balance of payments difficulties to which the government responded with tight monetary policies. In 1965 the economy was emerging from a stop phase. This upturn was reinforced by loose monetary policy and fiscal expansion, strongly directed towards investment by both government and business. The result was phenomenal growth: real

GDP grew by 55 per cent in the four years to 1969. The profit rate rose throughout the expansion. Wholesale prices rose by only around 1½ per cent per annum until 1969, when they accelerated to an annual rate of growth of 5 per cent.

By the end of the period, then, there existed a fairly synchronized upswing which was clearly 'excessive'; it constituted over-accumulation for the system as a whole. This increased synchronization was in part brought about by developments in the US external account, which removed balance of payments constraints elsewhere. Between 1964 and 1969 Japan had a positive swing of $2½ billion on its current account and Europe one of $6 billion. But at the close of the sixties, even before the strains in the international trade and payments system caused it to fracture, a remarkable development in industrial class struggle swept across Europe.

Strike waves and wage explosions

A wave of strikes swept across Europe between 1968 and 1970. The May 1968 events in France triggered a three-week general strike. Next year Germany and the Netherlands were drenched by waves of wildcat strikes, and Italy sweated through a Hot Autumn of industrial unrest. In the United Kingdom the Wilson government's incomes policy broke down in 1969–70 in a 'Winter of Discontent'.

The strikers won big wage increases, around twice those of the preceding years (Table 12.1). These gains were all spearheaded by settlements negotiated to conclude key strikes: the Grenelle agreements of May and June 1968 in France, the agreement between IG Metall and the iron and steel producers in September 1969 in Germany, the metal-working agreements of December 1969 in Italy, and the public sector settlements of winter 1969–70 in the United Kingdom.

The phenomenon was confined to Europe. The United States and Canada did experience more industrial unrest in the early seventies than in the fifties and sixties, and money wages rose faster. But the shift began earlier and was far more gradual. The number of strikes in Japan did not noticeably increase.

But within Europe the experience was remarkably uniform. The strike waves took place at around the same time and all won major

Table 12.1 The European wage explosions, 1965–70

	Strikes[1]	Money wage[2]	Real wage[2]
France			
1965–67	2,569	5.8	2.9
1968–69	76,000[3]	11.0	5.4
Germany			
1966–68	147	5.6	3.3
1969–70	171	12.0	9.2
Italy			
1966–68	10,761	6.9	4.3
1969–70	29,356	11.3	7.3
UK			
1967–69	4,774	6.9	2.4
1970–71	12,265	12.0	3.9

1. Thousands of days occupied in strikes, annual averages.
2. Average annual percentage change during the years shown.
3. Kendall's estimate (p. 365).

Source: Allsopp, Table 3.4.

wage increases. Many strikes were headed by groups of workers who had previously been fairly quiescent. Many were in white-collar jobs, often in the public sector. Often the workers were unorganized, or organized only weakly. The strikes were sparked off by the rank and file, most were unofficial, and often they were resisted at the outset by national trade union leaderships. So they should be seen essentially as a unified development.

They also marked a watershed in industrial relations, showing clearly that the consensus had failed to unite divergent class interests. Since 1968–70 there have been more strikes than in the fifties and sixties, and more of them have been unofficial (Table 17.1). The wage explosions also had an immediate economic impact: by jacking up costs they squeezed profits further and boosted inflation.

So the industrial turbulence of these years is important. But why did it happen?

At first glance it looks like a straightforward consequence of overaccumulation (Chapter 11). Europe as a whole was booming by the late sixties. As we saw, labour markets were tight. Accumulation could be maintained only if wages rose and scrapping accelerated. Otherwise there would be a shortage of workers to operate newly installed machines. So faster wage rises were needed if the system was to function smoothly.

The effective full employment also provided the mechanism to push up wages. By tilting bargaining power towards labour, it encouraged big pay claims. Capitalists resisted, which was an instinctive response, but also a rational one. Real wages had to rise somewhere if less efficient plant was to be scrapped and the labour shortage contained. But it was clearly to any one firm's advantage if somewhere was elsewhere. Workers backed up their claims with strike action. And they won, because employers could not find substitute labour and because, with demand for commodities high, they lost heavily from any interruptions of production. Capitalists were forced to concede the wage rises which for the system as a whole were needed to sustain accumulation.

But actually the situation was more complicated. The money wage increases which workers won exceeded those required to generate enough scrapping to ease labour shortage. The result was not only an increase in real wages but also a higher rate of inflation.

And the strike waves did not all occur in particularly tight labour markets. Those in Germany, Italy and some smaller countries did, but those in France and the United Kingdom did not.

The wage explosions were certainly a product of overaccumulation in a general sense: more or less full, and rapidly expanding, employment during much of the long boom was a necessary backdrop. It bred a new generation of workers with no memory of mass unemployment. But to go beyond this general observation we must examine the pattern of accumulation since the late fifties.

Europe underwent a sustained boom from the mid-fifties through to the early sixties. Prices and wages accelerated upwards and wage explosions occurred in Germany in 1961–2 and in Italy and France in 1962–3. Balance of payments difficulties followed in Italy in 1963, France in 1964–5 and Germany in 1965–6. The profit share fell sharply from 1960.

As we argued in the previous chapter, this profits squeeze fundamentally reflected overaccumulation. Labour markets became very tight and money wages rose rapidly. Firms were unable to pass these increases on fully in prices because of international competition. The US economy was stagnant with fairly stable prices, and its export prices dominated those for world manufacturing. The formation of the EEC in 1958 also saw substantial tariff reductions by member countries which increased competitive pressure on their industries. The fact that unemployment did not result prior to deflationary policies suggests that real wage rises did not exceed those required to adjust scrapping to the pace of accumulation and labour supply.

Governments responded to the profits squeeze and loss of competitiveness by deflation and incomes policies. The Bank of Italy clamped down on monetary policy in 1963, generating a major recession in 1964–5. Unemployment jumped from a low of 2.7 per cent to a high of 4.3 per cent in 1966. In France, Debré's 1963 Stabilization Plan embodied deflation. Unemployment rose slowly from 1.4 per cent in 1961–3 to 2.7 per cent in 1968. The Bundesbank tightened monetary policy sharply in 1965. By mid-1966 unemployment in Germany exceeded vacancies for the first time since 1959. Deflation in the United Kingdom began with the 'July measures' of 1966 aimed at staving off a devaluation of sterling. Unemployment rose from 2.3 per cent in 1965 to 3.8 per cent in 1967.

The French government tried to negotiate a voluntary incomes policy with the unions in 1964. When this 'dialogue of the deaf' broke down the authorities imposed limits on the public sector. In Germany the unions cooperated with the 'concerted action' programme initiated when the SPD entered the government in 1966. This involved long-term contracts and ceilings on increases. The Italian government did not attempt an incomes policy, but it did persuade the metal workers, whose settlement traditionally sets the pace for other sectors, to postpone the renegotiation of their three-year contract from 1965 to 1966. The British Labour government introduced a statutory incomes policy in 1966. A six-month freeze was followed by six months of 'severe restraint'. Further stages operated until 1969.

Incomes policies are often presented as a preferable alternative to deflation since they need not reduce output. But the real success of either policy depends, from the employers' perspective, on the extent to which real wages are held down and the potential profitability improved. Holding down money wage increases can reduce both inflation and real wage rises, as lower cost increases enable employers to raise profit margins where competition is weak. But in reality the two approaches more often go together. Incomes policies aim to persuade workers to accept lower money wage increases; deflation aims to weaken their bargaining position, and so offer them no choice. The threat of deflation as the only alternative to incomes policy is also more powerful when supported by a taste of the deflationary medicine.

Incomes policies alone can seldom weaken labour or prompt rationalization. Deflation can do both, albeit at the expense to capital of short-term profitability as markets are reduced (Chapter 18).

Employers also launched an offensive on working practices and plant-level bargaining machinery. In Germany and Italy this shows clearly in cuts in plant-level wage supplements. In France it seems mainly to have taken the form of rationalization during a major merger boom. In Italy it also involved a major intensification of labour. In the United Kingdom it took the form of productivity deals aimed at eroding shopfloor control over working practices.

These developments occurred against the background of a temporary relaxation of international competition. The US economy had moved into the Vietnam boom and its export prices had begun to rise significantly. This helped European capital to hold down real wages by raising prices. The policies were successful. The fall in both the share and rate of profit was reversed in 1966. Profitability then rose until 1969.

But resentment built up among workers. Deflation, incomes policies and attacks on plant bonuses held down wages. Incomes policies eroded differentials, and trade union action was limited by long-term contracts. The employers' offensive worsened job conditions and hamstrung plant-level union representatives.

The strike waves were the delayed expression of this resentment. In Germany and Italy better conditions for a fight back were provided by a tightening of labour markets in the boom of the late sixties. But British and French workers did not have to wait for an economic upturn.

The students' revolt provided the catalyst in France. The French working class also has a tradition of sudden quasi-general strikes. It struck in this way in 1953 and in 1936. Finally the workers who had suffered most were in the public sector, where incomes policy had held wage growth well below that of elsewhere. Most of the early strikers were state employees.

Public sector workers played a similar role in the United Kingdom. Incomes policy had been applied more rigorously in the state sector there too, and the winter of 1969–70 saw the novel spectacle of group after group of public sector workers rejecting settlements negotiated by their leaderships. The strength and traditions of the British labour movement are the other key factors. Shop stewards would lead unofficial disputes even in a downturn, confident that management would not dare attempt victimization.

The attacks of the mid-sixties also explain the wildcat nature of the strikes. Many trade union leaderships had become enmeshed in participation in incomes policies and arrangements for long-term contracts. The employers' offensive was also, almost by definition, at plant level. It was to be expected that resistance would begin here too.

There is also a rough correlation between the groups most hit by the austerity measures and those in the vanguard of the strikes. Public sector workers in France and the United Kingdom have already been mentioned. The other prominent group in the United Kingdom was motor industry workers, who had also borne the brunt of the attack on shopfloor organization and working practices. In Italy unskilled migrant workers from the centre and south both suffered most and fought back most tenaciously.

The wage explosions were the price of industrial peace. In France, they also bought political stability.

We have so far stressed the similarity of strike waves. But it is worth looking at two major examples in more detail to get a flavour of those heady days.

Italy's Hot Autumn

Italy is particularly interesting. The Hot Autumn marked a greater shift in the balance of power between labour and capital than occurred elsewhere. Before 1968 Italian unions were very weak. Their membership was low and they had failed to organize the immigrants from the centre and south who increasingly provided the majority of semi-skilled and unskilled labour in the industrial north. The unions had almost no influence on the factory floor and were ineffective in collective bargaining. They were divided politically into communist (CGIL) and non-communist (CSIL) federations. Their nearest counterparts were the French unions.

But since the beginning of the seventies the semi-skilled have become highly organized. Shopfloor bargaining has become standard in large plants and effective national negotiations have become the norm. The two federations have worked together fairly closely. The obvious comparison is now the United Kingdom.

The Hot Autumn also marks a greater turning point in economic performance than occurred elsewhere. Only the United Kingdom economy performed as badly during the seventies and it has always been near the bottom of the league. Italy, on the other hand, underwent an 'economic miracle' during the fifties and sixties. Yet during the seventies the 'gap' between the rate of growth of real wages and of productivity in Italy was three times that for France and Germany and twice that for the United Kingdom. The shift in the balance of forces reflected in the wage explosion of 1968–70 was almost certainly the chief factor behind Italy's precipitate tumble down the league. Indeed, the story of Italian economic policy in the seventies is largely one of attempts to adapt to or reverse this shift.

The Italian labour movement suffered enormous defeats in the late forties (Chapter 6) and the trade unions remained ineffective throughout the fifties. Membership figures are unreliable but suggest that no more than 10–15 per cent of the work force was unionized. More reliable data for the metal workers, the most powerful sector, show only 20–25 per cent unionization. Almost all negotiations were at industry or national level, and ineffective. Agreements on conditions at work were either disregarded by employers (for example the 1950 national agreement on dismissals) or used to undermine links between trade union representatives and employees (for example the 1953 National Agreement on Works Councils which made these, and not union structures, the official plant representatives for employees). Industrial agreements on minimum wages were imposed by employers' confederations, dominated by small firms, which set them 'at rates which employers could afford to pay' (Kendall, p. 164).

So workers were very much at the mercy of employers. Many large firms deliberately used 'wage drift' to obtain shopfloor quiescence.

Fiat allocated housing to employees on the basis of 'managerial judgements of the worker's union affiliation, politics and docility. . . . [For] some time Fiat systematically transferred all known members of FIOM, its CGIL metal workers union, to a particular plant which was shortly afterwards shut down. . . . If there are Communists in a man's family, he is not hired. . . . There are no doubt exceptions, but some such policy is commonly found throughout Italian industry' (Edelman and Fleming, quoted Flanagan *et al.*, p. 512).

Tough measures were encouraged by the United States, which threatened to withdraw contracts from companies with CGIL majorities on works councils.

So, it is hardly surprising that real wages rose less rapidly than productivity and hence that profitability and competitiveness improved. Nor is it surprising that the accumulation of capital was accompanied by an accumulation of employee grievances. Social steam was building up in a situation in which no effective institutional safety valves existed.

An opportunity for some of this pressure to vent itself was provided in the early sixties. Italy shared in the European boom of the period and the consequent general tightening of labour markets. In the key northern industrial region of Lombardy official unemployment fell to 1.7 per cent in 1962 and 1963.

This strengthened labour's hand. Workers could now press for improvements. The government could have clamped down at an early stage with tough deflationary policies. But it pursued accommodating policies at first and did not deflate until 1964.

The Christian Democrats wanted an alliance with the Socialists. They had consistently failed to push through reforms when governing alone. They were also losing votes to the left: in 1948 the Christian Democrats received 49 per cent of the votes while the Communists and Socialists together polled 31 per cent; by 1963 the Christian Democrats' share had fallen to 38 per cent and the Socialists and Communists' had risen to 39 per cent. Finally, the Socialists had become more acceptable to the Christian Democrats because they had begun to distance themselves from the Communists after 1956.

The Socialists' price for the deal was a redistribution to labour. The Christian Democrats paid up by accommodating the wage explosions. The governor of the Bank of Italy – a Christian Democrat and strong supporter of rapprochement with the Socialists – relaxed monetary policy during the strike wave to 'permit' the wage rises of 1962 and 1963.

The big wage increases were led – not for the last time – by the metal workers, who concluded a new agreement late in 1962. Manufacturing money wages skyrocketed, with national rates rising by 10.7 per cent in 1962 and 14.7 per cent in 1963, accompanied by significant wage drift.

Since manufacturing productivity rose by only 3.6 per cent a year between 1961 and 1964, this implied some combination of higher inflation and lower profitability. With world manufacturing prices growing at less than 1 per cent a year, international competition prevented much passing on of higher unit labour costs. So labour's share in the value of manufacturing output rose from 80 per cent in 1960 to 87 per cent in 1964. Profits and international competitiveness suffered accordingly.

Neither the government nor the employers were prepared to accept redistribution on this scale. Both tried to reverse it.

The government deflated sharply in 1964 and unemployment began to rise steeply, reaching 5.4 per cent in 1965. This severely weakened the unions. Nationally, this can be seen most clearly in the poor settlement achieved by the metal workers. Their three-year agreement was due for renegotiation in 1965. But the employers persuaded them to hold off until 1966, when they settled for a mere 5 per cent rise over the three years to 1969. National no-strike agreements were also concluded for continuous process industries.

Weakness at plant level was reflected in sharply negative wage drift in 1964 and 1965. Employers also took the opportunity to launch an assault on working practices.

'If one reads the union press; if one follows case histories of individual factories, one obtains the impression of a general intensification of the work process, which came in different ways and used different methods: reduction in labour-time on a particular machine operation; supervision of an increased number of machines; increased assembly line speeds; spread of incentive payments systems; increase in heavy and onerous work loads' (M. Salvati, quoted Flanagan *et al.*, p. 519).

These policies achieved quite a lot: 'By 1966 businesses had begun to re-establish profits through policies which aimed at reducing unit costs. The method most frequently applied was an increase in assembly line speeds unaccompanied in general by a proportional increase in wages. Similar changes were observed in almost all the factories studied' (M. Salvati, quoted Flanagan *et al.*, p. 519). Unit labour costs fell by 2.3 per cent in 1965 and 1.9 per cent in 1966.

Labour's share of manufacturing output fell from 87 per cent in 1964 to 82 per cent in 1968. International competitiveness rose: between 1961 and 1963 Italian export prices rose by 1.2 per cent relative to the EEC export price index; between 1964 and 1968 they fell by 5.4 per cent. The key role played by intensification is indicated by the sharp increase in manufacturing productivity achieved during the downturn. Between 1961 and 1963 output per head rose by 4.2 per cent; between 1965 and 1967 it rose by 7.1 per cent, despite a lower rate of accumulation in the latter period.

But this improvement in Italian business performance was once again only achieved at the expense of a powerful buildup of shopfloor grievances. As the general secretary of the CISL put it, 'In the years 1965–66, especially, a process of rationalization in the industries caused serious tensions to arise and was the cause of a new awareness of the problems of working life, this process having taken the form of a balance of forces highly unfavourable to the workers' (Reggio, quoted Flanagan *et al.*, p. 520).

These grievances were to find expression in the strike wave that occurred once economic conditions improved. This happened in 1968. Italy shared in the general European boom of the late sixties and, as labour markets tightened, the balance of industrial power tilted towards the workers. Resistance began in spring 1968 but developed only slowly. Commentators spoke of Italy's 'creeping May'. It was to take a year and a half to build up the momentum for the Hot Autumn. A milestone on the way was the onset at Pirelli in the summer of 1968 of an avalanche of wildcat strikes. Another was a dispute at Fiat in spring 1969.

A number of important changes took place over the eighteen months. One concerns the workers taking part. Grievances were felt particularly strongly by migrant workers who bore the brunt of the hardship because they were almost completely unorganized. They also suffered most from the centre-left government's failure to push through reforms – in particular, its failure to modernize the badly overstretched social infrastructure in the northern cities to which the migrants had flocked.

But they did not initiate the resistance. At the beginning their lack of experience and poor organization hampered mobilization, and so other workers struck first. The spring of 1968 strikes mainly involved older, skilled workers. The Pirelli strike was started by printers, and the Fiat dispute was led by skilled, indigenous northern workers. The young migrants first became heavily involved in the winter of 1968–9. Student activists and dissident trade union officials initially played an important role, formulating and popularizing demands. But by the autumn of 1969 the migrants dominated events.

Workers also developed new tactics. At first, industrial action took the form of short strikes – the unions' traditional weapon since the early fifties (although by the spring of 1968 the level of picketing and violence was unusually high). Later more imaginative tactics were adopted to try and achieve maximum disruption for a small loss of earnings. All-out strikes gave way to 'spot strikes', 'rolling strikes' and 'go slows'. Favourites were 'confetti strikes', where different workers struck for a set period at a time determined by the last digit or colour of their registration cards.

Picketing gave way to marches through factories, when workers would chase blacklegs and occasionally kidnap managers.

Public sector workers tried to hit at the state with minimum disruption of services to consumers. So ticket collectors would strike while train drivers worked normally.

Workers' relationships with the trade unions also changed. The unions were initially caught on the hop, because the disputes arose on the shop floor where few if any formal union representatives worked. The strike committees which mushroomed from the summer of 1968 did so outside whatever trade union structures existed (although individual union activists played a key role). The trade unions did not respond to events in a unified way until the summer of 1969.

When they did, they centred their national claims around the four basic demands coming from the shop floor. These were for higher wages, reduced differentials, greater workplace control and more shopfloor participation in bargaining. They also worked hard to channel shopfloor activity through new plant-level union structures. They demanded, and often won, access to factories for trade union officials. Workers would sometimes carry the officials, who had previously been barred from entry, shoulder-high through the gates. The unions then organized massive workplace meetings to discuss national claims – something unknown since the immediate postwar period. Two or three thousand such meetings were held.

The metal workers' agreement of December 1969 was the key breakthrough on pay and conditions. It included a flat-rate increase of 65 lire an hour (nearly 10 per cent of average hourly earnings), a progressive reduction in weekly working hours to forty by 1972, equal treatment of blue- and white-collar workers when sick, and overtime limits with compensation for lost earnings. It required, for the first time, shopfloor ratification. It also broke the dam for other sectors.

Another crucial agreement was the 1970 Workers' Charter. This removed all obstacles to union activity at plant level and granted time and facilities. It formed the basis for the development of plant-level bargaining in the big factories, which was to characterize the Italian economy throughout the seventies.

May 1968

Unlike the steady buildup in Italy, the French general strike of May-June 1968 was wholly unexpected.

On 22 March 1968 students at Nanterre University formed the Mouvement du 22 Mars during an occupation over the state of higher education. This new organization united the previously fragmented student left. On 2 May the dean closed Nanterre indefinitely, saying, 'There is a strange climate in the faculty . . . a very real war psychosis' (quoted Posner, p. 64). Communist Party leader Marchais denounced the students in these words, 'The pseudo-revolutionaries of Nanterre and anywhere else labour in vain, they will change nothing of historical reality' (ibid.). The authorities evidently felt less sanguine. They ordered 500 riot police (CRS) to surround the building.

Next day the rector of the Sorbonne summoned police to a student protest against the closure of Nanterre. The CRS fired tear-gas canisters and arrested 600 students. The Sorbonne and science faculty were closed. The National Union of University Teachers called a protest strike.

On 6 May the CRS broke up a 60,000-strong demonstration by students and teachers in Paris. Over seven hundred demonstrators received treatment in hospital. Students erected barricades and strikes began to spread throughout the nation's universities and high schools (*lycées*). The second largest trade union federation, the CFDT, supported the students. The largest, Communist Party federation, the CGT, did not. The next day the Communist Party denounced the demonstration as the act of pampered adventurists.

On 8 May a student demonstration in Marseilles was attended by a large number of workers. The next day the CGT in Dijon supported a student demonstration, against the instructions of head office.

On Friday 10 May students occupied the Latin quarter of Paris and built sixty barricades. The CRS attacked, reportedly raping several women on the streets. Twenty of the thirty Paris *lycées* were now on strike, and over three hundred and fifty were occupied nationwide. The trade union federations called a general strike for 13 May to protest at government repression.

The strike was a major success. Demonstrations were the largest since the war. The CGT failed in its attempt to separate worker and student contingents. The CRS withdrew from the Sorbonne, and students occupied the building, decking it out with red flags and a barrier proclaiming 'Labourers and workers are invited to come and discuss their common problems with the university students'. It became the headquarters and shop window of the movement. Students' action committees began coordinating demonstrations and contacting workers' organizations. Immediate relations were established with workers at Renault, Citroën, Air-France, Rhône-Poulenc and the Paris metro.

On 14 May workers at Sud-Aviation in Nantes locked the director in his office and occupied the plant. Broadcasting workers voted to strike in protest at media coverage of events. By the end of the day almost all universities were occupied or on strike, as were many hospitals.

On 15 May CFDT leaders shared a platform with students at Sorbonne. Prime minister Georges Pompidou said that 'groups of enragés [roughly "rabid extremists" – the term used to describe the extreme left in the French revolution of 1789] are encouraging the spread of disorder with the aim of destroying society . . .' Students adopted the slogan, 'Nous sommes de plus en plus enragés'. By then all the Renault plants had been occupied and students and workers held joint meetings to plan future action at Renault and Sud-Aviation. The CGT was rapidly losing control of even its most loyal factories.

By 17 May all air traffic had been halted and the Post Office workers had struck. Many occupied factories were organizing crêches and discussions for local residents. In the Loire-Atlantique region distribution had broken down entirely. Students, workers and peasants formed a joint committee to organize supplies. The police trade union warned that its members were close to striking. Students set out on a 'Long March' across Paris from the Sorbonne to the Renault works. Despite CGT opposition they were warmly received. By the next day the railways were paralysed and Paris bus stations, metro lines and post offices had been occupied. The actors' trade union demanded the right to decide democratically on what plays to perform. French film makers broke up the Cannes festival in solidarity. Radio journalists took control of news bulletins. The CFDT called for democratization of industry.

The government set up Committees for the Defence of the Republic. Extreme right-wing groups offered support in exchange for the release of imprisoned right-winger, General Salan. A public opinion poll showed 55 per cent support for the students and 60 per cent for a 'new society'.

On 19 May Socialist Party leader Mendès-France demanded the resignation of the government. De Gaulle announced, 'Les réformes, oui, le chienlit [untranslatable army vulgarity] non!' Students adopted the slogan, 'Le chienlit, c'est lui!' Strikes now covered all transport, nationalized industries, metals, banking and public services.

Next day all mines and ports closed, Michelin and Peugeot workers struck and the non-union work force at Citroën occupied the plant. CGT secretary Séguy announced that he was not concerned with such 'vacuous ideas as workers' control, reform of society and other inventions'. Rather, 'going the whole hog means a general rise in wages, guaranteed employment, an earlier retirement age, reduction in working hours without loss of pay, and defence and extension of such trade union rights in the factory'. But the CGT technicians' section came out in support of the students and for workers' control.

By 21 May 10 million workers were on strike. The employers association headquarters was occupied. Young magistrates formed a union and voted to establish an independent judicial system. The government withdrew facilities for independent radio stations.

On 24 May police stations were sacked and the stock exchange set alight. Police attacked bystanders and Red Cross workers. The largest peasant demonstrations in French history took place. Workers at the right-wing newspaper *Le Figaro* refused to print an article by sociologist Raymond Aron unless he had 'more respect for the facts'.

Next day the government began negotiations with trade union leaders. The Socialist Party's François Mitterrand demanded elections. On 26 May the left made big gains in local elections in Dijon.

On 27 May the government, the employers and the CFDT and CGT concluded the 'Grenelle agreements' embodying a 10 per cent across-the-board wage rise, an increase in the minimum wage, a small cut in working hours and a marginal extension of trade union rights. Up and down the country factory meetings debated the agreements and rejected them overwhelmingly. The Loire-Atlantique CGT left the federation, declaring that 'the struggle is not economic but political'. The CFDT then refused to sign the agreements and called for intensification of the strike movement.

The government halted the distribution of petrol and the Committees for the Defence of the Republic began distributing arms. De Gaulle left the country for Baden-Baden to consult with French army commander General Massau, who agreed, in return for the release of General Salan, that the army would support any legal government but would not intervene openly unless the Communist Party called for insurrection. In reporting what little was known about these discussions at the time, the *Economist* warned of 'the danger that some as yet unknown army officer, drumming his fingers in some provincial headquarters, will decide that enough is enough' (1 June 1968).

Meanwhile the communists refused to support the left's call for a transitional government headed by Mendès-France on the grounds that he was too closely associated with the new movement. The national news agency and the major publishing houses struck. The strike movement had reached its peak.

On 30 May pro-Gaullists were supplied with petrol for carefully organized massive demonstrations (1 million in Paris alone). Slogans included 'Cohn-Bendit [a German Jewish student leader] to Dachau'. Right-wing groups fired on left-wing demonstrators. De Gaulle dissolved the National Assembly, announced elections for 23 June and 30 June and formed a new government of similar complexion to the old.

Negotiations began in most factories. The CGT promised to respect any agreements reached. A despondent Renault worker remarked, 'It seems to me that we came very close to something new.' Close, but not quite close enough. On 7 June the CRS occupied the Renault plant at Flins after pitched battle. Two days later the exiled leader of the extreme French settlers in Algeria, Georges Bidault, returned to France. Many foreign students and workers were deported. On 11 June two workers were killed at Peugeot and a student at Melun. Several left-wing organizations were banned. On 15 June Salan was released. On 16 June the CRS took the Sorbonne. Next day Renault returned to work. On 20 June Peugeot went back and the first sackings of trade union leaders occurred. On 23 June the Gaullists took a big lead in the first round of the elections. One million workers were still on strike. On 30 June the Gaullists completed their election victory. France had returned to work and to bourgeois normality.

The underlying cause of the French general strike was the same as that of the other strike waves. France, like Italy and Germany, had experienced a wage explosion in the European boom of the early sixties. In 1962 and 1963 private sector wages rose by 10.8 and 11.1 per cent respectively and those in the public sector by 17.0 and 14.6 per cent. With prices rising by only 4.8 per cent in each year, this implied considerable real wage increases and a sharp fall in profitability. The share of profits in manufacturing fell from 23.9 per cent in 1960 to 19.8 per cent in 1963. For business as a whole the fall was from 24.0 per cent to 21.9 over the same period. Since French prices were rising considerably more rapidly than those in the United States and Germany, it also implied a loss of competitiveness.

The 1963 Stabilization Plan was designed to restore profits and competitiveness. These policies were incorporated into the Fifth Plan, formulated in 1964 and 1965, which aimed at an annual rate of growth of profits of 8.6 per cent between 1964 and 1970. Planned wage growth was restricted to 3.3 per cent a year. After abortive negotiations on a voluntary incomes policy between October 1963 and January 1964, the government adopted four major policies towards this end.

One was deflation. Registered unemployment rose from 1.4 per cent in 1961–3 to 2.7 per cent in 1968. Another policy was control of public sector wages. The Toutée procedure, adopted in May 1964, fixed an aggregate figure for wage increases in particular sectors, leaving the distribution of the overall increase to be negotiated between unions and management. A third device was the use of 'Contract Programme' agreements negotiated with major companies. These covered pricing policy and the principle was that companies were allowed to raise prices sufficiently to rebuild profit margins, providing they gave certain guarantees on employment, exports, investment and wages.

The agreements were confidential and their content unknown to the work force. By 1969 some 85 per cent of industry was covered by them.

The final policy was the encouragement of a major merger drive to promote rationalization. This was part of de Gaulle's attempt to modernize an industrially backward France – 'to make her marry her century', as he put it.

The policies were fairly successful. The rate of growth of real wages in the private sector fell to 3.9 per cent a year in 1965 and 1966, and 3.4 per cent in 1967. Public sector wages were squeezed tighter still, and in four years fell 9 per cent behind the private sector. The annual value of mergers more than trebled from a fairly stable trend in 1966 and 1967.

French inflation slowed to a rate comparable with that in Germany and the United States. Deflation hit productivity growth which slowed down somewhat. The share of profits in both manufacturing and business showed little change, despite lower capacity utilization. As in most deflationary periods, profitability did not rise immediately. But the potential for profitable production did improve, as the post-May 1968 expansion demonstrated.

This modest success was bought at the expense of mounting employee grievances. These included the slow growth of real earnings overall and, for public sector workers, the deterioration in their position compared to the private sector. The dislocations resulting from rationalization were also important. A government report, issued shortly after the May events, summarized their causes as: 'a failure to comprehend the resistance to change, to prepare the groundwork for unprecedented dislocation resulting from mergers, combinations, business failures and dismissals, which accompanies modernization. The changes on the labour market had come with greater rapidity than anticipated, too much reliance had been placed on the automatic adjustments, the mobility, of the market mechanism' (quoted Flanagan *et al.*, p. 605). In this sense May 1968 was the price de Gaulle paid for his attempt at a shotgun wedding between French industry and the twentieth century.

Two main differences, besides the obvious ones of speed, scale and aspirations, distinguish the French strike waves from the Italian. One is the fact that, while in Italy a tightening of the labour market played a key role, in France the strike occurred in the context of the highest levels of unemployment and excess capacity since 1960. The other difference is that the Hot Autumn permanently altered both industrial relations and economic performance in Italy, whereas the altogether more dramatic French experience brought no comparable long-term changes.

The students' revolt was clearly important to the timing of events in France. This was itself closely linked to the accumulated grievances of the workers, being also largely a product of de Gaulle's modernization strategy. In the fifties university student numbers had risen only slowly, from 135,000 in 1949 to 220,000 in 1960. In the sixties the pace accelerated: 520,000 enrolled in the autumn of 1967. This growth far outstripped the provision of facilities. In the academic year 1967–8 there were 30,000 too many students in Paris alone.

The government's response was a plan to replace the baccalauréat system, which guaranteed places to those obtaining certain qualifications, with one of competitive selection roughly along British lines. The occupation at Nanterre which gave birth to the 22 Mars movement was to protest against this proposal. The government's repressive response played a role in building sympathy for the students. Workers would probably have been less inclined to support them if their protests had met with reasoned discussion rather than tear gas.

Finally, the structure and traditions of the French labour movement were important. Collective bargaining hardly existed under de Gaulle. Union membership fell rapidly to around half of the immediate postwar level. In 1968 only around 15 per cent of the work force was unionized. Throughout the fifties and early sixties the level had been lower still. This did not reflect a few well-organized sectors and a larger number of unorganized ones as was the case in the United States, for example, where the average level of unionization was similar. In the private sector printing was the only heavily unionized industry. Unionization was high in the public sector but union activity restricted to dealing with individual grievances and the empty version of wage bargaining embodied in the Toutée procedures. So employers and the government could virtually ignore trade unions if they wished. Under de Gaulle they opted almost unanimously to do so.

The low level of unionization did not simply reflect apathy or a lack of militancy. All companies with more than fifty employees were required by law to have enterprise committees elected annually by the work force (their function being largely consultative, with some responsibility for health and safety). In 1967 and 1968 turnout for these elections was around 75 per cent, with 80–90 per cent of the vote going to union candidates.

But the low level of unionization did influence the form of industrial struggle. It meant that major strikes almost invariably began from the bottom up and were largely outside the control of the unions. As one commentator put it, the unions 'functioned as skilled surfboard riders'.

Strikes were often imitative, a few key factories providing a 'signal'. In 1968 that initiating role was played largely by the Renault and Sud-Aviation plants.

The chief reason why the May events failed to transform the industrial relations structure – let alone society as a whole – is the behaviour of the CGT and the Communist Party. The CGT was far and away the most powerful union federation. It had around three times the membership of the CFDT and received about half of the votes cast in enterprise committee elections. The Communist Party was a major force in French politics. We have already seen the role that these organizations played at key stages of the struggle.

The *Economist* described the situation vividly: 'Whenever one hears somebody on the French radio vituperating against "'adventurers" one can be sure that M. Cohn-Bendit or some other leftist student is the target. But one cannot guess the political colour of the speaker. It might be a Gaullist or it might be a Communist. On the other hand, if somebody talks about revolution, structural changes or socialist society, one is safe in assuming he is not a Communist' (25 May 1968).

It also provided an astute analysis:

A Revolution set alight by students, snuffed out by Communists
A modern revolution requires the coincidence of a revolutionary situation and a party or organization ready to seize power. As France comes virtually to a halt, the situation might look revolutionary. But the party which has always claimed the revolutionary role now shows no signs of fulfilling it. The Communists have climbed on the bandwagon, but only to put the brakes on. This is not because they want to preserve General de Gaulle's regime. It is because they are using a revolutionary

weapon – general and unlimited strikes – in order to achieve a parliamentary aim, the formation of a popular front government (*Economist*, 25 May 1968).

No one can be certain what would have happened if the Communist Party had tried to lead a revolution in May 1968. Indeed such a question is virtually meaningless. The Communist Party's behaviour was no sudden aberration. Its attempts to strangle the revolutionary movement at birth during May 1968 were consistent with the approach taken over the previous thirty years, including the immediate postwar period (Part I). Two things are clear, however. Its strategy was an abject failure on its own terms, for the Gaullists romped home in the June elections. Secondly, by denouncing the CFDT's demands for industrial democracy and restricting negotiations to the traditional issues of pay and hours, the CGT ensured that the May events would have little impact on the future structure of industrial relations. Presented with a spontaneous, unlimited general strike, the CGT failed even to build a mass shopfloor union movement.

Clampdown and the 1970–1 recession

For the ACCs as a whole, both monetary and fiscal policy swung sharply towards restriction between 1968 and 1969. This picture is dominated by developments in the United States, but a definite shift towards restriction is observable elsewhere, prompted by the acceleration of prices noted above and by growing economic and social unrest.

The effect of this shift was a highly synchronized but relatively mild recession. Idle capacity rose by about 3 percentage points between the second halves of 1969 and 1971; rather more in the United States and Japan and considerably less in Europe. From peak to trough, registered unemployment rose from 3.5 per cent to 5.9 per cent in the United States and from 1.8 per cent to 3.0 per cent in Europe. Inflation peaked at 5.0 per cent in the United States in 1970. As a result of the recession and price controls it fell to a trough of 3.3 per cent in 1972. In the wake of the wage explosions inflation rose more in Europe. It peaked at 7.5 per cent in 1971 and thereafter fell in only a few countries.

Policy-makers felt general disappointment with the stubbornness of prices in the face of rising unemployment. The term 'stagflation' became common parlance and increasing doubts were expressed about the effectiveness of Keynesian 'fine tuning'.

The breakup of Bretton Woods

We left the fortunes of the international financial system and of the dollar with the 1968 decision – implemented in 1970 – to issue special drawing rights (SDRs) on the IMF (Chapter 10).

This might have shored up the dollar for a time had the US balance of payments improved as expected. But it did not. The current account deteriorated as the trade balance shrank; business investment overseas doubled between 1965 and 1970. The situation was concealed in 1968 and 1969 as short-term capital was attracted to US banks by high interest rates: $12 billion flowed in during those two years, more than covering the long-term capital outflow. Simultaneously, foreign central banks' dollar holdings fell. But this policy was drastically reversed in 1970 when monetary policy became extremely permissive. The US money supply was allowed to grow at 10 per cent per year or more for the next four years, having been virtually unchanged in 1969. Predictably, the $12 billion 'hot money' left US banks as interest rates fell. Added to an already heavy outflow of long-term capital, the flight of dollars became a rout. In 1970 foreign central banks acquired $17 billions of dollars, and the United States lost $2½ billions of reserves. Reserve backing for the dollar deteriorated more in 1970 than during the previous decade.

In May 1971 the publication of figures showing a marked worsening of the US current account coincided with a further reduction in interest rates. Money flowed out of the United States into almost all OECD countries, but especially those with strong currencies – Germany, Switzerland, Austria and the Netherlands. Germany alone received $9 billion in 1970 and $4 billion in the first five months of 1971.

The countries receiving the dollars were largely powerless to do anything about it, despite their fears that credit would expand and inflation rise. The sums involved made it difficult to prevent the inflows from boosting the money supply by selling bonds, and in any case, if this were attempted it would only prevent interest rates from falling and keep the currency attractive to those anxious to get out of dollars. Initially many central banks made the best of a bad job by loaning the dollars to borrowers in Europe via the so-called Euromarkets, where a premium over US interest rates could be obtained. This stimulated the growth of these 'offshore' markets for dollar loans. The funds were often borrowed by speculators who then reinvested them in strong currencies in the expectation of revaluations, a hideous spiral by which central banks were providing funds to speculators who stood to make a profit from them if the currency was revalued.

In March 1971 central banks agreed to freeze the deposit of reserves on the Euromarkets. But speculative pressure continued and high demand for Eurodollar loans pushed interest rates on the market well above the usual 0.5 per cent premium on US rates. This in turn led to further withdrawals of dollars from the United States for deposit on the Euromarkets. Between April and June 1971 speculation against the dollar ran at an annual rate of $14 billion. A number of foreign exchange markets closed temporarily and hasty exchange-rate adjustments were made, with strong currencies being revalued or, as in the case of the Deutschmark, floated. This proved to be only a warm-up.

Action began in earnest in the summer. United States trade figures for the second quarter of 1971 showed a deficit for the first time. Between July and September hot money flowed out of the dollar at an annual rate of $35 billion. During the first two weeks of August non-US central banks began welshing heavily on their agreement not to convert dollar reserves into gold, and US gold reserves fell alarmingly. President Nixon, whose grasp of such matters was immortalized on tape in 'Well, I don't give a [expletive deleted] about the lira' (quoted Williamson, p. 175), responded on 15 August 1971 by suspending indefinitely the convertibility of the dollar into gold. He also introduced a 10 per cent surcharge on imports. For the next four months all major currencies floated.

After some hard bargaining, in December 1971 the major capitalist powers signed the Smithsonian Agreement which established a new system of fixed exchange rates. The United States accepted a cosmetic increase in the price of gold following European insistence that it must be seen to devalue. But nobody seriously proposed the convertibility of the dollar into gold. Indeed, it was out of the question given the dollar's enfeebled position. The events of that year, combining as they did an enormous outflow of dollars (the overall deficit for 1971 of $30 billion exceeded by 70 per cent the cumulative total for the previous ten years) with considerable 'cashing in' of dollars for gold in the weeks preceding the suspension of convertibility, reduced massively the extent of potential gold backing for the dollar. At the beginning of 1971 US gold reserves had been sufficient to cover 32 per cent of foreign dollar holdings. Twelve months later they could cover only 18 per cent.

The further diminution of the role of gold amounted, then, to little more than a recognition of the existing situation. The main benefit to the United States of the Smithsonian Agreement lay in the new exchange rates which embodied a 9 per cent devaluation of the dollar in relation to other currencies compared with the pre-August rates and thus increased US competitiveness. This devaluation was much smaller, though, than the United States had wanted. During the negotiations the United States indicated that it was seeking a rate for the dollar that would yield a $13 billion boost to the US current account. This would give a current account surplus of $9 billion a year, enough to finance a capital outflow of $6 billion a year and to improve confidence in the dollar by reducing liabilities to central banks by $3 billion a year.

The United States continued with its permissive monetary policies and dollar outflows began to mount again in the second half of 1972. The crunch came early in the next year. The events of 1971 assume the proportions of a small-town poker game in comparison to the speculation of February and March 1973. In February the Smithsonian Agreement was seriously breached when the yen was floated (sterling had already been floated in June 1972). The dollar was also devalued by a further 10 per cent in recognition that the Smithsonian Agreement, hailed by Nixon as 'the most significant monetary agreement in the history of the modern world' (quoted Gilbert, p. 164), was insufficient to restore US competitiveness. This had been demonstrated by the rise in US imports of manufactured goods, which rocketed by 27 per cent in 1972 following a 20 per cent rise in 1971: 'it was evident that industry abroad was making major adjustments and marketing efforts to enlarge its share of the US market' (Gilbert, p. 105). Even this further devaluation failed to restore confidence as the US treasury secretary announced that the United States would not intervene to support the dollar and intended to remove all controls on capital exports.

On the single day of 1 March 1973, Germany absorbed $2.7 billion, and in the first quarter of 1973 as a whole the US reserve position deteriorated by $10 billion.

On 19 March the major central banks renounced the commitment to maintain their exchange rates within a band of ± 2.25 per cent with respect to the dollar. This constituted the formal abandonment of the second and, since the suspension of dollar/gold convertibility in 1971, the only remaining basic principle of the Bretton Woods system which was thus now dead.

Dollar devaluation

The determination of the US authorities to secure a substantial devaluation of the dollar against other currencies and consequent improvement of the US trade balance is beyond doubt. Whether their monetary policy from as early as 1970 was designed to force such a devaluation is another question. On the one hand, driving interest rates down would predictably lead to a dollar outflow. It has been argued that the form the expansion took – monetary expansion rather than tax cuts – is proof of this intention. On the other hand, the United States carried out a series of crisis measures apparently aimed at shoring up the dollar. In the last week before convertibility was suspended in 1971, $2 billion was borrowed by the United States from other central banks to try and hold the line. The United States certainly pursued a policy of 'benign neglect' towards the dollar, expanding the economy for domestic reasons with little regard to the effect on the exchange rate. By early 1973 it was clear that they would do little or nothing to protect the exchange rate from the impact of domestic policies, and indeed increasingly resented the attempts of European and Japanese central banks to prevent the dollar rate from finding its own level.

Such a position would be quite incomprehensible if the main thrust of US policy was an attempt to run as large as possible a balance of payments deficit (on current and long-term capital account) in order to grab real resources from the rest of the world in exchange for paper dollars. On the contrary, given the heavy and increasing rate of capital exports, which was a major concern of many of the dominating US multinationals, it was far better from the United States' point of view that these capital exports should be mainly financed by a current account surplus rather than by endless piling up of US liabilities abroad to foreign central banks. The return paid on these liabilities was certainly low (the short-term interest rate in real terms averaged 0.4 per cent over the years 1968–74). But the onslaught of European and Japanese competition made it far more important to attempt to maintain the position of domestic manufacturing industry with a lower exchange rate. This would help domestic industry to maintain both its market share and its profitability, as European and Japanese firms would be obliged to increase their dollar prices to compensate for a fall in the dollar against their currencies. Indeed, the huge capital exports by US business provided a 'justification' for the United States running a current account surplus and were used as such during the Smithsonian discussions over the size of adjustment of the exchange rate. This argument was to be repeated in succeeding years during discussions over reform of the international monetary system, in which the United States consistently held that balance of payments targets should be defined in terms of current and capital account combined.

So the United States 'needed' a current account surplus to finance its capital exports. Indeed the United States could, and did, also claim that it actually required a greater surplus than this so that it could begin to chip away at the huge 'overhang' of dollar liabilities with a view to restoring convertibility of the dollar to the SDR once confidence had been restored. The basic negotiating position of the United States, presented to the IMF in November 1972, was that countries should peg their currencies to the SDR, but that they would be obliged to devalue or revalue if their reserves fell below or rose above certain predefined warning levels. This was directly aimed at the 'surplus countries', especially Japan and Germany, and was an attempt to bind them into a system where they could not pile up persistent surpluses.

The surplus countries

Such a 'reserve indicator plan', as it was called, was never a very serious possibility. Under it, major changes in reserves would have created an overwhelming presumption that a change in the exchange rate was around the corner, and thus encouraged speculation on what was in effect a certain bet. But the significant point is that it underlines the United States' determination to prevent the persistent undervaluation of the mark or the yen. Such a concern is explained by the fact that these countries had repeatedly demonstrated their willingness to go to enormous lengths (in effect taxing imports of capital, encouraging exports of capital and, even in the case of Japan, organizing plans for importing huge stockpiles of raw materials) in order to prevent an upward movement of their currencies. If these countries felt they were being exploited by having to run a surplus and thus provide finance for the US deficit, such behaviour would be quite incomprehensible. On the contrary, their exporting sectors, extremely powerful in both countries, had a very strong interest in maintaining the exchange rate at a low level in order to generate the maximum possible export surplus. This was not primarily due to some old-fashioned desire to pile up reserves, however comforting that might be for central bankers and useful when it came to securing influence by making loans to weaker countries. The fundamental concern was rather their export sectors' immediate interest in sales of, and profits on, exports. Revaluation, while cutting the cost of living for workers as the price of imported goods fell, would reduce their ability to compete profitably abroad, especially in the American market if the revaluation was with respect to the dollar.

Although the Europeans and Japanese firmly resisted the reserve indicator plan which would apply heavy pressure on surplus countries, they insisted that the United States should in effect reinstitute convertibility. 'From the US standpoint, the demand for dollar convertibility was simply the demand for an exchange value guarantee on the fiduciary instruments [dollars] that financed their deficits, while surplus countries retained their freedom to allow their surpluses to pile up' (Gilbert, p. 185). What they were not prepared to countenance was that 'the United States should redeem its unwanted dollars in goods, by undervaluing the dollar and thereby running a large and persistent export surplus: such a treatment was wholly unacceptable to export interests in Europe which would suffer the increased US competition' (Tew, p. 192). Precisely the same fear of revaluation underlay the continual reluctance of the German and Japanese authorities to see their currencies held as reserves by other countries. Quite simply, such an additional demand for the currencies concerned would help keep them at a higher level, with a consequent reduction in their export surpluses. Whatever prestige and influence might be gained by being a reserve currency was wholly insufficient to compensate for export profits being lost by overvaluation.

US competitiveness and payments

The successive downward movements in the relative value of the dollar brought a marked improvement in US competitiveness. The dollar fell by 24 per cent against the yen between 1970 and 1973, and 24 per cent against the Deutschmark; against currencies on average (weighted by their importance in US trade) the fall was 15 per cent. Moreover, since unit costs actually rose less in the United States than in competing countries over the same period, the improvement in US cost competitiveness was actually 27 per cent on average. In dollar terms, unit labour costs in US manufacturing rose by 6 per cent, in Japan by 72 per cent and in Germany by 64 per cent.

This improvement in competitiveness undoubtedly contributed to arresting the deterioration in the US balance of payments. For several years after 1972 the level of net imports of consumer goods stabilized. Net exports of capital goods doubled between 1972 and 1974 (assisted by strong demand from the oil producers). As demand for food rose, the United States suddenly became a major exporter of agricultural goods, the surplus on that account rising from $1½ billion in 1972 to $10½ billion in 1974. A large surplus would have resulted but for the $20 billion rise in the cost of oil imports as the OPEC price increases coincided with – indeed, were encouraged by – rising US oil imports (Chapter 13). Even though the current account was back in surplus in 1974, it was not nearly enough to cover the outflow of capital, and the result was that dollar liabilities rose by nearly $9 billion.

The story of the US balance of payments during the breakup of the old international monetary system is summarized in Table 12.2.

Despite the huge amount of interest received (nearly $9 billion a year), there was on average over the period hardly any current account surplus. To the long-term capital outflow of $42 billion had to be added a new element, a short-term capital outflow of $22 billion, as foreign firms and individuals either withdrew their cash from US banks or increased their borrowing from them. The total outflow of some $60 billion was financed by increases in the reserves held by the central banks of the industrial countries.

Of course, no foreign central bank was compelled to hold a single additional dollar – indeed, they could have unloaded part of their existing holdings. When they could not get gold for their dollars after 1971 (the US gold stock fell by only $2½ billion over

Table 12.2 US balance of payments, 1968–74

$ billion

Merchandise trade	− 9.3
Services and remittances	−10.2
Net military transactions	−19.8
US government grants (ex. military)	−16.7
Net interest and dividends received	61.4
Current account balance	5.4
Direct investment (net)	−42.2
Investment in shares and bonds (net)	10.8
Government loans	−11.1
Long-term capital	−42.5
Balance on current and long-term capital	−37.1
Dollars held abroad by private sector[1]	−22.5
Financed by	
Dollars held abroad in official reserves	58.1
Reduction in US reserves	1.5
(of which gold)	(2.4)

1. Includes net short-term capital.

Source: US, *Survey of Current Business*, June 1982.

the whole period), they only acquired these dollars because they were prepared to sell their own currencies in order to prevent them rising further. The reason why they maintained these holdings in dollars, rather than selling them for some other currency, was that dollar investments in New York remained attractive despite the decline in the relative value of the dollar in the early seventies. In 1974 the reserves of the industrialized countries stopped growing, while simultaneously the reserves of the OPEC producers shot up by $31 billion. Most of these reserves were held in the Eurodollar market, which meant that rather than deposit them in New York the central banks of the oil producers deposited them in banks outside the United States. Many of these were the overseas branches of US banks which made a healthy margin in acting as the go-betweens between the OPEC members, who wanted to lend dollars, and the countries with balance of payments deficits which wanted to borrow them.

US capital undoubtedly benefited from its ability to borrow via foreign central banks' holdings of dollar securities. Between 1967 and 1974 net US receipts of profits and interest rose from $5.3 billion to $15.5 billion. In contrast to the preceding period, none of this rise can be attributed to the investment of current account surpluses. A substantial part of the increase certainly represented increased profits in money terms on the existing stock of US industrial investment abroad. But a substantial part must also have resulted from the new investment overseas which was now being wholly financed by borrowing overseas at a very low real rate of interest. Shorn of all element of compulsion, now that the United States was no longer even pretending that the dollar was convertible into gold, the rise in official holdings of dollars showed that dollars were the best asset to hold. The United States was reaping the benefit of its industrial and financial might without having to resort to any crude use of political power.

When the issue of international monetary reform had been seriously debated in 1972 the United States started from the position that 'the system should neither bar nor encourage official holdings of foreign exchange', suggesting that 'the United States still thought of the SDR as providing a substitute for gold rather than for the dollar' (Williamson, p. 176). Although the United States accepted the case for the dollar eventually being convertible into SDRs, in its view this had to result from the dollar being sufficiently competitive to generate enough capital and current account surpluses over a period to make convertibility a reality. The European (and Japanese) unwillingness to accept this is shown at a theoretical level by their refusal to accept proposals which would have required revaluations, and in practice by their preparedness to pile up dollar reserves.

The Europeans suggested that the IMF should convert their existing dollar holdings into SDRs. This would protect the holdings against a future decline of the dollar, but at the cost of pushing the risk on to the United States if it were required to compensate the IMF (which would take over these dollar holdings) for any losses. This was simply keeping their cake (dollars earned by running of vast surpluses through refusal to revalue) and eating it (obliging the United States to guarantee the value of the assets they accumulated via these surpluses). There has never been any reason why the United States should accept this type of proposal. Limiting the size of US deficits by forcing revaluations (as in the US proposals for a 'reserve indicator plan' in the context of fixed exchange rates) or making official statements that the dollar is too high (the 'open-mouth policy', subsequently implemented on occasion under floating exchange rates) is quite consistent with the dollar maintaining an international role. Such a role, which inevitably involves the dollar's use as a reserve currency, is the product of US industrial and financial power, and was hardly eroded by the end of dollar convertibility and of the fixed exchange rate system.

The 1972–3 mini-boom

1972 and early 1973 was a period of very rapid growth throughout the world capitalist system. Between the first halves of 1972 and 1973 world capitalist output rose by 7 per cent and industrial production by 10 per cent. This 'mini-boom' had three distinctive features, which culminated in an unprecedented rise in commodity prices.

*It was highly synchronized, occurring in all major capitalist countries at about the same time.

*It was very rapid. Although the *level* of capacity utilization reached at the height of the upswing was lower than in the previous boom (and so the extent of 'overheating', as conventionally measured, was less) the *rate* of expansion was faster than at any time since 1958–9. Moreover, capacity utilization was considerably lower when the previous upswing had begun than it was at the start of the mini-boom of 1972–3.

*It had a greater impact on prices than previous upswings of comparable magnitude. Inflation for the system as a whole, which had fallen to 4 per cent a year in the first half of 1972, rose to an annual rate of 7 per cent in the first half of 1973.

The reasons for these characteristics are complex and interrelated.

The *synchronization* happened when most governments simultaneously moved from a tight monetary and fiscal stance to expansion. US fiscal policy was expansionary in 1970 – it gave some tax relief and additional transfer payments to households – but this stimulus was subsequently eroded by rising tax bills. Elsewhere fiscal policy was generally expansionary in 1971 and 1972. This was enormously reinforced by monetary developments. The opening years of the 1970s were *the* period of easy money. In the ACCs, the money supply began to accelerate at the beginning of 1970. It grew by 12 per cent in 1971 and slightly more in 1972. Short-term interest rates halved between early 1970 and early 1972.

The expansionary policy of nearly all governments resulted from three main factors. First, the synchronized nature of the 1970–1 recession meant that governments found themselves simultaneously at a similar, recessionary phase of the cycle. Traditional Keynesian fine-tuning criteria for output and employment thus suggested expansionary policies for each country at around the same time. Second, the enormous increase in international liquidity generated by the exodus from the dollar (see above) meant that the countries which still had weak payments balances could borrow easily. Finally, an unusually large number of major elections took place in 1972. There was a presidential election in the United States, and elections for the principal legislative assemblies in Canada, Germany, Italy and Japan. Taken together, these economies produce about 70 per cent of OECD output. Electoral considerations prompted 'give-away' budgets and hence expansionary policies.

The *speed* of the upswing was largely the result of the scale of monetary and fiscal stimulus given to the system as a whole. This, in turn, was chiefly the result of two main factors. First, the high degree of synchronization. The fact that other economies are expanding adds an external stimulus to any internal impetus provided by reflation. The degree of reflation 'required' will therefore tend to be overestimated by governments in a synchronized upswing, if they rely on past experience derived from periods of less international synchronization of business cycles.

Second, the exodus from the dollar created more expansionary monetary conditions than would otherwise have been adopted by some governments. Here we can distinguish two broad groups of countries. One consists of those for whom the expansionary repercussions on domestic liquidity of balance of payments surpluses, resulting from dollar inflows, did not exceed the degree of stimulus felt desirable. The United Kingdom, Italy and, initially, France, fall into this category. For these countries, the *scale* of expansion was not affected by the dollar crisis (although the *form* may have been – the 'automatic' nature of the monetary expansion generated by dollar inflows may have bred a more monetary, and less fiscal, policy mixture than would otherwise have been adopted, and thus contributed to the easy money regime).

The other group consists of countries for whom the deterioration of the US payments balance and the inflow of speculative funds generated a faster rate of monetary expansion, and lower interest rates, than would have been adopted on purely domestic criteria. In Japan expansionary monetary policies were adopted in 1972 to offset the expected deflationary impact of the Smithsonian yen revaluation and, later, to reduce the still large payments surplus achieved under the short-lived Smithsonian regime. In Germany the maintenance of a fixed, and clearly unsustainable, exchange rate in the face of massive speculative inflows rendered domestic monetary management virtually impossible from the late 1960s to March 1973 when the Deutschmark was floated.

The rapid acceleration of prices was the result of the interaction of a number of developments. In contrast to the last fillip to inflation in Europe provided by the wage explosions at the close of the sixties, this price acceleration clearly began in goods, rather than labour, markets. Indeed, wages only began to catch up and threaten a widening wage/price spiral in 1973. The very speed of the upswing helped to push up prices because bottlenecks developed, the prices of those goods rose and 'feed-through' effects followed. But the major inflationary impetus was provided by the conjunction of two factors:

(1) Low profits (and their failure to rise during a rapid upswing) led to and combined with poor business confidence. Firms reacted to the expansion of demand by raising prices, as well as expanding output, in order to try and raise profit margins. Because low profits also militated against the use of available money for productive investment, investors were encouraged to search for short-term speculative 'killings'.

(2) The existence of very slack monetary conditions (due mainly to the dollar crisis discussed above) led to negative real rates of interest. In principle, this made profitable the speculative holding of stocks of goods whose price rose only at the average rate. More significantly, in practice it encouraged speculation in the more traditional sense – on assets whose prices were expected to rise by considerably more than the overall price level (and would indeed do so if enough speculators made similar judgements). Initially, this speculative money found its way into fairly traditional havens. The London gold price rose two and a half times between early 1972 and the middle of 1973. New house prices rose by around 50 per cent in the United Kingdom between early 1972 and early 1973. The price of developed building land in Germany rose by more than one-third between 1970 and 1972.

If speculation had been restricted to these traditional fields then the effect on the overall price level would probably have been relatively insignificant, since the feed-through effects to other goods would have been modest. But it was not. The prices of another, broader category of goods began to rise faster than the general price level and attracted enormous sums of speculative funds. The result was the commodities boom and a major upward twist to inflation.

The commodities boom

Prices on the major US and UK commodity exchanges began to rise very rapidly in 1972 and maintained the pace through 1973. In 1973 and 1974 this price rise fed through to contracts between major producers and users. The magnitude of the increase was very similar, with both types of prices more or less doubling in 'real dollar' terms. No rises of this scale have previously been recorded in peacetime.

There are a number of reasons why primary product prices should have begun to rise in real terms around this time. On the supply side, there had been underinvestment in many areas of primary production for some years. This was the result of the expectations of inadequate and wavering returns, due to gently deteriorating terms of trade between primary products and manufactures, and fear of investing in politically volatile, or potentially volatile, third world countries. There had also been a long-term rundown of producer stock levels, especially of US grain buffer stocks. Finally, specific short-term shortages arose in the early

1970s, the most important being the 1972 crop failures (when grain output was down 3 per cent on the previous year, against a trend growth rate of 3 per cent a year). Anchovies – an important source of protein for animal feed – also mysteriously disappeared from the Peruvian coast around this time.

On the demand side, the effects of the rapidity of the synchronized upswing were reinforced by the fact that the materials processing sector responded less rapidly than others. User stock levels were also historically low as a result of steady improvements in stock control techniques and expectations of relative price falls (as a result of the previous trend deterioration in the terms of trade for primary products). Finally, materials stockpiling was encouraged by the Japanese government in 1972–3 in an attempt to hold down the yen exchange rate.

Taken together, these factors were sufficient to generate commodity price rises considerably in excess of the general rate of inflation. This attracted speculative funds. Many commodity markets are institutionally well suited to speculation, having developed facilities for buying crops before they are harvested (futures markets) for small down-payments (margin trading). This speculation pushed prices up further.

There is no way to measure the significance of speculation in the commodities boom. But it must have been considerable. The scale of price rises is quite out of line with that which could plausibly be required to balance 'real' supply and demand; and quite out of line with previous responses to fluctuations in industrial production.

We know that speculation was rife in this period, for example in currencies, gold and real estate, and a number of highly publicized incidents took place in commodities markets. The tendency of official commentators, such as the OECD, to play down the role of speculation is totally unconvincing.

The above discussion does not distinguish between different primary products or markets. This reflects the fact that the commodities boom was highly generalized, and therefore unlikely to have been a freak coincidence of very different developments in different markets. But it is nevertheless worth looking at one market in some detail – that for grains. This market is quantitatively the most important (after oil, which is discussed separately in Chapter 13), and is well documented. Moreover, it was the acceleration of food prices – largely as a result of developments in the grain market – which, of any (non-oil) commodity price rise, had the greatest overall effect on inflation.

The grain market

Grain is big business, in more senses than one. In 1975 around 160 million tons were traded internationally for about $50 billion. Before the war the volume of grain exported seldom exceeded 30 million tons a year. So growth of trade had been rapid. Production for the international market is concentrated in the most powerful capitalist state: the United States accounts for around 50 per cent of world grain exports. Finally, the trade is dominated by a handful of the world's largest – and most secretive – multinationals: Cargill, Continental, Louis Dreyfus, Bunge and Andre. Frank Church, chairman of the Senate Subcommittee on multinational corporations, has said of these companies, 'No one knows how they operate, what their profits are, what they pay in taxes and what effect they have on our foreign policy – or much of anything else about them' (quoted Morgan, p. ix). Cargill boasts in its company brochure that 'some of our best customers have never heard of us' (ibid., p. 4).

During the Second World War, the United States operated a 'bare-shelves' policy towards grain stocks, fearing a repeat of the price crash which followed the First World War. But this approach was rapidly changed in the reconstruction period. Enormous bonuses and premiums were offered to farmers.

Between 1945 and 1949 the United States provided one-half of world wheat exports. Nevertheless persistent surpluses became a problem from 1948 onwards.

The strength of the farm lobby prompted the US administration to operate a price support system. Internationally it entered into a *de facto* cartel agreement with Canada, whereby export prices were kept low enough to discourage new producers.

In the 1950s, the main way of disposing of the surpluses was as 'aid'. Public law 480, passed in 1954, gave governments cheap credit when they bought US grain, initially repayable in domestic currencies. (The United States built up huge rupee balances which it eventually wrote off.) At first, one-quarter of US wheat exports and one-fifth of rice were financed under PL480. By 1959 four-fifths of wheat and nine-tenths of soyabean oil exports were paid for in this way.

In the 1960s policy moved away from PL480 towards boosting commercial exports. The United States broke the unofficial cartel with Canada and tried to shoulder her out of markets. From 1964 onwards US wheat prices were subsidized enough to undercut all comers on world markets.

In the late 1960s almost all major exporters began to cut back production, apparently believing that surpluses would otherwise become unsustainable. World food output had grown steadily in the fifties and sixties (except in 1965 and 1967, after Indian droughts). Prices were stable and stocks mounting. The prospects for the 'Green Revolution' appeared good. There was talk of India soon becoming a grain exporter and she discontinued PL480 shipments in 1971 because of shortage of storage capacity.

So the four big wheat producers (United States, Canada, Australia and Argentina) all offered large subsidies in return for acreage reductions. Their combined wheat production fell from 80 million tons in 1968 to 60 million in 1970.

But this reckoned without developments in the USSR. In the 1950s Russia was a small net exporter (there were often shortages but these were met by cutbacks in consumption, and sales were sometimes made for hard currency). But in 1962 major strikes and demonstrations against food price rises took place in Novocherkassk. Troops were brought in, about seventy-five people were killed and their families deported to Siberia. In 1963 Exportkhelb – the USSR grain trading agency – bought 6.8 million tons of wheat from Canada and 1.3 million tons from Australia. US president Kennedy was annoyed that the United States – with 16 million tons of grain in store – had lost out and authorized the sale of up to 4 million tons a year to the USSR.

At the time this was not regarded as the start of a new trend. Soviet grain production doubled between 1955 and 1972. But after the successful Polish food riots of 1970, the USSR bought 7.8 million tons from the United States, despite bumper crops. The stage was set for a major Soviet shopping spree in the event of a bad harvest.

In 1971 the USSR indicated to the United States that it was interested in regular grain purchases. The United States responded enthusiastically, offering credit (which the Russians had not asked for) in return for guaranteed sales worth $0.75 billion over three years. Negotiations moved slowly at first.

Then, in June 1972, Exportkhelb officials suddenly flew to the United States and asked Continental to quote for 4 million tons of wheat and 3 million tons of corn. Now the way the system worked was that the Department of Agriculture fixed a 'gateway' (i.e. export) price and paid the companies for any excess of inland purchasing price over this. Obviously sales of the volume requested by the Russians would push up inland prices and raise the cost of the subsidy. (Continental claimed that the assistant secretary of agriculture had guaranteed the maintenance of the subsidy system.)

This put Continental at a big advantage. They sold the Russians 8.5 million tons of grain at a slight discount on the gateway price. They could afford this because the system allowed the trader to claim the difference between inland and gateway prices either at the time of purchase *or on delivery*. Clearly, if you wait until delivery you are gambling on a rise in inland prices. Equally clearly, this is not much of a gamble if you – and only you – know you have an order for 8.5 million tons.

Six days later the United States announced that the USSR had accepted credit and the attached terms of minimum sales of $0.75 billion over three years. It did not add that the Russians had already spent almost that much. A few days later they flew home, owning the equivalent of one-third of annual US grain exports. A week later they were back. This time they bought another 6 million tons.

The US administration claimed not to have known what was going on and subsequently accused the companies of misreporting (there are limits on the volume in which companies are supposed to deal on the US grain futures markets). But contemporary CIA reports – now public – show that the CIA knew what was happening and told the Department of Agriculture.

The United States certainly benefited from the transaction. Between 1971 and 1975 the global grain trade grew by nearly 50 per cent in volume, most of the increase coming from the United States. Their farm exports rose in value from $7.6 billion in 1971 to $17.6 billion in 1973, and grain stocks fell from 23.5 million tons in the middle of 1972 to 7 million one year later. The price rises wiped out the need for farm subsidies. The companies did particularly well. Cargill's after-tax profits rose from $19.4 million in fiscal year 1971–2 to $150 million in fiscal year 1972–3. Dreyfus paid its top trader a 'special bonus' of $1.2 million and two underlings $0.75 million each. Arguably the only losers in the United States were workers faced with higher food prices.

End of an era
The mini-boom marked the end of an era. It was the last upswing before the onset of slump, stagnation and mass unemployment. So we shall briefly stand back and assess its significance.

Many of its effects are fairly obvious and generally acknowledged. Most commentators agree that the rapid price acceleration played an important role in generating high inflationary expectations, which remained remarkably resilient even under later conditions of mass unemployment. It generated further disillusionment with fine tuning and, indeed, with Keynesianism in general. This contributed towards the shift in policies of the late 1970s and early 1980s. The easy money regime focused attention on monetary policy and contributed to the significance accorded to the money supply in later years. And high demand for basic inputs including oil provided an important condition for the 1973–4 oil crisis (Chapter 13).

But conventional discussion of the breakup of the boom and its underlying causes are generally inadequate. The most influential view is that expressed by a report for the OECD, which sees the intensifying economic difficulties of these years as resulting from 'an unusual bunching of unfortunate disturbances unlikely to be repeated on the same scale, the impact of which was compounded by some avoidable errors in economic policy' (McCracken, p. 14). The 'unfortunate disturbances' are the breakup of the Bretton Woods system and the commodities boom, while the 'errors in economic policy' refer primarily to the 'all systems go' monetary policy which so many countries adopted in 1971 and which 'was the most important mishap in recent economic policy history' (McCracken, p. 51).

This account is at best naive and at worst apologetic for the behaviour of the Organization's largest member – the United States. For the 'unfortunate disturbances' were in no sense 'random shocks' and the easy money regime was only in part a policy preference. The breakup of the Bretton Woods system at the time and in the form in which it occurred, to a large degree forced an easy money regime on the rest of the system, and thereby fuelled the speculation that in turn fuelled the commodities boom. The commodities boom also affected the major capitalist powers in different ways. Commodity exporters, including the United States, benefited from the boom. Major importers, most notably Japan, were worst hit. The most obvious manifestation of this fact was a substantial reduction in the US payments deficit, a corresponding reduction in the Japanese surplus, and an increase in the deficit of a number of European countries. As the next chapter shows, the subsequent oil price rises were also to hit Germany and Japan much more heavily than the United States.

13. Oil and the Crash of 1974

The mini-boom of 1972–3 proved to be the final and most feverish phase of the long postwar boom. The 'oil crisis' of winter 1973–4 and an international crash in the summer of 1974 brought the golden years to an abrupt and painful halt.

The oil crisis

In October 1973 war broke out in the Middle East. The conflict bred solidarity among Arab oil states and gave a new impetus to the Organization of Petroleum Exporting Countries (OPEC), a cartel of the major non-US oil producers which had previously been rendered ineffective by internal divisions.

In an attempt to reduce support for Israel, OPEC announced a 10 per cent across-the-board cut in oil exports (later briefly raised to 25 per cent) and a selective embargo, directed chiefly at the United States. The oil companies dutifully followed OPEC instructions to the letter.

'When they were told to cut production, they did so without quibble. When Aramco was told to cut production by 10 per cent and then, on top of that, shut in liftings equivalent to that which had been produced for ultimate sale to the USA in pre-embargo months, the company dutifully cut production back 23 per cent below September levels. When the Saudis insisted that Aramco impose tight control over the destination of its oil, the company got tanker captains to sign affidavits as to their destination and arranged to receive cabled acknowledgements of each ship's eventual arrival at the approved port or terminal' (Turner, pp. 135–6). Exxon even acceded to a Saudi request to provide information on their supplies to US military bases worldwide.

The selective embargo, however, proved ineffective because the companies transhipped oil from one destination to another, spreading the cutbacks equally. Despite widespread fears to the contrary (see below), the cutback in supplies of some 5 million barrels a day, or 9 per cent of non-Eastern bloc output, caused few lasting problems. But its effect on spot oil prices – which sky-rocketed – was used by the producers to justify a general price rise.

OPEC succeeded in imposing and maintaining a major increase: oil prices quadrupled during the winter of 1973–4, raising the oil producers' annual revenue by around $64 billion – enough money to buy 1½ per cent of world capitalist output.

This price rise occurred in the context of restrictive policies, rapidly decelerating output and double-digit inflation. Restrictive policies were introduced in all major countries in 1973 in response to the price acceleration of the mini-boom and the large wage claims that were beginning to be submitted in its wake. The measures were largely monetary: the annual rate of growth of the ACCs' money supply fell from 14 per cent at the end of 1972 to 8 per cent at the end of 1973; short-term interest rates rose from 4 per cent in early 1972 to 10 per cent in mid-1973. Fiscal policy also moved towards restriction, with the important exception of the United States: in Europe and Japan, policy became more restrictive to the tune of around 1½ per cent of GDP.

ACC real GDP growth fell from an annual rate of 8 per cent in the first half of 1973 to one of 3 per cent in the second half of the year (though the latter figure was reduced by output losses resulting from the oil embargo). Unemployment began to rise in the autumn of 1973.

Materials and food prices began to drift downwards from the summer of 1973. But world inflation rose to an annual rate of 10 per cent in the second half of the year as previous materials price rises fed through to final goods markets.

The oil price rise worsened the conditions both for producing surplus and for realizing it. It raised input costs, thereby tending to reduce profitability, and intensifying the pressure on industry to raise prices (much fixed capital could no longer be operated profitably at existing output prices). It also transferred, at a stroke, 1½ per cent of world purchasing power to OPEC. The recipients did not, and in the short run simply could not, spend the majority of their extra revenue. So world demand fell.

These pressures were intensified by the introduction of yet more restrictive policies: monetary conditions were further tightened in most economies in the spring of 1974. Nevertheless, inflation rose for some months, and production continued to grow in all major economies except the United States during the first half of 1974. In part this resulted from increased opportunities for exporting to the periphery. The commodities boom had increased many less developed countries' (LDC) export earnings, and imports rose with some lag. Also a number of non-oil-producing LDCs borrowed unspent OPEC reserves, channelled through the ACCs' banks.

The oil price rise reactivated the boom in commodity prices and boosted inflation, which reached an annual rate of 15 per cent in the spring of 1974.

Many accounts of the 1970s present the oil crisis as *the* key development. OPEC is often cast as a super-villain, holding the world economy to ransom for political motives. Similarly the price rise is portrayed as a lightning bolt from the blue, striking and severely damaging an engine of growth which had previously been performing well. It is true that the oil crisis dealt an important blow to the functioning of the system and had a major impact on the form and timing of the crisis – constituting a trigger for the crash which separates the period of overheating from the subsequent one of mass unemployment and stagnation. But this picture is nevertheless misleading in two important ways.

First, it seriously underplays the extent to which the system was in severe difficulties prior to the oil price rise. The basic problems – overaccumulation in relation to the labour supply and sharp decline in profitability – preceded the oil crisis and would not have evaporated in its absence. Nor is there any reason to assume that the system would have adjusted smoothly to the onset of overaccumulation had the oil crisis not occurred. The feverish character of the mini-boom hardly augured smooth adjustment.

Second, it ignores the extent to which the oil crisis had its roots in previous developments. The Middle East war which prompted the actions of OPEC was, of course, itself a product of the economic and political history of postwar capitalism. But there are more direct economic connections. For one thing, it is doubtful if OPEC could have successfully imposed the price increase at the time it did in the absence of the high levels of demand that accompanied the mini-boom. In addition, the dollar devaluations worked to encourage a price rise, because most oil was priced in dollars which were being eroded in value.

Furthermore, OPEC would almost certainly have been unable to sustain massively higher prices in the context of the subsequent crash had US policy towards oil imports not changed dramatically in the seventies. Throughout the sixties the United States limited imports of oil and petroleum products by law (the legislation was enacted in 1959 to bolster the dollar). Until 1970 the United States was 90 per cent self-sufficient in energy. The policy was then radically reversed. In 1971 price controls on domestic production were imposed and the legislation limiting imports was repealed. Oil imports soared in 1972. In August 1973 a two-tier pricing system was introduced: the price of oil from wells already functioning in 1972 was fixed at a maximum of $4.35 per barrel; oil from wells begun in 1973 or later and oil imports were exempted from the price ceiling. Following the OPEC price rise, the oil companies preferred not to work pre-1973 wells very intensely. This preference was reinforced by the announcement that the controls were temporary and would be lifted by the end of 1985. In 1976 the imposition of price controls on natural gas led to further substitution of oil imports for domestic energy sources.

The net result was that the United States moved during the 1970s from being 90 per cent self-sufficient in energy to importing 50 per cent of its needs. By the end of the decade it was importing 8–9 million barrels per day, or about 30 per cent of OPEC output. This cost some $40 billion a year before the 1979 oil price rises. Although the United States is the single largest exporter to OPEC (supplying about 15 per cent of its foreign purchases), its deficit with those countries largely accounted for its overall trade deficit in the second half of the seventies.

Finally, the price rise was a product of the boom in a more general and fundamental sense. The tremendous increase in oil consumption which accompanied the great burst of accumulation threatened to deplete reserves: by the early seventies considerable disquiet was expressed about the possibility of the 'depletion horizon' of known reserves being reduced below the conventional level of twenty-five years' supply. These worries were reinforced by the influential Club of Rome's 1972 report *Limits to Growth* which popularized the notion that the world was running out of essential materials and fuels, including oil. BP's exploration manager argued that oil production would peak in the early 1980s and that demand would outstrip supply by 1978. Within the industry it became a commonplace to point out that the discovery of 'a Libya a year' would be required to maintain the depletion horizon. A major price adjustment was needed to encourage both energy-saving and exploration.

*

The above account of the effects of the oil price rise applies to the system as a whole. But the impact varied considerably across industries and countries.

The most important division between industries is that between the oil companies and the rest. Whereas the bulk of industry faced higher costs and a squeeze on profits, the oil majors had a profit bonanza. Returns on their operations rose from $3.9 billion in 1972 to $12.1 billion in 1974. Those on investments in OPEC increased from $2.6 billion to $6.1 billion over the same period. Chase Manhattan estimated that the worldwide rate of profit for leading oil companies rose from 9.7 per cent in 1972 to 19.2 per cent in 1974 and 24.0 per cent in 1979.

But when viewed in the context of other changes in the industry, the oil price rise appears more of a mixed blessing for the seven major oil companies. The rise of OPEC brought changes in ownership and operation as well as in price. Direct exports by OPEC national oil companies rose from a negligible proportion of production within the area to some 50–55 per cent over the course of the 1970s. Host government ownership of oil production in OPEC rose from some 2 per cent in 1970 to 60 per cent in 1974 and 80–90 per cent in 1980. By the end of the decade the majors had secure ownership rights to crude oil only within the OECD area.

And, despite the boost given by the price rise to exploration and production, OECD oil output rose only from 5 million barrels a day in 1973 to 6.3 million in 1980, providing only 35 per cent of the seven majors' refining needs. Furthermore, OECD governments also began to demand an ownership stake in production. The share of world refining accounted for by the majors fell from 51 per cent in 1973 to 38 per cent in 1980.

The differing impact of the price rise on consumer countries is exemplified by comparing Japan with the United States.

Japan is almost entirely dependent on oil imports for all its basic energy requirements, having no fossil fuel deposits. So the oil price rise enormously increased its import bill. The additional exports required to earn the extra foreign exchange constituted a drain from domestic incomes. Since this deduction would have to come from either wages or profits, it therefore worked to intensify distributional struggle and to reduce the rate of accumulation. In addition, the larger cost in foreign exchange worked to increase balance of payments constraints and hence to reduce the room for manoeuvre over domestic economic policies.

For Japan, then, the 'oil shock' was a major blow without mitigating benefits.

The United States fared differently. For a start, the oil companies are predominantly US-owned. Furthermore, the USA's large oil reserves allow it, unlike its major rivals West Germany and Japan, to be self-sufficient in oil. In addition, the two-tier pricing system allows US domestic industry to purchase oil well below world market prices (some 40 per cent below in the first half of 1979). This obviously gives it a competitive advantage. Finally, in a longer-term perspective, the United States possesses enormous energy reserves in the form of shale oil and bituminous schists. The development of these was not remotely economically viable at pre-1974 oil prices. The 1979 round of oil price rises made extraction more or less economically feasible. Shale extraction could make the United States self-sufficient in oil for the foreseeable future, thus eliminating dependence on foreign supplies which has increasingly worried the Pentagon.

So, while the oil crisis caused major difficulties for the system as a whole, its impact – like that of the commodities boom and the dollar crisis – was uneven. The United States suffered less than its major rivals.

The crash

A major crash began in the summer of 1974. ACC industrial production fell by 10 per cent between July 1974 and April 1975. In the first half of 1975 ACC output was 3½ per cent down on the level of a year earlier, and international trade was 13 per cent lower. For 1975 as a whole, output was marginally lower than in 1973 (1½ per cent lower in the United States and some 1½ per cent higher in Japan). The previous worst postwar two-year period ended in 1958, with output 4½ per cent higher than in 1956. The crash of 1974 was far and away the biggest since 1929.

Most economic crashes are kicked off by a collapse in investment, especially in inventories, and this one was no exception. So any explanation of why it started must focus on the collapse in investment.

In the long run, investment is closely tied to profits. So the underlying cause of the fall in investment is the decline in profitability. But that does not explain the precise timing. Profits had been falling for some years; investment collapsed suddenly in summer 1974.

Capitalists invest because they hope to make profits. So the level of investment depends on expectations about future profitability. These expectations will usually be heavily influenced by past profits, but they are not the only consideration. A host of factors shape capitalists' confidence in the future.

The loss of confidence in the mid-1970s is usually put down solely to the oil crisis. Although this was an important factor, accounts which focus on it too narrowly are unsatisfactory.

Confidence is in one sense a delicate psychological state. Once it has been shattered, it is hard to re-establish, as we tried to show when discussing the origins of the boom. But confidence, like trust, is also fairly robust. Once firmly established, it tends to justify itself, as we tried to show in the section on the strength of the boom. It then takes a major blow to fracture it.

The oil crisis alone could not have shattered the confidence which capitalists felt during most of the golden years. The blow was so crippling because confidence had already taken quite a few knocks. And even then, it did not produce an immediate crash.

Over the previous few years capitalists had been hit by the European wage explosions and a general worsening of industrial relations. They had experienced the breakup of the Bretton Woods system and increasing international financial uncertainty. Inflation had accelerated and commodity prices had gone through the roof. Profitability had fallen by one-third and the fast and highly synchronized boom of the previous couple of years had failed to restore it.

But worsening expectations had not yet led to a collapse in investment. They had brought a modest decline in the face of extreme boom conditions, but no collapse. Their most obvious effect had been a massive increase in speculation as more capitalists tried to make money by wheeling and dealing rather than by productive investment. Hence the huge foreign exchange dealings and the booms in share prices, gold, land, real estate and commodities. The acceleration of inflation, the soft monetary stance of the authorities and the commodities boom all worked to boost stockbuilding.

The oil crisis undermined confidence further. Initially, worries centred on securing supplies in the face of the cutback and selective embargo. Most governments, having projected a fall in supplies of around one-fifth for 1974, rushed through emergency legislation to economize on the use of oil. In December 1973 the oil companies claimed that OPEC had cut supplies by 17½ per cent.

There was a run on all major stock exchanges. Prices on Wall Street fell by 5 per cent a week in November. The gold price soared again, shooting up by nearly one-fifth in the first week of 1974. The *Economist* commented, 'For years the gold enthusiasts have been regarded as barbarians. Now that it is fashionable to talk of the imminent collapse of civilization, their day has come on Wall Street' (16 February 1974). It described the mood in Japan as one of 'considerable panic'.

From January 1974 the oil once more began to flow freely. There was a mild stockbuilding boom, probably to make up for dislocations over the winter, and commodity prices took off again. Worries now shifted to the higher prices and to what became known as the 'recycling problem'.

It was clear that OPEC would be unable to spend much of its new revenues and would lend massively on international financial markets. Many countries would also need to borrow heavily to pay for oil imports. The problem was that OPEC was likely to lend mainly in US markets whereas the potential borrowers were concentrated in Europe and the third world. There was widespread scepticism about whether private financial institutions could successfully channel funds from lenders to borrowers, and general agreement that the IMF should play a major role.

Italy soon found difficulties in borrowing, as the *Economist* described: 'Another sign of possible 1929-style international financial crisis is upon us. Eurobankers are beginning to be chary of lending to the nationalized industries and state authorities of even big countries in balance of payments deficits. Italy seems to be coming close to that point of no return; it is rapidly exhausting its reserves of international goodwill as well as its reserves of foreign currency. Where Italy is being given a cold shoulder today, could other deficit countries with particular political problems – a Mitterrand France, a Wilson Britain, a post-Franco Spain, a Denmark with a parliament of all-sorts – be jilted tomorrow?' (20 April 1974).

The chances of the IMF organizing a major recycling programme were poor. At the time of the Smithsonian Agreement the Group of Ten – the leading central bankers – had announced that discussions would begin promptly on a new long-term monetary reform. After US obstruction, a Committee of the Board of Governors of the IMF was eventually set up for this purpose late in 1972. It had twenty members. British finance minister Barber remarked that reaching an agreement would only be twice as difficult in the new forum as in the old. Little was achieved.

Revelations of the Watergate affair, which dominated the world's media in spring 1974, did not help. The country with the largest single vote in the IMF, the largest recipient of OPEC funds and the key issuer of international money was being run by a president whose attentions were more and more focused on saving his own skin. Meanwhile doubts about the private banks' ability to cope caused mounting worries.

While recycling dominated economic discussions, developments elsewhere were hardly comforting. Output was decelerating, inflation rising, and governments everywhere (except the United Kingdom) deflating sharply. Commodity prices tumbled in May 1974, led by copper and given a push by official Japanese encouragement to firms to sell stocks to improve liquidity. A crash in share prices, which was to prove greater than that of 1929, was well underway: between September 1973 and September 1974 they were to fall by between 23 per cent in Japan and 55 per cent in the United Kingdom. With consumer prices rising by some 15 per cent over the period, the fall in the real value of the shares was considerably greater. Real share prices in the United Kingdom fell to the level of the wartime blitz.

The international banking system began to crack. On 26 June Germany's largest private bank, the Herstatt, collapsed as a result of speculative foreign exchange losses. US banks, which also lost heavily, were furious with the Bundesbank for refusing to compensate them. The German commercial and central banks refused to bail out Herstatt and many depositors lost money.

The ramifications were enormous. The international banking community was so nervous that for a while no forward foreign exchange markets operated properly anywhere. The lion's share of all foreign exchange dealing was restricted to a few New York banks, who refused to deal with many smaller banks and with most French and Italian ones. The volume of foreign exchange transactions plummeted (Chart 13.1). Money was moved out of small banks all over the world. The *Economist*'s assessment of the mood six weeks later was that 'the first whiff of even a false rumour is liable to cause a run' (3 August 1974). But by then the crash had already started.

Chart 13.1 World foreign exchange trading volume, 1970–9

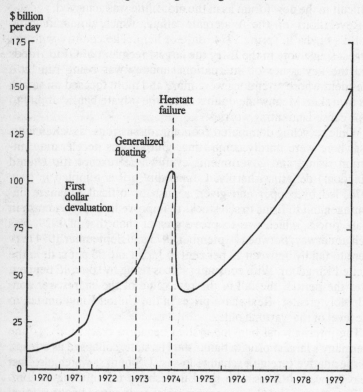

Source: UNCTAD, *Trade and Development Report*, 1981, Chart 14.

It is hard to explain why confidence broke precisely when it did. Searching for the elusive final straw is not a very fruitful activity. So it would be a mistake to place too much emphasis on any one event, such as the Herstatt collapse. All that can sensibly be said is that, given everything capitalism had gone through over the previous few years, a collapse of confidence was to be expected at some point.

SO, WHAT'S IT ALL ABOUT?

The play is a high-energy political farce. A Maniac impersonator turns police headquarters into a personal playground when he tricks senior police officers into thinking he is the magistrate sent to investigate the death of an anarchist, who - wait for it - 'fell' out the fourth floor window of police headquarters while under interrogation. You will hear lots of references to the 'fourth floor'.

The play was based on the police investigation of a bomb throwing incident in Italy more than 30 years ago, but each time it is performed - and it has been performed all over the world - the play is updated to mirror the current political situation. The Poets' Theatre has therefore brought the play right up to date.

The bomb throwing in 1969 killed sixteen people and injured about a hundred. The police arrested an anarchist who was in fact subsequently killed when he 'fell' from the fourth-floor window of the police interrogation room. The militant left-wing newspaper, Lotta Continua, accused a police inspector of 'murder' and was sued for defamation. The trial dragged on for ten years until the court finally implicated fascists (not anarchists) as authors of the bombing. The inspector was assassinated (by the left?)

In Accidental Death of an Anarchist, based on this scandal, Fo produced a piece in which his skill at writing farce and his gifts as a clown were put brilliantly at the service of his left wing politics, playing on the tension between the real death of a prisoner and the farcical inventions advanced by the authorities to explain it.

The resulting slump left a considerable proportion of productive capacity idle. By the autumn of 1975 around 11 per cent of fixed capital was gathering dust. Registered unemployment in the ACCs rose from around 8 million at the end of the mini-boom to about 15 million in the spring of 1975. Even this increase is a severe under-estimate of real job loss: participation rates fell sharply, under-employment rose and the number of migrant workers in Europe fell by over a million.

Two other developments generated concern at the time – and have continued to do so. One was the maintenance of high in-flation rates despite the collapse of output. Minerals and metals prices fell by 30 per cent between May 1974 and the end of the year. Food prices fell by 33 per cent between November 1974 and June 1975. But, while inflation slowed from the summer of 1974, prices as a whole continued to rise at an annual rate of 10 per cent during the depths of the slump. Inflationary expectations and processes had become extremely stubborn.

The other development which caused consternation was the beginning of large public sector deficits. Government revenues fell as the slump reduced taxation yields, while public spending rose as unemployment benefit payments rocketed. If governments had not run such deficits then the slump would have been far deeper, since the deficits worked partially to offset the collapse in demand which resulted from the big increase in OPEC savings and fall in investment. Nevertheless, obsession with the size of public sector borrowing requirements began at this time.

The most important effect of the crash, however, received less attention at the time – a further collapse in profits. In the two years 1974 and 1975 the profit rate fell by as much as in the previous five (Table 13.1). By 1975 it was only 60 per cent of the 1968 level. The fall was significantly smaller in the United States, where capital was hit less hard by the oil price rise. In manufacturing industry by 1975 the profit rate had fallen to only half of its 1968 level (Table 13.2).

The large increase in the price of oil – an important input into production – and the sharpness of the subsequent crash made in-evitable an immediate fall in the rate of profit. The worsening of the terms of trade for the ACCs, largely as a result of the oil price rise, reduced the resources available for profits and wages by around ½ per cent of output per year. The crash also brought a slight decline in productivity. A prerequisite for the profit share

Table 13.1 Business profit rates, 1968–75

Percentages

	ACC	USA	Europe	Japan
1968	17.2	19.4	13.5	31.7
1973	13.6	14.8	11.3	19.6
1975	10.2	12.3	7.3	13.5

Source: see Appendix.

Table 13.2 Manufacturing profit rates, 1968–75

Percentages

	ACC	USA	Europe	Japan
1968	23.6	28.9	14.8	46.0
1973	19.3	22.5	12.1	33.5
1975	11.6	16.7	7.9	10.4

Source: see Appendix.

being maintained was a fall in real wages of about 1 per cent a year between 1973 and 1975 (Table 17.2). In the event, high inflation and sharply rising unemployment worked to halve the rate of growth of real wages in comparison to the previous five-year period (the effect was particularly marked in the manufacturing sector in Europe and Japan). But real wages were not cut. So the profit share fell. The crash also pushed down the output-capital ratio, by an average of some 10 per cent, as excess capacity mounted. The combined result was a sharp decline in the profit rate.

This further sharp decline in profitability, following on that of earlier years, and taking profits to levels well below those which had come to be expected during the boom, is the key to the sustained sluggishness of accumulation in the latter half of the 1970s and the early 1980s. This sluggishness is in turn the key to the mounting unemployment of those years.

Part III

Things Fall Apart
1974 –

14. Unemployment Mounts

Unemployment

The crash of 1974–5 was a major turning point for the advanced capitalist economies. In the decade following 1973 production grew less than half as fast as in the sixties. This slowdown represented an enormous loss of potential output. If the ACCs had grown as fast after 1973 as in the previous decade then their output in 1983 would have been almost one-third higher. The extra goods and services would have exceeded the combined annual output of Germany and Japan.

The decade falls into two broad phases: fragile recovery, followed by renewed downturn in the wake of the second major oil price rise of 1979. In response to the crash, governments in the major countries initiated expansionary tax cuts and spending increases early in 1975. Recovery began in the middle of the year. Growth was rapid at first: industrial production rose by 10 per cent between June 1975 and March 1976, almost regaining the previous peak reached in November 1973. But the expansion lost momentum and only a moderate recovery continued until 1979, by which year output was 17 per cent above the 1973 level.

The further doubling of oil prices in 1979 then took its toll, lopping 2–3 per cent off OECD output in 1980. Rapid growth of exports to OPEC and to non-oil LDCs helped to maintain demand. However, tax increases and spending cuts, followed by tight monetary conditions and high interest rates, further depressed spending in 1981 and 1982. OECD output grew by less than 1 per cent per year over the period 1979–82. A strong US recovery in 1983 only boosted the overall growth rate to about 2 per cent.

Much the most visible, and for many millions of people the most painful, symptom of the much slower growth since 1973 has been the re-emergence of mass unemployment. Registered un-

employment in the OECD countries rose from around 8 million at
the end of the mini-boom to 15 million in the spring of 1975. It
then fell slightly during the recovery, largely because of a big
increase in employment in North America. A further rapid increase in unemployment followed the slowdown in growth after
1979. Between 1980 and 1983 the ACC average rate rose from 5½
per cent of the work force to 8½ per cent. In 1983 some 32 million
people were unemployed in the OECD area as a whole (Table
14.1).

Table 14.1 Unemployment rates, 1973–83[1]

Percentages

	ACC	USA	Japan	EEC
1973	3.4	4.8	1.3	3.0
1975	5.5	8.3	1.9	4.5
1980	5.6	7.0	2.0	6.0
1981	6.5	7.5	2.2	8.0
1982	7.9	9.5	2.4	9.3
1983[2]	8.4	9.8	2.7	10.1

1. Adjusted by OECD to secure comparability between countries.
2. First nine months.

Source: OECD, *Economic Outlook*, December 1983, Table R.12.

Official unemployment data do not tell the whole story. For one
thing, they include only certain categories of the unemployed. In
the United Kingdom, for example, only those 'signing on' at job
centres are counted. These practices lead to a very significant
undercounting of the real numbers of jobless. It has been
estimated that one in three new jobs created in Europe in the early
1980s was filled by one of the non-registered unemployed. Detailed studies of particular countries confirm that the official figures should be substantially increased to yield a more accurate
estimate of unemployment. But so long as this systematic understatement of absolute numbers of jobless is borne in mind, shifts in
official unemployment figures do illustrate the trend.

Unemployment results from an imbalance between the number of jobs available and the number of people seeking work. Rising unemployment indicates a growing imbalance. Its onset can result from either a drop in the rate of growth of jobs or a faster rate of increase in the number of those looking for them. Both factors have played a role in unemployment growth since 1973. The slowdown in the rate of provision of jobs has been the most important. The number of people in work has not actually fallen. In the ACCs, employment rose by 0.8 per cent per year between 1973 and 1982. But this was nearly ½ per cent a year lower than in the early seventies (Table 14.2). Employment growth slowed down in all the blocs, although it remained high in the United States.

Table 14.2 Population, labour force and employment, 1960–82

Average annual percentage growth rates

	1960–68	*1968–73*	*1973–82*
Population aged 15 to 64			
USA	1.6	1.8	1.6
EEC	0.6	0.5	0.7
Japan	2.0	1.1	0.8
ACC	1.1	1.2	1.1
Labour force			
USA	1.7	2.2	2.3
EEC	0.1	0.5	0.7
Japan	1.4	1.0	0.9
ACC	1.0	1.3	1.4
Employment			
USA	1.9	1.9	1.7
EEC	0.1	0.5	0.2
Japan	1.5	1.0	0.7
ACC	1.1	1.2	0.8

Source: OECD, *Historical Statistics*, 1960–81, Tables 1.2, 1.3, 1.6; OECD, *Employment Outlook*, Tables 4 and 5.

The labour force also grew a little faster after 1973 than before (Table 14.2). The growth of the number of people categorized as of working age (fifteen to sixty-four) fell slightly, but this was more than offset by an acceleration in the proportion of those in or seeking work. Had this 'participation rate' not risen at all (so that the population of working age and the labour force rose in parallel) then unemployment would have grown only half as fast as it did.

The rise in the participation rate is the product of very different trends for men and women (Table 14.3). The male rate declined, largely as a result of early retirement. Germany was the extreme case: the proportion of men aged sixty to sixty-four who were in the labour force fell from 75 per cent in 1970 to 40 per cent in 1979. But a rapid rise in the female participation rate more than offset the decline in the male rate. The sharpest increase was in the United States, up from 51.5 per cent in 1973 to 61.5 per cent in 1982.

Table 14.3 ACC participation rates, 1960–82[1]

	1960	1968	1973	1979	1982
Total	69.7	68.1	68.5	70.2	70.4
Women	46.8	47.6	49.7	54.4	55.9
Men	93.5	89.5	87.8	86.2	85.2

1. Percentage of population aged between fifteen and sixty-four who are in the labour force (employed or registered unemployed).

Sources: OECD, *Historical Statistics*, 1960–81, Tables 2.6, 2.7, 2.8; OECD, *Employment Outlook*, Table 3.B.

Part of the explanation for the increase in female participation is that the sectors in which women's employment is concentrated (particularly services) have been less seriously hit than those employing mainly men. But this is by no means the whole story. For the period 1973–82 the average female unemployment rate in the ACCs has grown almost as fast as the male rate (4.2 to 8.2 per cent and 2.8 to 7.4 per cent respectively). So the number of women seeking jobs rose faster than female employment. Many families sought a second income as male earnings either grew more slowly or were stopped by unemployment. A US study showed that women whose husbands are unemployed are much more likely to be in the labour force than those whose husbands have jobs. The resilience and dynamism of new social attitudes towards women and waged work born of the long boom probably also played a role.

The relative importance of slower growth of jobs and of further growth of the labour force varied considerably over the period. Between 1973 and 1975 employment in the ACCs did not grow at all, while the number of job-seekers rose by 1.1 per cent a year. Between 1975 and 1979 employment grew fractionally faster than the labour force (1.8 and 1.7 per cent a year respectively) and so unemployment fell slightly. Between 1979 and 1982 employment barely rose (by 0.1 per cent a year), while the number seeking work grew by 1.1 per cent a year.

The structure of jobs

Rising unemployment has coincided with a substantial decline in the proportion of jobs provided by the industrial sector. In the ACCs industrial employment fell by 1.6 million between 1973 and 1981; 4 million industrial jobs were lost in the big four European

Table 14.4 Sectoral employment changes, 1973–81

Millions

	USA	Japan	Europe	ACC[1]
Agriculture	−0.1	−1.5	−1.9	−3.5
Industry	2.0	0.1	−4.1	−1.6
Services	13.4	4.6	6.0	25.8
Total	15.3	3.2	0.0	20.7
Labour force	19.2	3.8	4.6	30.2
Unemployment	3.9	0.6	4.6	9.5

1. ACC includes Canada and thus exceeds sum of the blocs.

Source: OECD, *Labour Force Statistics*, 1970–81, Tables 5, 6, 7.

countries while 2 million were created in the United States and the number more or less maintained in Japan. Service employment rose rapidly but not fast enough to provide jobs for all the new entrants to the labour force and those moving out of agriculture or losing jobs in industry.

This decline in the relative importance of industrial jobs began in the 1970s. In the 1960s the share had remained fairly constant. So it is not surprising that the rising unemployment since the early seventies has been blamed on 'deindustrialization', especially as job losses in large manufacturing plants have been daily news items.

This deindustrialization is often blamed on poor competitiveness. But the fact that there has been a decline in the relative importance of industrial jobs in all countries shows that this cannot be the explanation. Industrial employment declined as a proportion of the total from 33.2 per cent in the United States in 1973 to 30.1 per cent in 1981, and from 41.6 per cent to 37.1 per cent in the EEC over the same period. But it also fell from 37.2 per cent to 35.3 per cent in Japan, despite that country's phenomenal success in exporting manufactures (Chapter 16). Indeed, the Japanese experience shows the need to interpret the term 'deindustrialization' with care. Industrial production there grew faster between 1973 and 1981 than total output (4.9 per cent a year and 3.9 per cent respectively). Jobs grew slower in industry than in the economy as a whole because productivity grew faster, and this was not compensated for by sufficiently rapid output growth. Deindustrialization there was caused by rapid industrial productivity growth rather than slow growth of output.

In Germany, industrial production grew more slowly than output as a whole. But most of the relative loss of industrial jobs was still due to faster productivity growth than in services. During the boom this differential productivity growth had been accompanied by rapid increases in industrial output, so industry maintained its share of jobs. Since 1973 slower growth and, in particular, the stagnation of investment, held down market growth for industrial products. Higher industrial productivity led to relative job loss in industry.

Once unemployment sets in, structural changes, which would otherwise pass unremarked, are accused of causing the dole queues. Agricultural employment declined rapidly during the boom. However, since the workers 'released' from farms found jobs elsewhere, the rundown of agriculture was never regarded as being responsible for unemployment. Changes in the employment structure are a constant feature of economic development, but are never in themselves the cause of slow overall growth in jobs. They are widely accepted as an explanation for unemployment both because they are widely canvassed as such and, more fundamentally, because people who lose their job in industry and cannot find another are obviously inclined to blame their predicament on the rundown of their sector.

Who is out of work?

Persistent unemployment is more pernicious than a temporary job-shortage. For one thing, people tend to be out of work for longer. In France, to take the extreme example, the proportion of the unemployed out of work for twelve months or more rose from 22 per cent in 1973 to 40 per cent in 1982. But not all the rise in unemployment is explained by people being out of work for longer. More and more people have experienced spells on the dole. So mass unemployment has cumulative effects. Being out of work today is also an experience qualitatively different from that of the sixties. It is more frightening because the chances of getting another job are much lower. By 1981 a UK man aged between twenty-five and forty-four who lost his job could expect to spend ten months on the dole.

Average unemployment figures for a given year also distort the picture by ignoring group differences. Global figures for unemployment can be broken down in various ways: by country, region and town; by industry, trade, educational attainment and skill; by age and sex; by ethnic origin. The effect of being disadvantaged on more than one of these criteria can be devastating, as any black teenager in Harlem knows only too well.

This unequal burden of unemployment obviously has considerable economic, social and political implications. Perhaps the most explosive issue is youth unemployment. In 1982 people under twenty-five in the ACCs as a whole were 2.6 times as likely to be unemployed as adults. (Seven times as likely in Italy.) Throughout most of Europe unemployment among young people has risen faster than among their parents. Rates there are now comparable to those in the United States (Table 14.5).

Table 14.5 Youth unemployment rates, 1973–82[1]

Percentages of youth labour forces

	1973	1982
USA	9.9	17.0
Japan	2.3	4.4
France	4.0	20.3
Germany	1.0	7.0[2]
Italy	12.6	27.4[2]
UK	3.3	19.8[2]

1. Age sixteen to twenty-four.
2. 1981.

Source: OECD, *Labour Force Statistics*, 1970–81.

Both demographic trends and developments in industrial relations have contributed to a very high level of unemployment among young people. As trade union strength grew during the boom, many unions negotiated 'first in, last out' arrangements, which protect the older workers at the expense of the younger. Severance payments deals lead employers to opt for so-called 'natural wastage' rather than sackings, thus hitting new entrants into the labour market particularly hard.

Politicians have expressed considerable concern about this feature of European unemployment and have come up with numerous 'make-work' schemes for youth (Chapter 19 contains a critical discussion). As Belgium's labour minister asked rhetorically; 'Who can say when we will reach the point when the flames start?' (quoted *Financial Times*, 17 January 1983).

The next chapter explains why mass unemployment has returned to haunt workers in the ACCs. The following chapters assess the implications of the major slowdown in growth since 1973. Relations between the advanced capitalist countries, and between them and the rest of the world, have been shaken up (Chapter 16). The balance of power on the shop floor has moved against workers, leading employers to attempt to reorganize production and to import the much-vaunted Japanese system of industrial relations (Chapter 17). Conservative parties have attempted to consolidate this shift in power by rolling back many of the gains that workers made during the boom years (Chapter 18). Workers' parties have been unable to defend, let alone extend, those gains in the face of the strength of pressures for retrenchment (Chapter 19). Prospects are gloomy (Chapter 20).

15. Unemployment and Accumulation

New technology

One widely canvassed explanation for the re-emergence of mass unemployment is the adoption of 'new technology', based largely on microelectronics. It is easy to see why this account is popular.

Fears about possible malign effects of technological change generally arise when unemployment develops and fade away when jobs are plentiful. The 1950s closed with an 'automation scare' in the United States which disappeared as soon as the slow growth and high unemployment of those years gave way to more rapid expansion in the 1960s. Similarly, there was strikingly less concern about microelectronics and employment in the 1970s in the United States, where employment was buoyant in comparison to Europe.

Many workers have personal experience of losing a job because of new investment. To them, new technology seems the clear culprit. Finally, numerous studies of particular industries show overall job loss to be a result of technical innovation.

But in reality matters are less clear-cut. In the 1950s and 1960s new investment, often of a directly labour-saving variety, was taking place faster than in the late 1970s and early 1980s. Yet overall employment was rising because the growth of output exceeded the reduction in the amount of labour required to produce each unit of output. No one displaced by technical change found much difficulty obtaining a job elsewhere.

It is very difficult to draw macroeconomic conclusions from studies of the form and rate of adoption of technical change. These difficulties have given rise to two opposing analytic errors. The fact that technical change typically raises productivity has led some people to conclude that employment in the industry must fall. In effect this ignores possible output growth. More sophisticated variants allow for some output growth, reducing the employment effect in the industry in question, but fail to allow for employment growth in other sectors.

At the other extreme, it is pointed out that firms at the forefront of technical change gain competitive advantage and so may experience employment growth. Although correct, this analysis says nothing about the overall pattern of employment in the economy. When the argument is also applied to countries, it says nothing about what is happening in the rest of the world and hence nothing about the economic environment in which the country operates. To do better than a poor average may be little consolation.

The impact of new technology on employment will be shaped by such factors as the extent to which requirements of labour and other inputs per unit of output are reduced, the extent to which innovation affects processes or products, and the extent to which changes in skill requirements are industry-specific or general throughout the economy. Most fundamentally, the extent to which unemployment is increased depends on whether the new technology is introduced in a context of expanding or of stagnant markets.

No one yet knows just how qualitatively different, in economic terms, today's emerging technologies really are, let alone the overall economic context – stagnation or expansion – in which their future widespread introduction will take place. The necessarily speculative nature of the discussion is probably another reason why the media give such attention to microelectronics as a possible cause of unemployment.

Although it is too early to say whether microelectronics and associated technologies will have employment effects different from those generated by previous technical change, we can be sure that any effects to date have had a relatively trivial influence on unemployment. Productivity growth has been much slower than in the fifties and sixties. Thus, far from new technology reducing labour input requirements faster than before, the labour required to produce a given unit of output has been falling far more slowly than in the previous decades. If each worker had continued to produce an extra 3¾ per cent a year, as during the sixties, then the 2½ per cent annual output growth achieved after 1973 would have implied a 1¼ per cent a year fall in employment. By 1981 official unemployment would have reached a staggering 25 per cent of the labour force, rather than the 6½ per cent actually recorded.

The story of mounting unemployment over the last decade is not one of technology suddenly destroying jobs at an unprecedented pace. Quite the contrary.

Real wages

A second popular explanation for rising unemployment is that it is the result of workers' wages rising too fast. In early 1983 the West German economics minister, Otto Lambsdorff, was in no doubt that workers were to blame: 'Our economies are still carrying the burden of an excessive real wage level from the seventies. A considerable part of current unemployment is due to the fact that labour has now become too expensive' (quoted Sachs, p. 255).

Since 'excessive real wages' is another way of describing 'insufficient profits', our analysis of overaccumulation and the onset of the crisis of the mid-seventies (Chapters 11 and 12) seems consistent with this stress on the role of real wages. But the argument of Chapter 12 was that it was the disproportion between accumulation and the available supplies of labour which lay at the root of the decline in profitability in the early seventies. Rising real wages were a symptom of this situation, not an independent element.

Moreover, in the period of rapid growth in real wages prior to 1973 there was no substantial increase in unemployment. In the eight years 1965–73 product wages (the real cost of employing labour) grew by 4.1 per cent per year in the ACCs as a whole (Table 15.1). In the succeeding eight years up to 1981, product wages actually grew much more slowly than before, and yet un-

Table 15.1 ACC productivity and wages, 1965–81

Average annual percentage growth rates

	Productivity	Product wage
1965–73	3.5	4.1
1973–81	1.3	1.7

Source: see Appendix.

employment soared. It was because of the drastic slowdown in the growth of productivity that even the much slower growth of product wages after 1973 still implied some further squeeze on profits.

Yet in two important respects this continuation of the profits squeeze contributed to rising unemployment. On the one hand, it further discouraged new investment and thus dampened demand. Secondly, it added to the pressure from stagnation on the older, less efficient plants, and thus hastened the process of plant closure. Such a process of rationalization and the concentration of production on the higher-productivity plants reduced average labour requirements and thus added to the dole queues.

But this is only one side of the picture. Rising product wages also implied rising real wages in terms of what workers could buy; the fact that product wages grew a little faster than productivity helped to maintain the market for consumer goods. So rising real wages, while an important aspect of the development of the crisis of the seventies, had contradictory effects on the growth of employment after 1973. It was by no means the central factor behind rising unemployment in the seventies and early eighties.

The stagnation of output

The most immediate constraint on production, and therefore on job opportunities, since the crash of 1974 has been the sluggishness of markets. Employers have been very hesitant about increasing output because of the difficulty of finding buyers. But to explain the stagnation of output we must ask who or what is responsible for the stagnation of spending power. Any number of scapegoats have been suggested.

Table 15.2 shows the contribution of the major categories of expenditure to the slowdown in the growth of overall spending.

Consumers to blame?

At first sight it would seem that slower growth of consumption expenditure is the main cause. Of the 3½ percentage point deceleration in output, a full 2 percentage points are accounted for by slower growth of sales of consumer goods and private housing – goods bought mainly by workers.

Table 15.2 ACC contributions to increased sales, 1960–82

	1960–73	1973–82	1973–75	1975–79	1979–82
Average percentage increase in GDP	5.5	1.9	−0.7	4.3	0.5
Accounted for by[1]					
Household consumption and housing	3.5	1.4	0.3	2.7	0.5
Government expenditure	0.9	0.4	0.5	0.4	0.2
Business Sector					
Fixed investment	1.0	0.1	−0.9	0.7	0.0
Stockbuilding	0.1	−0.2	−1.2	0.4	−0.6
Net exports	0.0	0.2	0.6	0.0	0.4

1. Figures show the extent to which each element of expenditure accounts directly for the percentage growth of GDP.

Source: OECD, *Economic Outlook*, December 1983, Table 5, and earlier years.

But workers as consumers play an essentially passive role (Chapter 8). The markets provided by other types of spending – investment, exports and government spending – largely determine the level of employment and hence the wage bill at any point in time. This, together with tax rates, is the main influence on workers' consumption. Over time, the rate of accumulation largely determines the rate of growth of labour productivity, which in turn is the predominant influence on the growth of real wages. The slowdown in the rate of growth of productivity, from 3¾ per cent a year during the sixties to less than 1½ per cent a year in the decade after 1973, held down the growth of real wages. The slower growth of productivity meant a faster growth of costs; so in order to maintain profitability, firms had to offset a higher proportion of money wage increases by price rises. Workers' purchasing power was further hit by rising import prices and taxes. It rose some 3 per cent a year slower than in the years before 1973; had product wages grown only as fast as productivity, the shortfall would have been 0.5 per cent a year more.

The smaller deceleration in spending on consumption and housing than in real incomes is explained by a fall in the proportion of those incomes saved. Between 1960 and 1973 the proportion of personal income saved had risen from 8.5 to 12.9 per cent. It continued to rise until 1975, reaching a peak of 13.6 per cent, as workers set more aside to offset the erosion through inflation of the real value of past savings. As inflation slackened, the savings ratio fell. By 1980 it was down to 11.4 per cent.

Since workers have more control over the proportion of their incomes saved than over the rate of growth of those incomes, their contribution to overall spending should really be viewed as positive. If the savings ratio had continued to rise along the pre-1973 trend, consumption would have grown more slowly – to the tune of nearly ¾ per cent a year.

This positive impetus was particularly powerful in the United States. There the savings ratio did not rise with the higher inflation of the mid-seventies, and it fell thereafter – from 8½ per cent in 1975 to around 6 per cent in the early eighties. Consumer debt fell sharply as a percentage of personal disposable income in 1975, but recovered strongly in the upswing which followed. Mortgage debt rose even more strongly, jumping from 45 per cent of personal disposable income in 1975 to 54 per cent in 1979. These developments helped to maintain overall spending, especially on housebuilding, in the face of the sluggishness of other categories of expenditure.

. . . or foreigners?

Foreigners have proved handy scapegoats ever since they were discovered, and in the 1970s Arab oil sheiks seemed perfect for the role. As already indicated, the advanced countries' terms of trade deteriorated after 1973 as a result of higher oil prices, and this worked to reduce overall spending. But for the years 1973–81 the effect of this deterioration on the purchasing power of advanced countries' incomes was fairly small, only ½ per cent a year. Moreover, it was partly offset by a faster expansion in the volume of exports than of imports – itself in large part a result of increased sales to OPEC (Chapter 16). This is reflected in Table 15.2 in a positive average contribution to total spending from net exports of ¼ per cent a year.

The combined effect of the negative impact on spending of worsened terms of trade and the positive impact of improved net exports can be seen in changes of the balance of payments. The OECD as a whole moved from a surplus – equivalent to 0.3 per cent of GDP – in 1973, to a deficit – equivalent to 0.3 per cent – in 1981. So there was a real, but small, negative net effect. Therefore, from the point of view of direct influence on overall spending, while the oil sheiks were a depressing influence, they were a very small one.

. . . or governments?

In the 1960s increased state spending on goods and services provided markets for a 1 per cent a year growth in output. Since 1973 it has provided for only ½ a per cent annual growth. Current expenditure began to decelerate in the early seventies as US military spending wound down. Since 1973 current civil spending on health, education and so on has also grown more slowly, and many capital programmes, such as housebuilding and road construction, have been cut back sharply.

Despite this slower growth in expenditure, state budgets moved from balance in the early seventies to deficits averaging over 2–3 per cent of GDP from 1975 onwards. The slow growth of incomes depressed the rise in government revenues. This was less than fully offset by an increase in the proportion of incomes taken in taxation. On the other side of the balance sheet, rising unemployment jacked up the cost of unemployment benefit and other transfers, which rose by ½ a per cent of GDP a year after 1973, twice as fast as before.

The economy would have been even more depressed in the decade after 1973 had governments not run up these deficits. But the deficits resulted solely from those features of state budgets in recession described in the previous paragraph. Overall, governments did not make deliberate moves to stimulate total spending. Indeed, after boosting spending in 1975 (and again, though by much less, in 1978), governments introduced restrictive policies.

The slowdown in welfare expenditures was in line with capital's needs. Employers opposed higher tax rates because of their impact on profits. Even if levied on workers, their effect is to raise costs as trade unions seek higher wage rises to try and maintain real take-home pay. The only other way to maintain spending growth in the face of stagnation is to finance it by borrowing. At high rates of interest, government bonds can provide a lucrative form of investment for some capitalists. But such an accumulation of financial assets offers no solution for the system as a whole. Unlike the accumulation of productive assets, it contributes nothing to raising productivity and potential surplus. Most importantly, boosting spending to maintain employment would have strengthened workers and hindered capital's attempts to re-establish the basis for profitable production. We return to these issues in Chapter 17.

In sum, the deceleration of state spending contributed significantly to the stagnation of markets after 1973. But it was as much a response to underlying difficulties as an independent cause. It is to these more fundamental problems that we now turn.

Investment and accumulation

After 1973 the growth of business fixed investment contributed the equivalent of a mere 0.1 per cent of GDP a year to the growth of overall spending, only one-tenth of the impetus it exerted in the sixties. And even this tiny boost was more than offset by a running down of stocks. Total business investment fell slightly (Table 15.2). This was crucial to the stagnation of markets.

The process was not smooth. The collapse in the investment rate was concentrated in 1974–5 (Chapter 13). But even in the 're-covery' years of 1975–9, business investment rose at only a third of the average rate achieved between 1960 and 1973. Between 1979 and 1982 there was no increase at all. The stagnation was common to all the major blocs. The faster business investment grew before 1973, the sharper the contrast thereafter.

The stagnation of investment not only inhibited market growth, it also steadily undermined the rate of accumulation. While one year of flat investment causes no more than a hiccup in the accumulation process, ten years brings about a significant loss of momentum. A stagnant level of gross investment adds less each year to the capital stock. Since the stock is still growing, in each succeeding year more of the investment is needed simply to replace what has been scrapped.

The decade after 1973 therefore saw a substantial decline in the rate of accumulation. It had averaged 5.3 per cent a year between 1965 and 1973. During 1974–82 it averaged 4.1 per cent a year, and by 1982 it had fallen to 3.5 per cent.

This major slackening is central to the period since 1973. So why did it occur?

Profits

Profits are the prime motive for accumulation. After the nose-dive of 1974–5, the profit rate increased a little as pressure from import prices and wages eased and capacity utilization inched up.

But for every country, and for both manufacturing and the total business sector, the rate was still lower in 1978 than it had been in 1973 – significantly lower for the ACCs as a whole. In 1979 it began to fall again as capacity utilization declined after the second oil price increase. By the early 1980s the manufacturing profit rate was considerably below even the 1975 level, and that for the business was no higher. The full extent of the fall can be seen by comparing the 1981 level with that of the year before the decline set in (Table 15.3). In each bloc the business profit rate was around half the peak level, and the manufacturing profit rate about one-third.

In the manufacturing sector the trend of the accumulation rate turned downward after 1970, soon after the slide in the profit rate began (Chart 15.1). For the business sector as a whole, however, accumulation was maintained right up to 1973, despite the fact that the profit rate had already begun to fall. But after the buoyant expectations of the boom had been snuffed out by the events of 1973–4 (Chapter 13), the accumulation rate for business as a whole tumbled down alongside the profit rate (Chart 15.2).

Just as the high profit rate firmly established by the end of postwar reconstruction had levered up the accumulation rate to unprecedented heights by the mid-sixties, so the decline in profits which

Table 15.3 Profit rates, 1960–81

Percentages

	ACC	USA	Europe	Japan
Business				
Peak year[1]	17.2[2]	22.3[3]	16.3[4]	32.0[5]
1981	10.2	11.8	7.6	14.2
1981/peak year	0.59	0.53	0.47	0.44
Manufacturing				
Peak year[1]	23.6[2]	34.9[3]	19.9[4]	46.5[5]
1981	8.9	10.3	5.2	13.3
1981/peak year	0.38	0.30	0.26	0.29

1. Year before sustained decline in profitability.
2. 1968. 3. 1966. 4. 1960. 5. 1970.

Source: see Appendix.

then set in dragged accumulation down in its wake. The fact that the conditions for accumulation had radically changed, summarized in the fall in profitability, is highlighted by accumulation's failure to recover in the mid-seventies despite some other pressures which observers believed would lead to a recovery.

The period 1974–5 saw rapid increases in materials and labour costs relative to output price increases; that is, in 'real' materials costs and product wages. (Table 15.4 illustrates these developments with UK data.) This must have led to accelerated scrapping and increased the need for replacement of old plant. The 1979 oil price rises must have had similar but more muted effects as real wages rose more slowly (Table 17.2). These developments could have been expected to have stimulated cost-cutting investment, especially in techniques to economize on materials and fuel.

Certainly the OECD believed as late as the close of 1974 that investment would behave 'more satisfactorily than in the 1956–58 downturn. Important strains on capacity developed during the exceedingly strong 1972–73 boom when higher levels of capacity utilization were reached and maintained longer than in the past'

Chart 15.1 ACC manufacturing accumulation and profit rates, 1951–80

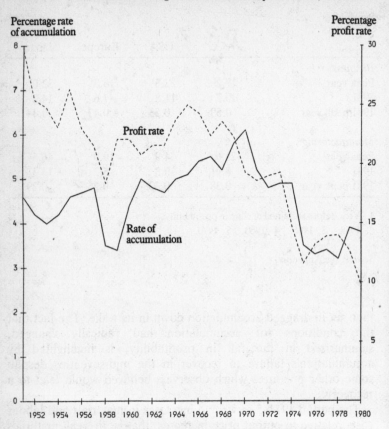

Percentage rate of accumulation

Percentage profit rate

Source: see Appendix.

(*Economic Outlook*, December 1974, p. 21). The Organization was wrong. The level of investment stagnated and the rate of accumulation slid down.

Profits, finance and confidence

Profits data always concern the past. The profits with which capitalists are mainly concerned when making investment decisions,

Chart 15.2 ACC business accumulation and profit rates, 1951–81

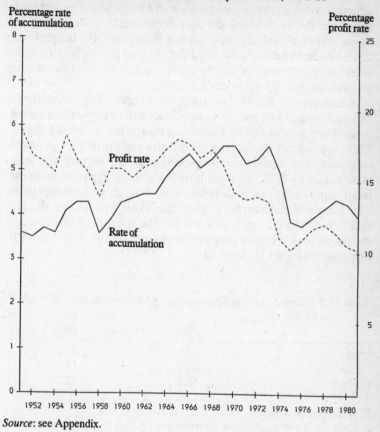

Percentage rate of accumulation

Percentage profit rate

Profit rate

Rate of accumulation

Source: see Appendix.

Table 15.4 UK manufacturing shares of gross output, 1973–5

Percentages

	Fuel and materials	Wages	Gross profits
1973	33.0	49.4	17.6
1975	36.8	52.2	11.0

Source: UK, *National Income and Expenditure*, 1983.

344 *Things Fall Apart, 1974–*

on the other hand, are expected future returns. And, while the actual income in the recent past clearly helps shape expectations about the future, it is not the only determinant. 'Confidence' is a more complex and slippery animal (Chapter 14). Insights into some relations between the hard data of past profits and the more nebulous psychology of future expectations can be gleaned from an examination of investment financing.

Actual profits directly constrain the amount of investment that can be financed internally. So capitalists can only maintain investment when profits fall by increasing borrowing or issuing shares. This they did not do. Borrowing did rise rapidly in 1974 as profits collapsed, and investment projects could only be trimmed more slowly. But by 1981, far from borrowing more to maintain investment, capitalists, except in Japan, were financing a higher proportion from internal sources (Table 15.5).This was despite the fact that in both the United States and Europe the sum of taxation and dividends took a higher proportion of gross profits, leaving less to be ploughed back (Table 15.6).

Table 15.5 Internal funds as a percentage of fixed investment, 1973–81[1]

	1973	1981
USA	80.0	85.1
Japan	57.8	53.0
Europe[2]	68.8	72.3

1. Non-financial companies.
2. Unweighted average of France, Germany and UK.

Source: OECD, *National Accounts*, 1981, Vol.I, Table 13.

Even in Japan, where borrowing increased as a proportion of investment, this did not compensate for the drain from taxation nor for dividends taking a sharply increased share of gross profits. So what inhibited corporations from raising more money externally?

Share issues were discouraged by depressed share prices. Adjusting for inflation, 'real' share prices fell by around one-third in 1974 (Chapter 13) and did not recover thereafter (Table 15.7). So,

Table 15.6 Taxation and distributions as a percentage of gross profits, 1973–81[1]

| | Taxation | | Dividend and interest payments | |
	1973	1981	1973	1981
USA	17.6	10.5	39.0	48.1
Japan	12.8	16.1	43.3	48.9
Europe[2]	14.2	20.0	50.8	47.0

1. Non-financial companies.
2. Unweighted average of France and UK.

Source: as Table 15.5.

despite the accumulation of productive assets that had taken place by the early eighties, the stock market was still valuing expected profits from those assets at only two-thirds of the 1973 level. This was a clear indication that share-owners expected the current depressed level of profits to continue.

The alternative to share issues was borrowing from banks or issuing bonds. The high nominal interest rates of 1974 (Chapter 12) were maintained until 1979, especially for long-term borrowing, and then rose further. Real interest rates, calculated on the basis of current inflation, were low and often negative until 1981. But, whatever the real rate, high nominal rates imply a heavy burden on cash flow in the early years of a loan. Also the 'real' rate

Table 15.7 Real share prices, 1973–81[1]

Index numbers

	1973	1974	1979	1981
USA	100	70	58	58
Japan	100	69	70	76
Europe[2]	100	64	66	56

1. Share price indices divided by indices for consumer prices.
2. Unweighted average of France, Germany and UK.

Source: calculated from OECD, *Main Economic Indicators*.

that matters is the rate over the lifetime of the loan. Long-term borrowing at high nominal rates can turn out very costly if inflation subsequently falls. Expectations about inflation then interact with those about profitability.

In response to this risk, a substantial swing towards short-term borrowing occurred in the United States, where its share of total debt rose from 35 per cent in 1973 to 42 per cent in 1981. It did not happen in Germany or Japan, however, where inflation rates were lower and relationships between corporations and banks were closer.

Fixed-interest borrowing assumed an increased importance as a source of external finance. Debt-equity ratios rose – by about one-fifth in Germany and Japan and nearly one-half in the United States. But clearly capitalists did not feel sufficiently confident about future returns from investment to increase borrowing enough to offset the fall in profits, so the accumulation rate failed to recover. This pessimism became more entrenched as the years of poor returns dragged on.

Accumulation and productivity

Productivity growth weakened in the early seventies (Chapter 11), and a much more pronounced slowdown set in after 1973 (Table 15.8). For the business sector as a whole, productivity grew only half as fast in the decade following 1973 as in that preceding it. In the United States, still with the world's highest level of productivity in many sectors, there was virtually no increase at all in productivity after 1973. Even in manufacturing, productivity grew at not much more than half the pace of the 1960s.

Falls in capacity utilization held back productivity, especially in 1974–5 and again in the early 1980s. The underutilization of capacity (visible in the fall in the output-capital ratio) also involved underutilization of labour. Much overhead labour, such as sales and office staff, is not reduced when output falls, and production workers are not automatically dismissed. The labour force will only be trimmed appropriately when the decline in output is expected to persist, when costs of dismissals, such as redundancy payments, are thought worthwhile and when the opposition of the work force can be overcome. Many companies opt to cut back only

Table 15.8 The productivity slowdown, 1960–81

Average annual percentage growth rates

	ACC	Europe	Japan	USA
Manufacturing output per hour				
1960–73	5.1	5.7	10.5	3.4
1973–81	3.3	4.2	5.8	1.6
GDP per head				
1960–73	3.7	4.3	8.4	2.0
1973–81	1.3	1.9	2.9	0.1

Sources: see Appendix; US Bureau of Labor Statistics, *Underlying Data*.

slowly via so-called natural wastage (not replacing workers who retire or leave). In the meantime, productivity is depressed.

In principle, as the slump deepens, accelerated scrapping of plant and sacking of workers should be a factor making for faster productivity growth. Closing older and less productive plants should raise average productivity levels, just as shooting short soldiers would raise the average height of an army. But the slower growth of product wages after 1973 suggests that the pressure to scrap, generated by rising labour costs, diminished. Higher materials costs, on the other hand, must have intensified pressure to accelerate scrapping.

The effect of deepening slump on productivity on previously installed plant is further complicated by developments in those that continue in operation. Lower output brings increasing under-utilization of more efficient plant alongside accelerated scrapping of less efficient. More efficient firms could secure full order books only by engaging in a ferocious price war. This could drive out enough older plants to maintain sales, but only by raising real product wages and hitting profits. So it is only likely to happen to a limited extent.

The development of productivity does not, of course, depend solely on what is happening within existing plants. It also depends crucially on the installation of new ones. The progressive decline in the accumulation rate has meant a slower rate of introduction of new plants, partially reflected in the slowdown in the growth of the capital-labour ratio. But this indicator actually underestimates the slowdown in mechanization. This is because the faster scrapping of old plant as a result of the slump is not captured in the statistics for the capital stock which are based on assumptions of 'normal' rates of scrapping. So the decline in the accumulation rate has been an important contributing factor to the slowdown in productivity.

A more difficult issue is whether such new plants as were installed generated productivity increases as large as previously. Increases in mechanization seem to have yielded smaller productivity increases in the early seventies than in the sixties (Chapter 11). It is impossible to know whether this trend continued after 1973 on the basis of aggregate statistics, because of the complication of low levels of capacity utilization. But even if it did, most of the slowdown in productivity growth can be attributed in one way or another to the weakening of accumulation, both because of its direct effects and because it generated the stagnation of output which compounded the problem. The stagnation of output further depressed accumulation and discouraged research and development spending, unravelling the virtuous circle of rapid accumulation and productivity growth fostered by the boom. New technologies have been introduced more slowly, and have been reflected in lost jobs rather than rising living standards or shorter working hours.

Living standards and inflation

The slower rate of accumulation and growth of productivity after 1973 led to a slower growth of living standards. Despite a substantial increase in the wage share in 1974–5 (the profits squeeze from another angle, again), workers' take-home pay grew in those years only half as fast as previously (because total output was contracting). This slower rate of growth continued subsequently.

The rapid fall in the rate of growth of money wages (Chart 15.3) undoubtedly reflected the sharp rise in unemployment. This weakened workers' bargaining position. With continuing inflation, they were forced to accept relatively small real wage rises (Chapter 17).

The initial resilience of inflation in the face of sluggish markets reflected inertia in the system. Despite high unemployment, work-

Chart 15.3 ACC money wages and prices, 1973–83

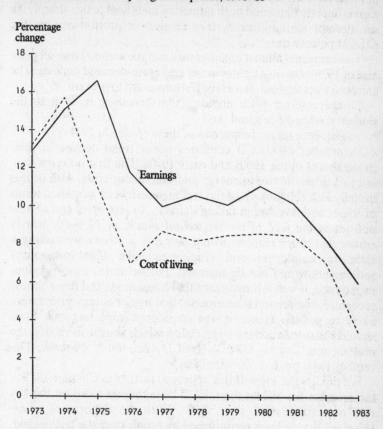

Source: OECD, *Economic Outlook* and *Historical Statistics*.

ers would not accept wage cuts, and fought for wage rises which would maintain or slightly improve their real wages in the face of the past year's inflation. Employers conceded and were then able to pass on most of the cost increase in higher prices. Until 1979 monetary policy played the essentially passive role of allowing credit to grow enough to finance a modest expansion of production without interest rates going through the roof. Inflation only inched down slowly.

After the 1979 round of oil price increases things changed. Governments tightened both monetary and fiscal policy sharply, in an attempt to minimize further erosion of profitability, as the OECD pointed out:

'Governments almost unanimously met the second large oil price rise of 1979–80 with a tightening of aggregate-demand policies. The purpose was two-fold. It was judged important to prevent

' – the external price impulse from becoming built in to the domestic wage-price spiral, and

' – a squeeze on profit margins of the sort seen in 1974–75.

'A number of OECD countries saw a trend decline in their profit shares in the 1960s and early 1970s. The first oil crisis then led to a dramatic rise in energy and unit labour costs, with profits initially absorbing much of the real income loss of worsened terms of trade, and investment falling sharply. *An important aim of tight policies in the face of the second oil shock, in 1979–80, was to ensure that profit margins would be better protected* by making it clear to employers and employees alike that inflationary settlements would not be financed. Furthermore, from previous experience, it was felt necessary that households and firms should recognize, the second time around, that higher energy prices were likely to persist. Hence it was considered important that firms should resist inflationary wage claims which sought to recoup the real income loss to OPEC' (OECD, *Economic Outlook*, December 1981, pp. 6–7, our emphasis).

We discuss the logic of this approach further in Chapter 18. For the moment we will let the OECD have the last word on the key role of accumulation since 1973: 'With the importance of investment having been reconfirmed by events over the last decade, a major policy concern in many countries has been to achieve higher rates of capital formation. Stepping up the rate of investment in an essentially market-oriented economy is not, however, straightforward' (ibid., p. 8). This observation must qualify as the understatement of the decade.

16. International Relations

The mould of international relations set in the immediate postwar years showed few cracks during the boom. The cold war thawed a little, but neither Eastern Europe nor China became a significant market for capitalist goods. Many colonial countries achieved independence, but this seldom jeopardized economic relations with the advanced countries. Even protracted and bloody independence struggles rarely disrupted supplies. The West, led by the United States, ignored the East and dominated the South. Growth was uneven between the advanced countries but, with rapid expansion overall, such divergences could be accommodated. The subsequent years of stagnation, however, fractured this structure.

The Eastern bloc

Despite a marked deterioration in political relations and the onset of the 'second cold war' in the early 1980s, economic relationships between the West and the USSR, Eastern Europe and China changed little. The 'eastern trading area' – as GATT delicately describes these countries – emerged fleetingly in the mid-1970s as a significant market for commodities and capital made idle by stagnation in the West. The proportion of advanced country exports going to the East had only edged up slightly in the sixties. Between 1973 and 1975 it increased by one-half. In 1976, the Eastern bloc took around one-fifth of the machine tool exports of Germany, France, Italy and Belgium. Citroën and Fiat signed major contracts to produce cars in Romania and Poland respectively, exports of which to the West were to cover the cost of imported machinery and know-how. General Motors licensed the manufacture of rear axles in Hungary to be exchanged for Bedford trucks. Over sixty contracts were signed in the years 1974–80 by European, Japanese and US firms to build chemical and fertilizer plants.

The trade deficit of the Soviet Union and Eastern Europe jumped from $3 billion in 1973 to $9 billion in 1975.

The novelty of the trade, the ideological capital to be gained from Russian purchases of Pepsi-Cola concentrates or Western technology and the size of individual deals led to some exaggeration of the importance of Eastern markets. Even in 1975 the bloc absorbed less than 6 per cent of advanced country exports (up from 4½ per cent a couple of years earlier).

Later years saw sharp cutbacks. By 1982 the East's trade deficit had declined to negligible proportions. The expansion had been financed largely by borrowing. Debts to the West rose from $20 billion in 1974 to $90 billion in 1981. Between 1975 and 1980 Western banks lent over $5 billion per year. This represented a substantial accumulation of capital. By 1981 interest totalled $9 billion a year. The East became less willing to borrow more and, being unable to export more to stagnant Western markets, cut back imports sharply. OECD exports to the bloc fell by some 14 per cent in 1982, and the East's share of advanced countries' exports slipped back to around 4½ per cent.

Poland was the most dramatic example. It had incurred one-third of the total Eastern bloc debt and its debt-service ratio (interest and repayments as a percentage of exports) exceeded 100 per cent in 1982. A major rescheduling of debt repayments had to be carried out, and all the Eastern European countries suddenly found it virtually impossible to borrow. Hungary's central bank lost over $1 billion of deposits early in 1982 as panic grew as to whether these deposits could be repaid.

The problem was the East's inability to export enough to underwrite the payment of the interest and eventual repayment of principal. Lenders will only increase the value of outstanding loans if they bear a 'safe' ratio to foreign exchange earnings. Loans and interest payments can grow rapidly without problem only if exports grow in parallel.

Deals whereby Western companies supplied plant in exchange for a share in the product – popular in the seventies – were an attempt to circumvent this problem. For the host countries they were a way of generating exports. For the Western companies they provided a cheap and reliable source of supply. However, estimates by the United Nations suggest that products supplied under these 'buy-back' agreements constituted only around 5 per cent of exports to the West (10 per cent of the Soviet Union's). By the mid-1980s natural gas supplied under these contracts is expected to cover around one-fifth of gas requirements in Germany, France and Italy. Around 6 million tons of coal a year will be supplied to Japan. Over $1 billion worth of chemicals a year will be exported, mainly by the USSR.

In the case of such products as chemicals and cars, these supplies will compete directly with spare capacity in the West. Eastern bloc exports could only grow fast enough to pay the interest on further Western lending if advanced countries' markets for those exports also grew rapidly.

The less developed countries

Many commentators suggest that developments in the LDCs contributed significantly to stagnation and unemployment in the advanced economies. This argument is frequently used to excuse the problems in the advanced countries. It is quite mistaken, however. Developments in the South initially alleviated the slump in the West, and the subsequent failure of the LDCs to continue playing this role was itself a product of stagnation at the centre.

There are obvious parallels with the Eastern bloc, but also two important differences. One is that the West's economic relations with the South were on a far larger scale. By the early 1980s, for example, Brazil and Mexico each owed as much to international banks as did the entire Eastern bloc. The other important difference is that Western relations with the South changed more radically than they did with the East.

During the sixties accumulation proceeded roughly in parallel in the advanced and less developed countries. Between 1960 and 1973 investment grew by 6.2 and 7.6 per cent a year respectively. After 1973 this pattern was transformed. In the advanced countries investment levelled off, whereas in the LDCs it bounded ahead – by 10.7 per cent a year between 1973 and 1979. The share of world capitalist investment carried out in the LDCs rose from 16½ per cent in 1973 to 23¼ per cent in 1979. In the early seventies accumulation in the LDCs was close to the 5½ per cent rate achieved in the advanced countries. By the end of the seventies it was running at about twice the 4 per cent a year to which the advanced countries had slipped.

But rapid growth was concentrated in the major oil exporters and a few countries with successful manufacturing export sectors. For most LDCs the seventies were worse than the sixties. About half achieved GDP growth per head of more than 2 per cent a year, whereas two-thirds had reached this level in the sixties. At the extreme, the 'least developed countries' (thirty of the poorest, accounting for nearly one-tenth of the population of the developing world) saw their real incomes per head fall (Table 16.1).

Table 16.1 Growth rates of less developed countries, 1960–80

Average annual percentage growth rates

	1960–70	1970–80
GDP		
Total developing countries	5.7	5.6
Fast-growing exporters of manufactures	6.4	7.1
Least developed countries	2.6	3.2
GDP per head		
Total developing countries	3.1	3.0
Fast-growing exporters of manufactures	3.6	4.5
Least developed countries	0.0	0.6
Real income per head[1]		
Total developing countries	2.4	4.5
Major oil-exporting countries	0.9	11.1
Fast-growing exporters of manufactures	3.5	4.0
Least developed countries	0.0	−0.3

1. Real income per head is GDP per head of the population, adjusted for changes in the purchasing power of exports.

Source: UNCTAD, *Trade and Development Report*, 1981, p. 34.

Foreign exchange was the crucial constraint for many LDCs. Commodity prices held up in the wake of the first oil crisis and many LDCs began to borrow OPEC surpluses channelled through Western banks. For a time their high import demand provided much-needed markets for Western exports. But developments in the ACCs prevented this situation from lasting. Commodity prices remained at more or less 1974 levels for the remainder of the decade, and by 1980 were three times higher than in 1970. But inflation in the advanced countries meant that their prices relative to manufactures were no higher in 1980 than in 1970. By 1982 the recession had pushed them 20 per cent lower. The LDCs also suffered from the oil price rises. The terms of trade of the least developed countries fell by 1.7 per cent a year between 1970 and 1980 and their export volume by 0.8 per cent a year. So the purchasing power of their exports deteriorated by 2½ per cent a year. By the early eighties this had become the most pressing issue between the advanced countries and the LDCs. We return to it below.

The oil producers

The oil price rises of 1973 and 1979 pushed up the oil producers' real incomes. Between 1970 and 1980 the purchasing power of the major oil exporters' exports grew by 18 per cent a year, despite a stagnation of export volume caused by slow growth and energy-saving measures in the advanced countries. Between 1973 and 1980 the oil exporters' share of non-Eastern bloc incomes doubled, reaching 12 per cent. Most of these extra oil revenues accrued to governments, either as profits or as taxes on foreign oil companies. The share of profit incomes in Saudi Arabian GDP rose from 82 per cent in 1972 to 90 per cent in 1974.

Oil-exporting governments embarked on huge schemes of economic and social development. The ratio of domestic investment to GDP rose from 21.4 per cent in 1970–3 to 28.0 per cent in 1979–80, implying that about one-third of the extra income generated by the oil price rise was invested (Table 16.2).

This burst of growth initially provided welcome relief in the advanced countries for industries hard pressed by the recession. ACC exports to OPEC grew in volume terms by a phenomenal 14 per cent a year. OPEC's share of the total rose from 4 to 8 per cent. The OPEC market was particularly important for the engineering industries. By 1980 it absorbed over 10 per cent of US and EEC exports of machinery and 13 per cent of Japanese. Western companies also provided much vital, and profitable, know-how for OPEC investment programmes. Imports of such private services as civil engineering rose tenfold in value during the seventies.

Table 16.2 Oil producers' investment growth, 1960–79

Average annual percentage growth rates

	1960–73	*1973–79*
Saudi Arabia (construction)	8.1[1]	23.6
Kuwait	n.a.	21.3
Iran	13.0	28.9[2]
Venezuela	7.3	14.1
Nigeria	n.a.	27.6[2]

1. 1963–73.   2. 1973–7.

Source: UN, *Yearbook of National Accounts Statistics,* 1980, Vol. II, Table 6A.

For the advanced countries the ideal form of 'accumulation' by the oil producers was apparently a buildup of military hardware. This should have provided export markets, created no problems of competitive capacity and eased the burden of 'policing' the region. But the oil producers could remain free from political turmoil only if they harnessed oil wealth to development schemes capable of meeting popular aspirations. Events in Iran – the centrepiece of Western strategy in the Middle East – showed that even the most expensive and elaborate techniques of repression could only delay, and thus render the more ferocious, explosive opposition to rotten dictatorships. The fall of the Shah raised the spectre of profitable arms exports being deployed against their suppliers.

Political instability was not the only problem. Much OPEC investment was concentrated in heavy industry. In the late seventies about one-fifth of investment by five major oil producers went into petroleum refining, petrochemicals, fertilizers, basic metals and cement. While plant sales boosted badly depleted Western order books, the end result was bound to cause further difficulty. Saudi Arabia alone aimed to corner 4 to 5 per cent of the world petrochemical market by the 1990s. Such additions to world capacity could have been absorbed without much difficulty had markets grown rapidly. But stagnation meant that even marginal increments to capacity – especially when backed by assured access to inputs – posed serious problems for industries in the advanced countries.

The newly industrializing countries

The other pole of accumulation in the LDCs was the so-called newly industrializing countries (NICs). These countries began to present problems for the West well before OPEC heavy industry capacity came on stream. Within OPEC rapid accumulation was a product of enormously increased export earnings. The NICs, in contrast, boosted exports through rapid accumulation (Table 16.3). Their success seemed to rival Japan's, with export growth of 11 per cent a year between 1970 and 1980.

Table 16.3 Investment growth in the newly industrializing countries, 1960–79

Average annual percentage growth rates

	1960–73	*1973–79*
South Korea	20.4	18.9
Hong Kong	4.6[1]	13.3
Singapore	16.6	4.6
Taiwan	14.2	5.0[3]
Brazil	12.4[2]	6.5
Mexico	9.3	4.1

1. 1968–73. 2. 1965–73. 3. 1973–7.

Sources: UN, *Yearbook of National Accounts Statistics*, 1980, Vol. II, Table 6A; World Bank, *World Tables*.

The NICs are a select group of countries in Asia and Latin America. The three biggest Asian exporters – Taiwan, South Korea and Hong Kong – together account for about half of all LDC exports of manufactures to the advanced countries. Brazil and Mexico provide another 15 per cent, and Singapore, Yugoslavia, Malaysia and the Philippines account for a further 15 per cent. (In the following discussion, Taiwan is excluded due to lack of data.) The share of manufactures in LDC exports to the advanced countries more than doubled over the seventies, rising from 22.1 per cent to 45.0 per cent. By 1980 8.5 per cent of manufactures imports into the advanced countries came from the third world as compared with 4.5 per cent in 1970.

But despite this development, the LDCs as a whole remained enormous importers of manufactures from the advanced countries. In 1980 the imbalance was $175.5 billion, up from $27 billion in 1970 (representing nearly 20 per cent of advanced countries' manufactures exports in 1980 as compared to 17 per cent in 1970). In 1980 the ACCs sold thirty-one times as many vehicles to the LDCs as they bought from them, nine times as many chemical products, seven times as much steel and six times as much engineering output.

The only products with which the LDCs stole a march on the ACCs – selling significantly more than they bought from them – were leather and footwear (three times as much) and clothing (five times). Developments in these sectors – plus a few branches of engineering – are what generated problems in the advanced countries. For hard-pressed producers of clothing in Germany, electronic goods in Britain or TV sets in the United States, the fact that the LDCs as a whole were importing vast amounts of manufactures from their countries was cold comfort. Their markets were being gobbled up by the NICs. In 1980 Mexico, Hong Kong, Singapore and South Korea each sold over $1 billion of engineering goods to the United States. Hong Kong and South Korea sold over $1 billion of clothing. South Korea persuaded the United States to buy $1 billion of light manufactures. Hong Kong sold over $1 billion of engineering products and of clothing to the EEC. Korea persuaded Japanese buyers to accept at least $300 million of engineering products, textiles and clothing. Since markets in the advanced countries were growing only at a snail's pace, imports inevitably displaced home production. Those on the receiving end of factory closures and unemployment inevitably blamed the NICs.

Moreover, although the dynamic NICs did not run huge trade surpluses with the OECD as a whole, they did with the USA and the EEC, alongside deficits with Japan (Table 16.4).

So the problem was not so much that the NICs were selling much more to the advanced countries than they were buying from them, but rather that they were selling consumer goods to the EEC and, especially, the United States, while buying capital goods from Japan. So friction between the advanced countries and the NICs was largely a reflection of friction between Japan on the one hand and the United States and EEC on the other. The NICs were the terrain on which competition between the advanced countries

Table 16.4 Newly industrializing countries' trade balances, 1980

$ billion

with	USA	EEC	Japan	OECD
South Korea	0	+1.4	−2.4	−1.0
Hong Kong	+2.5	+1.9	−4.2	+0.9
Taiwan	+3.3	+1.8	−2.9	+2.7
	+5.8	+5.1	−9.5	+2.6

Source: calculated from OECD, *Trade by Commodities*, Series C, 1980.

was fought out. Substantial portions of the export sectors of some NICs were owned by transnational companies: over 70 per cent in the case of Singapore, over 40 per cent in Brazil; around 30 per cent in Mexico and South Korea, and about 10 per cent in the case of Hong Kong. Many of the Asian NICs' exports to the USA and Europe were by Japanese companies.

The potential problem posed by the NICs is underestimated by the above data to the extent that imports from them have been held down by special measures. Tariffs are no longer the major weapon. Customs duties in 1979 represented 1.1 per cent, 2.9 per cent and 3.5 per cent, respectively, of the value of imports of the EEC, Japan and the United States. But much trade is now limited by 'non-tariff barriers' – measures which restrain import volumes directly or indirectly – preventing imports from undercutting domestic producers (Table 16.5).

The average frequency of such controls is 26 per cent for labour-intensive commodities (typically exported by the LDCs) and only 9 per cent for capital- and technology-intensive products (typically exported by the advanced countries). Around 9 per cent of products in the EEC face price controls, and around 15 per cent volume controls specified in terms of country of origin, and usually directed against the NICs. Apart from foodstuffs and armaments, these controls are most widespread in clothing and textiles (nearly 80 per cent of such products being covered in the EEC) and in footwear (70 per cent coverage in the United States).

Table 16.5 Trade controls, 1983

| | Percentage of product groups covered by | |
	Volume controls	*Price controls*
All advanced countries	23.2	7.5
USA	6.2	9.7
EEC	37.5	14.8
Japan	10.4	0.3

Source: UNCTAD, *Protectionism*, Table 7.

As far back as the mid-1950s, Japan agreed to limit textile exports to the United States, and the United Kingdom concluded bilateral agreements with Hong Kong, India and Pakistan. In 1962 the United States negotiated a long-term agreement limiting import growth of cotton products to 5 per cent a year, and providing a framework for various bilateral agreements. In 1971–2 the United States negotiated agreements with Japan, Hong Kong, South Korea and Taiwan covering artificial fibres. In 1973 the Multi-Fibre Agreement extended the restraint to wool products. It offered an import growth target of 6 per cent a year, but facilitated much more stringent limitations on 'sensitive' products. The agreement was extended and tightened in 1977 with the EEC threatening to redistribute the quotas of countries refusing to accept the terms offered.

'Once governments assumed responsibility for the industry by selective regulation of imports of some products from some countries, regulations inevitably spread until there was global control of imports from low-cost sources. The LTA [long-term agreement] and MFA [multi-fibre agreement] were originally justified on the grounds that selective measures were needed in order to avoid market disruption caused by a surge in imports from a particular source, hence the derogation from the GATT principle of non-selectivity. Selective import regulation, however, stimulated new sources of supply or diversification into other products. These new products were then controlled (under the MFA), as were any new producers. A system of trade regulation has thus developed which has become progressively more global.

Initially applied selectively against a few exporters, it has grown to include all developing countries, has been extended to EEC-associated countries and outward processing, and is now threatening intra-AIC [advanced industrial country] trade in the form of US-EEC trade' (Woolcock, p. 46).

In the 1970s really dynamic accumulation was confined to the East Asian NICs. They managed to maintain rapid export growth despite the recession of the early 1980s and increased protectionism. While South Korea, in particular, borrowed heavily overseas to finance accumulation, the fact that the borrowing was ploughed back into productive capacity, some of which found outlets in world markets, meant that growing debts could be serviced. The Latin American NICs – second-division export manufacturers – proved less capable of weathering the recession of the early eighties. Bankers, who a few years earlier had regarded them as dream clients, began to get nightmares about their credit-worthiness.

Debt

Borrowing implies lending. The LDCs' enormous buildup of debt after 1973 was made possible by surplus OPEC funds. As well as accumulating at home (exchanging oil for petrochemical works) the oil producers piled up financial assets overseas (oil for 'petrodollars'). Their balance of payments surpluses peaked after the major oil price rises (reaching $65 billion in 1974 and $107 billion in 1980), and then declined as spending and import costs rose. Their surpluses totalled some $500 billion over the years 1973–81, about 15 per cent of their incomes.

Capitalists in the advanced countries could have borrowed the oil surpluses to maintain accumulation despite lower profits (although at the cost of raising their already stretched external financing ratios). Faced with stagnation, they did so only to a limited extent. Nor were advanced countries' governments prepared to expand borrowing enough to maintain demand. So the non-oil LDCs, facing depressed export markets and hugely inflated fuel bills, were forced to run massive balance of payments deficits if they were to expand. Between 1974 and 1981 these countries together ran twice as big a deficit as the advanced capitalist world.

Their debts represented the cumulative effect of these deficits. One estimate put their total at $750 billion. The most rapidly growing component was to private Western banks. Between the close of 1973 and 1981 LDC debt to Western governments and such international agencies as the World Bank rose about three times, while that to private banks rose nine times. It had reached around $400 billion by early 1983.

The banks, faced with limited outlets for profitable lending in the advanced countries, competed madly to attract OPEC deposits to lend on to the South. It seemed safe enough. Many loans were at variable interest rates, guaranteeing a profit regardless of interest rate changes.

The borrowers were then hit by rising interest rates, looming repayment obligations and stagnant export earnings. Higher interest rates cost the LDCs an estimated $20–25 billion over the three years 1979–81. By 1981 total debt servicing on long- and medium-term debt for the thirteen biggest borrowers represented about 25 per cent of export earnings, up from 18 per cent in 1974. In 1981 LDCs were due to repay loans of $129 billion, practically double their foreign exchange reserves. Mexico was due to repay $28 billion. Its reserves stood at $4 billion.

The debt crisis also had a strong political element. Many regimes – whether military and dictatorial as in Brazil and Argentina, or populist as in Mexico – borrowed partly to head off rising popular discontent. Some of the money also found its way into Swiss bank accounts and other safe havens; $100 billion is estimated to have left Latin America during 1981 and 1982.

But problems would have arisen even if all loans had been invested productively. A single country may avoid such difficulties. South Korea has piled up more debts in proportion to its size than the 'problem' Latin American borrowers. But continued export success had ensured it a high credit rating. Were all borrowers to have accumulated on a Korean scale, however, excess capacity would have skyrocketed. Not even productive investment will show a return if markets cannot be found for the output. And the West would almost certainly have responded to signs of a successful LDC export drive with a barrage of protectionist measures (see below).

Unable to make repayments or to borrow enough elsewhere to keep their creditors at bay, the debtors were forced to demand revised terms. And the creditors were forced to concede them – to 'reschedule' the debts for, at least hypothetical, later repayment. In 1981–2 ten new countries undertook debt reschedulings, more than in the whole of the fifteen years 1956–70. Total reschedulings covered $250 billion of debt.

The situation is highly fragile. The capital of the largest hundred banks in 1983 was some $160 billion, around half of Latin American debt. The largest nine US banks have lent the equivalent of half their capital to Mexico, and most have lent much more than their total capital to Mexico and Brazil together. If these countries defaulted, the banks would be bankrupted. They admit privately that making provision in the accounts for bad debts would 'have a devastating effect on bank profits and perhaps also on the confidence in the banking system' (*Financial Times*, 18 February 1983). This obliges banks not only to reschedule existing debts but also to lend even more to enable the borrowers to meet interest payments.

'The International Monetary Fund wants the world's banks to stuff yet more dollars into the stocking of Latin America's debt. The banks have little choice but to concede. They know as they do it, however, that the money will probably not be seen again; indeed, they will be lucky even to get paid the interest. . . .

'In all about $300 billion of debt is owed by Latin America. The new money that is now being poured in is being lent not for productive long-term capital investment but for a more immediate purpose: to prevent a horrendous jolt to the world's banking system. That jolt would follow if any major debtor – in Latin America alone, count Mexico, Brazil, Argentina, Venezuela – failed to meet its interest payments. Constant last-minute injections of cash by central and private banks have managed, just, to keep that time at bay. So far. Should that time come, however, it would send a hurricane through Wall Street; it would cause the certain collapse of a number of US banks; it would set the price of gold flying; it would produce political chaos in the defaulting country; and, worst of all, through a crisis in confidence, it would put off hopes of a world economic recovery' (*Economist*, 11 December 1982).

Rescheduling and new loans have had strings attached. The IMF has provided some of the additional finance ($5 billion to Brazil, $4 billion to Mexico; $2 billion to Argentina). In return it has demanded that governments agree to tough IMF policies – reductions in government deficits, limits to money supply growth and currency depreciations to improve trade. Mexico agreed to cut its budget deficit from 16 per cent of GDP in 1982 to 3.5 per cent in

1985 and to cut inflation from 100 per cent a year to 70 per cent. These policy packages are the lineal descendants of the policies implemented in Europe and Japan thirty-five years before under the Marshall Plan, with even more devastating effects on employment.

'The Mexican economic and social landscape meanwhile looks as though a hurricane had swept through it. Hundreds of firms are going bankrupt every month. Private investment declined by 15 per cent last year. Unemployment is reckoned to have jumped from 8 per cent to around 13 per cent in the space of a few months, in an economy in which underemployment anyway probably stands at around 45 per cent' (*Economist*, 30 April 1983).

The fundamental point is that the bulk of the loans could not have been invested in ways capable under existing world economic conditions of yielding sufficient returns to enable debt servicing and eventual repayment. Thus someone has to foot the bill. There are three candidates. One is the banks. If loans are simply written off then bank shareholders suffer, with the attendant risk of a collapse of the credit system. If governments bail out the banks then Western taxpayers pay. The only other possibility is for the LDCs to depress their economies enough to cut imports to the point where net foreign exchange receipts are sufficient to cover debt servicing and repayment; in other words, to make the third world masses pay. All plans for resolving the international debt crisis involve juggling these three possibilities.

The IMF, at the bidding of the ACC governments which control it, is trying to impose the third option. But there is no guarantee that it will succeed. If third world resistance is too great, or the world economic climate so hostile that even draconian policies cannot generate sufficient LDC foreign exchange receipts, then ACC governments and banks will have to find some of the money. Either way, IMF policies will have given a further contractionary twist to the world economy.

The advanced countries

Uneven development

The fall in accumulation since 1973 has been mainly located in Japan and Europe, the powerhouses of the boom. By 1982 the stagnation of investment pulled down the rate of business accumulation in Japan to 5.7 per cent, less than half that of the early seventies. In Europe it fell from 5½ per cent to 3.1 per cent. In the United States the 4 per cent rate of accumulation achieved in 1980 matched that of the early seventies and it only declined to 3.2 per cent in 1982 (Chart 16.1).

Chart 16.1 Business accumulation, 1970–82[1]

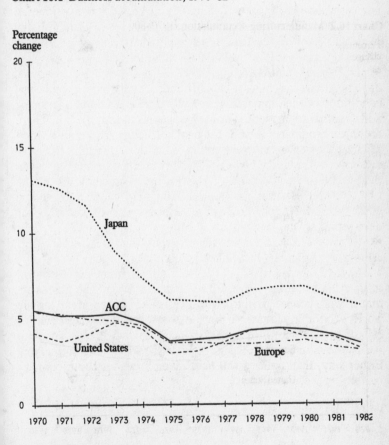

1. Growth rate of gross fixed capital stock.

Source: see Appendix.

The pattern is even more striking in manufacturing, the decisive sector for international competitiveness. By 1980 the rate of manufacturing accumulation in the United States was double that of the sixties. In the EEC and Japan it had fallen to one-half or less. The rate of accumulation in the United States was now similar to the Japanese and double the European – an astounding turnaround (Chart 16.2).

Chart 16.2 Manufacturing accumulation, 1970–80[1]

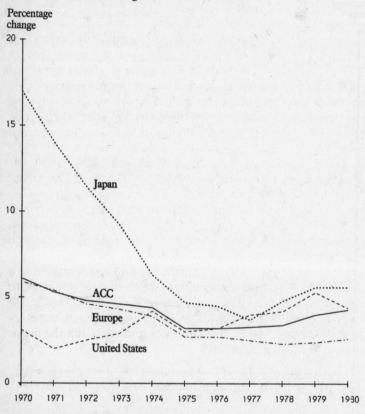

1. Growth rate of gross fixed capital stock.

Source: see Appendix.

But US business was neither back on terms with Japan nor restoring its earlier advantage in relation to Europe. For one thing, employment rose rapidly in the United States: manufacturing employment rose by 0.4 per cent a year between 1973 and 1981, whereas it fell by 0.3 per cent a year in Japan and 1.7 per cent a year in Europe. So capital stock per worker, our indicator of mechanization, grew at around 6 per cent for Japan, 5 per cent for Europe and 4 per cent for the United States. Nevertheless the difference is much less than in earlier years (and is probably exaggerated by the fact that a faster rate of scrapping of old equipment in Japan and Europe is not reflected in the capital stock statistics).

But the difference in productivity performance was enormous. Productivity growth in US manufacturing was far slower than in the period before 1973 (Table 15.8), despite the faster growth of capital stock per worker. It was also slower than its rivals, despite a not much lower rate of mechanization. Japanese capital achieved rapid productivity growth by expanding production fast (though far more slowly than in the sixties). European industry maintained a more modest productivity growth by sacking workers. US business failed to do either, and productivity stagnated despite the accumulation. Explanations canvassed ranged from the impact of energy prices, the effect of anti-pollution measures and other legislation, and the slowdown of research and development spending. None was very convincing. US capital, more concerned with treatment than explanation, attempted to solve the puzzle through an onslaught on the factory floor (Chapter 17).

So in terms of productivity growth, US business remained at a disadvantage as compared to Europe, which in turn continued to lag behind Japan. But competitiveness also depends on the exchange rate, so we must look at how the international monetary system developed, before the pattern of trade between the major blocs can be assessed.

International money
The collapse of the fixed exchange rate system in 1973 (Chapter 12) did not have the disastrous consequences for trade sometimes predicted. Exchange rates between the major currencies have fluctuated considerably on a day-to-day basis despite government intervention to smooth out 'disorderly markets'. But these movements – averaging ½ per cent per day between the dollar

and the mark, for example – are thought to have had only a minor effect in discouraging trade. More serious have been the trends in exchange rates from year to year, which have not simply balanced out different inflation rates in the various countries. Measures of real competitiveness, calculated in terms of relative unit labour costs, have shifted substantially (Chart 16.3). Since 1973 the

Chart 16.3 Real competitiveness, 1970–82[1]

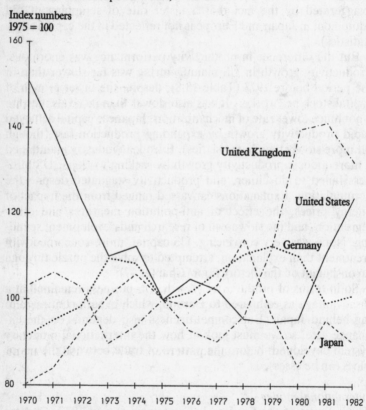

1. Unit labour costs in manufacturing relative to competitors. Thus a *rise* in the index implies a *fall* in competitiveness.

Source: IMF, *International Financial Statistics*, 1983.

current balances of the United States, Japan and Germany have all fluctuated from year to year in the range of plus \$10–15 billion to minus \$10–15 billion. The yen and the mark both rose against the dollar up to 1979 and 1980 respectively, much more than their low rate of cost increase warranted. The dollar appreciated sharply after 1978, especially under Reagan's tight money policies. So by 1982 the relative unit labour costs of the three were back to the pattern of 1973. Further, taking the period as a whole, the fluctuations seem to have balanced out. Between 1974 and 1981 the United States averaged a current account surplus of \$¼ billion a year, Japan a surplus of \$1¼ billion, and Germany was in balance.

While exchange rate movements have kept the current payments position of the major countries in rough balance over the years, the United States was still able to finance a heavy capital outflow. This has run at double the rate (in money terms) of the years of the breakup of the fixed exchange rate system (Table 16.6). Reserves of foreign exchange held by governments nearly trebled between 1973 and 1982. Although an increasing proportion of these are now held in marks and yen (12.5 per cent and 4.1 per cent respectively at the end of 1981), around 70 per cent are still held in dollars, and two-thirds of these dollars are held in New York. The dollar has remained the major international currency, being used by the private international banks to conduct their business and held by central banks as the major component of reserves.

The benefit to US business of being able to finance the continuing long-term capital outflow has been a continued buildup of profit and interest receipts from abroad without a US current account surplus. US capital received \$161 billion of net profit and interest from abroad between 1975 and 1981. Annual receipts rose from \$15½ billion to \$33 billion between 1974 and 1981. Part of the increase was simply higher money profits on the existing industrial investments abroad. But part was profits on \$42 billion (net) additional foreign investment, financed at a relatively low interest rate by other countries accumulating dollar reserves (the average real short-term interest rate in the United States over the years 1974–80 was minus 0.1 per cent).

The cost was that the dollar was higher than it would have been had the long-term capital outflow driven the exchange rate down. The United States (until the election of Reagan, at least) would

Table 16.6 US balance of payments, 1975–81

$ billion

Merchandise trade	−145.5
Services and remittances	12.1
Net military transactions	− 4.1
US government grants (ex. military)	− 24.7
Net interest and dividends received	161.5
Current account balance	− 0.7
Direct investment (net)	− 41.8
Investment in shares and bonds (net)	− 26.0
Government loans	− 19.6
Long-term capital	− 87.4
Balance on current and long-term capital	− 88.1[2]
Dollars held abroad by private sector[1]	− 14.3
Financed by	
Dollars held abroad in official reserves	91.3
Reduction in US reserves	− 12.5
(of which gold)	(−0.2)

1. Includes net short-term capital.
2. Since 1979 the US accounts do not distinguish between the short-term and long-term nature of certain asset holdings. However, the long-term component is relatively small and a rough estimate has been made.

Source: US, *Survey of Current Business*, June 1982.

probably have preferred an even lower dollar, allowing current account surpluses. But this proved impossible to achieve. Attempting to 'mouth' the dollar down in 1977 nearly led to disaster: the dollar overhang is so huge that once speculation gets going it is almost impossible to control. At the end of 1980 the US money supply stood at $1656 billion. Foreign monetary authorities held an estimated $240 billion ($157 in the United States, the rest in Eurodollar markets). Other foreigners held $700 billion in dollar deposits outside the United States. Its gold and foreign exchange reserves would last a matter of seconds if all that money began to move out of the dollar. In 1978 the United States had sharply to arrange $30 billion support from foreign central banks to stave off a threatened dollar collapse. Other governments were willing to help because a declining dollar was eroding their export competitiveness. Reagan's tight money policies would have been a blessing to Japanese and German exporters if they had not reduced the US market alongside US competitiveness (Chart 16.3).

Trade

The growth of world trade slowed considerably from the mid-seventies. It grew by 3.5 per cent a year between 1973 and 1981, down from 8.7 per cent a year in the previous decade. World trade in manufactures, the arena of sharpest competition, grew at 5.1 per cent a year as compared to 10.8 per cent during the boom. With markets growing more slowly and excess capacity mounting, competition intensified.

The usual way to distinguish winners and losers in the struggle for markets is by shares of manufactures exports. The EEC's share declined significantly during the 1970s. Japan gained most, but the US share also recovered slightly after a long period of decline (Table 16.7). All the major European countries, except Italy, scored a lower share by the early 1980s. By 1982 Germany's share was only a couple of percentage points higher than that of the United States and Japan; in 1973 it had exported one-third more than the United States and two-thirds more than Japan.

Both the EEC and the United States are also major importers of manufactures, but while the United States imported about as many manufactures as it exported in 1973, the EEC exported many more, contributing nearly two-thirds of *net* manufactures

Table 16.7 Manufacturing export shares, 1973–81

Percentage of total for three blocs

	USA	EEC	Japan
1973	18.2	67.5	14.4
1981	20.4	60.0	19.6

Source: calculated from GATT, *International Trade*, 1982, Tables A19, A20, A21.

exports (exports less imports) of the three blocs. Japan, which has consistently imported a tiny proportion of manufactures, contributed over one-third of net exports (Table 16.8).

Table 16.8 Imports and net exports of manufactures, 1973–81

Percentage of total for three blocs

	USA	EEC	Japan
Imports			
1973	25.3	69.1	5.6
1981	27.8	67.0	5.2
Net exports			
1973	−1.8	62.8	39.0
1981	3.9	44.3	51.9

Source: as Table 16.7.

Japan's hugely increased export share, combined with no increase in the import share, brought its share of net exports up to over one-half. The EEC's share dropped by a little more as the United States moved to a slight surplus on manufactures. The shift reflected Japan's enhanced competitiveness, but it was also required by other developments in the trading position of the advanced countries.

All three major blocs faced similar increases in fuel import bills as a result of the oil price rises. Between 1973 and 1981 net fuel imports rose by $66 billion in the United States, $63 billion in Japan and $81 billion in the EEC. They also all faced increased raw materials costs. But whereas Japan had to pay an additional $10 billion for imported food, the United States' net food exports rose from $6 to $21 billion. So the net import bill for primary products rose by $52 billion in the United States, $88 billion in the EEC and $81 billion in Japan. The United States also gained in net 'exports of services' (basically interest from abroad) almost as much as it lost on primary products. The EEC showed a much smaller improvement, and Japan a small deterioration, on 'services'. So, while the United States would have required only a $12 billion increase in net exports of manufactures to maintain the current account balance as in 1973, the EEC would have required an increase of $74 billion and Japan one of $89 billion. In the event the United States gained $10 billion in net manufactured exports, the EEC $61 billion and Japan $94 billion.

If the EEC and Japan had increased their net exports solely in markets outside the advanced countries – such as OPEC and other LDCs – then little friction need have occurred. This is roughly what the EEC did. Net exports of manufactures to the major oil exporters rose by $41 billion, those to other developing countries by $20 billion, those to the Eastern bloc by $5 billion, and those to the smaller industrialized countries by $15 billion. Japan was more or less as successful in all these markets except OPEC, where its net exports rose by only $19 billion. The United States, which did not need to export more manufactures, also sold another $14 billion to the oil producers and $8 billion to other LDCs. So the EEC and the USA did better in third world markets than they needed to, whereas Japan did markedly worse. The system balanced only because Japan succeeded in penetrating the US and European markets. Net Japanese exports of manufactures to the United States rose by $22 billion and those to the EEC by $10 billion (Table 16.9). This bred demands for protectionist measures in Europe and the United States.

Yet the rise in Japan's import bill for primary products made a corresponding rise in net manufacturing exports essential if even the slower rate of growth was to be maintained without an escalating balance of payments deficit. And US and European success in third world markets meant that they were bound to run a larger deficit with Japan in net manufactured exports.

Net flows of manufactures are not the only influence on protectionist sentiment. The fact that ACC exporters of capital goods are expanding sales rapidly is of little comfort to clothing producers in the advanced countries who face import competition from the NICs. Nor were US car producers, facing nearly $5 billion worth of imports from the EEC in 1981 ($4 billion net), impressed by the fact that US office and telecommunications equipment firms were selling $7 billion to the EEC ($5 billion net). And, while net flows of manufactures between the EEC and United States have been small, gross flows have been large

Table 16.9 Net exports of manufactures to various markets, 1973–81[1]

$ billion

Importer

	Japan	EEC	USA	Oil exporters	Other LDCs	Total
Exporter						
USA						
1973	− 6.9	− 3.3	–	2.4	2.5	−1.1
1981	−29.8	0.7	–	16.0	10.4	8.9
EEC						
1973	− 1.8	–	2.3	6.6	11.1	39.8
1981	−13.2	–	− 4.0	47.1	31.8	100.8
Japan						
1973	–	1.9	5.6	2.5	7.7	24.7
1981	–	12.3	27.3	22.0	32.7	118.3

1. Figures for net imports differ from the corresponding figure for net exports due to statistical discrepancies.

Source: as Table 16.7.

(around $40 billion in 1981) – as big as gross manufactures imports from Japan in the case of the United States, and twice as big in the case of the EEC. They have also been growing rapidly – about one-half in volume between 1973 and 1981 – considerably faster than manufacturing output. So all major European countries and the United States experienced increases in import penetration when production was growing more slowly and unemployment rising (Table 16.10). This added to the clamour for protectionism.

Protectionism

Since 1973 more and more trade has become subject to some form of control. The proportion of manufactured trade so covered rose from about 13 per cent in 1974 to some 30 per cent in 1982.

Table 16.10 Share of imports in apparent consumption of manufactures, 1970–80

Percentages

	1970 Total	1970 from LDCs	1980 Total	1980 from LDCs
EEC	20.4	2.5	31.8	4.6
Japan	4.7	1.3	6.2	2.4
USA	5.5	1.3	8.6	2.9

Source: IMF, *Developments in International Trade Policy*, Table 4.

The classic technique has been to negotiate 'voluntary' export restraints. The most comprehensive so far implemented cover trade between the EEC and Japan, but the United States has also used the device. The *Economist* discussed these developments under the headline 'Import or Die':

'Because of existing agreements, in any year only 11 out of every 100 British car buyers (and only three in 100 French) can choose a new Japanese car. America sins, too. Despite its free-enterprise, free-trade bombast, the Reagan administration prevents Americans from buying more than 1.68 m cars from Japan in a year (a limit that was extended this month for a third year).

'Europe's latest agreement goes further than America's. It extends protectionism far beyond the old geriatric wards of textiles, steel, shipbuilding and cars into the maternity wards. The Japanese have been coerced into promising "moderation" over a product range that extends from quartz watches to fork-lift trucks to machine tools (where they "will pay special attention to the French market"). It imposes limits on the number of Japanese video tape recorders (VTRs) sold in the common market and guarantees a minimum share of the market to Europe's own producers. This year the Japanese are not allowed to sell more than 4.55 m videos in the EEC, including around 600,000 sets exported in kit form for final assembly at Japanese VTR plants in Britain and West Germany. European manufacturers will have guaranteed sales in the common market for 1.2 m sets, and the price of these sets will not be undercut by the Japanese' (19 February 1983).

At the end of 1982 the United States House of Representatives passed a Bill which would force companies selling more than 100,000 cars in the United States to make or buy a minimum of 10 per cent of their value in the United States, rising by 1 point for every additional 10,000 to a maximum of 90 per cent for sales of 900,000.

The stiffest battle between the EEC and the United States has probably been that over steel. In June 1982 the United States government found that nine foreign governments were 'unfairly' subsidizing their steel industries (with British Steel alleged to be the worst offender). After months of wrangling a quota system was agreed, but the limitations of such deals were spelt out in a report on the negotiations: 'Relief from European competition will not give the American steelmakers the relief from imports they expect. Tariffs and quotas are like rocks placed in a fast running stream. They provide only a temporary diversion. The European companies shut out of America will compete in markets outside the United States, sometimes against American companies. And producers not subject to quotas, notably the Japanese, South Koreans and Canadians, will react to this competition by shifting more of their efforts to the American market' (*Economist*, 25 December 1982).

Tension also mounted over agricultural products. The EEC's share of world food exports rose from 8.3 per cent in 1976 to 18.3 per cent in 1981, with exports of meat, milk products, grain and sugar receiving subsidies of some $8 billion.

The trend towards increased protectionism brought a sharp increase in direct investment in the United States. Japanese investment there rose from $0.7 billion in 1979 to $2.7 billion in 1981. Western European investment increased from $8.2 billion to $12.4 billion over the same period. The low value of the dollar in the late seventies provided an incentive by making US plant cheaper for foreigners. It also worked to reduce US investment abroad (down from $25 billion in 1979 to $9 billion in 1981). But it was not the only factor. OECD comments: 'While direct investment abroad in the 1970s was mainly related to the supply of raw materials and the availability of cheaper labour in neighbouring countries, in the more recent period Japan has increasingly shifted the production of export goods to the United States and other OECD countries – a move apparently related to increasing trade frictions and threatened protectionism'

(*Economic Outlook*, December 1982, p. 60). But overseas investment, and even cooperation with domestic producers, may only push the problem one stage back. There has been pressure inside the EEC to redefine 'domestic products' so as to extend tariffs and quotas to Japanese cars produced by joint ventures with European producers (such as that between Honda and BL).

'Voluntary restraint' appears increasingly inadequate. Whatever the gains to a particular industry – and these are likely to be limited by increased competition in third world markets – the overall impact is much less than the sum of the gains in the industries covered. Keeping out Japanese cars weakens the yen and thereby increases the competitiveness of other Japanese exports. Relief for car producers is offset by increased pressure on other sectors. Given the dynamism of accumulation in Japan, and her pattern of imports and exports, surpluses on manufactured trade with other advanced countries are inevitable, as is the pressure towards protectionism which they generate.

17. Capitalists and Workers

As labour markets tightened in the late sixties, class conflict re-emerged as a major problem for employers. The years after 1973, by contrast, saw unemployment mount and industrial struggle gradually recede. Western employers sought to capitalize on the new balance of forces by bypassing or weakening unions in order to secure the 'flexibility of labour' enjoyed in Japan. But a decade after mass unemployment re-emerged they have yet to break the power of organized labour in a decisive fashion.

Labour in retreat

Workers did not accept the effects of stagnation on jobs and living standards willingly or easily. Strike rates remained high throughout the seventies. But the pressure of unemployment forced concessions, and strike rates fell in the early eighties (Table 17.1).

Table17.1 Days occupied in strikes, 1953–82[1]

	1953–61	1962–66	1967–71	1972–76	1977–81	1982
USA	113	79	165	105	90	n.a.
Japan	45	25	19	21	5	2
France	41	32	350	34	23	26
Germany	7	3	8	3	8	0
Italy	64	134	161	200	151	192
UK	28	23	60	97	112	47

1. Average number of days per year occupied in strikes per 100 workers in industry and transport.

Source: *Employment Gazette*, October 1963, October 1972, March 1983, March 1984.

At first, in response to pressure from the labour movement, governments in several countries provided aid to alleviate unemployment. Redundant workers received incomes equivalent to their previous earnings, and firms were subsidized to retain labour (although these latter schemes were often ineffective – Chapter 19). In January 1975 the Giscard administration in France enacted a law requiring that dismissals be justified to the Labour Inspectorate. This followed hard on government pressure which forced employers to pay redundant workers up to 90 per cent of their earnings, financed mainly by increased employers' contributions. In late 1974 Italian employers and unions signed an agreement, under government pressure, guaranteeing workers 80 per cent of gross pay (93 per cent of net) for all idle time between zero and forty hours a week. Firms directly involved were to contribute a maximum of 8 per cent of earnings. At the same time wages were completely indexed to changes in the cost of living under the *scala mobile*.

But as the seventies progressed and unemployment mounted and the scale and persistence of stagnation became widely appreciated, the employers moved on to the offensive. In France the 1976 'Barre Plan' attempted to hold real wages constant and rebuild profit margins. In 1978 the government facilitated redundancies and presided over wholesale reorganization of steel and textiles. The deflation which accompanied the plan increased unemployment but had the short-term contradictory effect of holding back productivity growth and profit margins (a problem Thatcher was to experience a few years later – Chapter 18). The Barre experiment ended with the defeat of Giscard and the installation of the Mitterrand government in June 1981.

In Germany the unions pulled out of the so-called 'concerted action' sessions in which guidelines for wage increases were discussed with the government and employers. The president of the German union federation, the DGB, complained that the 'honeymoon is over' and said that 'if the social market economy isn't capable of re-establishing full employment one must wonder whether such a system will remain defensible in the future' (quoted Flanagan *et al.*, p. 285). A strike wave, major by German standards, followed in 1978 and early 1979 as unions resisted new technology (in printing), downgrading of jobs (engineering), and fought for better pay (engineering) and a thirty-five-hour working week (steel). The employers retaliated by locking out vast numbers of workers. In engineering alone nearly 200,000 workers were locked out, three times as many as were on strike. In steel, where the strike lasted six weeks, the employers reacted to strikes in plants supplying the car industry by locking out the rest of the work force. The resulting financial pressure helped to force the workers back on substantially the employers' terms. In the printing industry reporters were to be allowed to type straight on to computers. In engineering, technologically displaced workers were to be transferred or retrained. In steel the work-week remained intact. Fewer than half the strikers voted for the settlement and this was widely regarded as a vote of no confidence in the union leadership. The steel and engineering union was forced in 1979 to accept a moratorium on all non-wage issues until 1983 – an indication of the scale of the defeat.

The Italian unions also suffered severe defeats at the end of the seventies. From 1976 to 1979 the Italian Communist Party (PCI) cooperated with the Christian Democrat government in an attempt to realize its 'historic compromise'. One facet involved the unions holding back on pay and accepting redundancies. The communist secretary-general of the main union confederation, the CGIL, said that pay 'will have to be very restricted' and that 'we can no longer force firms to keep on a number of workers which is superfluous to their productive possibilities'. He called for 'sacrifices, not marginal but substantial sacrifices' (quoted Flanagan *et al.*, p. 555).

But electoral reverses forced the PCI back into opposition. The employers then moved on to the offensive, with what was described as a 'new sense of identity and cooperation'. In the autumn of 1979 Fiat fired sixty-one workers for misconduct (alleging intimidation, insults to foremen and sabotage) and union officials failed to win support for strike action. A British observer noted that 'Fiat's action has already produced a marked change on the factory floor: the general attitude to foremen has changed, and there has been an end to the insults to which they were previously subjected. It is clear that the Fiat episode has also made a strong impression on workers in some other large companies such as Pirelli, Alfa Romeo and Italsider' (Incomes Data Services, November 1979).

In September 1980 the Fiat unions were forced, after a thirty-three-day strike, to accept 23,000 lay-offs and the transfer of surplus labour to other jobs in the area. The decisive event was a march of foremen and plant managers opposing the strike, at which some 3000 were expected. This turned into the 'March of the 40,000' with many rank-and-file workers demonstrating opposition to the union line. The *Economist* reported that 'Because of Fiat's size and symbolic importance in Italy, the outcome is already being described as the "hot autumn in reverse"' (25 October 1980). It also noted that 'when full production resumed on October 20th, absenteeism – scourge of Fiat in the past – dropped to 5 per cent'. In January 1983 agreement was reached to reduce by one-seventh the protection for inflation granted by the *scala mobile*. Although the employers had aimed to cut the protection by one-half, the union concession was still hailed as 'one of the most significant agreements in industrial relations since the war' (Incomes Data Services, February 1983). British and American workers also suffered setbacks under Thatcher and Reagan (Chapter 18).

The extent to which the labour movement had been weakened is exemplified in its different responses to the two oil crises. In both the mid-seventies and early eighties stagnant productivity and higher costs of oil and other imports meant that real wages could only grow very slowly without squeezing profits (Table 17.2, columns 1–3). In the mid-seventies, however, aggressive wage bargaining in Japan and Europe secured considerable money and real wage increases so that the share of wages in the value of output grew rapidly (columns 4 and 5). By the time of the second oil crisis, however, workers' bargaining position was much weaker. Real wages grew much more slowly than in 1973–5 and profits were squeezed much less.

Although the labour movement was on the defensive almost everywhere by the early eighties, the defeats had not amounted to a rout. Workers had not deserted their unions in large numbers, as had happened in the thirties. The union movement had not fragmented into ineffectiveness, as had happened in much of Europe in the late forties. The employers had not achieved the fundamental reshaping of industrial relations which they sought.

Table 17.2 Real wages, productivity and terms of trade, 1972–82

Annual percentage growth rates

		(1) Productivity	*(2)* Effect of terms of trade	*(3)* 'Warranted' real wage[1]	*(4)* Actual real wage	*(5)* Share of wages
				(1)+(2)		(4)−(3)
USA	1972–75	0.2	−0.4	−0.2	0.1	0.3
	1979–82	0.0	0.1	0.1	0.3	0.2
Japan	1972–75	2.7	−1.5	1.2	5.4	4.2
	1979–82	2.3	−0.8	1.4	2.2	0.8
Europe[2]	1972–75	2.0	−0.8	1.3	3.5	2.2
	1979–82	1.6	−0.5	1.1	1.7	0.7

1. The 'warranted' growth of the real wage shows the rate at which real (pre-tax wages) can grow given the growth of productivity and the effect of import prices on domestic purchasing power, while maintaining the share of wages in the value of output.
2. Unweighted average of four biggest countries.

Source: OECD, *Economic Outlook*, July 1982 and earlier issues.

After Japan?

In Europe and the United States the goal was to secure as pliable a labour force as that available to Japanese employers. The Ford company went so far as to describe its new strategy as 'After Japan'. So we shall next examine industrial relations in Japan, not least in order to explode the myth of classless harmony.

The contrast between real wage growth before and after 1973 is starkest in Japan. Here, workers' living standards rose by 9½ per cent a year between 1970 and 1973. In the following decade the annual rate of increase was only 1½ per cent. Money wage growth fell from a peak of over 25 per cent a year in 1974 to less than half that rate the next year. Productivity rose by nearly 10 per cent a year after the 1974–5 recession as Japanese industry continued rapidly to accumulate and Japanese workers accepted the new machinery and work practices. Profit margins, which had been eroded by the real wage increases of 1970–3, and then slashed by the recession of 1974–5 (Table 17.3), were steadily rebuilt. All this was achieved without a formal incomes policy and in the context of only a tiny rise in registered unemployment (up from 1.4 per cent in 1973 to 1.9 per cent in 1975 and 2.2 per cent by 1981).Unions apparently posed few problems. Business magazines like the *Oriental Economist* scarcely mentioned them. The 'self-restraint' of Japanese workers was promoted in Europe and the United States as the key to recovery.

Table 17.3 Profits, wages and productivity: Japan, 1970–82

	Manufacturing profit share[1]	*Money wage*[2]	*Real wage*[2]	*Manufacturing productivity*[2]
1970	40.7			
1973	32.9	17.5	9.5	11.6
1974	26.3	26.1	1.3	0.8
1975	15.3	11.5	−0.2	−4.1
1980	19.0	8.4	1.8	9.3
1981	19.1	5.6	0.7	3.5
1982	n.a.	4.8	2.1	1.6

1. Percentage of net output.
2. Annual average percentage growth rates since previous date.

Sources: Japan: *Annual Report on National Accounts*, 1982, Table 17; *Japan Statistical Yearbook*, 1982, Tables 55A, 292; *Monthly Statistics of Japan*, Tables B4, B5.

The conventional explanation for this 'self-restraint' is that Japanese traditions encourage rank-and-file workers to identify their interests closely with those of the enterprise for which they work. A Japanese industrial relations expert has pointed out that the US occupation authorities reinforced semi-feudal attitudes towards authority by their postwar reforms designed to spread Western capitalist culture throughout the working class. He argues that 'the "democratic" educational system established at that time continues as one of the most efficient systems for the inculcation of extremely competitive attitudes even among working-class families' (Totsuka, p. 11). Managerial authority, in other words, is legitimized by close association with educational achievement.

But traditions and culture alone did not rule out militant trade unionism. Indeed, trade unionism spread like wildfire after the war. Only an employers' offensive, fully supported by government, crushed the shopfloor control established in those years (Chapters 4, 6 and 8). But the fact that it could be crushed owed much to the weak tradition of working-class activity.

By the early sixties private sector militancy had been almost completely destroyed. But it survived in the public sector, especially on the railways, where shop floor strength successfully rode out a coordinated managerial onslaught in 1971. Strikes, although illegal on the railways, occurred regularly. Between 1953 and 1973, 361 union officials were prosecuted for leading them. Each year, up to fifty railway workers were dismissed for union activities, up to three hundred suspended, and hundreds or thousands more (29,000 in 1972) penalized by wage cuts.

But private sector employers developed an industrial relations system which prevented the revival of militancy which occurred elsewhere towards the end of the boom. This helped Japanese business to adapt to the difficulties of the seventies. During the boom high rates of accumulation and productivity growth allowed Japanese workers to receive large real wage increases without shopfloor struggle. In Nissan, for example, the union secured 100 per cent of its wage claim each year without industrial action. And the gains were substantial.

The Japanese wage system, in which both length of service and management evaluation of the worker's efficiency help determine his or her wage, encouraged workers to go along with company initiatives. Management also put initiatives for reorganization of production through a process of shopfloor consultation. This acted as 'a kind of buffer system to evade the real growth of trade union control of the shop floor' by inducing the expectation among workers that 'their complaints or discontent will be "democratically" dealt with by the consultation bodies' (Totsuka, p. 9). The Japan Productivity Centre, founded in 1955, organized a nationwide consultation campaign. Management was enthusiastic, seeing consultation as a way of minimizing shopfloor bargaining.

'[Management] conceded that the concrete measures for "rationalization" as well as all problems arising from "rationalization" should be matters for consultation provided the trade union accept the "managerial prerogative". It seems that they wanted to widen the sphere for consultation so as to restrict the sphere for collective bargaining. In fact most of the big enterprises developed a unique combined system of consultation and collective bargaining where all matters should be discussed first by the consultation body and only unresolved matters should be transferred to the collective bargaining body' (Totsuka, p. 3).

In the 1960s management began to organize employees into small groups – Quality Circles and the Zero-Defect movement – to discuss and implement productivity improvements and cost savings. 'Originally the leaders of such group activities were mainly senior foremen or foremen but soon quite a few rank and file members also came to be involved in these small circle activities' (Totsuka, p. 3).

This system proved resilient enough to survive difficulties of the 1970s. Workers were persuaded that only minimal real wage increases were possible, despite continued rapid reorganization of production processes, if their companies were to prosper in the harsher economic environment. No doubt many workers accepted this because they identified their own interests with those of the company. But the trade unions themselves also fostered this view and suppressed the idea that company and workers' interests were opposed. Many unions had no real independence from the company, functioning largely as adjuncts of the industrial relations department. There was even a well-recognized career pattern of movement between the two. Much of the 'consultation' and 'bargaining' had long been little more than a ritual. Prominence in the union frequently led to promotion to the upper echelons of the company. An analysis of a group of university graduates in Nissan suggests the following typical structure. First, seven years on the staff of the industrial relations section. Then a spell as a full-time union officer in the wages section. Next, promotion to a vice-presidency in the union (head of the planning department or secondment to a position in the Japan auto workers' union). Then back to the company to head the industrial relations section at factory level or as vice-chief of industrial relations at company level. A real high-flyer might end up running the company's industrial relations department. In 1978 ex-members of the trade union executive committee had risen in the management to secure a seat on the board of directors of two-thirds of major companies. The average was four per company, or nearly one-quarter of board members.

The wearing of two hats is also common at lower levels. Rank-and-file workers are often represented by their immediate superiors: '. . . in most cases the shop stewards of big enterprise unions in the private sector are mainly foremen with the remainder comprised primarily of charge-hands who are soon to be appointed foremen. In other words, in the consultation body on the shop floor, usually the management side is represented by a superintendent and the union side is represented by foremen or charge-hands. Such a consultation between a superintendent and foreman might be expected to work smoothly without any serious friction' (Totsuka, p. 10).

Some commentators would consider this simply as confirmation of very different cultural attitudes from those prevailing in the West. In fact, Japanese workers have little alternative since 'their' unions are thoroughly undemocratic. Elections in the Nissan workers' union, for example, reveal a unanimity of opinion rivalled only by elections in the Soviet Union. In August 1972 182 candidates stood for 182 places on the Nissan workers' union committee. Of the 60,000 or so workers eligible to vote, 99.7 per cent did so. Successful candidates gathered an average of 98.6 per cent of votes cast. By 1978 the work force was apparently even more united: 218 candidates stood for 218 seats; the turnout was 99.96 per cent; the average successful candidate received 99.7 per cent of the votes cast.

Two Nissan workers explain: 'When we vote, we are asked to gather around the supervisor's desk in a group of several at a time, and write out our voting slips right on the spot, on the desk, in front of everybody. The desk is an ordinary office desk of about 1 metre in width. And standing beside the desk are the election administrators, I mean, the assistant manager and the shop steward, who watch closely to see if we write down the right name. . . . If blank votes or invalid votes are found, the shop steward is forced to submit a written apology to the top union leaders. That is why he keeps an eye on how we fill in the voting slips. He even fills out the ballots for new employees, saying that they mis-wrote the characters or that they may not know who the candidates are' (quoted Yamamoto, 1980, p. 30).

The union leadership justifies this surveillance on the ground that votes critical of the existing leadership would 'reveal disunity in the union to the management'.

At Toyota, too, most shop stewards are foremen or 'team chiefs', and members of the union committee are supervisory staff – in effect, company appointees. In 1971 a rank-and-file member with the temerity to stand against the union's president secured a fifth of the votes. The union responded by changing its rules. In future candidates must be nominated by fifty workers: 'As it now stands, you can't run for chief executive unless you find fifty supporters who have the courage to openly oppose the union, which emphasizes cooperation with the management' (Kamata, p. 183). Such a stand would endanger promotion. The unsuccessful candidate for president found himself stuck at the bottom of the wage scale.

So collective bargaining is a largely meaningless ritual, despite the presence at the Nissan annual wage negotiations of many union members. An academic observer explains: 'At the bargaining session the management and the union cross swords. The content of the discussions is, however, well understood by both sides beforehand; this is because those union officers in charge of the wage problems (the career category) frequently exchange information with the company's personnel affairs section, besides Shioji [the union president] himself directly meets with chairman of the board of directors, Kawamata Katsuji, and the company's officers handling the wage problem and gathers information from them. In the light of such a procedure we are forced to conclude that the collective bargaining has a ceremonial function designed to mobilize the union members rather than constituting an occasion for meaningful negotiations' (Saga, p. 4).

Any disagreement with the union line is ruthlessly suppressed. A worker at a Nissan truck plant explains: 'Seven years ago we used to have some fun at work. Work control was not so strict as it is today. But, since the oil crisis, the atmosphere in the workshop has completely changed. It was around that time when I began to feel dissatisfied. After the oil crisis, the Nissan Labour Union announced settlement of the wage claim. The agreed amount was smaller than what they had originally requested, for the first time in company history. At the time of the wage campaign, I opposed the suggested settlement. The chairman said, "Now for confirmation, if you are for this suggestion, please raise your hand,

and if you are not, please raise your hand next." Then, when I raised my hand for negative side, I was immediately surrounded by 5 or 6 managerial personnel in front of all the members. They yelled harshly at me, saying, "Hey! Stop that! What's the big idea?" or, "What are you opposed to?" This was how I came to be involved with the labour movement at workshop level for the first time. After this, all members on a line except me were gathered together. A section chief, a chief clerk, a foreman, a trainer, executive members of the union and a chief of the workshop stood in a group before my colleagues, and said, "Kayama is a radical subversive and is trying to provoke you. So, you should not talk to him at all." Apparently my friends had to undergo an intensive scolding for about one and half hours. They were told not to exchange greetings with me in the morning, not to talk to me during work and not to eat with me. Therefore, the company was trying in this manoeuvre to cause division among the workers' (AMPO, Vol. 13, No. 2, 1981).

Another worker explains what happened at the same plant in 1981: '6 March (Fri.) Today was the day of the meeting to determine the attitude of the car industry union on its wage demand. The second machine section's number one workplace – to which I belong – met at 12.20.

'A group including Executive Committeeman Takahashi, foremen Takada, Inoue and Otsuka, Mukaida and Takada of the factory committee came crowding around me, and I felt something was amiss.

'A vote was taken at once by a show of hands after Yagisawa explained the attitude on the wage increase demand (a 10 per cent increase), with no time allowed for questions. I was the only one to raise my hand to vote against the proposal, whereupon the fellows sitting to my right stood up and moved around in front of me, while supervisor Toyoda pushed people aside and came rushing up to me, shouting: "Give me a reason! If you want to oppose us you can quit the company. Go off and join your mates. You are a trouble-maker. Quit!" I was sitting there, flabbergasted. The others too looked down at me, shouting: "Quit if you can't think and behave like the rest of us. When we are all voting for something, what do you mean by opposing it? You are a trouble-maker." I had no chance to say anything in reply. Mukaida stuck his face in front of me and challenged me saying: "Go on, hit me if you want. We are ready for you!"

'I said, "I do not have to resign and have no intention of doing so." As the end of the lunchbreak approached I went to my locker. They followed me, however, and this harassment continued even after time to resume work came round (13.00). There were about 15 of them. Several times I repeated my request "Let me go and do my work," but they completely ignored me. "Quit! Quit while we are all in a good mood and we will even cook special red rice to celebrate," said Takahashi. They were yelling right in my face.

'At about 15 or 20 minutes past one, work chief Ikesawa, supervisors Sata, Shiraishi and Tozaki, and factory committeeman Kodaira came up to me looking rather tense. The kangaroo court grew to about 30 or 40 in number. I was so anxious that my knees shook. When Kodaira said, "I want to hit you so much I can hardly restrain myself," I was even more alarmed, expecting his right fist to strike out at me. Abuse, and the cry "Quit the company" continued till about 13.30. Then Takahashi said, "Tomorrow I will bring the necessary forms for you to sign to resign from the company. You had better think hard about it. The papers will be on the foreman's desk." I was upset all day having been so much abused by so many people' (AMPO, Vol. 13, No. 2, 1981).

Harassment of this sort, including frequent physical assaults, was commonplace for two weeks.

A worker at a different Nissan plant recounted his experiences: 'I am not the only one who has been unfairly treated by the union. A certain Mr T. uttered at a shopfloor mass meeting that "I do find the whole thing rather odd" and was afterwards called to the union office where abuse was hurled at him. I myself have also been "persuaded" by the chief steward. At the same bloc discussion a few workers at first opposed the executive committee's proposal but all suffered the fate of being "persuaded". All of them quit the company. After some time I was temporarily shifted to another shopfloor' (quoted Saga, p. 7).

Nissan probably has a particularly ferocious union bureaucracy. But incidents of that kind are not unique to that company. The following report concerns a Toshiba plant:

'When Mr Ueno, a 25-year-old press operator in a section making console boxes for computers took issue with the authoritarianism of the shop union system, he found himself branded as a dangerous subversive. One day last spring Mr Ueno handed out a single handbill to a colleague. It expressed criticism of the low wage demand made by the company union. The union's reaction to this "challenge" was swift and heavy handed. First Mr Ueno's supervisor ordered the spiky-haired young man to sign an apology: "I realize I was wrong to hand out a pamphlet without permission. . . . In case I ever repeat such a thing I am ready to accept any punishment." He refused. Then he was summoned to the union office, threatened with ejection from the union (and thus from the firm) and told he would be placed under surveillance by shop stewards.

'He was continually harassed. "I was even followed when I went to the toilet, and the shop stewards recorded how long I stayed there." His shop floor supervisor brought him more letters of apology to sign, some thirty times. He was sent to Coventry, and workmates were instructed not to talk to him either during or after factory hours.

'In July last year he was attacked by the supervisor and his minions, resulting in a bloody nose and a haemorrhage in the upper arm: hospital treatment was required, and police notified. A psychiatrist advised him to take time off to rest. Back at work, he was given only the most monotonous of tasks in the workshop. In January this year he filed a civil suit against the supervisor who, he says, orchestrated the harassment and against Toshiba, who deny the charges. An official at Toshiba's Fuchu plant refused to comment' (*Guardian*, 11 May 1982).

The Nissan union has usurped some management functions in the company's interest. In the mid-1970s it launched the '3-P movement' – Productivity, Participation and Prosperity. It has also trespassed on management's absolute prerogative over promotion, insisting that 'one's record of union activities' and 'one's standing in the union hierarchy' are criteria where transfers and promotions are discussed – an important device to secure rank-and-file loyalty to the union. In other companies management does its own job. At the Japan Steel Company the most frequent questions at promotion interviews are: 'What do you think of strikes?' 'What do you think about trade unions?'

This system of labour control proved very robust in the seventies and early eighties. Some extended struggles against redundancy occurred in small- or medium-sized plants, involving occupations and cooperative production. Professional staff facing transfer occupied a Toshiba plant in Yokohama claiming that the company was 'waging a vendetta against the house union, which in most Japanese companies are compliant, but which in the Yokohama plant had some record of confrontation with the management' (*Financial Times*, 20 May 1983). But little effective resistance in the large private sector firms surfaced. Disputes over redundancy and plant closures continued to run at the rate of around 150 a year in the early 1970s, the majority of strikes being formal affairs of a day or so at the time of the annual wage round. This was despite the fact that the system of lifetime employment was under strain. Larger numbers of older workers were being transferred, sometimes to lower-paid jobs in subsidiaries or subcontractors. Others were 'loaned out' (as were several hundred steel workers on loan to a car company). Others were sacked. While the total number of workers leaving their jobs each year fell by more than one-fifth between 1970 and 1980, the number with over ten years' service with the firm rose by more than one-third. This weakening of the system of 'lifetime employment', supposedly the core of the industrial relations system, provoked little response.

Nor was effective opposition developing in the unions. At the end of 1982 right-wing union control in the private sector was further consolidated with the formation of a new trade union federation comprising the main private sector trade unions from the traditionally left-wing Sohyo federation as well as the right-wing Domei. This increased the influence of the IMF-JC (International Metal Workers Federation – Japan Committee), which since the mid-1960s has brought the main export industries together, and which has in some respects a more pro-business attitude than the government. The Committee supports rationalization and cost-cutting not only in the public sector (notably the railways) but also in agriculture and in distribution and services. These sectors, with low productivity by international standards, undoubtedly constitute a drag on Japanese growth. But it is a drag with a heavy political pay-off: it maintains a large *petit bourgeoisie* of peasants and small shopkeepers, which consistently supports he right-wing government.

The Japanese industrial relations system is not based on harmony but on subservience. Western management has failed to achieve a similar dominance. But since the mid-seventies it has increasingly sought both to bypass and to undermine organized labour, often borrowing heavily from Japan for its methods.

Table 17.4 Manufacturing plant size, 1958–73

Median number of employees

	1958–61	*1970–73*
All manufacturing		
UK	470	440
Germany	350	410
USA	390	380
Light industries		
UK	220	240
Germany	120	140
USA	190	210
Heavy industries		
UK	1140	820
Germany	1140	1080
USA	1110	810

Source: Prais, 1981, Table 3.4.

Relocating production

One response to effective work-force organization has been to disperse production geographically. Even during the boom, management often opted to spawn new plants on fresh sites rather than enlarge existing ones. In the United Kingdom, for which systematic data are available, the share of net manufacturing output contributed by the largest hundred plants only crept up from 9 to 11 per cent during the fifties and sixties, while that contributed by the largest hundred firms jumped up from 22 to 41 per cent. Trends appear to have been similar in the United States. In Germany average plant size continued to rise in the sixties, but only in so-called 'light industries'. In 'heavy industry' average plant size fell in all three countries (Table 17.4).

One factor inhibiting the growth of plant size was the difficulty in controlling labour. A crude indicator of such difficulty is the incidence of strikes. In the United Kingdom in 1971–3 only 0.2 per cent of plants with between eleven and twenty-four employees had strikes, while 75.8 per cent of those employing more than five thousand did. The average number of days occupied in strikes was 0.3 and 29,400 respectively, representing 15 and 3708 days per thousand employees. It is unlikely that this difference arises solely from plant size. Some of the most repetitive and alienating jobs are housed in giant plants. But labour control problems have undoubtedly encouraged firms to limit plant size. The growing sophistication of product ranges (see below) has probably contributed too. Some of the new technology can be used very effectively on a tiny scale.

Again, as the *Engineer* magazine reports, Japan is in the vanguard. Mr Iguchi has a plastics factory in his back garden. The mouldings are handled by robot arms, and the only tasks he has to perform are to fill the hopper with raw materials and replace the boxes for the mouldings to fall into. This allows him plenty of time to play golf and entertain Western TV crews.

The most publicized type of relocation over the last decade has been movement to the third world. Many people believe this has caused a major loss of jobs in the advanced countries.

Between 1973 and 1980 total direct investment from abroad in non-oil-producing LDCs did rise by 188 per cent (in dollars) while net investment within advanced countries rose by only 72 per cent. But in 1980 the former amounted to only $11 billion while the latter amounted to $800 billion (with total net business investment of $500 billion). Furthermore, some investment by advanced countries in LDCs is for resource development, which does not compete with jobs at home. So the 'flight of jobs' has been small. Even in the important case of the German garment industry it was estimated that by 1975 only 5 per cent of the employees of German companies were in 'low wage' countries. Fear of protectionist measures against exports from factories overseas (Chapter 16) probably inhibited overseas investment and encouraged a system of subcontracting, whereby only part of the product is made abroad. This yields the benefits of cheap and docile labour while minimizing the threat posed by protectionism.

Within the advanced countries, capital has migrated away from areas with strong traditions of industrial militancy. In the United Kingdom, a shift away from conurbations to smaller towns began in the sixties. Labour relations almost certainly played a part. In the United States manufacturing has been attracted to the Southern 'Sunbelt' states where labour organization is weak.

More work has been 'put out' to small subcontractors within the advanced countries too. In Italy management embraced 'decentralized production' as a conscious antidote to working-class strength, especially after the 'Hot Autumn' (Chapter 12). Small factories could often avoid union control, state measures to protect workers (important parts of the Statute of Workers' Rights do not apply in firms employing less than fifteen workers), and taxes and social security contributions. In the Modena area of Italy the number of small workshops quadrupled between 1963 and 1975. Ironically, many were set up by union militants victimized in the fifties. The author of an enthusiastic account of this 'high-technology cottage industry' has described these firms:

'Most of the shops and factories in these areas employ from 5 to 50 workers, a few as many as 100, and a very few 250 or more. Some recall turn-of-the-century sweatshops: the three or four workers are children scarcely fifteen years old, supervised by an adult or two, perhaps their parents; the tools are simple, the product crude, the hours long, the air full of dust and fumes. But many of the others are spotless; the workers extremely skilled and the distinction between them and their supervisors almost imperceptible; the tools the most advanced numerically controlled equipment of its type; the products, designed in the shop, sophisticated and distinctive enough to capture monopolies in world markets. If you had thought so long about Rousseau's artisan clockmakers at Neuchâtel or Marx's idea of labour as joyful, self-creative association that you had begun to doubt their possibility, then you might, watching these craftsmen at work, forgive yourself the sudden conviction that something more utopian than the present factory system is practical after all' (Sabel, p. 220).

But even he admits that artisanal creativity is limited to the top stratum of skilled workers. The firms are reluctant to train un-skilled workers, because 'once they possess the generally applic-able skills that innovative work requires, nothing prevents the newly minted craftsmen from moving to another firm or going into business for themselves' (Sabel, p. 228).

In Japan subcontracting is more extensive and tightly organized than elsewhere. The average manufacturing firm employing more than a thousand people has 160 subcontractors. Even those employing less than four workers have on average three subcontractors. Subcontracting gives parent firms great flexibility. In downturns it is more difficult to cut staff and overheads in the parent than to cancel orders from subcontractors. A further advantage is steep wage differentials by firm size. In 1981 the average manufacturing wage in firms employing between five and twenty-nine people was only 57 per cent of that in firms employing more than five hundred. Between 1973 and 1980 the number of manufacturing workers in factories with less than ten employees rose by 70,000 while that in factories employing more than 1000 fell by 470,000 (one-quarter). Only about one-third of this increase can be accounted for by slower productivity growth in small firms.

The relationship between Japanese subcontractors and parent companies is often very close, and becoming more so: 70 per cent or more of parent companies specify daily deliveries from their subcontractors. In 1982 a reported 10 per cent were even designating delivery by the 'hour'. Parent companies are also heavily, and increasingly, involved in keeping subcontractors' technical standards up to scratch. After the 'oil shock', an electronic condenser manufacturer developed an automatic assembly machine and insisted that its subcontractors installed it. 'The parent company set forth a policy that subcontractors not investing 5 million yen per worker ($25,000) would cease to receive orders' (Ikeda, p. 68). This in turn radically reduced the subcontractors' use of home workers from neighbouring farms. The Toyota company is famous for its highly organized and sophisticated system of subcontracting. Technical levels and quality controls are closely monitored.

Much Japanese subcontracting takes place inside the core plants. Data are hard to come by. But one-quarter of the workers in one Toshiba factory are reportedly employed through subcontractors or as part-timers, with very low wages and no union protection, and 9.5 per cent of non-agricultural workers are classified as casual workers or day labourers, an increase of 1 per cent over the decade.

396 Things Fall Apart, 1974–

Reorganizing work

Throughout the history of capitalism the central problem for management has always been how to make workers work hard enough. What capitalists buy on the market with a wage is only an employee's capacity to work. The work itself must be squeezed out on the factory floor.

The production line tried to achieve this by allowing the worker only a certain time to perform the allotted task before whisking the product-in-process on to the next work station, a technique immortalized in Chaplin's *Modern Times*. But individual workers could jeopardize the steady flow by absenteeism, rapid turnover and shoddy methods, producing a high proportion of defects. When they organized themselves, they could haggle over line speeds and operating levels.

This production-line system of work organization came under increasing strain as labour reserves dried up towards the end of the sixties (Chapter 11). The difficulties were signalled in a 1970 article in *Fortune* magazine headlined 'Blue Collar Blues'. A notorious 'revolt' at General Motors' Lordstown plant in 1972 further highlighted the problems, which took their most extreme form in the Fiat workers' struggles for control over work organization in the late sixties and early seventies. Management responded most radically in Sweden where the labour market was especially tight and workers' expectations particularly high. Volvo's Kalmar plant was based on an apparently revolutionary new system of work organization which replaced the line with work groups.

Then, in the mid-seventies, the issue disappeared from view. The obvious explanation was that management had decided to use mass unemployment to break down union opposition. British Leyland was a classic example. The *Sunday Times* (21 March 1982) described as a 'miracle' the transformation at Longbridge where 'a marriage of men and machines has dramatically improved the productivity of BL'. One Longbridge worker – transferred to five different departments in one year, and ten different jobs in one department in three months – described the 'miracle' as follows:

'In the past management couldn't shift you without the agreement of the union; now it's done without consultation . . . it means that you never get to know any of the blokes, it breaks up any unity. . . . In the old days the target was set by timing the operator, now the target is based on the gross potential of the machine, that means they set the machine as fast as possible, the only limit being quality, and you have to keep up with it. They give you targets you can't reach. The gaffer comes to check your counter every hour; blokes have been suspended for failing to have an adequate explanation of why they haven't reached their target' (*Militant*, 23 April 1982).

Increased labour flexibility – widening the range of tasks a worker undertakes – is as important a goal for management as pure speedup. Ford, for example, developed a plan for production workers to carry out quality control, rectification of faults and maintenance of machinery. Demarcation lines between skilled workers were to be abolished.

It is labour flexibility which big non-union firms in the United States value so highly, and which earns Japanese firms so much envy. It both saves labour on current production processes and, perhaps more important, clears the way for introducing new technologies in the most profitable way.

Flexibility is difficult to organize on a large scale. Dividing work into parcels, carried out by a small group of employees who each perform a number of tasks, widens the scope. An enthusiast explains: 'As a manager I love that. If you look at fork lifts in traditional plants they never have more than 20 to 25 hours of running time on the clock at the end of the week. So what are the operators doing in the other 15 hours? Here we don't have that' (*Fortune*, 27 July 1981).

The traditional assembly line is ill-suited to complicated model mixes. Slight variations in production patterns require considerable reorganization and rebalancing of the track. But where assembly is carried out by parallel work groups, the schedules of one or two can be adjusted without affecting the rest. Fixed capital costs rise because machinery cannot be used as intensely – increases of 10–30 per cent are mentioned – and more stocks of materials may be needed. But reductions in labour costs often more than offset these disadvantages.

In Chevrolet's gear plant in Detroit, 'while a worker might have stood in one place all day tightening bolts on a rear brake assembly, he is now responsible with other team members for the production and quality of an entire brake system' (ibid.). This type of reorganization was part of GM's 'Quality of Work Life Program', the key feature of which from management's point of view was flexible job assignments. Its impact in another GM plant was described as follows:

'Livonia [USA] is one of nine General Motors Corp. plants that use the "pay-for-knowledge" team concept to make factory work less boring and more productive. This approach differs radically from the practice in most union shops, where workers perform narrow functions. At Livonia, production workers can learn all of the jobs in one section, giving management flexibility in assigning work and filling in for absent workers. Workers are paid according to the skills they acquire, giving them an incentive to learn new ones.

'Livonia uses less manpower per engine than the Detroit plant while producing higher-quality products. It hit the breakeven point after one year, instead of the anticipated two years. The scrap rate has fallen by 50 per cent. And in 1982 worker suggestions saved Cadillac more than $1.2 million.

'The plant, which cranks out 1200 engines a day, is divided into 15 departments that are in turn subdivided into business teams of 10 to 20 workers each, consisting of production workers who assemble the engines and perform nonskilled maintenance duties. The engines are still produced on an assembly line, but the employees have varied routines and participate in decision-making. Moreover, dress codes are passé: almost no one wears a tie, and some supervisors wear jeans. Managers and workers share the same cafeteria and compete for parking spots.

'The teams meet weekly on company time to discuss issues such as safety and housekeeping. They decide when to award raises and rotate jobs, and they may even suggest redesigning the work flow. . . . The 23 members of [one] team rotate among 12 or 13 jobs on the line, 6 engine-repair jobs, and 4 or 5 housekeeping and inspection jobs. In the old Detroit plant, there were 45 job classifications, each with its own wage rate. In Livonia, there are four wage levels for experienced workers, ranging from $9.63 an hour to a maximum of $10.08 for a "job setter" – a worker who sets up and changes tooling on the line. A worker reaches the top rate after learning all the skills on two business teams' (*Business Week*, 16 May 1983).

Labour flexibility often had to be bought by raising wages. Increases of 10–20 per cent were fairly typical. But direct labour requirements fell drastically (10–40 per cent), as did overtime. Supervision costs were slashed (25–50 per cent) and reductions reported in scrap, wastage and reject rates and in inventories of goods waiting to be checked. Accounts of such schemes indicate productivity improvements in half the cases, cost improvement in one-third and improvements in quality, labour turnover and absenteeism in about one-fifth each. They represent the imposition of a new, less splintered division of labour on trade unions in a weak position to resist resulting job losses. The point is to make each worker do more work. The more varied nature of the work is a by-product. Nevertheless, some of the schemes will have improved working conditions. 'Restrictive practices', imposed by trade unions to protect jobs and work speeds, seldom make work less monotonous. But when mass unemployment exists, even those schemes of work reorganization which do yield benefits for the workers involved do so at the expense of those put out of a job.

Work groups appear to involve a movement away from the hierarchical (arbitrary authority of the foreman) and technical (determination of work pace through machine speeds) systems of control. They may indeed have considerable flexibility in allocating tasks among members, deciding the pattern of work during a day, and so forth. But this autonomy is constrained strictly within the straitjacket of management work norms and targets. Granting work groups autonomy in detailed matters costs management little and may save on supervisory costs. The groups typically carry out evaluation functions by checking the work for quality. Workers operating below par will be obvious to the rest of the group who are often obliged to make up the difference themselves – by putting right mistakes, for example. So workers performing below par, or frequently absent, will face pressure from other group members, especially when bonuses are organized on a group basis. In one small, non-union, plant team members were even reported as having initiated sackings. Encouraging team members to acquire a range of skills, on which pay structures and perhaps promotions are based, also helps bind workers to individual firms, especially when the skills are firm-specific. Employees not only perform more work, but also, ideally, reduce the need for managerial control over detail by exercising collective 'self-discipline'.

Where work groups cover whole departments, with a definable cost structure, they are sometimes represented by management as being separate businesses which set their own goals and whose members are responsible to each other for its success. This is utterly misleading. Basing bonuses on team output no more makes the team a business than piecework makes the worker self-employed. But the market can be used to ensure that work groups do perform the function of work evaluation effectively. Faults which do get through can be readily traced to the group concerned. Having switched from assembly line to team assembly, the expensive ranges of Raleigh bicycles were sent out bearing the name of the skilled craftsman in charge of the team. By 'personalizing' the product, the market was brought into the factory as a direct discipline on the individual groups of workers.

Quality Circles (QCs) also became a vogue Japanese import in the late seventies. Small groups of workers meet to analyse and solve detailed production problems. By 1981, 750 US companies and government bodies and 100 firms in Britain had set up QCs. Many reported improvements in layout and design of equipment, design of products and modification to work practices. The management of one GM plant which introduced a more comprehensive scheme of employee involvement in work reorganization reported an 'entirely positive' result from the point of view of costs. But, as an American trade unionist pointed out, QCs give workers 'no real transfer of power over their work environment'.

Management Today's correspondent noted that 'it is precisely this feature which explains the noisy QC bandwagon' (March 1982). The wholly negative response of the management of Lucas Aerospace to the combine committee's alternative plan for the company, involving the substitution of socially useful for military production, was instructive. Even in cases where there *would* be a payback to the company, management would have no truck with suggestions which transgressed the absolute prerogative of management to determine all essential elements of corporate strategy.

These developments all share an important feature. Management reacted to the crisis of the seventies by focusing attention 'on how goods and services are *actually produced* – a basic concern that has been sloughed aside to an astonishing degree by a generation of executives pre-occupied with finance, marketing, strategic redeployment . . .' (*Fortune*, 15 June 1981). US management schools noticed a shift in students' choice of courses: marketing and finance slipped down in the popularity polls, while production management gained in status.

The labour movement suffered many setbacks in the decade

following 1973. Important changes also took place in the location of production, in relations between small and large firms, and in work organization within core plants. But Western management was unable to import wholesale the highly successful Japanese organization of labour. Worker resistance remained too powerful for individual firms to impose their will. The project of smashing trade unions and atomizing the labour movement devolved increasingly on to governments. The most determined of these were the Thatcher and Reagan administrations.

18. Thatcherism and Reaganomics

During the boom a broad consensus was established. Major parties of both left and right generally accepted the notion of a 'mixed economy' – that is, a capitalist economy with some state enterprise. They also recognized certain rights for workers as workers, notably the right to free trade unions. In addition, they accepted certain responsibilities as governments, notably the responsibility to provide various welfare services and to maintain more or less full employment. The precise parameters of this consensus varied from country to country and shifted a little over time, and they were contested at the margin. Nevertheless, broad agreement existed across the major political parties; in Britain the consensus was labelled 'Butskellism' after a leading Tory, Butler, and the Labour leader, Gaitskell.

By the end of the seventies that consensus had come under increasing strain because the economy was no longer delivering to order the jobs, living standards and welfare services. In some countries it had clearly broken down. Two opposing approaches had emerged, or were in the process of so doing. The left-wing alternative, so far pursued only hesitantly, is the subject of the next chapter. Here we examine the economic policies of the New Right, which were implemented vigorously in the early eighties.

The first major government to espouse this approach was the Tory government elected in 1979 in Britain. A year later a US president was elected on a similar programme. So the approach became linked with two names: Thatcher and Reagan.

To understand Thatcherism and Reaganomics we must go beyond the simplistic sloganizing frequently used to present them. We therefore begin by discussing both the rhetoric and the political and economic theories used to justify the policies before looking at their real nature and logic.

Rhetoric

The catch-phrases that politicians use to promote the policies mainly centre around two ideas. One is that inflation is both immoral and Public Enemy Number One. So Thatcher talked about the need to restore 'honest money', and her appointee as governor of the Bank of England, Robin Leigh-Pemberton, said that inflation was a greater danger to the 'free world' than communism. The main purpose these slogans serve is to justify restrictive monetary policies.

The other central idea is that previous governments and the nation as a whole have been profligate. So the tautology that 'we cannot pay ourselves more than we earn' is presented as a profound insight, and schoolchildren hit by education cuts are not the only ones to be told that 'there is no free lunch'. We all need to 'tighten our belts' in the interests of 'good housekeeping'. The main purpose these homilies serve is to justify attacks on jobs, living standards and welfare provision. The high moral tone helps instil guilt in anyone reluctant to make the sacrifices required.

Political economy

The theoretical justification for the approach caught in such phrases is provided by a body of political economy, whose most distinguished contributor is F. A. Hayek.

The central thrust of this approach is the need to 'get the state off people's backs'. The increased government intervention implied by the consensus is seen, in the words of the title of one of Hayek's books, as inevitably leading down 'The Road to Serfdom'. Once governments become involved, economic outcomes cease to reflect impersonal market forces and become politicized. Coalitions of interest groups impose their wishes on others in an essentially arbitrary and dictatorial fashion. This is inherently incompatible with economic efficiency and with freedom.

Very radical policy conclusions can be drawn: 'Those libertarians who wisely retain the idea of state authority would confine it to "night watchman" activities, mainly law and order, and defence. . . . There would certainly be no conscription, no anti-drugs legislation, and no interference in private sexual behaviour. But there would also be no social security – not even the provision of the barest minimum – and nothing remotely resembling a health service. There would be no place for town-and-country planning rules' (Brittan, p. 55). Hayek himself advocates the abolition of the state monopoly of issue of cash and the competitive circulation of rival, privately issued currencies.

Neither Thatcher nor Reagan go this far. But they do accept the basic philosophy, shorn of any genuinely libertarian overtones.

Within this broad approach to political economy, two narrower economic theories can be distinguished. One is *monetarism*. Its starting point is that the cause of inflation is a too rapid rate of growth of the money supply. The key economic task for governments is therefore to rein in the rate of growth of money and credit. The best way to achieve a slower growth of the money supply is to reduce government deficits (the public sector borrowing requirement, PSBR). Deficits are bad because they must be financed by creating more money or by borrowing. In the former case the money supply grows too fast. In the latter, the state absorbs funds which would otherwise go to industry, interest rates rise and so private investment is 'crowded out', leading to lower employment and incomes in the long run.

Fiscal policy is held to be largely ineffective. Deficit spending to boost employment, in particular, is seen as disastrous. Employment gravitates anyway to a 'natural' rate, based on free market forces of demand and supply, so any jobs created are, after a very short space of time, fully offset by job losses elsewhere in the economy. The only net effect of more government spending is less private investment or a higher inflation rate. Governments cannot, and should not, attempt to provide fuller employment than the economy spontaneously generates.

The policies of the Thatcher government were initially defended in pure monetarist terms, although its arguments later became more pragmatic. The Reagan administration has always been divided between monetarists and *supply-siders*, who advocate the second of the theories that make up the New Right's approach to economics.

The term 'supply-side economics' is confusing for Europeans, who associate it with government intervention in industry. That is almost the opposite of what it means in the United States.

The core of supply-side economics is the belief that slashing taxes is the way to economic recovery. Lower income tax means a greater return for saving, working and investing. So with lower taxes people will work longer and harder and invest more. Output will rise and unemployment will decline. Despite the lower rates of taxation, rising incomes will, supply-siders believe, increase the tax base to such an extent that total tax receipts will, paradoxically, rise. Government spending should still be pruned, however, both to allow still more tax cuts and, more fundamentally, because much government spending, especially on welfare benefits, destroys incentives by reducing the need to work. Far from explaining unemployment by lack of demand – the cornerstone of Keynesian economics – the supply-siders assert that unemployment derives from lack of incentive to work, and stagnation from lack of incentive to invest. While most monetarists share the supply-siders' preference for tax cuts and increased incentives, they take a much more cautious view of the extent to which this will reduce the 'natural rate of unemployment', and of the speed with which it might happen. So they do not believe that tax rates should be cut in advance of corresponding cuts in government spending because the government deficit would rise leading to higher inflation or interest rates or both. Supply-siders, on the contrary, believe that keeping monetary policy too tight would damage recovery by pushing up interest rates and sabotaging the good work of the tax cuts in increasing investment.

The real project

Although the ideas outlined in the last section do influence Thatcher's and Reagan's thinking, they also obscure the joint goals of the administrations quite as much as they illuminate them. This is because the theories systematically avoid any mention of classes.

Thus the central fear of the New Right is not the politicization of decision-making itself but politicized decisions in which the working class has a big say. The worry is not coalitions of any old interest groups but the political power of the labour movement.

Hayek is explicit: 'Public policy concerning labour unions has, in little more than a century, moved from one extreme to the other. From a state in which little the unions could do was legal if they were not prohibited altogether, we have now reached a state where they have become uniquely privileged institutions to which the general rules of law do not apply. They have become the only important instance in which governments signally fail in their prime function – the prevention of coercion and violence . . . the whole basis of our free society is gravely threatened by the powers arrogated by the unions' (Hayek, pp. 66–8).

Similarly, the aim is not to get the state off any and everyone's back but to get the labour movement, and the progressive legislation enacted at its behest during the boom, off the employers' backs. In our view this approach constitutes a coherent, and very radical, attempt to resolve the economic difficulties of the last fifteen years on capitalism's terms. It seeks to cope with major problems generated by the end of the boom years – workers' increased ability to secure improvements in wages, state services and working conditions – by shifting fundamentally the parameters previously accepted by all parties. In other words, it is an attempt to return relations between capital and labour to how they were thirty years ago. Again, Hayek is very clear about what is involved.

'This path is still blocked, however, by the most fatuous of all fashionable arguments, namely, that "we cannot turn the clock back". One cannot help wondering whether those who habitually use this cliché are aware that it expresses the fatalistic belief that we cannot learn from our mistakes. . . . Nothing less than a re-dedication of current policy to principles already abandoned will enable us to avert the threatening danger to freedom' (Hayek, pp. 87–8).

For Hayek 'freedom' can only mean 'capitalism'. If the re-establishment of conditions for profitable production and sustained accumulation requires a return to pre-consensus politics then so be it, says the New Right.

The most important policies designed to achieve these ends are outlined below, and contrasted with the orthodoxies of the 1960s.

Restrictive monetary policy. Far from being the guarantor of full employment, the government's responsibility is to prevent the consequences for prices and profits of, in their words, 'overfull' employment. Traditional demand management, in Hayek's words, simply 'passes the buck, in an irresponsible manner, on to our successors. We are of course in this respect already reaping the harvest of the man [Keynes] who set this fashion since we are already in that long run in which he knew we would be dead' (Hayek, p. 109).

Cutbacks in welfare provisions. Rather than ensuring improved welfare services, the government should cut them back to the lower standards which are all the economy can afford, without 'damaging' the 'wealth-generating' private sector.

Tax cuts. Far from levying whatever taxes are necessary to finance welfare services in a way which bears more heavily on the better-off, taxes should be cut, especially at the top end, to reduce government 'interference' with the income distribution which the market both generates and requires for its efficient working.

Privatization and deregulation. Rather than limiting the ways in which firms can seek profits at the expense of workers and consumers, the government should widen the field for, and not constrain, private profit-making.

Weakening trade unions. Far from recognizing the power of organized labour in legislation which safeguards trade union rights, the government should water down that legislation to allow employers freer rein to bust union organization, and should give a lead in its own relations with the increasingly important public sector unions.

In examining the implementation of these policies in the United Kingdom and United States we focus on their logic and coherence. Since both administrations remain in office at the time of writing it is too early to attempt a definitive balance sheet.

Restrictive monetary policy

In the early days of the Thatcher government it was fashionable to suggest that tight money would reduce inflation without affecting anything else. The idea was that the simple announcement of a tough target for the growth of the money supply would be enough to hold down wage and price increases. The leading theoretician of monetarism, Milton Friedman, talking of Britain, asserted in 1980 that 'only a modest reduction in output and employment will be a side effect of reducing inflation to single figures by 1982' (quoted Stewart, p. 172). Not surprisingly, this proved ludicrously optimistic. Tight monetary policy operates through causing recession or even slump. Fear has always proved a more effective cure for economic problems than has magic.

If the government holds the growth of credit below the prevailing rate of inflation then interest rates tend to rise. This reduces the returns from business investment, makes hire purchase and mortgages more expensive, and encourages firms to sell off stocks which are now dearer to finance. The strength of these effects has been disputed for years, but a really sharp credit squeeze undoubtedly reduces spending. This deflationary impetus has been bolstered by floating exchange rates. High interest rates tend to attract foreign funds which push up the value of the currency. This makes exports uncompetitive and imports more attractive. Sales of domestically produced output fall further. The impact is greater on a country like the United Kingdom, where foreign trade is large in relation to production, than on a country with a less open economy, such as the United States.

The purpose of engineering a slump is to restore the profitability of production and investment. Its success depends not primarily on the extent to which wage *and* price increases are reduced by the slump (reducing inflation), but the extent to which wage increases are reduced *more* than price increases (squeezing real wages and raising profits). The effect the slump may have in increasing productivity is equally important.

In a recession, the weakest firms, with lowest productivity, tend to go bust first. Their demise raises average productivity. Tough deflation also puts pressure on management to force through changes in working practices – to reduce operating levels, impose speedup and so on. The mechanism is fear. Managers rightly believe that the firm's survival may be at stake. Most importantly, deflation weakens workers' resistance to such changes. Again, fear is the key. Workers rightly believe that opposition may lead to redundancies or closure, and that it may be impossible to get another job. Pay rises are held down, hopefully below the rate of price increases, by the same pressures.

The emphasis on monetary rather than fiscal policy to promote deflation and cause a slump is of secondary economic importance; in any case, cuts in government expenditure operate in the same direction, so long as extreme supply-siders are curbed in their enthusiasm for tax cuts. But using monetary policy, with its alleged direct impact on inflation, can be a crucial element in the presentation of the overall economic policy. A major difficulty with the approach is how to win electoral support for a programme of squeezing the economy. This is where academic doctrines like monetarism come in. They serve as a rationale for abandoning a fundamental feature of the postwar consensus – government's responsibility to maintain full employment.

J. S. Fforde, an adviser to the governor of the Bank of England, outlined the strategy in an article for the Bank's prestigious *Quarterly Bulletin*: '. . . it would have been possible to initiate such a strategy with a familiar "Keynesian" exposition about managing demand downwards, and with greater concentration on ultimate objectives than on intermediate targets. But this would have meant disclosing objectives for, *inter alia*, output and employment. This would have been a very hazardous exercise, and the objectives would either have been unacceptable to public opinion or else inadequate to ensure a substantial reduction in the rate of inflation, or both. Use of strong intermediate targets, for money supply and government borrowing, enabled the authorities to stand back from output and employment as such and to stress the vital part to be played in respect of these by the trend of industrial costs. In short, whatever the subsequent difficulties of working with intermediate targets, they were vitally important at the outset in order to signal a decisive break with the past and enable the authorities to set out with presentational confidence upon a relatively uncharted sea' (June 1983, p. 207). So monetarism played as important a role in the marketing of Tory strategy as did the party's advertising agency.

The early years of the Thatcher government certainly saw savage monetary deflation. Interest rates soared from about 5 per cent less than the inflation rate to nearly 10 per cent more. This hit sales opportunities, and hence production and employment, in various ways. The high cost of borrowing discouraged fixed investment, which fell by the equivalent of 1½ per cent of output between the second quarter of 1979 and 1981. The strain imposed on companies' cash position led to a massive rundown of stocks, which fell by 3½ per cent of output over the same period. High interest rates, combined with confidence in sterling engendered by its new status as a petro-currency, sharply reversed the previous decline in the value of the pound. The competitiveness of UK manufacturing industry deteriorated by a staggering 50 per cent. This hit exports, which fell by 2 per cent of output over the two years. Imports also rose by 2½ per cent of output, displacing domestic production. These developments reinforced each other, and their combined dynamic was the motor force of the 1980–1 crash.

The effects were dramatic. Output fell by more than in any other downturn for sixty years, including the crash of 1929–32.

Official unemployment doubled, reaching 12 per cent of the labour force by the spring of 1981. By 1982 company liquidations were running at 12,000 a year, 2½ times the 1979 rate. The industrial sector was hardest hit. Manufacturing output fell by a colossal 15 per cent in twelve months from December 1979. This compares with a maximum fall in any single year during the 1930s of 5.5 per cent. By the beginning of 1983 imports of manufactures were 24 per cent higher than in 1979, while production stayed 16 per cent lower.

The concentration of the crash in industry, and especially manufacturing, is important. These sectors are most subject to international competition. They must experience the pressures most strongly, and respond to them most positively, if the strategy is to succeed.

The US recession of 1982 was of similar intensity to the United Kingdom's recession of 1980–1. But, being less prolonged, it only reduced output by about 2 per cent as compared to 4 per cent in the United Kingdom. Again, interest rates were pushed up very high – around 10 per cent in real terms – quite unprecedented for the United States. As in the United Kingdom, the rundown of stocks was the most important contributing factor, reducing output by over 1 per cent. Private investment also fell sharply. The competitiveness of US industry was reduced by 20 per cent as the dollar rose, contributing to a sharp fall in exports. As in the United Kingdom, public expenditure on goods or services grew a little, and transfers a lot, helping to moderate the impact on consumption of the fall in incomes. Industry was worst hit. Industrial production fell by 8 per cent in 1982. Unemployment rose to over 10 per cent.

Dismantling welfare

Both the Thatcher and Reagan administrations have significantly eaten away at state welfare provision. Under the first Thatcher government many cash benefits were scrapped. The earnings-related supplement to unemployment benefit was abolished. In 1983 it would have been worth £18.60 a week to someone on average earnings. Industrial injury benefit was abolished.

Many other cash benefits were reduced in real value, and arrangements linking them to prices or earnings weakened or broken. Pensions are no longer linked to movements in average earnings. This change had cost a pensioner couple £2.25 a week by

1983. Invalidity benefit was cut by 5 per cent and the link with earnings snapped. This had cost a married invalidity pensioner £4.25 a week by 1983.

Reduced grants to local authorities and spending limits produced a 3.5 per cent cut in the real value of current spending by local councils. Capital spending by local authorities fell by 40 per cent. This severely hit provision of housing, schools, old people's homes and so on.

In education, 18,000 teaching posts were axed by Thatcher between 1980 and 1982. Between 1978–9 and 1981–2 spending on books fell from £22.70 to £19.90 per secondary pupil, a huge fall when inflation is taken into account. School meal prices were decontrolled and on average doubled. Open University fees rose by 79 per cent between 1981 and 1983.

In health, standards deteriorated, despite an increase in real spending, mainly because of the changing age structure of the population (someone over seventy-five costs the health service nearly eight times as much as someone of working age, and this section of the population has been growing by some 45,000 a year). Prescription charges were raised by 600 per cent. Routine dental charges rose by 170 per cent.

In the United States, Reagan suffered his first major Congressional defeat in 1981 when he tried to cut social security spending. He then retreated on this issue. But many other aspects of welfare provision have been axed.

Trade Adjustment Assistance used to provide a year's unemployment benefit to people whose jobs were lost due to higher imports. When Reagan came into office the programme covered half a million workers, most laid off from the motor industry and its suppliers. The 1982 budget cut the programme by more than half. In 1981, 140,000 people who had recently left the army were collecting unemployment benefit. Benefits are now denied anyone eligible for re-enlistment or discharged for bad conduct.

Washington has also encouraged 'workfare' programmes, adopted by many states. These require people either to spend many hours a week looking for work – by forming 'job clubs' which people must attend for forty hours a week to read job-ads and fill in applications, for example – or to work for the state for enough hours at minimum wage rates to 'earn' the money paid in benefits.

Workfare saves money mainly by harassing recipients of programmes rather than by finding them jobs. In a New Jersey programme, 2879 people found jobs while 9016 lost benefits. In a programme in Michigan every single person who left the programme was thrown off for 'uncooperative behaviour'.

The earnings limit above which a family of four lose eligibility for food stamps has been cut from $14,000 to $11,000. Cost-of-living increases in benefits have been postponed. Eligibility rules for subsidized school lunches have been tightened and funds reduced. As a result, during the first year of the administration the average price of school meals rose from 50 cents to 85 cents in Massachusetts, and the number served fell by a third.

A 1983 Census Bureau report on poverty in the United States reported that 34.4 million people were living below the official poverty line ($9862 a year – around £6500 – for a family of four). This represented about one American in seven and was the highest level recorded since 1965.

Cuts in welfare take many forms and hit individuals in different ways. They may reduce what an individual is entitled to, in the form of cash or kind, as a citizen or as a member of a particular subgroup of citizens. An example would be a cut in the real value of pensions. Cuts may make it harder to obtain that right without formally withdrawing it. Longer hospital waiting-lists would be an example. They may make a right more expensive to obtain (and thus harder or impossible for low-income groups). Prescription charges are an obvious example. But all welfare cuts represent a reduction in the state's responsibility to ensure adequate welfare standards for its citizens. As such they amount to an attempt radically to undermine one of the parameters of the postwar consensus. This undermining fulfils two main functions.

First, cuts in welfare mean the government does not have to spend so much. This is deflationary, holds down deficits and, if taken far enough, can make tax cuts possible.

Second, cuts in welfare, unlike other forms of government spending, make it more imperative for people to hold down a job. The more intolerable being unemployed is, the worse pay and conditions people will accept. Cuts in entitlement to benefits strengthen the link between work and the ability to acquire enough goods and services to survive. They thus help reinforce the central discipline which capitalism imposes on workers – the need to work for their employer on their terms in order to obtain a living.

Tax cuts

Reagan's campaign promised a dramatic 30 per cent across-the-board cut in personal income taxes. He said he would institute 'an equal reduction in everybody's tax rates', not a 'shift of wealth between different sets of taxpayers'. What actually emerged was not only a smaller cut, 23 per cent over three years, but one which benefited the rich quite disproportionately. In the first place the top tax brackets were cut by 29 per cent, more than the average. Secondly, a given percentage cut in the tax bill has a much bigger effect, the higher the tax bracket (so, for example, halving all tax rates would double the take-home pay of somebody paying two-thirds of their income in tax, but have no effect at all on people paying no tax). Thirdly, there was no proposal to link to inflation either the level of personal allowances or the level at which successive tax brackets operated. This meant that the poorest people would travel up the tax brackets faster than the rate which was being applied at each bracket was reduced. One calculation showed that families on $10,000 a year in 1980 would actually pay more in tax, whereas those on $250,000 a year would increase their post-tax incomes by about one-fifth.

Reagan's budget director, David Stockman, was very candid: 'The hard part of the supply-side tax cut is dropping the top rate from 70 to 50 per cent – the rest of it is a secondary matter. The original argument was that the top bracket was too high, and that's having the most devastating effect on the economy. Then, the general argument was that, in order to make this palatable as a political matter, you had to bring down all the brackets. But, I mean, Kemp-Roth [the original cuts proposal] was always a Trojan horse to bring down the top rate' (quoted Ackerman, pp. 43–4). The Trojan horse, it will be remembered, was not sugar to sweeten a bitter pill but an exercise in deceit.

New loopholes were opened up for particular groups. Exemptions from the windfall oil profits tax, for example, should save the oil companies $3 billion a year from 1986. David Stockman summed up the lobbying for tax cuts by special interest groups as follows: 'Do you realize the greed that came to the forefront? The hogs were really feeding. The greed level, the level of opportunism, just got out of control' (quoted Ackerman, p. 50).

The biggest tax cut for business is accelerated depreciation allowances. This will cost the US Treasury $53 billion a year by 1986, and far more in later years.

The president's *Economic Report* actually admitted that instead of corporate taxation reducing the rate of profit by about one-third, the effect of all these concessions would be to leave the rate of profit after tax *higher* than the return before tax. As one commentary put it, 'we should all get such incentives!' (Bowles *et al.*, p. 185).

Thatcher did not produce a grand plan along the lines of Reagan's phased, across-the-board tax cuts. Her government, while repeatedly stating that the long-term aim is 'substantial' cuts in the basic rate of income tax, tended to avoid announcing precise targets or time schedules.

Income tax was cut under the first Thatcher administration. The basic rate was reduced from 33 to 30 per cent in 1979. Personal allowances also rose by 5 per cent more than prices over the four years. But the VAT rate was raised from 8 to 15 per cent in 1979. National insurance contributions were raised in three stages from 6.5 to 9 per cent, and the rate on the first £750 of taxable income was raised from 25 to 30 per cent. The average level of rates also rose.

The net effect of all these changes was similar to that of Reagan's programme. Most people finished up paying more in tax. The overall burden for a worker on average earnings rose from 44 per cent in 1979 to 48 per cent in 1983. But those on high incomes ended up paying less. The top rate of income tax was cut from 85 to 60 per cent. A typical company director on £45,000 a year enjoyed a £120 a week rise in real take-home pay, an increase of a quarter.

The tax changes that have so far taken place on both sides of the Atlantic thus amount to a redistribution from the less well off to people from backgrounds similar to those of members of the administrations.

So all the talk of tax cuts has turned out to be little more than a cover for massive redistribution from poor to rich. As J. K. Galbraith pointed out, it was a most convenient theory that suggested that the way to improve incentives was to make the rich richer and the poor poorer. General tax cuts would have an economic logic in terms of buying wage moderation from workers whose take-home pay would be increased; any gains in terms of more slowly increasing labour costs would tend to improve competitiveness and profits. But short of an attack on the welfare state far greater than anything which has proved politically possible in the United Kingdom or United States, massive tax cuts would mean correspondingly huge deficits, thereby undermining the deflationary stance of fiscal policy. So they have so far either not been implemented or have been more than offset by increases in other forms of taxation. The shrinking of the tax base caused by the recession has meant that taxes have actually risen in relation to GDP – from 39 per cent in 1979 to 43 per cent in 1981 in the United Kingdom.

Privatization and deregulation

Both administrations adopted a 'hands off' approach to management, taking the view that production decisions are best made by capitalists in an environment as unfettered by government 'interference' as possible. In the United States, moves in this direction have mainly taken the form of 'deregulating' the activities of existing private capital. In the United Kingdom the thrust has been to 'privatize' operations previously under state ownership and control. This difference in emphasis largely reflects the greater importance given in the United States to state control of private industry by regulation rather than by nationalization (electricity generation being a good example).

'*Don't just stand there, undo something.*' The words are those of the first chair of Reagan's Council of Economic Advisors, Murray Weidenbaum, chief crusader for deregulation. In 1981 the administration jettisoned the legal requirement on manufacturers to incorporate air bags, or other passive safety restraints, in all cars. GM says that this move will save it $500,000 a day. If so, the total savings to all US auto companies over four years should be around $1.5 billion. The cost to consumers of extra deaths, medical bills, insurance premiums and so on has been put at $4.5 billion.

The supply-siders claim that business has become stitched up in a red-tape cobweb of regulations, and that this is stifling innovation and investment, and restricting individual freedom. Their main targets are controls on job safety, energy, the environment and consumer health and safety, described by Weidenbaum as the 'newer areas of social regulation'.

These controls have certainly cost firms money. One estimate is around $12 billion. But they have also had tangible benefits for the quality of life. During the 1970s particle emissions into the air fell by a half, and sulphur dioxide by a sixth. Average pollution per car mile fell by something between a third and a half. Aquatic life began to revive in important stretches of water. Conventional analyses of the social benefits of four of the agencies have valued the annual benefits from the Clean Air Act at $21 billion, those from water pollution controls at $12 billion, the reduction in deaths from auto safety standards at $6 billion and reduced workplace accidents at $10 billion. All these agencies are seen as prime targets for deregulation.

The energy industry is a particularly powerful deregulation lobby. The American Petroleum Institute, representing the oil companies, is pressing for the opening up to the oil majors of the third or so of US land owned by the federal government. They assure us that national parks, forests, prairies and so on can only benefit. Animals love oil companies: 'Caribou, moose and their calves can be seen grazing within a few hundred yards of drilling rigs, or resting and browsing beneath the elevated portions of the trans-Alaska pipeline, because it is warmer there and the grass is literally greener' (quoted Ackerman, p. 131).

Enthusiasm in the administration for deregulation seems almost boundless. In 1980 James C. Miller III co-authored a report which argued that: 'Avoiding defects is not costless. Those who have low aversion to risk – relative to money – will be most likely to purchase cheap, unreliable products. Agency action to impose quality standards interferes with the efficient expression of consumer preferences' (quoted Ackerman, p. 119). He was later appointed to chair the Federal Trade Commission.

Privatization took two main forms under the first Thatcher government. One was the sale of public assets, or of substantial minority shareholdings in such assets, to the private sector. British Aerospace, Cable and Wireless, Amersham International and Associated British Ports were fully privatized and shares sold on the stock exchange. The National Freight Corporation was sold to 'employees' (mainly management). The British Technology Group (formerly the National Enterprise Board) sold off several high-technology companies and shares in Ferranti, ICL, Fairey and twenty-four smaller firms. The biggest single sale in cash terms was of shares in the British National Oil Corporation.

Subsidiaries of nationalized industries were also disposed of. British Rail divested itself of its hovercraft service, laundries, hotels and its Superbreak holiday venture. British Gas put its 50 per cent stake in the Wytch Farm oil field on the market. Government departments also offered assets for sale, including the National Maritime Institute, eleven Royal Ordnance factories, twenty-four motorway service stations, a pub in North London and a cattle-breeding centre.

Public buildings and land were also sold off. Over 400,000 council houses were disposed of at up to 50 per cent below market price. Whole estates were sold to private developers, including a 3312-dwelling estate in Merseyside. NHS buildings and land were also put up for sale.

The second main form of privatization was the hiring of private contractors to undertake work previously done by public employees – that is, contracting out. Government departments, the National Health Service and some Tory-controlled local authorities contracted out operations ranging from cleaning, refuse collection, laundering and sewer maintenance to catering, security, typing, photocopying and vehicle maintenance to computer services, photographic and design work and auditing. The Reagan administration has taken this idea a little further. It is going to pay Corrections Corporation of America $23.50 a day for each inmate in its $4 million purpose-built Texas gaol.

The function of deregulation is very simple – to allow capital to make more money by legally cutting corners. The enormous social costs are seen as acceptable because very few of them are borne by business. Deregulation thus represents a rolling back of one of the responsibilities accepted by governments during the postwar consensus – that of protecting workers from 'excessive' pollution, danger at work and shoddy products.

Privatization has more complex effects. It opens up profitable areas of activity to private capital, but its impact on the total resources available for private accumulation is less obvious. It certainly reduces the amount of government borrowing during the years in which the assets are sold, and in subsequent years if the enterprises were borrowing in order to invest more than their current profits. But it does not matter fundamentally if private capital lends to a government enterprise or to a private one carrying out the same functions. If the government sells off the assets cheaply then clearly the investors – or speculators who bought the shares – gain, at the expense of the taxpayers. But provided the government charges a true market value for the assets, then the private investors are merely switching from holding government bonds to shares of the same value.

Privatization can only increase the total surplus available for private accumulation if it increases the profitability of those enterprises. Fear of the sack under the new management may intimidate workers into accepting lower wages or more intensive work patterns, especially where strongly unionized public sector workers are replaced by weakly unionized private sector workers. Capital as a whole gains from the greater pool of profits which results. Workers in that industry pay. If it galvanizes management into cutting out loss-making services, through subjecting the enterprise to market pressures, then again the pool of profits increases; this time at the expense of the consumers. In the highly implausible case that private management is simply better at organization, so that efficiency improves without greater effort from the workers, then the greater pool of profits is at the expense of those put out of work. To the extent that workers in state industries have won favourable conditions, or the behaviour of those industries reflects social considerations, privatization is simply a way of attacking such gains.

Union bashing

In October 1980 the former star of *Bedtime for Bonzo* – soon to become the first US president to have been a trade union leader – wrote to the president of one of the few unions to endorse his candidature: 'You can rest assured that if I am elected President, I will take whatever steps are necessary to provide [your members] with the most modern equipment available and to adjust staff levels and work days so that they are commensurate with achieving a maximum degree of public safety . . . I pledge to you that my administration will work very closely with you to bring about a spirit of co-operation between the President and [your members]' (quoted Ackerman, p. 110). The union was PATCO – the Professional Air Traffic Controllers' Organization. Ten months later, on 3 August 1981, Reagan fired the entire 11,000 membership. Union leaders were hustled to gaol in chains.

Union busting has always been a feature of Reagan's approach. PATCO president, Robert Poli, would have done well to pay more attention to his candidate's speeches than to his correspondence. On 23 April 1980 Reagan had said: 'We should look very closely at whether [unions] should not be bound, as business is, by the antitrust laws. Labour has become so powerful and, bargaining on an industry-wide basis as they do, I've thought for some time they should be subject to the same restraints that are imposed on industry and business' (quoted Ackerman, p. 101). Reagan has not yet tried to use antitrust laws against unions. Nor has he moved to repeal minimum wage and other laws to protect labour (though he never tires of denouncing them). But he has put in the boot in other ways.

The PATCO affair was exemplary. Its roots stretch back to the early seventies when the Federal Aviation Administration (FAA) diagnosed morale difficulties in the control towers. A 1978 consultants' report blamed harsh management (controllers rated supervisors' 'tolerance of freedom' lower than soldiers rated their officers'). It recommended that a 'program be undertaken with joint union-management co-operation to improve work life'. The FAA opted instead to ride out an expected strike.

Air traffic rose by a fifth between 1978 and 1981, without any increase in controllers or equipment. To shift planes, you had to bend rules and risk lives. Strain like this takes a toll. Controllers get more ulcers than most people and more become alcoholics. Despite retirement after twenty-five years (twenty if over fifty years of age), only 11 per cent last the distance. Half drop out on medical grounds.

Reagan added two twists to the FAA's plans to beat the strike. One was immediate firings. (Carter had intended to *threaten* sackings.) The other was a crucial flight reduction plan that eased the pressure on traffic control. It also enabled the major airlines, suffering from around 50 per cent excess capacity and furious competition from the newly deregulated cut-price operators, to cut down on their losses. After the strike was defeated, new air traffic controllers had to sign an agreement not to engage in industrial action.

The treatment handed out to PATCO intimidated other state sector workers. In the private sector, workers have been forced to make major concessions to management in the form of wage cuts, wage freezes, premature regulations of existing contracts and easing of work rules. Major wage concessions took place in the trucking industry in 1982: no general wage increases were granted, and cost-of-living adjustments both covered a smaller proportion of inflation (70 per cent) than previously and were to be paid less frequently. Automobile workers accepted a deal with no general wage increases and a delay in the cost-of-living adjustments (which in this case gave 90 per cent protection). Probably of more long-term significance, important changes in work rules have been accepted – speeding up a process already underway (see Chapter 17). *Business Week* reported many examples – from steel, autos, railroads, meatpacking, rubber, airlines, construction and other industries – of jobs being 'enlarged' by adding duties or combining crafts, and management being granted greater flexibility to schedule hours of work and to change manning after the introduction of new technology. One observer remarked: 'You can go back to almost any recession and find examples of unionized companies more aggressively going after work rules. But you have to go back to the Depression to find as much of it as is going on now' (*Business Week*, 16 May 1983).

Thatcher's approach to public sector unions in her first two years contrasted sharply with Reagan's response to PATCO. She allowed a series of very high wage settlements in 1979–80, flowing from a comparability exercise set up by the previous Labour government. Even in 1981, the more powerful public sector groups won large settlements: miners and water workers each received 9 per cent, firemen 10 per cent and local authority workers 7½ per cent. Only in 1982–3 was the government prepared to ride out a water workers' strike and two rail strikes. Despite adopting the target of a 15 per cent cut in civil service employment between 1979 and 1984, Thatcher created almost no redundancies in the service in the first eighteen months. The early privatization moves centred on companies in which there was little union opposition, the most important being the British National Oil Corporation, British Aerospace, and Cable and Wireless. Other target companies in which strong resistance could be expected, such as British Airways and British Telecom, where initially kept on ice. At first sight this squares awkwardly with the government's overall radical approach.

The explanation is a desire to avoid an antigovernment alliance of public and private sector unions. Just such an alliance had thwarted the policies of the previous Tory administration of 1970–4, under Heath, and eventually brought it down. Since then the public sector unions had grown in strength and spearheaded the strike wave of winter 1978–9. So they were to be handled carefully until unemployment had weakened private sector unions enough to prevent them effectively assisting their brothers and sisters in the public sector. This was not judged to be the case until 1982.

The Heath experience also shaped the approach to private sector unions. His strategy had centred on legislation which would restrict union rights, shift power from plant to national level, and allow employers to take unions to court for breaches of the new restrictions. Employers generally refused to use the legislation, and towards the end of the administration the director-general of the employers' confederation, the CBI, explicitly condemned it. On the few occasions when legislation was used, unions refused to comply with legal judgements and the government was forced to back down.

Thatcher drew two main conclusions from the Heath fiasco. One was that legislation had limitations as a weapon with which to restructure industrial relations. She decided not to make major legal changes until other factors had weakened the unions. In other words, she saw anti-trade union legislation primarily as a way of buttressing changes in the balance of industrial power achieved by other means, rather than as a device for initiating such changes.

The Employment Acts of 1980 and 1982 were weaker than Heath's Industrial Relations Act. The first provided finance for secret strike ballots or elections but left such devices to the discretion of the unions. It limited picketing to six people, and removed certain types of secondary action from immunity to civil action. Finally, it made it illegal to expel workers from a union, or to refuse them admission, where a closed shop existed, and required an 80 per cent majority for the establishment of new closed shops.

The second Employment Act limited the definition of a trades dispute to exclude inter-union and political disputes, and made unions liable for illegal acts performed by representatives unless such acts were explicitly repudiated. It also outlawed commercial contracts stipulating the use of union labour and extended compensation to workers dismissed as a result of closed shops. No moves were made on the central issues of outlawing closed shops, making unofficial strikes illegal or requiring negotiated contracts to be legally binding.

Employment secretary James Prior summed up the three lessons from the Heath government as follows: 'The Conservative Party is not prepared to get itself into a position of trying to pass laws which employers ask us to pass and then don't use. . . . It would be a great mistake if we took certain actions now which merely united the trade union movement again in an anti-Conservative government posture' (*Business Week*, 16 April 1979).

The 'softly-softly' strategy which followed succeeded very effectively in dividing the trade union movement. Soon after the 1983 election the print union, the National Graphical Association (NGA), was taken to court by a small employer over union members' actions while trying to win a dispute over a closed shop. After exceptionally tough police action against mass pickets, fines imposed on the NGA totalling more than £½ million and a court order to seize all the NGA's assets, the TUC was faced with the dilemma of whether or not to give the union full support in its battle with the government. A previous decision of TUC conference to give such support was disregarded and the TUC agreed to back only lawful action, thus depriving the NGA of any means of winning the strike. This was a major victory for the government. But legal measures were auxiliary to the government's main strategy. It adopted a two-pronged strategy to bring about changes in employer-labour relations in the private sector. The key targets were large-scale industrial plants – those in which plant-level union structures were strongest and had wrested the most serious concessions from employers over procedures and operating levels.

One prong has been force of example. The government used its position of majority shareholder in BL to try and show what tough, new-style management could achieve even in such a bastion of plant union power as the motor industry. One observer sums up:

'The government let it be known that continuing financial subsidy depended upon satisfactory performance in reducing losses. BL management aimed at unilateral control on the shop floor in order to reduce overmanning both among skilled and semi-skilled workers and to introduce labour-saving machinery especially in welding and spraying. Their method was to communicate demands directly to shop-floor workers, threatening dismissal to those who wanted a strike and closure in the event of the withdrawal of government subsidy, and balloting the workforce when unions called strikes. In February and April 1980 strike calls by the TGWU [transport workers] and, less enthusiastically, the AUEW [engineering workers], were rejected by large margins. Since then management has operated a system of unilateral control (though with some variation between plants) which has resulted in a reduction in job demarcation for skilled workers, work intensification on assembly lines and heavy redundancies particularly for semi-skilled and unskilled workers' (Soskice, 1984, p. 26).

The other prong has been the savage deflation. This has forced managers who would otherwise prefer 'gentlemanly' negotiations with plant union structures to follow the example set at BL and tackle shopfloor power head-on.

Attempts to take on unions, to bypass them, to reduce their legal status or to weaken them by mass unemployment are central to the strategy of radically shifting the parameters of the old consensus. The right to effective representation by free trade unions was itself a significant component of that consensus. But the importance of weakening the unions is more general still – strong unions were always the main guarantee for workers of the other components – jobs and welfare services.

Militarism

Thatcher and Reagan are both committed to vastly increased military spending. Reagan called for an increase of 7½ per cent a year real growth for the five years from 1982. Thatcher aimed for a 3 per cent a year increase. Conflicting as it does with the general desire to reduce the role of government and with specific obsessions to reduce public sector deficits, it appears that such militarism is an aberration from their programmes for economic restoration. The explanation for this 'second cold war' lies in a complex set of factors including purely military aspects such as improved Soviet military capability. Undoubtedly the challenge faced by the United States in the third world has an economic dimension, access to key materials. Further, there is the desire of the United States to bring its allies into line over economic matters by reasserting the importance of 'defence' where its predominant position in the alliance is unchallenged. But there can be no doubt at all that militarism, just as during the first cold war, also plays an extremely important ideological role in the generalized assault on the labour movement through linking the left – the 'enemy within' – with the USSR.

Is it working?

It is too early to draw up any kind of final balance sheet on Thatcherism and Reaganomics. But a few points can be made.

First, the benefits to profitability of deflating sharply seem to have been limited to date. Productivity in UK manufacturing did grow by a remarkable 10 per cent in 1981, but this barely offset the decline in the early months of the recession when output fell faster than firms could organize sackings. During the four years of the first Thatcher government as a whole, manufacturing productivity did grow by 3.1 per cent a year, as compared to 1.4 per cent a year under the previous Labour administration. However, this was not the result of higher investment and faster introduction of new technology. In 1982, for the first time in postwar Britain, new manufacturing investment fell below the normal level of scrapping of old equipment. So the capital stock fell – by a considerable amount if extra scrapping due to forced rationalization induced by the slump is taken into account.

The productivity growth has therefore been achieved primarily by this process of rationalizing the less efficient areas and by schemes of work intensification and reorganization. Spectacular results have been claimed in a few companies, notably British Steel and BL where state ownership has been used to good effect by threatening closure if the workers do not accept the management's plans. It was still unclear after four years of the 'Thatcher experiment' whether these cases were the spearhead of a more general process. Some of the productivity gains would only be realized in an upswing which allowed capacity to be used more intensively. A 1981 survey indicated that firms could increase output by 10 per cent with only a 2 per cent increase in employment. A 19 per cent decline in industrial profits in real terms between 1979 and 1982, during the decline in production, was reversed during 1983, when output edged up a little and profits rose three times as fast as wages. But this still left the profit rate way below the level of the 1960s.

In the United States there was a sharp recovery of production in 1983, based on stockbuilding and consumer spending. Profits in the first three quarters of the upswing rose about twice as fast as the average recovery in previous upswings, reflecting 'the moderate uptrend in wages and by the intensive cost-cutting efforts many firms have made in the past four troubled years' (Morgan

Guaranty Bank, *Survey*, November 1983, p. 6). Productivity is reckoned to have increased about 3 per cent in 1983, reflecting 'cost-cutting – in response to rising imports, deregulation and the recession' (ibid., p. 11), after the stagnation of the late seventies. But the rise in profitability in 1983 no more than reversed the decline of the previous year, still leaving the rate far below peak levels and making it doubtful whether business investment would take off to the extent needed to maintain the momentum of the recovery in output and productivity.

In one important respect the practice of Reaganomics differed sharply from the deflationary policies championed most fiercely by Thatcher. While the governments of the other ACCs were busy cutting total government expenditure and increasing taxation, Reagan's supply-side tax cuts on high incomes, and military spending increases, pumped spending equivalent to 2½ per cent of GDP into the US economy over the period 1982–4. From being negligible at the end of the seventies, the US government deficit moved up to the ACC average of 4 per cent of GDP, and was forecast to increase further. The US Federal Reserve Board, dominated by financially orthodox bankers, felt obliged to hold the expansion in check. They squeezed hard on credit and kept real interest rates at unprecedentedly high levels. Without stringent controls to prevent capital flight, other countries had no option but to keep their interest rates up too. So while other ACCs' exports gained from the high value of the dollar, the high interest rates provided a convenient excuse for the sluggishness of the recovery elsewhere.

Finally, it is important to be clear about what would constitute success. The criteria are not those usually cited by politicians and financial commentators. Inflation is not the fundamental issue, and minor upswings, based largely on stockbuilding and housing and consumer credit, are almost irrelevant. Real success would consist of re-establishing the conditions for profitable production and sustained accumulation. This would involve inflicting a defeat on the labour movement severe enough to prevent it from fighting back effectively when and if accumulation took off and economic conditions improved substantially. By early 1984 this had not been achieved, and no general move to more expansionary policies was in sight.

19. The Left Alternative

Socialists have never confined their concerns to the economy; many broader socialist aspirations, however, depend on economic success. So the mounting economic difficulties of the 1970s and 1980s posed a formidable challenge to parties of the left. The apparently automatic growth of the 1960s, which had maintained employment and provided the resources to improve living standards and welfare services, was fading into the past. That prosperity depended on buoyant accumulation but, as we argued earlier (Chapters 11–13), the high rate of accumulation could not be sustained. The challenge was to recreate that prosperity while protecting the interests, and extending the rights, of working people.

The response of workers' parties to this challenge is exemplified by the UK Labour government of 1974–9 and the Mitterrand administration elected in France in 1981. Before discussing their initial achievements and subsequent failures, it is important to highlight the economic constraints they faced. Feebleness was not the essential problem. The most resolute approach could not have succeeded without adequate policies.

Maintaining full employment has always been the cornerstone of the economic policies of the left. Restoring it has been the priority since the mid-1970s. This is not only for the sake of the unemployed but also because of the benefits to the rest of society as a result of the additional output they would produce if at work. The welfare state has actually increased this gain from full employment. Since the state guarantees workers and their families a minimum standard of living when they are unemployed, their additional consumption when employed is that much less. If employed to produce goods and services for sale, the rest of society gains not only whatever surplus is received by the employer, but also the extra tax paid by the worker, and the savings on dole payments. If employed in the public sector, the real cost to the rest of society of the services the newly employed worker produces is not the gross wage paid, because the worker taken on loses dole payments and pays tax. Only the difference between take-home pay and the dole, frequently very little for low-paid public sector employees, represents a real cost. So workers making commodities for sale produce much more than the extra they consume when employed, and public sector workers' extra consumption when employed is rather little. It follows that the achievement of full employment can provide the resources for better public services and improvements in the position of the worst-off sections of society, together with increases in investment necessary to secure further gains all round in the future.

The problem faced by left parties was that, once the underlying conditions of high profitability and accumulation had disappeared, the effectiveness of Keynesian policies also evaporated. Increasing government spending, and cutting taxes, which had seemed the solution to the minor recessions of the sixties, no longer appeared to have the desired effect. The problem was stated explicitly by the leader of the Labour Party, James Callaghan, at its 1976 conference: 'We used to think that you could spend your way out of a recession and increase employment by cutting taxes and boosting government spending. I tell you in all candour that that option no longer exists and that insofar as it ever did exist, it only worked on each occasion since the war by injecting a bigger dose of inflation into the economy, followed by a higher level of unemployment at the next step.'

Traditional Keynesianism lacked policies to overcome difficulties with real wages and inflation, government borrowing, the balance of payments and investment. This chapter opens with a discussion of these difficulties. It then outlines how the problems manifested themselves under the Labour government in the United Kingdom and the Socialist one in France, and how these governments responded.

Obstacles to full employment

In conditions of low profitability and accumulation a major expansion of demand, via tax cuts and public spending increases, tends to generate inflation. Employers take advantage of higher spending to rebuild their squeezed profit margins. Some need to raise prices to make profitable additional production on old, less efficient, machinery. They do not take on additional workers without such a price increase. These price rises tend to reduce real wages. For their part, workers' confidence is increased by falling unemployment and the election of a government which they feel supports them. Faced with price increases, and after years of low real wage increases, militant wage bargaining is almost inevitable.

These two pressures interact. Big wage rises force firms to increase prices further. Price rises force workers to increase wage claims to maintain living standards. A price-wage-price spiral follows. Price controls, the obvious solution from workers' point of view, offer no easy solution, for if wage increases eat further into profits, jobs will be jeopardized in the low-productivity, low-profit plants. Investment would also be further hit, slowing down the provision of more productive jobs for the future. When profits are low, traditional Keynesian remedies to raise employment imply severe wage restraint.

Obviously there is a limit to the growth rate of real wages under any economic system. Take-home pay, the public services and investment cannot all grow faster than total production without an increasing and unsustainable balance of payments deficit. The special feature of capitalist production is that each additional worker taken on has to generate profits for the employer, by producing commodities to a value greater than the cost to the employer of that labour. This cost (the gross wage plus employers' social security contributions) to the employer is much greater than the cost to the rest of society of that employment (the extra consumption of the worker which is equal to the difference between the net wage and the dole). So employment which is highly beneficial to the rest of society (not to mention to the worker concerned) is blocked by the capitalist criterion of profitability. Moreover, firms will only invest if the real wage is sufficiently low to generate both a required level of profits to finance the investment and the expectation of what are regarded as satisfactory profits from the project. Again this criterion of private profitability diverges wildly from the criterion of social gain, especially in a situation of mass unemployment when the resources used to construct the investment project would otherwise have been idle.

The only way that workers can overcome this inherent characteristic of capitalism to decide employment and investment on the criterion of private profitability is to transform the basis on which the economy operates. This requires either the nationalization of the major sections of industry or the successful imposition on the private sector of sufficiently tight controls to achieve the same results. On this basis planning of the growth of real wages would form a part of the overall planning of production and expenditure priorities.

A major component of all the left strategies to reduce unemployment is a substantial expansion of public spending. As well as bringing much-needed improvement in the public services, this provides jobs both directly and indirectly because the spending of workers taken on in the public sector raises employment in consumer goods industries. The problem is how to finance this spending, how to raise the sums necessary to cover the increased budget deficit (PSBR). A substantial part of the extra government spending will be offset by lower dole payments and increased tax. If investment rises sharply, pushing up output even further, the PSBR could even fall. Such a process takes time, however, and so the government would be forced, temporarily at least, to increase its borrowing. Unfortunately the financial institutions who control the funds are convinced that a major increase in government borrowing will wreck the economy (Chapter 18). The dominant left response to this difficulty is to propose that the financial institutions should be obliged to cough up the funds the government requires, by nationalization if necessary.

Expansion would also threaten the balance of payments. Part of any increase in incomes will tend to be spent on imports, especially if industry is uncompetitive in the field of consumer goods. Even a highly competitive industry would require extra imported raw materials. One solution is to allow the exchange rate to float down (to make competitive the additional exports required to balance the import bill). But a lower exchange rate also means higher import prices eating into real wages. The threatened twist to the inflationary spiral will cause a flight of money capital from the country, tending to push the exchange rate down even further. Proposals from the left to meet these difficulties centre around exchange controls (to prevent capital flight) and import controls (to prevent the trade balance deteriorating). Obvious difficulties are those of implementing effective capital controls in highly internationalized capital markets and of avoiding retaliation to import controls.

Expansion could only be maintained if accompanied by an adequate level of investment. Without it there would not be sufficient increases in labour productivity to allow expectations about improvements in living standards and welfare services to be met. Further, the pressure of international competition impinges on any government through the necessity to trade. This imposes a certain pattern of modernization irrespective of domestic preferences.

If export industries fail to match international productivity gains then more and more labour may have to be expended in the export industries to cover even an unchanged bill for necessary imports. Suppose the United Kingdom exports cars to Australia in exchange for iron ore. If Japanese car producers double productivity, thereby halving costs, one car will exchange for roughly half as much iron ore as before (assuming no productivity growth in iron ore mining). If labour productivity in the United Kingdom car industry failed to rise, that would not prevent one UK car also selling for less and less iron ore. More and more labour would have to be devoted to producing cars for export if the same amount of iron ore was to be imported, implying that less labour could be devoted to other sectors like the public services. So the competitive world market makes standing still impossible. It imposes the necessity for modernization, and partially dictates its direction, regardless of domestic considerations.

So left governments need to raise investment to ensure the growth of resources necessary for their programmes, and are obliged to follow to some extent the patterns of modernization dictated by the evolution of the world market and their existing position in it. If this is to be done on a capitalist basis then the 'appropriate' balance between real wages and productivity has to be ensured, and employers persuaded that markets will grow smoothly and fast. The restoration of the conditions for profitable production precludes the substantial increases in real wages to which a left government will be committed in the eyes of its supporters. This means an inevitable clash between aspirations and the necessities imposed by the capitalist system. Together with the other problems already discussed, this makes it highly unlikely that the employers will be confident that the expansion will be maintained. Moreover, the election of a left government will tend to reduce the employers' freedom to introduce new technology in the most profitable way. Legislation over matters such as dismissals, union recognition, rights to information and even decision-making strengthens trade unions in relation to the employers. Together with renewed confidence among workers, this will all tend to sap the employers' degree of control over the shop floor. The effect of doubts by employers about the future of real wages, the sustainability of expansion and about control in the factories is much more likely to be an investment strike rather than an investment boom. The left's response to the probability of such problems is to propose that the government takes the powers to plan investment. The fundamental question is whether this can be achieved by government directions to private firms, which override their own assessments of what would be profitable for them. The alternative is extensive nationalization.

This discussion of the problems facing any left government attempting to restore full employment in the conditions obtaining since the mid-seventies forms the backdrop to the rest of this chapter, which evaluates the British Labour and French Socialist governments. It focuses on their programmes for expanding the economy and providing job opportunities by increasing public spending and raising investment by industrial policies. Since the Mitterrand government has been in office for only two and a half years at the time of writing, our analysis is necessarily provisional, although it appears all too ominously to be following the pattern set by Labour.

Jobs

Labour's election manifesto pledged it to 'increase social equality by giving far greater importance to full employment'. Faced with registered unemployment of 600,000 when taking office in the spring of 1974, it introduced a mildly expansionary budget, making Britain the only major country not to deflate significantly in the wake of the 1973–4 oil price increases. The employers' federation subjected the government to intense pressure immediately after the October election. Its director published an open letter to the prime minister, saying that 'price control, profit limitations and social threats would ensure that the economic crisis . . . could bring the country down within a year'. The budget granted big tax concessions to companies and slackened price controls. The chancellor of the exchequer announced that the growth of public spending would be restricted to 2 per cent a year over the next four years, insufficient to prevent unemployment rising. The April 1975 budget contained further cuts.

The most spectacular public spending cuts followed an agreement reached with the IMF in the autumn of 1976. A sterling crisis had forced the government to apply to the IMF for a loan when the major central banks refused to extend credits further. Arthur Burns, chairman of the US Federal Reserve Bank, explained the bankers' view: 'I had my doubts whether the British could correct the fault in their economic management on their own. You must remember that I am a neanderthal conservative, and naturally suspicious of a Labour Government. I thought it was a profligate government' (*Sunday Times*, 28 May 1978).

The chancellor agreed to cut spending by £3 billion over two years in return for the loan. The City, whose views coincided precisely with the IMF's, was delighted to have such policies 'externally imposed'. As a result of all those cuts, even the modest spending increases announced in February 1975 were not achieved. By 1978 housing spending had only grown half as fast as planned, and that on education not at all. Total government expenditure (excluding such transfer payments as dole, which rose rapidly) hardly increased at all between 1973 and 1978. The stagnation of government spending contributed substantially to the rise in unemployment, which reached 1½ million by 1977. Labour's retreat from expansionary policies was symbolized by prime minister Callaghan's speech already quoted.

As unemployment began to rise steeply, the government introduced a battery of special employment schemes and training measures. By the end of 1977, 177,000 workers were covered by the Temporary Employment Subsidy, 47,000 by the Job Creation Scheme and 80,000 by other programmes. But these schemes had severe limitations.

Most obviously, they did not prevent unemployment from shooting up. They also failed to reduce the overall level of unemployment by the numbers on the schemes. The Department of Employment reported a survey which found that three-quarters of those for whom employers claimed the school-leaver subsidy would have been taken on anyway. The Temporary Employment Subsidy, which paid £20 per week for a year for each worker retained who would otherwise have been made redundant, tried to avoid this by scrutinizing applications carefully. But, with a given level of overall demand, a job saved in one company usually meant one lost in another. To the extent that low-productivity firms are kept in business, employment may be a little higher than if output were concentrated on the more profitable firms. But the gain in jobs could only be small.

This is a general problem with 'make-work' schemes. If governments are not prepared to expand demand then the major effect of most such schemes are costs to the exchequer, subsidies to the employers and a chance for the government to influence the makeup – but not significantly the numbers – of those out of work.

So Labour clearly failed to defend the full-employment component of the consensus, although it did avoid savage deflation on the scale of Thatcher.

The Mitterrand government also intended to rely partly on Keynesian policies to reduce unemployment. Initially it boosted consumption by raising minimum wages and transfer payments, increasing public investment and expanding employment in the public sector by 80,000 in 1981 and 120,000 in 1982. It hoped that the boost to consumption, together with exports rising on the tide of a world recovery, would increase profits and stimulate investment. It was hoped that the economy would grow by 3 per cent in 1982 and that unemployment would begin to fall in 1983.

The first major blow to the plans for expansion came in June 1982, just a year into the government's term of office, when rapidly increasing imports and faster inflation than in the rest of the EEC fuelled speculation against the franc and led to a devaluation of 6 per cent following on the heels of a 3½ per cent devaluation the previous autumn. Social security contributions were increased and the duration of some unemployment benefits reduced. The government announced its intention to stabilize its deficit at 3 per cent of GDP and reduced its growth targets for 1982 and 1983 to around 2 per cent. In March 1983 a further squeeze accompanied the third devaluation of 8 per cent against the mark. This deflationary package, alleged to be the largest single dose of deflation in Western Europe since the Wilson government's post-devaluation package in 1966, reduced output by around 1 per cent. Increases in taxes and nationalized industry prices were accompanied by a slowdown in public investment. The aim was to reduce the budget deficit to about 2½ per cent of GDP. Employment, which hardly fell in 1982 (compared to a fall of around 2 per cent in Germany and the United Kingdom), declined by some ¾ per cent in 1983 (a similar fall to that in the United Kingdom, but a good deal less than in Germany). Reduced growth of the labour force (resulting partly from measures to encourage early retirement and to finance training) held down the rise in unemployment. After rising by around ¼ million in Mitterrand's first year in office, the unemployment rate then stabilized during the rest of 1982 and 1983. One specific policy which contributed was a reduction in the working week – to thirty-nine hours with no loss of pay – and a rise in paid holidays from four weeks to five in 1982. However desirable in themselves, such measures reduce unemployment only by spreading work around (reduced hours) or by reducing the length of the working life (early retirement), and not by increasing jobs.

So pressures to cut the government deficit, both to reassure capitalists at home and to preserve confidence in the currency, forced the Labour and Socialist governments to abandon reflationary policies centred on higher government spending. In order to reduce the dole queues, both administrations were forced back on piecemeal programmes which at worst were largely cosmetic and at best only shared work out more evenly. The Mitterrand government was forced into this retreat despite having extensive control over the banking system (see below) which should have alleviated the problems of financing its deficit and of controlling outflows of funds. Despite talk of 'reconquering the domestic market' the government explicitly rejected protectionism (apart from some temporary petty regulations such as requiring all imported videos to pass through an obscure customs post in Poitiers). Mauroy, the prime minister, explained: 'Reconquering is a slogan which was needed in the election campaign. But we have to adapt it because you can't use the phrase in the same way once you have governmental responsibilities' (*Financial Times*, 6 June 1982).

Wages

Neither government was thwarted in its attempt to increase employment by a failure to persuade its working-class supporters to hold back on wage claims. Wages rose rapidly in the early months of the Labour government in the wake of the 1974 miners' strike. These gains were eroded by high inflation, which peaked at an annual rate of over 25 per cent in the middle of 1975. The TUC then agreed to successive rounds of wage restraint. Earnings growth was halved – an unprecedented concession. Despite the resulting slowdown in inflation, real wages fell by 6 per cent in the second year of the policy. Frustrations built up over falling real wages and the government's failure to create jobs or improve public services and the pay policy collapsed amidst a series of bitter strikes, especially in the public sector. However, it had secured a sharp improvement in manufacturing profitability (it doubled between 1975 and 1978), and the retreat from expansionary policies occurred while the pay restraint was successful in holding back wage increases, not after it had broken.

The Mitterrand government increased the minimum wage by about 6 per cent shortly after taking office. But austerity measures followed. After the June 1982 devaluation, wage indexation agreements were suspended (with the exception of the minimum wage, although even here a promised 4 per cent real increase for 1982 was not forthcoming) and a four-month wage freeze imposed. This was the first time free collective bargaining had been suspended in France since 1950. The government then planned for wages to rise only in line with projected inflation (so that if it underestimated inflation, real wages would decline). This implied that the loss in real earnings during the freeze would not be made good and that the traditional system of close indexation of wages, which had been adjusted to actual previous consumer price rises every three to six months, would be broken. Further real wage cuts were also to be imposed in the public sector. In the year after the 1982 devaluation, real wages stagnated.

Despite moderation on the wages front, the French employers campaigned vigorously for more concessions. They claimed that shorter hours, longer holidays and increased taxes and social security contributions added some £10 billion a year to their costs, and demanded equivalent reductions in social security contributions over five years. Since the money would have to be raised by taxing workers, this implied making them pay for improved hours and welfare benefits by reduced take-home pay. The government accepted the logic of the employers' position and agreed to freeze their contribution levels (and exempt the textile industry from certain contributions) as a means to stabilize employment. In the autumn of 1983 the official statistical office described companies' financial situation as alarming, pointing to the fact that profit margins had declined to their lowest ever level.

Industrial democracy

In the fields of employment, living standards and welfare the initial objectives for both governments were simply to maintain the achievements of the boom years. They represented an attempt to hold the line in the face of severe economic difficulties and the assaults of previous administrations. The achievements were more modest still.

The initial approach to the role of trade unions, by contrast, was considerably more radical. Both parties envisaged going well beyond the traditional role for unions of free collective bargaining over pay and conditions. They promised a major extension of trade union influence in economic decision-making. In Britain the objective became known as 'industrial democracy' and was seen by many as central to the 'fundamental and irreversible shift in the balance of power in favour of working people and their families' promised in the 1974 manifesto.

Labour's approach to the issue had three strands. First, it pledged itself to repeal certain legal restrictions on trade unions dating from the previous Conservative administration. The Industrial Relations Act, the Pay Board and statutory incomes policies were scrapped soon after Labour came into office.

Second, Labour made much play of a 'Social Contract' with the unions. The idea was that in return for cooperation on pay, the TUC would become a partner in national economic and social policy-making. The origin of this supposedly novel arrangement was a 1973 TUC-LP Liaison Committee document entitled *Economic Policy and the Cost of Living*. This short and vague statement talked of the need for 'an alternative strategy to fight inflation . . ., to provide the basis for co-operation between the trade unions and the future Labour government'. Labour made a number of specific policy commitments (all later included in the February 1974 manifesto). The TUC agreed to help 'create the right economic climate for money incomes to grow in line with production'.

Union leaders did gain access to certain ministries in the early stages of the Labour government. *The Times*, commenting on Benn's early discussions on industrial strategy (see below), remarked that trade unionists had 'rarely been seen before crossing the portals of the Department of Trade and Industry headquarters' (quoted Forester, p. 79). But the only real fruits of the contract were the voluntary incomes policies described above. Ministers and civil servants continued to make economic policy. Although the unions were briefly able to cross the portals of DTI headquarters, they were never admitted to its corridors of power.

Labour's third strand was a proposal to give workers a much greater say in company-level decision-making. In 1971 Benn had proposed that continued registration as a limited company should become conditional on depositing annually a certificate of acceptability signed by workforce representatives. The two 1974 election manifestos were more wordy and vague on the subject. The October one said: 'We will introduce new legislation to help forward our plans for a radical extension of industrial democracy in both the private and public sectors. This will involve major changes in company law and in the statutes which govern the nationalized industries and the public services.'

In August 1975 the government set up a committee of inquiry on how, or whether, to meet this general commitment. It took six months to set up the committee under Lord Bullock. Its report was not published until January 1977.

The TUC had pressed for a 50 per cent share of company direction. The committee – comprising three TUC representatives, three heads of companies and a few 'neutral' lawyers and academics (including one who left prematurely to become director of the CBI) – opted for a watered-down version of this objective. Larger companies would have to appoint an equal number of worker and management representatives and a mutually acceptable group of 'independents', who would hold the balance. This became known as the '2x + y' formula. It seemed as if the committee had taken two years to decide that the best formula was the one on which it had itself been set up.

The unions divided sharply over the report. The 1977 TUC Congress passed a compromise resolution: '. . . Congress calls upon the General Council to press the Labour Government to provide for statutory backing to all unions wishing to establish joint control of strategic planning decisions via trade union machinery. This legislation would include the option of parity representation on the board, but would also link up with more flexible forms of joint regulation more clearly based on collective bargaining.'

In May 1978 the government produced a White Paper. This suggested that a code of practice might be drawn up by an Indus-

trial Democracy Commission 'if one is set up', or by the conciliation service, ACAS, 'with a view to its being submitted to
Parliament for approval'. It noted that: 'the object of participation
is understanding and co-operation . . . recourse to statutory fallback arrangements will be the exception.' No legislation was ever
put before parliament.

In France the Socialist Party's *Programme for the 80s* published
before the 1981 elections advocated some fairly radical changes.
Employees were to be given veto powers over hiring, firing and
working-time provisions. Workers were also to have a say on
mergers, closures and major investment programmes. The programme also noted that 'the real power which socialists want for
the workers must come through a break with capitalism'.

In office, the Mitterrand government commissioned the Auroux
report which was presented in September 1981. Six months later, it
introduced a watered-down version of the report as the Auroux
Bill. This proposed:

1. To limit managements' disciplinary powers. Rules concerning
   work practices were to be clearly specified and to relate to sub-
   stantive issues only. Petty regulations, such as bans on talking on
   the line, were to be outlawed. Fines were also to be banned.
2. To introduce mandatory annual negotiations on pay, hours and
   conditions for all firms employing fifty or more workers
   (although neither side would be obliged to reach agreement).
   Unions demonstrating 50 per cent support at company level for
   rejecting an agreement reached at industry level could veto its
   application to their company.
3. To compel companies to grant union delegates and staff representatives more paid time to carry out their duties and more
   protection against sanctions. Union delegates, staff representatives, works committees and health and safety committees
   were to have access to company books and extended powers.
   Industry-wide committees were to be set up with access to
   information on companies' performance.
4. To establish 'workshop councils' in the nationalized sector and
   to grant workers a statutory right to representation on boards.
   In the private sector, unions and management were to be given
   three years to negotiate a mutually agreeable form of industrial
   democracy.

The first two provisions, while important for the weak French unions (Chapter 12), were fairly standard trade union and employee protection measures. The third does in principle advance on the consensus. 'Industrial secrecy' was scarcely challenged in the fifties and sixties. But, important though access to information is, it is a far cry from real decision-making powers. It is no more acceptable as a substitute for real industrial democracy than is a freedom of information act as a substitute for parliamentary democracy. Only the final provision embodies any real elements of industrial democracy.

The French employers' association lost no time in roundly condemning the Auroux Bill as both enormously costly and liable to paralyse business decision-making.

Industrial democracy might seem the type of reform most easily conceded by the employers in a crisis, because it has no immediate economic costs. But their hostility is not really surprising. Such proposals seek to undermine the very foundation of the existing economic system – the employers' control over the deployment of capital.

Industrial policy

The industrial democracy proposals challenged the power of capital by seeking to give workers more control over decision-making. They sought to 'remix' power relations between labour and capital within firms. But not even their staunchest advocates would claim that they were capable of generating economic recovery.

But Labour in the United Kingdom and the French socialists argued that proposals for reshaping the mixed economy centred on industrial policies did offer hope. They aimed radically to 'remix' the balance of power between private capital and the *state*, and to use the latter's newly gained weight to promote investment and growth.

Other objectives of the programmes could have been achieved only if a high rate of accumulation was re-established. Improvements in living standards and welfare provision would also have soon run into difficulties – using idle resources and redistribution can yield only so much; further progress then depends on output growth. Even industrial democracy would have proved a two-edged victory if workers could only preside over the continued rundown of their companies. So industrial policy to buttress expansion by a rising level of investment directed to priority areas was crucial.

Labour's policy had two main strands. One was to nationalize at least one leading, profitable manufacturing company in each industry and then direct its operations through a National Enterprise Board (NEB). The idea was that these newly nationalized companies would undertake major investment programmes and innovations. The architect of these proposals, Stuart Holland, argued that they would exert a 'pull effect on other big firms' based on: '. . . oligopoly leadership, or the situation in which one of the new firms at the top end of an industry breaks from the pack and pioneers a new product or technique on a major scale. While the remaining leading firms might otherwise have hung around and delayed introducing a similar product or process, they cannot any longer afford to do so without risk of losing sales, profits and market share to the pioneer firm' (Holland, 1975, p. 185).

Planning agreements constituted the other main strand of the new industrial policy. The government would require all major firms to present corporate plans, detailing proposed levels of output, employment, investment and so on. It would then amend the plans to fit in with overall economic objectives, while leaving firms free to decide how to carry them out. This was supposed to provide the government with sufficient leverage to plan the economy without having to resort to the traditional socialist device of nationalizing the 'commanding heights'.

In April 1973 the Labour opposition proposed that the next Labour government take powers to impose compulsory planning agreements and talked of nationalizing between twenty and twenty-five of the largest one hundred manufacturing companies, accounting for around one-third of manufacturing output, with or without their consent. The 1973 Party Conference approved this position. The *Guardian* described the policy as 'little short of an industrial and financial revolution' (quoted Forester, p. 74). But, at the leadership's insistence, the word 'compulsory' was omitted from the section on planning agreements in the February 1974 election manifesto, as was any indication of the scale of NEB operations.

In office, Benn, at the Department of Trade and Industry, soon ran into difficulties on all fronts. The press was hostile. Civil servants at the DTI were also obstructive. Permanent secretary Sir Anthony Part reportedly greeted Benn with the words, 'I presume, Secretary of State, that you don't intend to implement the industrial strategy in the Labour Party's programme' (quoted Coventry Trades Council *et al.*, p. 33). Leaked documents were used by the press to whip up scares about 'Bennery'. Michael Clapham, CBI president, objected to the 'interventionist line' and registered the CBI's 'hostile stance'. The *Financial Times* reported that 'the CBI told Mr Wilson that there was absolutely no room for compromise or negotiation about further state intervention in industry and further nationalization' (16 September 1974).

The prime minister, Wilson, and chancellor, Healey, were also vociferous about the need to maintain confidence. Wilson said: 'Private industry must have the necessary confidence to maintain and increase investment to do their duty by the people. And confidence demands that a clear frontier must be defined between what is public and what is private industry' (quoted Forester, p. 81).

He also appointed the industrial tycoon Sir Donald Ryder to head the NEB. After the June 1974 EEC referendum, Wilson also removed Benn from the DTI. The official excuse was that his anti-EEC views made his position difficult. The industrial policy plans published in August 1974 represented a victory for business pressure. Planning agreements were to be purely voluntary, and the NEB's powers were severely restricted by the clause that 'holdings in companies . . . should be acquired by agreement'. The Board's borrowing was limited to £1 billion over five years, insufficient to buy a single company like ICI at prevailing share prices. The Board was also required to bid for shares in the open market unless company directors agreed to the takeover – hardly likely in profitable concerns.

The government transferred eight publicly owned companies to the NEB. Most had been acquired because they were close to bankruptcy. Two, BL and Rolls Royce, accounted for about nine-tenths of the Board's operations. It cut operating levels savagely in an attempt to restore profitability. In the Board's first two years of operation 19,000 jobs were lost at BL and 5600 at Rolls Royce. The NEB's other activities were peripheral and of a purely commercial nature. It lent money to small and medium-sized companies at commercial interest rates.

The only company to sign a planning agreement was Chrysler UK, in spring 1976. The US Chrysler Corporation had offered the government £35 million to take its loss-making British subsidiary off its hands, thereby avoiding redundancy payments and other closure costs. The government did not want Chrysler UK to close, with a loss of some 60,000 direct and indirect jobs, but it was also unwilling to nationalize the company. It opted to provide a £55 million loan for investment and to guarantee to cover a proportion of losses for three years, up to a ceiling of £72.5 million. In return, Chrysler UK agreed to sign a planning agreement. Its trivial significance is well illustrated by the fact that when Chrysler Europe, including Chrysler UK, was later taken over by Peugeot, the Labour government learned of it through the press.

Having abandoned its original industrial strategy, in November 1975 Labour presented the National Economic Development Council (a tripartite economic forum comprising employers, unions and the government) with an alternative long-term industrial strategy. About two-thirds of manufacturing was selected for treatment on the basis that it was either intrinsically successful, could be made so with appropriate action, or supplied essential inputs for the rest of industry. Forty or so 'sector working parties' were set up. The implication was that the other third must sink or swim.

The working parties served two main purposes. First, they provided a forum for industry to discuss with the government (and to a lesser extent the unions) how to allocate the £3 billion or so a year of state subsidies. Second, they made it possible to rationalize industry in a more orderly way than via cut-throat competition and bankruptcies. Rationalization involved job loss with no planned reallocation.

Labour's industrial policy was utterly inadequate to the problems faced. British industry continued to decline apace. Output per hour in manufacturing rose by only 5 per cent between 1973 and 1978 compared with 15 to 25 per cent in its major competitors. Manufacturing employment fell by 7 per cent between 1974 and 1978. Manufacturing investment was no higher in 1978 than in 1974. By mid-1979 imports of finished manufactures was 70 per cent higher than in 1973, while domestic production had not risen at all. This was the inevitable result of abandoning expansionary policies and failing to take control of industry.

*

The centrepiece of Mitterrand's policy has been a major extension of the public sector through the Nationalization Act of February 1982. The government has taken over five major industrial groups in electrical and electronic engineering and chemicals. It has also nationalized the two largest steel groups, thirty-nine banks, two major financial holding companies and a major firm in aircraft, armaments, computers, telecommunications and pharmaceuticals.

The proportion of industrial activity undertaken by the public sector has almost doubled. It now accounts for almost 30 per cent of sales. Its activity is concentrated in large enterprises, where it now accounts for almost one-half of output. It dominates tobacco, steel, artificial fibres, armaments and aeronautical construction (Tables 19.1 and 19.2). About 90 per cent of banking is in state hands.

Table 19.1 French nationalization, 1982

Percentage of industry in
nationalized firms

	Before	*After*
Sales	17.2	29.4
Employment	11.0	22.2
Investment	43.5	51.9
Industrial employment		
Firms with >2000 employees		47.7
Firms with 500–2000 employees		15.4
Firms with < 500 employees		2.7

Source: OECD, *Economic Survey of France*, March 1983, Table 18.

In no sense do these nationalizations amount to a policy of wholesale expropriation. First, the net has been spread more narrowly than had been mooted before the election. Certain pre-election nationalization proposals have not been carried out, including insurance and the taking of a blocking minority stake in Peugeot. Only parent companies have been fully nationalized; key subsidiaries remain open to private investors. Second, not all state

Table 19.2 French nationalization by industry, 1982

Percentages of turnover
in nationalized
firms

	Before	After
Cars	40	40
Tobacco	99	99
Iron and steel	80[1]	80
Non-ferrous metals	13	63
Basic chemicals	23	54
Artificial fibres	0	75
Pharmaceuticals	9	28
Glass	0	35
Construction materials	1	8
Paper and board	0	9
Machine tools	6	12
Industrial equipment	3	14
Armaments	58	75
Office equipment	0	36
Electrical equipment	0	26
Electronic equipment	1	44
Household equipment	0	25
Naval construction	0	17
Aeronautical construction	50	84

1. Allows for fact that state has had effective control of Usinov and Sacilov since 1978, i.e., before actual nationalization.

Source: Delion and Durupty, p. 191.

takeovers have been full nationalizations. The state is now the sole shareholder in the five major industrial groups. But it is only a majority shareholder in some of the other firms. Third, the government has constantly stressed its desire to avoid 'creeping nationalization' or 'nationalization by stealth'. It has argued that the new parameters of the 'mixed economy' must be clear to all if the private sector is to retain confidence.

Finally, compensation has been generous. The *Financial Times* commented that shareholders in the 'big five' received 'far too much compensation when the businesses were taken over' given the losses being made (24 May 1982).

The Interim plan for 1982–3 listed a number of objectives for the massively expanded state sector:

1. To increase research, development and innovation, and to play a 'locomotive role', leading the private sector in the necessary restructuring of the economy. (This seems a similar notion to Holland's 'oligopolistic leadership', see above.)
2. To help reduce working time, to bring youth into employment; to assist the promotion of retirement and 'balanced employment' policies and to improve working conditions.
3. To increase workers' involvement in management and to improve training.
4. To help achieve balanced regional development and to protect the environment.

The banking sector was to encourage more long-term savings linked to industrial lending, to be more sensitive to industrial needs, to disburse medium- and long-term credit in accordance with the government's planning priorities and to aim at lower interest rates.

One theme of the Interim plan is that the public sector would be able to take a long-term view of national economic needs, unconstrained by short-term profitability or liquidity. But this is effectively contradicted by other statements. The plan noted that nationalized companies would have to compete on equal terms with their private counterparts, both domestic and foreign. In summer 1982, industry minister Chevènement said that nationalized companies would be expected to make a profit and that there would not be 'a collection of unpaid bills'.

The key institutional structure for planning the state sector is a system of five-year 'plan contracts' between nationalized companies and the government. (There is an obvious similarity to Labour's proposals for planning agreements, see above.) Within the terms of the contracts, management is supposed to have complete autonomy. Indeed, the supposed autonomy is stressed by ministers more than are the constraints of the contract. Mitterrand said of management in nationalized companies that 'their autonomy of decision and action will be total' (*Financial Times*, 18 February 1982).

The top jobs in the nationalized companies were not generally given to socialists. The industrial groups were run by professional administrators from government or business, the banks by top bankers or civil servants. The chairman of the chemicals firm at Rhône-Poulenc was retained despite a long-running trade union campaign to oust him for presiding over heavy job losses, only to resign later over alleged excessive government interference. It was said that top salaries would be 'recognizably lower' than in the private sector. But at around £80,000 a year they can hardly have promoted close identification with the shop floor.

The government has adopted very ambitious targets for certain sectors. The plan contract signed with one major electronics firm in February 1983 included the targets of a doubling of turnover and exports over five years, electronics being singled out as having a strategic position in the industrial structure.

A plan for the machine tool industry announced in December 1981 aimed at reducing import penetration from 60 to 30 per cent, raising exports from 15 to 30 per cent of output and doubling production over three years. Other import-penetration targets include a reduction from 20 to 15 per cent of the market in furniture and from 25 to 10 per cent in shoes.

The government announced its intention to employ a whole battery of devices to achieve its ends, and made a lot of money available. The chairman of the nationalized computer firm Honeywell Bull said: 'One of the main justifications for the nationalizations is that it was the only means of organizing the transfer to the companies of the funds needed to make them internationally competitive' (*Financial Times*, 17 March 1983). The banks were required to contribute around £½ billion to the nationalized industry's financing requirements, but they were promised that this was a one-off loan.

The plan for machine tools, to give one example, includes: subsidized ten- to twelve-year loans and grants for customers, highly subsidized loans and a free machine hire scheme for companies investing in robots. There is also a scheme to introduce robots into the machine tool companies themselves and a public purchasing policy (pressure on nationalized companies to buy French). There are plans for amalgamation of the 150 or so manufacturers into larger units. Groups of companies are also being asked to specialize in different areas, and the government wants greater standardization of components and the pooling of research and development and sales networks. Financial assistance is available for research and training. The plan is backed with about £⅓ billion of government money. In the chemicals industry the nationalized firms have been involved in a major restructuring plan, involving plant closures and job losses estimated to cover some 10 per cent of the labour force. One company official gloomily told the *Financial Times*, 'Once we get past the restructuring we reach another stage – rationalization' (20 September 1983).

The government has displayed ruthlessness about jobs. It warned workers in the newly nationalized companies that they were not becoming civil servants; if necessary, they must face redundancy like their private sector counterparts. It carried this threat out in steel, among other sectors.

The importance accorded to the private sector and to the capitalist criteria of profitability has been a recurring, and indeed an increasing, theme. Just as Benn was replaced at the Department of Trade and Industry, so was the more radical Chevènement replaced by the aptly named Fabius (the Roman Emperor Fabius was called The Delayer, the avoider of head-on battles, after whom the Fabian Society named itself).

In autumn 1981 Mitterrand reassured industry that the economy would be merely 'a little more mixed' (*Financial Times*, 3 October 1981). Prime minister Mauroy told a gathering of industrialists in Paris that he expected industry 'to produce, to create jobs, to invest and to export'. He was, however, greeted with disbelieving laughter (*Financial Times*, 20 November 1981). Fabius has said that: 'The state must not substitute itself in the role of enterprises and of entrepreneurs, that politics must be kept out of industry, that the main effort in the form of job creation, innovation and development should increasingly in the future come from (largely private) medium and small companies . . . [and that] the notions of risk, profits, competitiveness, have nothing shameful about them – quite the contrary' (*Financial Times*, 13 April 1983).

A few months later he emphasized the implications: 'French industry needs to be given freedom to determine industrial prices to improve profitability' (*Financial Times*, 12 October 1983). Rocard, as minister for the plan, was credited with the view that the market is 'all-embracing and irreplaceable' (*Financial Times*, 22 July 1981).

The drift of Mitterrand's economic policy is clear. There will be a serious attempt at using state funds and pressure to restructure sections of French industry in order to increase competitiveness. In the absence of overall expansion, however, this process will be limited in depth by insufficient investment – between 1981 and 1983 industrial investment fell by 10 per cent. Moreover, without overall expansion, such rationalization as is achieved will lead to more loss of jobs. The best that French workers can look forward to is that, if there is a major recovery in the world economy in the mid-1980s (Chapter 20) and if rationalization is as effective in France as elsewhere, then French industry will secure its share of the fruits of an upswing.

Conclusion

The main conclusion from the experiences of left governments in France and the United Kingdom is the extreme difficulty of ensuring jobs, rising living standards, improved social services and trade union rights in conditions of chronic capitalist crisis. The logic of the economy's guidance system – private profit – presses remorselessly in the direction of wage cuts, rationalization, job losses, cuts in public spending and an employers' offensive to regain control over the shop floor.

The economic conditions which underpinned the consensus have disappeared. Left governments now face a stark choice. They can bow to economic (capitalist) 'reality', abandon expansion and try to restructure industry so as to strengthen its ability to take advantage of a future world upswing, while protecting workers' interests to the limited extent consistent with such a strategy. Alternatively, they can try to break the stranglehold of profitability by extensive nationalization and planning, replacing limited production for private profit by full production for social use. Such a strategy could succeed only by overcoming formidable opposition, both at home and abroad. Very real problems of developing democratic socialist planning would then present themselves.

20. Future Prospects

In 1945 the capitalist system was reeling from the effects of the war. By the early 1980s year after year of stagnation had left a mounting legacy of problems. In between, the most powerful boom in history had occurred.

Although the advanced countries were profoundly transformed by the boom, they continued to be driven by the logic of capitalism. Their motive force remained the accumulation of capital in which the technical aspects of mechanization and rising productivity are underpinned by particular relationships between the classes. Successful accumulation depends crucially on employers' ability to exercise sufficient control over employees to ensure smooth production and profits. For full advantage to be taken of such conditions, relations between countries must be orderly. Focusing on these relationships lends coherence to the story of the successive stages of capitalist restoration, expansion, crisis and unemployment since the Second World War.

Such an approach is essential to understanding the past; however it provides no simple formula with which to predict the future. In retrospect, the course of events often seems inevitable. But at certain decisive periods in the last forty years the future was highly problematic. The postwar radicalism was first contained and then decisively pushed back because on a world scale capitalist forces were stronger than socialist forces. With hindsight, the strengths and weaknesses of both sides can be evaluated clearly. At the time, however, the balance sheet could only have been guarded and conditional; the strengths and weaknesses would only be fully revealed in the clash of events. Study of the postwar period can clarify the crucial factors which will determine future developments. But it cannot predict the precise outcome of the conflicting forces.

The fundamental economic question is whether the stagnation of the past ten years will persist, or whether it will be succeeded either by a catastrophic collapse or by a period of renewed, sustained expansion.

A sustained recovery could only be based on an upsurge in accumulation. This alone could drive productivity growth towards the heights scaled in the fifties and sixties, providing the basis for a new period of prosperity, and accommodation with the working class. The essential precondition would be a restoration of a sufficient degree of capitalist control over the working class. Only then would employers feel confident that an upswing would not flounder on rising inflation and eroded profits. Emboldened with such confidence, they could press governments to prime the pump of expansion, providing additional markets to justify the investment, which in turn would push the expansion upwards. In our view a decade of mass unemployment has failed to restore this degree of control, let alone the confidence that it would be maintained in more favourable economic circumstances.

Nor would attempts at incomes policies and workers' collaboration in reorganizing production restore such confidence. The employers require more than good intentions. Any attempt to restore an acceptable degree of control by pushing monetarist policies much further than Thatcher and Reagan have so far dared would risk prompting a major political reaction from the working class. It would also risk pushing the capitalist economies into an unstoppable slide.

The possibility of a sustained capitalist expansion at some time in the future cannot be ruled out. But it is unlikely to be achieved without prolonged social turmoil. Lower strike figures, quality circles, micro-chip technologies and the election of some right-wing governments are certainly not evidence that the construction of such a basis is well on the way to completion.

Assuming that sustained recovery does not take place rapidly, might a collapse occur? Workers' consumption is too stable to trigger off a major downturn, unless a huge assault on workers' living standards were mounted. Cuts in government spending large enough to start the slide would involve virtually dismantling the welfare state. Both real wages and state spending have so far proved extremely resilient. The gains won by the working class in the fifties and sixties are not easily reversible, even in conditions of mass unemployment. A political defeat for the working class in the advanced countries, far in excess of anything inflicted so far, would be required to provide the basis for a cut in living standards and social services large enough to provoke a major slump (and even then the impact might be offset by massive increases in military spending). Such a Chilean-style defeat could only follow a period of massive social turmoil, and no pointers to it are discernible at present.

Could protectionism spark off a vicious downward spiral? It might seem that a major move by the United States and the EEC to block out imports from Japan, for example, would simply redistribute the effects of stagnation. Japan would for the first time face high unemployment in the mass-production export industries which have taken such a battering in Europe and the United States. These industries would recover a little there. But if Japanese industry were shouldered out of advanced countries' markets, it would be forced to launch an enormous export drive into third world markets (Chapter 17). European and US export industries would suffer, perhaps as much as industries competing with imports gained. Since exporting industries tend to be the more dynamic, severe curtailment of export possibilities would most probably reduce accumulation overall. Stock markets would be hit and confidence further reduced.

If the protectionism were successful, Japan might be forced into savage deflation in order to cut its import bill in line with lower export sales. There would be no guarantee of a compensating expansion elsewhere. All-out trade wars would at the very least increase stagnation substantially.

Investment is the most volatile component of total spending. Could a crash in investment initiate a major downturn? The most likely cause of a sharp fall in investment is a crisis in the international credit system. Firms rely on continually renewing credit in order to maintain stockholdings and investment levels – and on expanding it to finance growth. A ferocious credit contraction would occasion massive running down of stocks, pushing production far below sales. Firms would slash investment in new plant and machinery to enable them to repay loans out of cash flow. A rash of lay-offs would further cut consumer spending. A very severe fall in output and employment is quite conceivable.

An extreme application of monetarist policies could bring about such a credit collapse. But governments are unlikely to squeeze so hard as to provoke a crash within their own countries. Pressures on central banks to use the sophisticated techniques available to maintain the credit system in some sort of balance, and thus to prevent the effects of future downswings being multiplied by a credit crisis, would probably stave off disaster, as in 1974–5 (Chapter 13).

The international credit structure seems much more vulnerable. A major series of defaults by Latin American borrowers, for example, would threaten the viability of major US banks in particular. If the authorities could not prevent a banking collapse then the internal credit systems would be paralysed. The consequences for investment and workers' spending on durables and housing, which is heavily dependent on credit, would be disastrous. Recognition of this possibility has obliged the IMF to coordinate the activities of the banks and the policies of the debtor countries. The Fund has staved off disaster thus far. But it could get out of its depth. Transformation in a socialist direction of a substantial part of the heavily indebted countries, while not implying immediate repudiation of debts, would leave the IMF in a much weaker position to control the course of events. The US and other governments would then be compelled to try to maintain confidence in the banking system by spending huge sums of taxpayers' money to compensate the banks for loans whose repayment prospects were visibly jeopardized. Major defaults of this sort, with disastrous effects on the credit system in the advanced countries, cannot be ruled out.

Barring a collapse of this kind, the economic stagnation of the sort experienced over the last decade is not necessarily unstable. The development of cheaper production processes and new products may generate a low but steady rate of accumulation, despite excess capacity. Even a low rate of accumulation generates some productivity growth, allowing rises in real incomes for the employed, despite high, and perhaps rising, unemployment levels. If government expenditure is held back then taxes may be cut a little, boosting consumption. Even with profit rates far lower than in the boom, the level of investment can creep upwards, ensuring the realization of the slowly growing surplus. Continued trade between the advanced countries provides some scope for new capacity to drive out old, even with little overall growth in trade. Inflation may remain higher than in the fifties and early sixties, and threaten to take off if growth accelerates, without immediately jeopardizing the functioning of the economy.

Developments since 1975 have been broadly along these lines. They could well continue in the same groove. Short upswings and downswings could occur, particularly if governments try to break the pattern, either by expanding demand or by squeezing harder, hoping to prepare the way for renewed expansion along Thatcherite lines (Chapter 18). There is no inherent reason why capitalism must be in either a boom or a bust situation.

The persistence of stagnation over the last decade has resulted from a stalemate between the classes. Employers, faced by a working class enormously strengthened by the boom, have been unable to repeat their successes of the period after 1947 and reimpose the degree of control they require. Workers have been unable to secure full employment since the logic of capitalist crisis imposes itself on any left government elected to pursue this aim without a decisive rupture with capitalism. The terrible costs of continued stagnation, in terms of lives devastated by unemployment and deteriorating public services, more than justify the search for an effective socialist path to break this stalemate.

Data Appendix
Sources
Bibliography
Index

Data Appendix

Sources and methods

This Appendix first describes the basic series for profitability, capital accumulation and state spending which we constructed for the seven largest advanced capitalist countries since 1951. Many of the tables and charts in Parts II and III are based on these data. Appendix Tables A1–A6 present the series for profit shares, profit rates and the capital stock for each country, for both the manufacturing sector and the corporate business sector. Some discussion of sources and methods for these series follows this introduction. We also constructed aggregate series for the seven countries as a whole (labelled 'ACCs') and for the four European ones, France, Germany, Italy and the United Kingdom (labelled 'Europe'). The methods used are described below. Table A7 presents some series for consumption, investment and government spending as shares of GDP for the ACCs. The rest of the data used in Parts II and III come from standard international sources (notably OECD publications), as indicated in the tables and charts. The data for Part I was put together from a range of national sources listed at the end of this Appendix.

The stock of fixed capital at constant prices

Capital stock is calculated using the 'perpetual inventory' method. Each type of means of production is assumed to have a particular life, at the end of which it is scrapped. Each year the capital stock grows as the new investment is added to it, and shrinks as old means of production are retired. These figures are referred to as the *gross* capital stock. An alternative measure is the *net* capital stock. The essential difference is that when calculating the gross stock, means of production are assumed to retain their full initial value throughout their lives, whereas when calculating net stock the value is assumed to fall steadily, reaching zero at the point when they are retired (straight-line depreciation). Steadily falling values capture the fact that ownership of a means of production yields a steadily falling income as a result of competition from more modern equipment (see below). However, the productive capabilities of means of production change little with age. For this reason we have used changes in the gross stock to estimate accumulation.

The asset lives assumed in the different countries vary enormously. Since the statistical evidence on which the lives are based is very tenuous, there is little reason to believe that assumed differences accurately reflect real ones. The assumption of unchanging asset lives is also dubious. For these reasons cross-country comparisons of the level of the capital stock should be treated with caution. Maddison (1982, Appendix D) discusses the differences in estimation between the various countries and provides (Table D6) estimates for various countries assuming the same life of assets for all countries (and assets). However, estimates of the growth of the stock should be more reliable (see Maddison 1982, Table D2). In any case, they are the best available.

The main source of the capital stock data is the OECD's *Flows and Stocks of Fixed Capital 1955–1980*. National sources have been used where the OECD does not provide data, and in order to extend the series back to 1951. The series for Italy and the pre-1955 figures for France required extensive estimation and are less reliable. Business sector estimates have also been made for 1982 and 1983, using investment data and our estimates of the amount of capital retired from use.

Additional sources for gross capital stock at constant prices

United States:	*Survey of Current Business*, October 1982 and earlier issues.
Canada:	*Fixed Capital Flows and Stocks*, 1926–78 and later issues.
United Kingdom:	*National Income and Expenditure*, various issues and unpublished series supplied by the Central Statistical Office.
France:	Carré, Dubois and Malinvaud, *French Economic Growth*.
	Mairesse, *L'Evaluation du capital fixe productive*.
Germany:	*Volkswirtschaftliche Gesamtrechungen*, Revidierte Ergebnisse 1960 bis 1981 and earlier years.
	Deutsches Institut für Wirtschaftsforschung, *Anlageinvestitionen und Anlagevermögen*.
Italy:	*Annuario di Contabilita Nationale*, tomo 1, 1982.
	Bolletino Mensile di Statistica, January 1978.
Japan:	*Estimates of the Stock of Non-Residential Business Capital*, March 1976 and other issues.

The measurement of profit shares and rates

The capitalist advances capital in order to appropriate a certain amount of surplus. Part of the gross surplus goes to replace worn-out or obsolescent equipment. The rest is net profit. Some net profit is used to extend the amount of capital, in the form either of such fixed capital as machinery or buildings or of stocks of commodities. So the value of capital is simultaneously both reduced, as means of production wear out or become obsolete, and increased, as a result of gross investment in new means of production.

It is difficult to estimate, either conceptually or practically, the depreciation of fixed capital. To construct national accounts, a simple general depreciation rule has to be assumed. This usually takes the form of straight-line depreciation. Both net profits and net capital stock can then be estimated, and hence the net profit share and rate. In order to avoid the difficulties involved in calculating depreciation, some authors have used the gross profit rate, which makes no allowance for depreciation in the estimation of either profits or the capital stock. Means of production are valued at their initial cost (after allowing for inflation) throughout their assumed lives. Hill (1979) has even suggested that the gross profit rate may be superior to the net as an estimate of the true rate.

The true, or economic, rate of profit is that which would be obtained from a discounted cash flow calculation of profitability. On this basis the rate of profit is the discount rate which equates the current value of gross profits to the cost of investment. Depreciation in any year can then be calculated: given gross profits, depreciation is set to ensure that net profits divided by the capital stock at the beginning of the period equals the net profit rate (previously calculated from the discounted cash flow). Chart A1 shows the depreciated value of the capital stock over the lifetime of an asset. The middle curve, 'depreciated stock', is that obtained when economic depreciation is subtracted each period. It is given the shape typically found when annual gross profits remain constant throughout the life of the asset. The distance AB represents the economic depreciation during the year n, and CD the assumed depreciation in national accounts terms, which is then used to calculate net stock and net profits. With the gross stock there is no depreciation until the end of the life of the asset, at which point the whole value is depreciated.

However, gross profits are seldom constant throughout the life of an asset. Most means of production are scrapped because they no longer earn profits. As the equipment ages, output may decline and running costs increase. Moreover, newer machines embody technical change and may enable the production of a superior product at a lower price. The consequence of lower gross profits as machines age is more rapid depreciation. The curve representing the depreciated capital stock, in Chart A1, is flattened out, and more closely resembles the straight line of the net stock. So straight-line depreciation approximates closely to economic depreciation. The net capital stock is a good representation of the depreciated stock and net profits are a good estimate of true profits.

Chart A1 Economic and straight-line depreciation

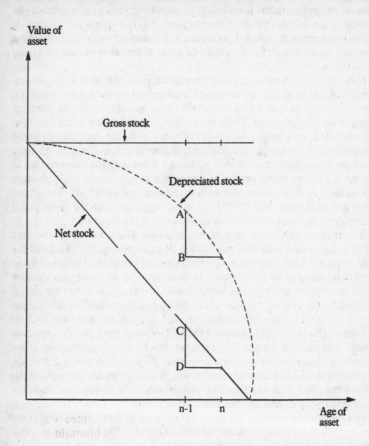

Our estimates overstate the level of the rate of profit in one important respect. Only the *fixed* capital advanced has been taken into account. But there is also a large amount of capital in the form of materials and fuels, work in progress, or finished goods waiting to be sold. (Capital is also advanced to pay wages, but this does not need to be considered separately. It very soon takes the form of commodities, which are sold or form part of the stocks.) Data on the value of the stocks held are rather sketchy. This is why they have not been included in the profit rate estimation. However, what data are available suggest that the ratio of stocks to net fixed capital varies little either over time or across countries, being about one-third of the value of fixed capital, for both manufacturing and total business. The United States is an important exception. It has a particularly high ratio of stocks to fixed capital in manufacturing, reflecting the very low ratio of fixed capital to output found there.

The basic OECD source for profit rates and profit shares is *National Accounts of Member Countries* vol. 2, 1964–81 (Paris, 1983) which gives net profits (value added less depreciation less employment incomes), net value added (gross value added less depreciation) and the net capital stock at current prices. It also calculates the net shares (net profits divided by net value added) and net profit rates (net profits divided by net capital stock). For countries not included in this publication, and for years prior to 1964, national sources have been used to construct the series needed (net profits, net value added and net capital stock). In some cases this has required a considerable amount of estimation on our part, especially the series for Italy (profit rates), Japan (profit rates) and France (manufacturing sector and corporate sector prior to 1960). In the cases of Canada, Germany and Italy, series for corporate business were not available and we had to construct series for non-agricultural business as a whole (including both corporations and unincorporated enterprises).

The national accounts series for profits in manufacturing, published by OECD and national sources, and for non-agricultural business which we have constructed from national sources are for 'net operating surplus'. This has an important weakness as a measure of profits: all self-employment income is included. Since self-employment is substantial in some countries, even in manufacturing (notably Italy and Japan), this inflates the estimates for the profit share. It can also substantially exaggerate the downward trend where the importance of self-employment declined. Self-employment is much more important in the non-agricultural business sector since services are included. So series for corporate business (which includes both public and private enterprises but excludes those operated by the self-employed) are preferable. Where these are not available we have calculated profits by subtracting an imputed 'wage' for the self-employed equal to the average wage in manufacturing or the business sector, whichever is relevant. For this reason our series for manufacturing profit shares and rates differ from those published by the OECD.

In addition to the national capital stock sources listed above, we have used the following national sources to construct the profits series needed to supplement those taken from OECD, *National Accounts*:

United States: *National Income and Product Accounts*, 1929–76 and later issues.

United Kingdom: *National Income and Expenditure*, various issues and unpublished series supplied by CSO.

France: *Les Comptes des entreprises par secteurs*, 1959–66, 1962–9.
    Les Comptes de la nation, various issues.
    'Les bénéfices industriels et commerciaux', *Statistiques et études financières*, various issues.
Germany: *Volkswirtschaftliche Gesamtrechungen*, various issues.
Italy: *Annuario di Contabilita Nationale*, various issues.
Japan: *Annual Report on National Accounts*, various issues.

Other series

We also derived series for productivity (GDP at constant prices per person in civil employment), capital stock per head (business capital stock divided by civil employment and manufacturing capital stock divided by manufacturing employment), manufacturing investment per head, and the product wage (productivity multiplied by the share of labour in net business output). The series for GDP were from OECD, *National Accounts*, and for employment (and self-employment) from OECD, *Labour Force Statistics*. We also calculated the ratios to GDP (at current prices) of various categories of government spending (transfers, military, investment, current civil spending), the government deficit (government savings less government investment), consumption, privately financed consumption (private consumption less transfers) and various categories of investment (government, housebuilding, manufacturing and other business). The data came from OECD, *National Accounts*, supplemented by national sources.

Aggregation for ACCs

To derive series for the ACCs as a whole, series for the seven individual countries have to be combined in a suitable weighted average. The simplest approach is to add up the component countries, with the individual country's contribution (to GDP, for example) weighted by the current exchange rate (for example, converting everything into dollars). But the exchange rate is a poor indicator of purchasing power, as detailed studies carried out by Kravis and his associates of the true 'purchasing power parities' (PPPs) of different currencies show. So absolute levels calculated using current exchange rates (for example, comparing GDP in Japan and the United States) would be unreliable, trends would also be masked (by progressive undervaluation or overvaluation) and totally spurious short-term fluctuations introduced (by rapid exchange rate gyrations, such as were experienced in the 1970s). The detailed studies are not available for each year. So the approach used here was to combine the PPPs for one year (1970) with *constant price* data for the individual countries. Therefore, to combine Japanese and US GDPs, the yen PPP in relation to dollars, calculated by Kravis *et al.* (Table 4.3) for GDP as a whole, is used to convert Japan's series for GDP at 1970 prices on to a 1970 dollar equivalent. When this is done for all of the big countries (for the United States, of course, dollars are used; and for Canada, where no PPP is available, we have used the 1970 exchange rate, which must be very close to PPP) the 1970 dollar-equivalent GDPs are added together to form the area figures, and the share of each component country in the total can be calculated.

These shares are both interesting in themselves and provide weights for constructing other area figures. For example, to calculate the ACCs' share of military spending in GDP the current price shares for the individual countries are weighted by these GDP shares. This is not ideal (for there is the implication that 100 yen of defence spending in Japan has the same dollar equivalent as 100 yen of spending on GDP as a whole) but it seems satisfactory for the purpose at hand. Some of these shares are presented in Table A7.

We have also applied PPPs directly to (1970 prices) manufacturing investment and to the capital stock (manufacturing and business) in order to calculate aggregates for the ACCs and Europe and to see how the different countries' shares have changed.

To calculate area profit shares and rates, we have simply weighted the figures for the individual countries using the shares of GDP. Current weights have been used in order to reflect the changing relative importance of the countries. The increasing weight of Japan (where the profit rate is high) means that the current weighted series declines slightly less than the fixed-weight one.

Table A1 Manufacturing net profit rate

Percentages

YEAR	ACC	ACC-USA	EUROPE	CANADA	FRANCE	GERMANY	ITALY	JAPAN	UK	USA
1951	N.A.	N.A.	N.A.	28.2	N.A.	35.2	17.7	N.A.	21.3	34.1
1952	25.4	21.6	21.6	29.7	16.8	36.8	12.6	15.3	19.5	29.0
1953	24.8	21.1	20.9	26.1	16.7	36.2	10.6	17.6	18.7	28.5
1954	23.1	21.3	21.3	23.5	17.5	34.8	10.8	23.7	19.5	24.5
1955	26.3	21.5	21.3	24.3	17.3	35.7	10.5	20.7	18.8	31.2
1956	23.0	20.1	19.2	25.0	16.5	32.2	8.3	23.6	16.7	26.0
1957	21.6	20.3	18.9	21.0	17.9	30.3	7.7	34.1	16.0	23.0
1958	18.4	19.1	18.3	18.4	16.3	29.5	8.2	28.0	15.4	17.5
1959	22.1	19.9	18.9	19.0	15.7	29.8	9.2	29.9	16.1	24.6
1960	22.1	21.9	19.9	17.4	18.0	28.8	11.4	43.8	17.5	22.3
1961	20.8	20.5	17.7	16.6	16.7	25.4	11.2	46.0	14.6	21.2
1962	21.6	18.5	15.3	18.4	15.2	21.0	9.6	40.4	12.9	25.6
1963	23.8	17.9	14.3	19.4	14.6	18.7	7.2	39.9	13.7	26.6
1964	25.8	18.8	14.8	20.1	14.4	20.0	6.6	41.4	14.6	30.9
1965	25.0	17.8	14.4	17.7	12.7	19.4	8.1	36.0	14.0	35.7
1966	24.3	17.4	13.3	16.4	13.9	16.6	10.4	37.3	12.1	34.9
1967	22.6	17.9	13.3	14.7	13.4	16.6	9.6	42.4	11.8	29.2
1968	23.6	20.2	14.8	17.1	13.5	20.4	10.7	46.0	11.8	28.9
1969	22.3	20.9	15.2	16.2	14.0	21.3	10.9	46.4	11.5	24.5
1970	19.3	20.3	14.0	13.2	17.1	18.6	8.9	46.5	9.6	17.7
1971	18.6	17.7	12.4	13.5	15.0	16.4	6.3	37.0	9.4	20.1
1972	19.0	17.1	11.9	15.3	13.1	16.9	7.3	34.0	9.8	22.5
1973	19.3	17.5	12.1	17.9	11.8	15.2	7.6	33.5	9.9	22.5
1974	16.7	10.9	10.7	18.8	12.5	13.5	11.0	21.6	5.4	16.0
1975	11.6	9.0	7.9	14.3	11.3	11.0	3.6	10.4	3.9	16.7
1976	13.2	9.9	8.2	11.5	5.2	13.2	7.9	13.3	4.3	19.5
1977	13.9	10.3	9.6	11.6	9.6	12.8	6.4	11.7	7.5	20.8
1978	14.0	11.0	9.3	12.5	6.4	13.1	7.7	14.8	7.7	19.8
1979	12.7	10.9	9.2	15.0	5.8	13.9	10.9	14.2	4.8	15.9
1980	9.8	9.6	7.4	14.7	3.3	10.5	12.8	13.6	3.3	15.1
1981	8.9	8.1	5.2	13.9	0.9	8.3	9.9	13.3	1.7	10.3

Table A2 Business net profit rate

Percentages

YEAR	ACC	ACC-USA	EUROPE	CANADA	FRANCE	GERMANY	ITALY	JAPAN	UK	USA
1951	18.5	14.4	14.6	12.4	10.3	21.7	15.3	15.0	12.9	22.4
1952	16.7	14.5	14.9	12.6	9.0	24.8	12.4	13.4	12.6	18.8
1953	16.2	14.7	14.8	11.5	8.6	24.0	12.0	19.3	13.0	17.6
1954	15.5	14.8	15.1	9.4	9.0	23.3	13.0	20.2	13.6	16.2
1955	18.1	15.8	16.0	12.9	9.3	25.8	13.1	18.6	13.9	20.2
1956	16.4	15.5	15.6	13.2	9.5	24.9	13.1	18.4	12.7	17.2
1957	15.5	15.6	15.6	10.6	10.8	24.4	12.6	22.5	12.3	15.5
1958	13.8	14.6	14.9	9.1	10.5	22.5	13.0	20.6	11.6	15.1
1959	15.8	15.1	15.4	9.4	9.8	23.2	14.1	20.7	12.3	16.6
1960	15.8	16.2	16.3	8.8	11.2	22.9	15.2	27.0	13.5	15.3
1961	15.2	15.0	14.6	8.9	11.0	20.2	14.7	26.8	11.2	15.4
1962	15.9	14.0	13.5	9.3	10.4	18.0	14.3	24.6	10.4	17.8
1963	16.3	14.0	13.4	9.9	10.4	16.0	12.1	23.4	11.4	19.2
1964	17.2	14.1	13.8	10.7	11.4	17.0	11.2	23.2	11.8	20.6
1965	17.9	13.8	13.3	10.0	11.6	16.5	12.1	21.2	11.2	22.6
1966	17.6	13.6	12.8	9.7	11.9	15.1	14.0	22.7	9.8	22.3
1967	16.6	13.4	12.6	9.6	13.2	14.3	14.0	26.2	9.5	19.8
1968	17.2	15.4	12.6	10.2	13.5	15.9	15.2	31.7	9.6	19.4
1969	16.1	15.5	13.8	9.7	14.8	15.6	15.9	29.9	9.3	16.9
1970	14.2	15.0	12.7	8.6	14.3	14.5	14.7	32.0	7.8	13.2
1971	13.7	13.5	12.0	8.2	14.6	13.3	12.3	24.8	7.8	13.9
1972	13.9	13.7	11.9	8.9	14.7	12.8	12.5	22.7	8.0	14.7
1973	13.6	12.7	11.3	10.7	14.2	12.2	11.0	19.6	7.8	14.8
1974	11.0	10.6	9.4	10.3	12.2	10.4	10.4	15.2	4.9	11.4
1975	10.2	8.6	7.3	8.3	9.4	9.2	6.1	13.5	3.6	12.3
1976	10.9	9.3	8.0	8.0	7.9	10.7	7.6	14.5	4.3	13.2
1977	11.7	9.7	8.7	7.5	9.3	11.0	6.4	14.4	6.9	14.3
1978	12.0	10.4	9.2	8.0	9.3	11.7	7.0	15.8	6.5	14.2
1979	11.4	10.3	9.5	9.9	9.6	12.2	9.6	14.7	5.5	12.5
1980	10.5	10.3	8.8	10.0	8.4	10.5	11.4	15.4	4.2	10.8
1981	10.2	9.1	7.6	8.2	7.1	9.3	8.3	14.2	5.0	11.8

Table A3 Manufacturing net profit share

Percentages

YEAR	ACC	ACC-USA	EUROPE	CANADA	FRANCE	GERMANY	ITALY	JAPAN	UK	USA
1951	N.A.	N.A.	N.A.	30.7	N.A.	30.7	27.9	N.A.	30.7	24.6
1952	24.0	28.1	28.8	31.8	27.6	32.8	21.8	21.7	30.3	20.9
1953	23.0	27.3	27.8	29.4	27.1	32.4	19.0	24.0	29.0	19.9
1954	22.8	27.9	27.6	28.7	28.0	31.4	17.9	29.1	29.2	18.8
1955	24.4	27.3	27.3	29.5	27.1	31.6	17.9	26.0	28.5	22.2
1956	22.4	25.8	24.8	30.4	23.0	30.2	14.6	27.7	26.4	19.7
1957	22.5	26.3	25.2	27.8	25.5	29.9	14.3	36.6	26.2	18.6
1958	20.7	26.8	24.7	27.9	22.8	30.0	15.5	33.4	26.0	15.9
1959	22.8	26.8	25.3	27.2	21.9	30.4	18.1	33.5	26.6	19.4
1960	22.8	28.7	25.9	25.9	23.9	29.3	19.8	41.5	27.6	17.4
1961	22.2	27.6	23.9	25.6	22.2	27.3	19.4	42.3	24.4	17.0
1962	22.1	25.6	21.7	27.2	20.5	24.4	16.9	39.2	23.0	18.7
1963	22.0	25.2	21.0	28.1	19.8	23.5	13.0	38.7	24.5	18.6
1964	23.5	26.0	21.6	28.8	19.7	25.2	12.7	39.4	25.1	21.0
1965	24.1	25.0	21.3	26.6	18.2	24.5	15.6	36.1	24.0	23.3
1966	23.8	24.8	20.8	25.3	19.6	22.3	18.9	36.7	21.6	22.8
1967	23.1	25.4	20.7	25.2	19.1	23.6	16.3	39.4	22.0	20.8
1968	23.7	26.7	21.4	24.6	18.9	26.0	17.8	40.8	21.8	20.7
1969	22.7	26.8	21.6	24.4	18.8	25.9	17.8	40.7	21.1	18.3
1970	20.6	25.6	19.6	21.8	21.8	22.5	13.8	40.7	18.2	15.0
1971	20.5	23.3	18.0	22.8	19.4	21.1	10.3	35.8	18.5	17.4
1972	20.8	22.9	17.8	24.4	17.7	19.7	11.8	33.9	20.0	18.5
1973	20.6	23.0	17.9	26.7	16.0	19.4	10.6	32.9	20.7	17.8
1974	17.4	20.1	16.3	26.1	17.1	17.7	17.2	26.3	12.6	14.3
1975	15.4	14.3	12.5	24.4	16.5	15.3	6.4	15.3	9.3	16.6
1976	16.5	15.1	12.4	22.8	8.6	17.0	12.7	18.5	10.4	18.1
1977	17.2	15.9	15.0	21.0	14.5	16.2	10.9	16.4	17.5	18.7
1978	17.3	16.6	14.2	24.7	9.9	16.8	12.2	19.2	18.2	18.0
1979	16.0	16.5	13.8	26.1	8.9	15.2	17.3	19.0	12.3	15.4
1980	13.3	15.2	11.6	26.8	5.3	13.2	20.2	19.2	9.3	15.4
1981	12.5	13.3	8.3	26.4	1.5	11.2	15.8	19.1	5.5	11.6

Table A4 Business net profit share

Percentages

YEAR	ACC	ACC-USA	EUROPE	CANADA	FRANCE	GERMANY	ITALY	JAPAN	UK	USA
1951	24.9	26.4	25.7	23.2	27.5	27.0	28.3	32.6	22.2	23.8
1952	23.0	25.7	25.7	22.4	25.4	29.7	25.9	26.8	22.7	21.0
1953	22.2	25.6	24.5	22.3	22.2	28.2	23.9	32.3	22.9	19.6
1954	21.9	25.4	24.5	19.3	22.5	27.8	24.3	33.4	23.1	19.2
1955	24.1	26.2	25.2	25.7	21.8	29.6	23.4	31.4	24.4	22.4
1956	22.5	25.6	24.3	26.3	20.9	29.2	25.1	31.4	22.7	19.9
1957	22.3	26.4	24.6	23.2	22.0	29.6	22.7	36.7	22.5	18.9
1958	21.1	25.3	23.8	22.3	21.2	28.5	22.8	33.6	21.7	17.4
1959	22.8	25.8	24.5	22.9	20.1	29.7	23.7	33.1	22.9	20.1
1960	22.8	27.6	25.4	22.4	21.7	29.4	24.6	39.1	24.5	18.4
1961	22.4	26.5	23.6	23.0	20.9	27.3	23.7	38.8	21.5	18.6
1962	22.5	25.1	22.3	24.0	19.6	25.7	22.5	35.7	20.6	20.0
1963	22.7	24.4	21.7	26.0	19.0	24.5	19.1	33.6	22.5	21.0
1964	23.4	25.0	22.3	26.3	20.0	25.7	18.1	33.2	23.2	21.8
1965	23.6	24.2	22.3	24.8	20.1	25.2	19.8	30.4	22.3	23.0
1966	23.3	24.1	21.7	24.0	20.6	23.8	21.8	31.2	20.2	22.5
1967	22.9	24.8	21.8	24.7	21.3	23.8	20.8	33.2	20.5	21.0
1968	23.5	26.1	22.6	25.8	21.4	25.0	21.6	37.3	20.8	20.5
1969	22.3	26.1	22.6	25.0	22.4	24.4	22.5	34.8	20.6	18.4
1970	20.6	25.3	20.9	23.5	21.6	22.6	20.4	36.1	18.1	15.5
1971	20.3	23.7	20.5	23.1	21.6	21.5	19.5	31.1	18.8	16.6
1972	20.5	23.6	20.4	24.7	21.1	21.0	18.4	30.3	19.6	17.0
1973	19.9	22.7	19.5	27.4	21.8	19.8	16.8	28.1	19.7	16.7
1974	18.1	19.9	17.0	27.8	18.8	17.6	16.3	24.0	14.2	16.3
1975	16.9	17.1	15.8	23.8	15.7	16.5	10.5	22.0	10.8	16.7
1976	17.6	17.9	14.8	23.1	13.7	18.3	12.9	22.8	13.1	17.3
1977	18.4	18.7	16.4	22.8	15.3	18.6	10.9	22.5	19.2	16.0
1978	18.8	19.9	17.0	24.9	15.2	19.8	11.5	24.3	20.1	17.5
1979	18.1	20.3	17.4	29.6	15.7	20.8	15.0	23.4	16.8	15.7
1980	17.5	20.1	16.5	30.3	14.1	18.7	17.2	24.5	15.6	14.4
1981	17.3	18.7	15.1	26.9	12.3	17.7	13.5	23.3	16.4	15.7

Table A5 Manufacturing gross fixed capital stock

1970 dollars, 100 millions, beginning year

YEAR	ACC	ACC-USA	EUROPE	CANADA	FRANCE	GERMANY	ITALY	JAPAN	UK	USA
1951	3536	1778	1490	160	371	321	230	128	568	1758
1952	3700	1854	1554	167	380	342	239	143	591	1837
1953	3857	1945	1616	177	388	357	250	153	612	1911
1954	4013	2033	1683	187	394	393	251	153	634	1980
1955	4182	2131	1761	197	403	426	273	172	659	2051
1956	4375	2250	1862	208	411	457	289	180	695	2125
1957	4583	2372	1954	223	421	512	308	195	713	2211
1958	4801	2507	2052	237	435	557	329	218	731	2294
1959	4971	2634	2149	248	449	602	348	237	749	2338
1960	5140	2772	2252	258	463	654	359	261	766	2369
1961	5369	2961	2386	268	482	714	395	307	795	2408
1962	5636	3193	2546	278	507	781	431	369	827	2443
1963	5905	3421	2702	287	536	846	473	431	848	2484
1964	6184	3650	2862	297	565	937	515	491	875	2554
1965	6493	3895	3019	312	595	972	544	564	907	2598
1966	6826	4125	3174	332	625	1044	562	619	943	2701
1967	7196	4356	3332	355	658	1113	582	669	979	2840
1968	7594	4608	3474	376	692	1165	603	758	1014	2986
1969	7991	4892	3620	394	726	1218	627	877	1050	3099
1970	8458	5240	3809	413	771	1293	654	1019	1090	3218
1971	8974	5656	4034	433	823	1388	690	1189	1133	3318
1972	9443	6059	4253	454	877	1480	724	1353	1172	3383
1973	9894	6426	4449	474	934	1556	755	1503	1204	3448
1974	10375	6805	4639	495	990	1619	795	1670	1235	3570
1975	10881	7161	4819	519	1043	1665	839	1824	1271	3720
1976	11265	7432	4950	543	1082	1699	865	1939	1303	3833
1977	11635	7679	5084	565	1130	1734	887	2030	1332	3956
1978	12032	7919	5213	585	1171	1769	910	2121	1363	4113
1979	12421	8134	5332	602	1208	1800	927	2200	1396	4286
1980	12902	8389	5461	621	1245	1836	950	2326	1431	4514
1981	13395	8682	5604	643	1288	1877	979	2435	1460	4714

Table A6 Business gross fixed capital stock

1970 dollars, 100 millions, beginning year

YEAR	ACC	ACC-USA	EUROPE	CANADA	FRANCE	GERMANY	ITALY	JAPAN	UK	USA
1951	12288	5900	4689	726	1206	1239	618	484	1627	6338
1952	12725	6090	4819	757	1225	1289	643	504	1652	6645
1953	13176	6296	4991	809	1243	1348	670	526	1699	6880
1954	13670	6530	5126	855	1262	1421	702	549	1741	7140
1955	14169	6795	5237	900	1290	1508	740	569	1789	7374
1956	14750	7103	5553	950	1319	1624	784	595	1831	7646
1957	15383	7459	5816	1011	1355	1754	832	632	1875	7924
1958	16044	7845	6098	1075	1397	1881	884	682	1927	8199
1959	16622	8229	6371	1133	1443	2013	937	725	1978	8393
1960	17274	8656	6637	1189	1490	2152	996	780	2039	8618
1961	18012	9146	7046	1244	1544	2320	1067	856	2115	8866
1962	18809	9709	7451	1296	1611	2495	1152	962	2194	9100
1963	19663	10288	7866	1348	1685	2673	1247	1074	2262	9375
1964	20547	10881	8293	1434	1764	2845	1349	1184	2335	9665
1965	21555	11543	8752	1470	1851	3036	1430	1321	2435	10012
1966	22668	12194	9203	1549	1940	3234	1493	1442	2536	10474
1967	23886	12874	9665	1639	2040	3424	1561	1570	2640	11012
1968	25108	13593	10119	1731	2144	3584	1640	1743	2751	11515
1969	26432	14485	10595	1822	2255	3749	1730	1968	2861	12047
1970	27923	15290	11138	1915	2389	3947	1828	2238	2974	12653
1971	29481	16311	11737	2014	2534	4183	1930	2560	3090	13170
1972	31027	17374	12362	2117	2689	4437	2033	2895	3204	13553
1973	32671	18465	12779	2228	2860	4675	2133	3258	3310	14206
1974	34488	19595	13609	2349	3023	4909	2250	3637	3427	14893
1975	36224	20078	14232	2482	3219	5094	2373	3965	3546	15546
1976	37638	21618	14740	2622	3370	5264	2453	4256	3654	16019
1977	39072	22554	15275	2763	3535	5444	2537	4516	3759	16518
1978	40616	23599	15816	2898	3698	5632	2614	4786	3873	17117
1979	42327	24469	16370	3035	3862	5832	2688	5066	3988	17859
1980	44191	25544	16965	3180	4028	6061	2771	5399	4105	18647
1981	46081	26702	17594	3343	4201	6272	2872	5765	4229	19379

Table A7 Share in ACC gross domestic product

Percentages

	Private consumption	Fixed investment				Civil consumption	Government				Surplus
		Total	Housing	Business	Manu-facturing		Transfers	Military	Investment	Total spending [1]	
1952	62.9	17.4	4.7	10.1	3.1	7.6	5.0	10.1	2.6	25.7	-0.3
1953	63.3	18.0	4.8	10.4	3.0	7.7	5.1	10.0	2.7	25.6	-0.9
1954	64.3	18.6	5.2	10.4	2.9	8.1	5.7	8.5	2.8	25.2	-0.7
1955	63.5	19.0	5.5	10.8	3.1	8.1	5.7	7.5	2.7	24.0	-0.9
1956	62.9	19.7	5.0	11.9	3.6	8.2	5.8	7.4	2.8	24.2	1.2
1957	62.8	19.7	4.8	12.0	3.7	8.5	6.2	7.3	2.9	25.0	-0.7
1958	63.7	19.2	4.9	11.2	3.1	9.0	7.0	7.9	3.1	26.4	-1.3
1959	63.0	19.7	5.3	11.3	3.2	9.0	6.9	6.9	3.1	25.8	-0.3
1960	62.6	20.1	4.9	12.1	3.8	9.2	6.9	6.6	3.0	25.7	1.0
1961	61.9	20.5	4.9	12.6	4.0	9.3	6.8	6.4	3.0	25.4	0.4
1962	61.8	20.7	5.2	12.5	3.8	9.6	6.8	6.5	3.4	25.8	-0.3
1963	61.9	20.8	5.3	12.5	3.8	9.6	6.9	6.1	3.4	26.0	0.3
1964	61.4	21.8	5.2	12.5	3.7	9.3	6.8	5.6	3.5	25.8	-0.3
1965	61.2	21.3	4.9	12.6	3.7	10.0	7.1	5.3	3.5	26.0	0.0
1966	60.7	21.3	4.8	12.9	3.9	10.2	7.2	5.7	3.6	26.6	0.0
1967	60.6	21.0	4.9	12.8	3.9	10.5	7.7	6.1	3.5	26.8	0.9
1968	60.3	21.0	5.1	12.4	4.3	10.5	7.9	5.8	3.5	27.7	-0.1
1969	59.9	21.8	5.1	13.4	4.3	10.6	7.9	5.4	3.3	27.3	-1.1
1970	59.9	22.0	4.9	13.7	4.4	11.2	8.4	4.9	3.4	27.9	0.2
1971	60.0	22.2	5.5	13.2	3.9	11.6	8.8	4.3	3.3	28.4	0.0
1972	60.1	22.4	6.0	13.1	3.9	11.8	9.1	4.5	3.3	28.6	-0.4
1973	59.5	22.1	6.1	13.6	3.9	11.7	9.2	4.1	3.3	28.3	0.0
1974	60.1	22.4	5.4	13.6	3.9	12.4	10.0	4.1	3.4	29.2	-0.5
1975	61.4	21.1	5.0	12.7	3.3	13.2	11.6	4.1	3.4	32.4	-3.9
1976	61.2	20.9	5.3	12.5	3.3	13.0	11.7	4.0	3.1	31.7	-2.6
1977	61.1	21.1	5.5	12.6	3.2	12.8	11.6	3.9	2.9	31.2	-1.1
1978	60.7	21.6	5.5	13.0	3.0	12.7	11.6	3.8	3.0	31.0	-1.9
1979	60.9	21.7	5.5	13.6	3.8	12.6	11.6	3.8	3.0	31.0	-1.3
1980	61.5	21.1	5.0	13.7	3.8	12.9	12.2	4.0	3.1	32.2	-2.0
1981	61.5	21.1	4.7	13.5	3.8	13.0	12.7	4.1	2.9	32.8	-2.2

1. Excluding debt interest and subsidies.

Series for Part I

The major sources for the data on investment and capital stock (Tables 2.1, 4.1 and 6.1, and Chart 6.2) are as follows:

United States:	*Survey of Current Business*, March 1980, February 1981.
	Long-term Economic Growth 1860–1970.
United Kingdom:	Feinstein, *National Income, Expenditure and Output of the United Kingdom 1855–1965*.
France:	Carré, Dubois and Malinvaud, *French Economic Growth*.
	Mairesse, *L'Evaluation du capital fixe productive*.
Germany:	Krengel, *Anlagevermögen, Produktion und Beschäftigung 1924–56*.
Italy:	Fua, *La Sviluppo Economico in Italia*, vol. III.
Japan:	Ohkawa and Rosovsky, *Japanese Economic Growth*.

These series are not always directly comparable to those used in Part II and described earlier in this Appendix.

We also used UNECE, *Economic Survey of Europe Since the War* for changes in stock of machine tools (plus Cohen, *Japan's Economy in Wartime and Reconstruction*) and OEEC, *Statistics of National Product and Expenditure 1938 and 1947–55*.

The series for industrial production, employment, productivity and real wages and profits etc. (Tables 4.2–4.5, 6.2–6.8 and Charts 6.1, 6.3 and 6.4) are calculated from:

United States:	*Long-term Economic Growth 1860–1970*.
United Kingdom:	Feinstein, *op. cit.*
	National Income and Expenditure, 1946–51.
France:	Rioux, *La France de la Quatrième République*.
	Mouvement économique en France de 1938 à 1948.
	Annuaire statistique de la France, rétrospectif.
	UNECE, *Economic Survey of Europe*, various.
Germany:	Bank Deutscher Länder, *Monthly Report, Annual Report*, various.
	UNECE, *Economic Survey of Europe*, various.
Italy:	Fua, *op. cit.*
	UNECE, *Economic Survey of Europe*, various.
	Campanna, 'Economic Problems and Reconstruction in Italy'.
Japan:	Ohkawa and Rosovsky, *op. cit.*
	Allen, *Japan's Economic Recovery*.
Europe:	OEEC, *Statistics of National Product and Expenditure 1938 and 1947–55*.
	UNECE, *Economic Survey of Europe*, various.

Table A.8 Dollar values

	Percentages of Gross domestic product			Percentages of Imports		
	USA	Japan	Large European[1] country	USA	Japan	Large European[1] country
In 1952 $1 billion represented	0.3	5.8	4.7	6.3	50.3	26.7
In 1970 $10 billion represented	1.0	3.2	5.4	18.4	51.5	38.9
In 1982 $10 billion represented	0.3	0.8	1.8	3.4	6.6	7.4

1. Unweighted average of France, Germany, Italy and United Kingdom.

Sources: OECD *National Accounts*, 1982 and earlier issues.

Sources

For full details of publication, see the Bibliography.

Part I: Postwar Reconstruction, 1945–50
Basic sources of statistical information used throughout Part I:

J.-J. CARRÉ, P. DUBOIS AND E. MALINVAUD, *French Economic Growth*

K. OHKAWA AND H. ROSOVSKY, *Japanese Economic Growth*

C. FEINSTEIN, *National Income, Expenditure and Output of the United Kingdom 1855–1965*

US GOVERNMENT, *The National Income and Product Accounts of the United States 1929–76*

US GOVERNMENT, *Balance of Payments, Statistical Supplement*

US GOVERNMENT, *Long-term Economic Growth 1860–1970*

G. FUA, *La Sviluppo Economico in Italia*, vol. III

UNECE, *Economic Survey of Europe*

UN, *World Economic Review*

OEEC, *Statistics of National Product and Expenditure 1938 and 1947–55*

FRENCH GOVERNMENT, *Annuaire statistique de la France, rétrospectif*

See Appendix, page 471, for further details on the more specific sources used for the tables and charts.

1. *Chaos and Despair*
The main sources for economic development after the First World War are:

A. LEWIS, *Economic Survey 1919–39*

D. ALDCROFT, *From Versailles to Wall Street 1919–29*

A general survey of conditions in Europe at the end of the Second World War is:

R. MAYNE, *Postwar*

See also the sources cited for Chapter 2.

2. *Behind the Chaos*
The major sources used for the immediate economic consequences of the Second World War are:

UNECE, *Economic Survey of Europe Since the War*
J. COHEN, *Japan's Economy in Wartime and Reconstruction*
W. ABELSHAUSER, *Wirtschaft in Westdeutschland 1945–48*

The political and social consequences of the war are discussed in:

W. GRAF, *The German Left since 1945*
J. MOORE, *Japanese Workers and the Struggle for Power 1945–47*
J. HALLIDAY, *A Political History of Japanese Capitalism*
S. WOOLF (ed.), *The Rebirth of Modern Italy*
A. WERTH, *France 1940–55*
G. ROSS, *Workers and Communists in France*
A. PREIS, *Labor's Giant Step*
D. PRITT, *The Labour Government 1945–51*
J.-P. RIOUX, *La France de la Quatrième République*

International relations, focused on the United States, are discussed in:

G. KOLKO, *The Politics of War*
G. KOLKO AND J. KOLKO, *The Limits of Power*
D. YERGIN, *Shattered Peace*

3. *Great Power Policies*
On the reconstruction of the world monetary system, see:

R. GARDNER, *Sterling Dollar Diplomacy*

On occupation policy in Japan:

J. HALLIDAY, *op. cit.*
J. MOORE, *op. cit.*
J. COHEN, *op. cit.*

In Germany:

J. GIMBEL, *The American Occupation of Germany*
H. ZINK, *The United States in Germany 1944–55*

On the policy of the Soviet Union:

I. DEUTSCHER, *Stalin*
F. CLAUDIN, *The Communist Movement*
M. DJILAS, *Conversations with Stalin*

On Czechoslovakia:

J. BLOOMFIELD, *Passive Revolution*

4. *The First Two Years*
Sources are as for Chapter 2, plus the following.
On Japan:

G. ALLEN, *Japan's Economic Recovery*
S. LEVINE, *Industrial Relations in Post-war Japan*
JAPANESE GOVERNMENT, *Economic Survey of Japan*

On Germany:

U. SCHMIDT AND T. FICHTER, *Der Erzwungene Kapitalismus 1945–48*
H. WALLICH, *Mainsprings of the German Revival*

On Italy:

A. CAMPANNA, 'Economic Problems and Reconstruction in Italy'
E. SIMPSON, 'Inflation and Deflation and Employment in Italy'
M. POSNER AND S. WOOLF, *Italian Public Enterprise*

On France:

R. KUISEL, *Capitalism and the State in Modern France*
FRENCH GOVERNMENT, *Mouvement économique en France de 1938 à 1948*
UNIR, *Histoire du PCF*
G. LEFRANC, *Le Mouvement syndical*

On the United Kingdom:

J. DOW, *The Management of the British Economy 1945–60*
D. WORSWICK AND P. ADY, *The British Economy 1945–50*
A. ROGOW, *The Labour Government and British Industry*

5. *Marshall Aid: the United States Changes Tack*
See particularly:

G. KOLKO AND J. KOLKO, *op. cit.*
D. YERGIN, *op. cit.*

Also:

J. JONES, *Fifteen Weeks*
R. MIKESELL, *United States Economic Policy and International Relations*
F. BLOCK, *The Origins of International Economic Disorder*

6. *The New Turn in Europe and Japan*
Sources are as for Chapters 2 and 4, plus:

T. BALOGH, 'Germany: an Experiment in Planning by the "Free" Price Mechanism'
H. MENDERSHAUSEN, 'Prices, Money and the Distribution of Goods in Post-War Germany'

7. *Towards the Boom*
On the American recession of 1949, see:

H. VATTER, *The US Economy in the 1950s*

On the devaluations of 1949, see:

BANK FOR INTERNATIONAL SETTLEMENTS, *Annual Report*, 1949–50, Ch. 6
A. CAIRNCROSS AND B. EICHENGREEN, *Sterling in Decline*

On the Korean boom, see:

UN, *World Economic Review*
OEEC, *The Problem of Rising Prices*

Part II: The Great Boom, 1950–74

The main statistical series used throughout Parts II and III, mainly derived from OECD national account, labour force and capital stock data, are described in some detail in the Appendix. Additional important sources of statistical material and analysis are:

OECD, *The Growth of Output 1960–80*
A. MADDISON, *Phases of Capitalist Development*
J. CORNWALL, *Modern Capitalism*
T. HILL, *Profits and Rates of Return*

8. *The Golden Years*
Much detailed information on individual countries (in addition to the sources referred to for Chapters 2 and 4) is contained in:

A. BOLTHO (ed.), *The European Economy*
M. FELDSTEIN (ed.), *The American Economy in Transition*

Perhaps the best known Marxist interpretation of the boom, with which we differ in many aspects, is:

E. MANDEL, *Late Capitalism*

The literature on postwar economic growth in Japan is vast. The best general account of the Japanese postwar economy is:

A. BOLTHO, *Japan, an Economic Survey*

For the section on Japan we have also used:

S. BROADBRIDGE, *Industrial Dualism in Japan*
R. CAVES AND M. UEKUSA, *Industrial Organisation in Japan*
E. DENISON AND W. CHUNG, *How Japan's Economy Grew So Fast*

JAPANESE GOVERNMENT, *Estimates of the Stock of Non-Residential Business Capital*

JAPANESE GOVERNMENT, *Annual Report on National Accounts*

R. KOMIYA (ed.), *Postwar Economic Growth in Japan*

R. MINAMI, *The Turning Point in Economic Development*

K. OHKAWA, B. JOHNSTON AND H. KAMEDA, *Agriculture and Economic Growth*

K. OKOCHI, B. KARSH AND S. LEVINE (eds.), *Workers and Employers in Japan*

H. PATRICK AND H. ROSOVSKY (eds.), *Asia's New Giant*

K. TAIRA, *Economic Development and the Labor Market in Japan*

K. YAMAMURA, *Economic Policy in Postwar Japan*

9. *A New, Managed Capitalism?*

There is an enormous literature on the increased importance of the postwar state, including:

I. GOUGH, *The Political Economy of the Welfare State*
A. SHONFIELD, *Modern Capitalism*

On welfare, valuable sources are:

P. KOHLER AND H. ZACHER (eds.), *The Evolution of Social Insurance 1881–1981*
OECD, *Public Expenditure Trends*
G. RIMLINGER, *Welfare Policy and Industrialisation in Europe, America and Russia*

On German codetermination:

R. ADAMS AND C. RUMMEL, 'Workers' Participation in Management in West Germany'

On French planning:

S. COHEN, *Modern Capitalist Planning*
J. DELORS, 'The Decline of French Planning'
S. ESTRIN AND P. HOLMES, *French Planning in Theory and Practice*

On Japanese industrial policy:

I. MAGAZINER AND T. HOUT, *Japanese Industrial Policy*
E. KAPLAN, *Japan – the Government-Business Relationship*
R. KOMIYA, 'Planning in Japan'

10. *The Eclipse of US Domination*

Comparative productivity levels are calculated in:

I. KRAVIS, 'A Survey of International Comparisons of Productivity'
A. ROY, 'Labour Productivity in 1980 – an International Comparison'

The development of trade patterns is analysed in:

A. MAIZELS, *Industrial Growth and World Trade*
R. BATCHELOR, R. MAJOR AND A. MORGAN, *Industrialisation and the Basis for Trade*

We based our factual analysis of multinational corporations on:

R. ROWTHORN AND S. HYMER, *International Big Business 1957–67*
J. DUNNING AND R. PEARCE, *The World's Largest Industrial Enterprises*

The very fundamental question of why US accumulation was so much lower than that in Europe and Japan has not received the systematic treatment which it deserves.

The major Marxist study of the US economy, emphasizing its monopolistic structure, is:

P. BARAN AND P. SWEEZY, *Monopoly Capital*

This work has been extended in a number of collections of articles from the magazine *Monthly Review*, the most recent of which is:

H. MAGDOFF AND P. SWEEZY, *The Deepening Crisis of US Capitalism*

A more recent analysis is:

M. AGLIETTA, *A Theory of Capitalist Regulation*

The literature on the contradictions in the international monetary system is huge. The analyses which we found most helpful were:

M. GILBERT, *Quest for World Monetary Order*
H. ROBINSON, 'The Downfall of the Dollar'
B. TEW, *The Evolution of the International Monetary System 1945–77*
J. WILLIAMSON, *The Failure of International Monetary Reform*

A Marxist analysis emphasizing the benefits to the United States of the Bretton Woods system is:

R. PARBONI, *The Dollar and its Rivals*

11. *Overaccumulation*

An analysis which discusses falling productivity, while putting more emphasis on technology and less (than ours) on the labour supply, is:

E. MANDEL, *op. cit.*

The next book reviews Mandel's in detail and also contains an excellent theoretical discussion of inflation:

R. ROWTHORN, *Capitalism, Conflict and Inflation*

A detailed analysis of the decline in US profitability is:

T. WEISSKOPF, 'Marxian Crisis Theory and the Rate of Profit in the Postwar US Economy'

An analysis rather similar to ours, though drawing very different conclusions, is:

J. SARGENT, 'Capitalist Accumulation and Productivity Growth'

12. *Overheating*
The classic description of the late 1960s and early 1970s is:

P. McCRACKEN, *Towards Full Employment and Price Stability*

The main source on the European strike wave of the late sixties is the extremely comprehensive study:

R. FLANAGAN, D. SOSKICE AND L. ULMAN, *Unionism, Economic Stabilisation and Incomes Policies*

together with:

C. CROUCH AND A. PIZZORNO (eds.), *The Resurgence of Class Conflict in Western Europe since 1968*

Events in Italy and France are also discussed (respectively) in:

C. SABEL, *Work and Politics*
G. ROSS, *Workers and Communists in France*
C. POSNER (ed.), *Reflections on the Revolution in France: 1968*
V. FISERA (ed.), *Writing on the Wall*

13. *Oil and the Crash of 1974*
Sources are as Chapter 12, plus the most comprehensive review of contemporary developments in OECD countries:

OECD, *Economic Outlook*

For the oil crisis:

J. BLAIR, *The Control of Oil*
A. SAMPSON, *The Seven Sisters*
L. TURNER, *Oil Companies in the International System*

On international banking:

A. SAMPSON, *The Money Lenders*

Part III: Things Fall Apart, 1974—

See sources for Part II for a note on the statistical series used.

14. *Unemployment Mounts*
Comparative material on the growth of unemployment and the pattern of jobs is presented in:

OECD, *Employment Outlook*

15. *Unemployment and Accumulation*
There is a vast literature on the stagnation since 1974. See:

M. BOYER AND J. MISTRAL, *Accumulation, Inflation, Crises*
A. MADDISON, *Phases of Capitalist Development*
C. FREEMAN, J. CLARK AND L. SOETE, *Unemployment and Technical Innovation*
R. MATTHEWS (ed.), *Slower Growth in the Western World*
J. CORNWALL, *The Conditions for Economic Recovery*
J. SACHS, 'Real Wages and Unemployment in the OECD Countries'
A. LINDBECK, 'The Recent Slowdown of Productivity Growth'

16. *International Relations*
A most valuable source for developments in the underdeveloped countries is:

UNCTAD, *Trade and Development Report*

We have also used the series of UNCTAD papers prepared in 1983 for that organization's June 1983 meeting, as listed in the Bibliography.
The debt crisis is analysed in:

D. LLEWELLYN, 'Avoiding an International Banking Crisis'

Very extensive data on the crisis is given in:

WORLD BANK, *World Debt Tables*

The position of the Eastern bloc has been analysed in:

R. PORTES, 'East, West and South'

A number of useful articles, especially one called 'Recent Developments in East-West Trade' (December 1982), are published in

UNECE, *Economic Bulletin for Europe*

The major study of the transfer to low-wage countries of manufacturing production is:

F. FRÖBEL, J. HEINRICHS AND O. KREYE, *The New International Division of Labour*

The development of trade patterns within the advanced countries is analysed in a very interesting way by:

CAMBRIDGE ECONOMIC POLICY GROUP, 'World Trade and Finance: Prospects for the 1980s'

Developments in the international monetary system are analysed in:

R. McKINNON, *Money in International Exchange*

They are also surveyed in articles in the *Midland Bank Review* (see especially Winter 1977, Autumn/Winter 1979, Autumn/Winter 1981).

17. *Capitalists and Workers*
The major source for European developments is:

FLANAGAN *et al.*, *op. cit.*

The real situation of Japanese industrial relations, which in our opinion is very different from the picture normally painted, is discussed in two papers from professors at Tokyo University:

H. TOTSUKA, 'Japanese Trade Union Attitudes towards Rationalisation'

K. YAMAMOTO, 'Labour-Management Relations at Nissan Motor Co. Ltd'

A very vivid description of working in a Japanese motor factory in the early seventies has recently been translated:

S. KAMATA, *Japan in the Passing Lane*

Among the vast literature on work organization, we found particularly useful:

H. BRAVERMAN, *Labor and Monopoly Capital*

C. COOPER AND E. MUMFORD (eds.), *The Qualtiy of Working Life in Western and Eastern Europe*

R. EDWARDS, *Contested Terrain*

D. MACAROV, *Worker Productivity*

18. *Thatcherism and Reaganomics*
Comprehensive descriptions of the economic policies of the Thatcher government, from a narrow, economic point of view, are given in:

W. BUITER AND M. MILLER, 'The Thatcher Experiment'

W. BUITER AND M. MILLER, 'The Macro-economic Consequences of a Change in Regime'

A broader account, written just before the 1983 election, is:

PLUTO PRESS, *Thatcher's Britain*

Our main sources for Reaganomics were:

F. ACKERMAN, *Reaganomics: Rhetoric and Reality*
S. ROUSSEAS, *The Political Economy of Reaganomics*
S. BOWLES, D. GORDON AND T. WEISSKOPF, *Beyond the Wasteland*

The last mentioned book discusses the nature of the crisis in the US economy. OECD's annual *Economic Surveys* on the United States provide regular and up-to-date analyses.

19. *The Left Alternative*
Our discussion of the Labour government was based on:

A. GLYN AND J. HARRISON, *The British Economic Disaster*, Chapter 4
D. COATES, *Labour in Power*
K. COATES (ed.), *What Went Wrong?*

Labour's Alternative Economic Strategy is also discussed in:

S. HOLLAND, *The Socialist Challenge*
CONFERENCE OF SOCIALIST ECONOMISTS, *The Alternative Economic Strategy*

and in numerous articles in the *Socialist Economic Review*.

The main source for the Mitterrand government was the press, especially the *Financial Times* (and its excellent index), plus OECD's annual *Economic Surveys* on France.

Bibliography

Note: official publications are listed under the government concerned.

ABELSHAUSER, W., *Wirtschaft in Westdeutschland 1945–48*, Deutsche Verlag-Anstalt, Stuttgart, 1975.

ABELSHAUSER, W., 'West German Economic Recovery 1945–51: a Reassessment', *Three Banks Review*, September 1982.

ACKERMAN, F., *Reaganomics: Rhetoric and Reality*, Pluto Press, London, 1982.

ADAMS, R. AND RUMMEL, C., 'Workers' Participation in Management in West Germany', *Industrial Relations Journal*, March 1977.

AGLIETTA, M., *A Theory of Capitalist Regulation*, New Left Books, London, 1979.

ALBER, J., 'Government Responses to the Challenge of Unemployment', in P. Flora and A. Heidenheimer (eds.), *The Development of the Welfare State in Europe and America*, Transaction Books, New Brunswick, 1981.

ALDCROFT, D., *From Versailles to Wall Street 1919–29*, Allen Lane, London, 1977.

ALLAM, P. AND SASSOON, D., 'Italy', in M. McCauley (ed.), *Communist Power in Europe*, Macmillan, London, 1977.

ALLEN, G., *Japan's Economic Recovery*, Oxford University Press, 1958.

ALLSOPP, C., 'Inflation', in A. Boltho (ed.), *The European Economy*.

AMPO, *Japan Asia Quarterly Review*, Tokyo.

APPLE, N., 'The Historical Foundations of Class Struggle in Late Capitalist Liberal Democracies', mimeo, Sydney, n.d.

BAGGULEY, J., 'The World War and the Cold War', in D. Horowitz (ed.), *Containment and Revolution*, Beacon Press, Boston, 1967.

BAILEY, R., 'Impact of the Euro-Soviet Gas Pipeline', *National Westminster Bank Quarterly Review*, August 1982.

BAILY, M., 'Productivity and the Services of Labor and Capital', *Brookings Papers on Economic Activity*, 1, 1981.

BAIN, G. AND PRICE, R., *Profiles of Union Growth*, Oxford University Press, 1981.

BALFOUR, M., *The Adversaries*, Routledge and Kegan Paul, London, 1981.

BALOGH, T., 'Germany: an Experiment in Planning by the "Free" Price Mechanism', *Banca Nazionale del Lavoro Quarterly Review*, April–June 1950.

BANK DEUTSCHER LÄNDER, *Annual Report, Monthly Report*, various issues.

BANK OF ENGLAND, *Quarterly Bulletin*, London, various issues.

BANK FOR INTERNATIONAL SETTLEMENTS, *Annual Report*, Basle, various issues.

BARAN, P. AND SWEEZY, P., *Monopoly Capital*, Penguin, Harmondsworth, 1968.

BARJONET, A., *La CGT*, Seuil, Paris, 1968.

BATCHELOR, R., MAJOR R. AND MORGAN, A., *Industrialisation and the Basis for Trade*, Cambridge University Press, 1980.

BATT, W. AND WEINBERG, E., 'Labor-Management Co-operation Today', *Harvard Business Review*, January–February 1978.

BAUM, W., *The French Economy and the State*, Princeton University Press, 1958.

BLAIR, J., *The Control of Oil*, Macmillan, London, 1977.

BLOCK, F., *The Origins of International Economic Disorder*, University of California Press, 1977.

BLOOMFIELD, J., *Passive Revolution*, Allison and Busby, London, 1979.

BLUMENTHAL, T., 'Scarcity of Labour and Wage Differentials in the Japanese Economy 1958–64', *Economic Development and Cultural Change*, October 1968.

BOLTHO, A., *Japan, an Economic Survey*, Oxford University Press, 1975.

BOLTHO, A. (ed.), *The European Economy: Growth and Crisis*, Oxford University Press, 1982.

BOWLES, S., GORDON, D. AND WEISSKOPF, T., *Beyond the Wasteland*, Anchor Press, New York, 1983.

BOYER, M. AND MISTRAL, J., *Accumulation, Inflation, Crises*, PUF, Paris, 1982.

BRANSON, W., 'Trends in United States International Trade and Payments since World War II', in M. Feldstein (ed.), *The American Economy in Transition*.

BRAVERMAN, H., *Labor and Monopoly Capital*, Monthly Review Press, New York, 1972.

BRECHER, J., *Strike*, South End Press, Boston, 1972.

BRITTAN, S., *The Role and Limits of Government*, Temple Smith, London, 1975.

BROADBRIDGE, S., *Industrial Dualism in Japan*, Frank Cass, London, 1966.

BRUS, W., *Post-war Reconstruction and Socio-economic Transformations in Eastern Europe*, St Antony's College Paper in East European Economies, **41**, Oxford, 1974.

BUITER, W. AND MILLER, M., 'The Thatcher Experiment: the First Two Years', *Brookings Papers on Economic Activity*, **1**, 1982.

BUITER, W. AND MILLER, M., 'The Macro-economic Consequences of a Change in Regime', *Brookings Papers on Economic Activity*, **2**, 1983.

Business Week, various issues.

CAIRNCROSS, A. AND EICHENGREEN, B., *Sterling in Decline*, Basil Blackwell, Oxford, 1983.

CAMBRIDGE ECONOMIC POLICY GROUP, 'World Trade and Finance: Prospects for the 1980s', *Cambridge Economic Policy Review*, December 1980.

CAMPANNA, A., 'Economic Problems and Reconstruction in Italy', *International Labour Review*, June/July 1951.

CANADIAN GOVERNMENT, *Fixed Capital Flows and Stocks*, Statistics Canada, Ottawa, various issues.

CANADIAN GOVERNMENT, *National Income and Expenditure Accounts*, Statistics Canada, Ottawa, various issues.

CAPDEVEILLE, P. *et al.*, 'International Trends in Productivity and Labour Costs', *Monthly Labour Review*, December 1982.

CARRÉ, J.-J., DUBOIS, P. AND MALINVAUD, E., *French Economic Growth*, Stanford University Press, 1976.

CATALANO, F., 'The Rebirth of the Party System', in S. Woolf (ed.), *The Rebirth of Modern Italy*.

CAVES, R., 'The Structure of Industry', in M. Feldstein (ed.), *The American Economy in Transition*.

CAVES, R. AND UEKUSA, M., *Industrial Organisation in Japan*, Brookings, Washington, 1976.

CLAIRMONTE, F. AND CAVANAGH, J., 'Transnational Corporations and Global Markets', *Trade and Development*, Winter 1982.

CLARKE, R., *Anglo-American Economic Co-operation in War and Peace 1942–49*, edited by A. Cairncross, Oxford University Press, 1982.

CLAUDIN, F., *The Communist Movement*, Penguin, Harmondsworth, 1975.

CLOSON, F.-L., '1938–48 ou les similitudes trompeuses', in French government, *Mouvement économique en France de 1938 à 1948*.

COATES, D., *The Labour Party and the Struggle for Socialism*, Cambridge University Press, 1975.

COATES, D., *Labour in Power*, Longman, London, 1980.

COATES, K. (ed.), *What Went Wrong?*, Spokesman, Nottingham, 1979.

COHEN, J., *Japan's Economy in Wartime and Reconstruction*, University of Minnesota Press, 1949.

COHEN, S., *Modern Capitalist Planning: the French Model*, University of California Press, 1969.

COLE, A., TOTTEN, G. AND UYEHARA, C., *Socialist Parties in Post-war Japan*, Yale University Press, 1966.

CONFERENCE OF SOCIALIST ECONOMISTS, *The Alternative Economic Strategy*, CSE Books, London, 1980.

COOPER, C. AND MUMFORD, E. (eds.), *The Quality of Working Life in Western and Eastern Europe*, Associated Business Press, London, 1979.

COOPER, R., 'The Gold Standard, Historical Facts and Future Prospects', *Brookings Papers on Economic Activity*, **1**, 1982.

CORIAT, B., 'The Restructuring of the Assembly Line', *Capital and Class*, Summer 1980.

CORNWALL, J., *Modern Capitalism: its Growth and Transformation*, Martin Robertson, Oxford, 1977.

CORNWALL, J., *The Conditions for Economic Recovery*, Martin Robertson, Oxford, 1983.

COVENTRY TRADES COUNCIL *et al.*, *State Intervention in Industry: a Workers' Inquiry*, 1980.

CROSLAND, A., *The Future of Socialism*, Jonathan Cape, London, 1956.

CROUCH, C. AND PIZZORNO, A. (eds.), *The Resurgence of Class Conflict in Western Europe since 1968*, 2 vols., Macmillan, London, 1978.

DALZELL, C., *Mussolini's Enemies*, Princeton University Press, 1961.

DE CECCO, M., 'Economic Policy 1945–51', in S. Woolf (ed.), *The Rebirth of Modern Italy*.

DELION, A. AND DURUPTY, M., *Les Nationalisations 1982*, Economia, Paris, 1982.

DELORS, J., 'The Decline of French Planning', in S. Holland (ed.), *Beyond Capitalist Planning*, Basil Blackwell, Oxford, 1978.

DENISON, E., 'The Interruption of Productivity Growth in the United States', *Economic Journal*, March 1983.

DENISON, E. AND CHUNG, W., *How Japan's Economy Grew So Fast*, Brookings, Washington, 1976.

DEUTSCHER, I., *Stalin*, Oxford University Press, 1967.

DEUTSCHES INSTITUT FÜR WIRTSCHAFTSFORSCHUNG, *Anlageinvestitionen und Anlagevermögen*, Beiträge zur Structurforschung, Heft 41, Berlin, 1976.

DJILAS, M., *Conversations with Stalin*, Hart-Davis, London, 1962.

DJILAS, M., *Wartime*, Secker and Warburg, London, 1977.

DOW, J., *The Management of the British Economy 1945–60*, Cambridge University Press, 1964.

DROUCOPOULOS, V., 'The Non-American Challenge', *Capital and Class*, Summer 1981.

DUNNING, J. AND PEARCE, R., *The World's Largest Industrial Enterprises*, Gower Press, Hants, 1981.

Economist, London, various issues.

EDELMAN, M. AND FLEMING, R., *The Politics of Wage-Price Decisions*, University of Illinois Press, 1965.

EDWARDS, R., *Contested Terrain*, Heinemann, London, 1979.

EINAUDI, M., BYE, M. AND ROSSI, E., *Nationalisation in France and Italy*, Cornell University Press, 1955.

ESTRIN, S. AND HOLMES, P., *French Planning in Theory and Practice*, Allen and Unwin, London, 1983.

FEINSTEIN, C., *National Income, Expenditure and Output of the United Kingdom 1855–1965*, Cambridge University Press, 1972.

FELDSTEIN, M. (ed.), *The American Economy in Transition*, University of Chicago Press, 1980.

FFORDE, J., 'Setting Monetary Objectives', *Bank of England Quarterly Bulletin*, June 1983.

FIELDHOUSE, D., *Unilever Overseas*, Croom Helm, London, 1978.

FISERA, V., *Writing on the Wall*, Allison and Busby, London, 1978.

FLANAGAN, R., SOSKICE, D. AND ULMAN, L., *Unionism, Economic Stabilisation and Incomes Policies*, Brookings, Washington, 1983.

FLEMMING, J., 'Trends in Company Profitability', *Bank of England Quarterly Bulletin*, June 1976.

FORESTER, T., 'Neutralizing the Industrial Strategy', in K. Coates (ed.), *What Went Wrong?*

FREEMAN, C., CLARK, J. AND SOETE, L., *Unemployment and Technical Innovation*, Frances Pinter, London, 1982.

FRENCH GOVERNMENT, *Mouvement économique en France de 1938 à 1948*, Ministère des Finances et des Affaires Economiques, Paris, 1950.

FRENCH GOVERNMENT, *Statistiques et études financières-annuaire 1930–1959*, Ministère des Finances, Paris, 1960.

FRENCH GOVERNMENT, *Annuaire statistique de la France, rétrospectif*, Paris, 1971.

FRENCH GOVERNMENT, *Les Comptes de la nation*, INSEE, Paris, annual.

FRENCH GOVERNMENT, *Les Comptes des entreprises par secteurs*, INSEE, Paris, various issues.

FRENCH GOVERNMENT, *Statistiques et études financières*, monthly.

FRIEDMAN, A., *Industry and Labour*, Macmillan, London, 1977.

FRÖBEL, F., HEINRICHS, J. AND KREYE, O., *The New International Division of Labour*, Cambridge University Press, 1980.

FUA, G., *La Sviluppo Economico in Italia*, vol. III, Franco Angeli Editori, Milan, 1969.

GARDNER, R., *Sterling Dollar Diplomacy*, Oxford University Press, 1956.

GARTMAN, D., 'Origins of the Assembly Line and Capitalist Control of Work at Fords', in A. Zimbalist (ed.), *Case Studies in the Labor Process*, Monthly Review Press, New York, 1979.

GENERAL AGREEMENT ON TARIFFS AND TRADE (GATT), *International Trade*, Geneva, annual.

GERMAN GOVERNMENT, *Volkswirtschaftliche Gesamtrechungen*, various issues, Statistisches Bundesamt, Wiesbaden.

GILBERT, M., *Quest for World Monetary Order*, John Wiley, New York, 1980.

GILMOUR, I., *Inside Right*, Quartet, London, 1977.

GIMBEL, J., *The American Occupation of Germany*, Stanford University Press, 1968.

488   *Bibliography*

GIMBEL, J., *The Origins of the Marshall Plan*, Stanford University Press, 1976.

GLYN, A. AND HARRISON, J., *The British Economic Disaster*, Pluto Press, London, 1980.

GLYN, A. AND SUTCLIFFE, R., *British Capitalism, Workers and the Profit Squeeze*, Penguin, Harmondsworth, 1972.

GOUGH, I., *The Political Economy of the Welfare State*, Macmillan, London, 1979.

GRAF, W., *The German Left since 1945*, Oleander, Cambridge, 1976.

GREEN, J., *The World of the Worker*, Hill and Wang, New York, 1980.

GRIMM, B., 'Domestic Non-financial Corporate Profits', *Survey of Current Business*, January 1982.

GRUNDROD, M., *The Rebuilding of Italy*, Oxford University Press, 1955.

GUERIN, D., *100 Years of American Labour*, Ink Links, London, 1979.

GUPTA, P., 'Imperialism and the Labour Government', in J. Winter (ed.), *The Working Class in Modern British History*, Cambridge University Press, 1983.

GWIAZDA, A., 'Some Characteristic Trends in East-West Economic Relations', *National Westminster Bank Quarterly Review*, August 1982.

HADLEY, E., *Anti-Trust in Japan*, Princeton University Press, 1970.

HALLIDAY, F., *The Second Cold War*, New Left Books, London, 1983.

HALLIDAY, J., *A Political History of Japanese Capitalism*, Pantheon, New York, 1975.

HARRIS, S. (ed.), *Post-war Economic Problems*, McGraw-Hill, New York, 1943.

HAYEK, F., *A Tiger by the Tail*, Institute for Economic Affairs, London, 1972.

HECLO, H., *Modern Social Politics in Britain and Sweden*, Yale University Press, 1974.

HELLER, W., 'The Role of Fiscal-Monetary Policy in German Economic Recovery', *American Economic Review*, Papers and Proceedings, 1950.

HENDERSON, P., 'Trade Policies: Trends, Issues and Influences', *Midland Bank Review*, Winter 1983.

HERDING, R., *Job Control and Union Structure*, Rotterdam University Press, 1972.

HILDEBRAND, G., *Growth and Structure in the Economy of Modern Italy*, Harvard University Press, 1965.

HILL, T., *Profits and Rates of Return*, OECD, Paris, 1979.

HOLLAND, S., *The Socialist Challenge*, Quartet Books, London, 1975.

HOLLAND, S. (ed.), *The State as Entrepreneur*, Weidenfeld and Nicolson, London, 1972.

HONE, A., 'The Commodities Boom', *New Left Review*, September/October 1973.

HOROWITZ, D., *The Free World Colossus*, MacGibbon and Kee, London, 1965.

IKEDA, M., 'The Subcontracting System in the Japanese Electronic Industry', *Engineering Industries of Japan*, 1979.

INCOMES DATA SERVICES, *International Report*, London, monthly.

INTERNATIONAL MONETARY FUND (IMF), *Developments in International Trade Policy*, Occasional Paper No. 16, Washington, 1982.

IMF, *Annual Report*, Washington, annual.

IMF, *International Financial Statistics*, monthly and annual yearbooks.

ITALIAN GOVERNMENT, *Annuario di Contabilita Nationale*, ISTAT, Rome, annual.

ITALIAN GOVERNMENT, *Bolletino Mensile di Statistica*, ISTAT, Rome, monthly.

ITOH, M., *Value and Crisis*, Pluto Press, London, 1980.

JAPANESE GOVERNMENT, *Annual Report on National Accounts*, Economic Planning Agency, Tokyo, annual.

JAPANESE GOVERNMENT, *Census of Manufactures*, Tokyo, various issues.

JAPANESE GOVERNMENT, *Economic Survey of Japan*, Economic Planning Agency/Japan Times, Tokyo, annual.

JAPANESE GOVERNMENT, *Estimates of the Stock of Non-Residential Business Capital*, Economic Planning Agency, Tokyo, periodically.

JAPANESE GOVERNMENT, *Japan Statistical Yearbook*, Office of the Prime Minister, Tokyo, annual.

JAPANESE GOVERNMENT, *Monthly Statistics of Japan*, Tokyo, monthly.

JAPANESE GOVERNMENT, *White Paper on Small and Medium Enterprises in Japan*, Ministry of International Trade and Industry, Tokyo, annual.

JONES, J., *The Fifteen Weeks*, Harcourt, Brace, New York, 1955.

KALECKI, M., *Essays on the Dynamics of the Capitalist Economies*, Cambridge University Press, 1971.

KAMATA, S., *Japan in the Passing Lane*, Pantheon Books, New York, 1982.

KAPLAN, E., *Japan – the Government-Business Relationship*, US Department of Commerce, Washington, 1975.

KATZENSTEIN, R., *Die Investitionen und ihre Bewegung in Staatsmonopolistischen Kapitalismus*, Berlin, 1967.

KENDALL, W., *The Labour Movement in Europe*, Allen Lane, London, 1975.

KENNAN, G., *Memoirs 1925–50*, Hutchinson, London, 1967.

KOHLER, P. AND ZACHER, H. (eds.), *The Evolution of Social Insurance 1881–1981*, Frances Pinter, London, 1982.

KOMIYA, R., 'Planning in Japan', in M. Bornstein (ed.), *Economic Planning East and West*, Ballinger, Cambridge, Mass., 1975.

KOMIYA, R. (ed.), *Postwar Economic Growth in Japan*, University of California Press, 1966.

KOLKO, G., *The Politics of War*, Vintage Books, New York, 1969.

KOLKO, G. AND KOLKO, J., *The Limits of Power: the World and US Foreign Policy*, Harper and Row, New York, 1972.

KOVANDA, K., 'Works Councils in Czechoslovakia', *Soviet Studies*, April 1977.

KRAVIS, I., 'A Survey of International Comparisons of Productivity', *Economic Journal*, March 1976.

KRAVIS, I., HESTON, A. AND SUMMERS, R., *International Comparisons of Real Product and Purchasing Power*, Johns Hopkins University Press, 1979.

KRENGEL, R., *Anlagevermögen, Produktion und Beschäftigung der Industrie im Gebiet der B.R.D. von 1924–56*, DIW, Berlin, 1958.

KUISEL, R., *Capitalism and the State in Modern France*, Cambridge University Press, 1981.

LEFRANC, G., *Le Mouvement syndical*, Payot, Paris, 1969.

LEONHARD, W., *Child of the Revolution*, Ink Links, London, 1979.

LEVINE, S., *Industrial Relations in Post-war Japan*, University of Illinois Press, 1958.

LEWIS, A., *Economic Survey 1919–39*, Allen and Unwin, London, 1949.

LICHTENSTEIN, N., *Labor's War at Home*, Cambridge University Press, 1982.

LINDBECK, A., 'The Recent Slowdown of Productivity Growth', *Economic Journal*, March 1983.

LLEWELLYN, D., 'Avoiding an International Banking Crisis', *National Westminster Bank Quarterly Review*, August 1982.

LOCKSLEY, G. AND WARD, T., 'Concentration in Manufacturing in the EEC', *Cambridge Journal of Economics*, March 1979.

MACAROV, D., *Worker Productivity*, Sage, Beverly Hills, 1982.

MADDISON, A., *Economic Growth in the West*, Twentieth Century Fund, London, 1964.

MADDISON, A., *Phases of Capitalist Development*, Oxford University Press, 1982.

MAGAZINER, I. AND HOUT, T., *Japanese Industrial Policy*, Policy Studies Institute, London, 1980.

MAGDOFF, H. AND SWEEZY, P., *The Deepening Crisis of US Capitalism*, Monthly Review Press, New York, 1981.

MAIRESSE, J., *L'Evaluation du capital fixe productive*, INSEE, Paris, 1972.

MAIRESSE, J. AND DELESTRE, H., 'Rentabilités économique et comptable des sociétés en France de 1959 à 1975', INSEE, Paris, 1976.

MAIZELS, A., *Industrial Growth and World Trade*, Cambridge University Press, 1963.

Management Today, London, monthly.

MANDEL, E., *Late Capitalism*, New Left Books, London, 1975.

MANDEL, E., *The Second Slump*, New Left Books, London, 1978.

MASON, E. AND ASHER, R., *The World Bank since Bretton Woods*, Brookings, Washington, 1973.

MATTHEWS, R. (ed.), *Slower Growth in the Western World*, Heinemann, London, 1982.

MAYNE, R., *Postwar*, Weidenfeld and Nicolson, London, 1983.

McCAGG, W., *Stalin Embattled*, Wayne University Press, 1978.

McCRACKEN, P., *Towards Full Employment and Price Stability*, OECD, Paris, 1977.

McKINNON, R., *Money in International Exchange*, Oxford University Press, 1979.

MENDERSHAUSEN, H., 'Prices, Money and the Distribution of Goods in Post-War Germany', *American Economic Review*, 1949.

Midland Bank Review, Sheffield, quarterly.

MIKESELL, R., *United States Economic Policy and International Relations*, McGraw-Hill, London, 1952.

Militant, London, weekly.

MILLER, D., 'Social Partnership and the Determinants of Workplace Independence in West Germany', *British Journal of Industrial Relations*, March 1982.

MINAMI, R., *The Turning Point in Economic Development*, Kinokuniya Bookstore, Tokyo, 1973.

MOORE, J., *Japanese Workers and the Struggle for Power 1945–47*, University of Wisconsin Press, 1983.

MORGAN, D., *Merchants of Grain*, Weidenfeld and Nicolson, London, 1979.

MORGAN GUARANTY BANK, *Survey*, New York, monthly.

MÜLLER-JENTSCH, W., 'Strikes and Strike Trends in the Federal Republic of Germany 1950–78', *Industrial Relations Journal*, July/August 1981.

NATIONAL RAILWAY WORKERS UNION (Japan), *The Japanese Railwaymen's Struggle,* Tokyo, 1980.

NOSWORTHY, J. *et al.*, 'The Slowdown in Productivity Growth', *Brookings Papers on Economic Activity*, **2**, 1979.

OHKAWA, K., 'Changes in National Income Distribution', in J. Marchal and B. Ducros (eds.), *The Distribution of National Income*, Macmillan, London, 1968.

OHKAWA, K. AND ROSOVSKY, H., *Japanese Economic Growth*, Stanford University Press, 1973.

OHKAWA, K., JOHNSTON, B. AND KAMEDA, H., *Agriculture and Economic Growth: Japan's Experience*, Princeton University Press, 1970.

OKOCHI, K., *Labour in Modern Japan*, Science Council of Japan, Tokyo, 1957.

OKOCHI, K., KARSH, B. AND LEVINE, S. (eds.), *Workers and Employers in Japan*, Princeton University Press, 1974.

ORGANIZATION FOR ECONOMIC AND COOPERATIVE DEVELOPMENT (OECD), *The Growth of Output 1960–80*, Paris, 1970.

OECD, *Public Expenditure on Income Maintenance Programmes*, 1976.

OECD, *Public Expenditure Trends*, 1976.

OECD, *Employment Outlook*, 1983.

OECD, *Flows and Stocks of Fixed Stocks 1955–1980*, 1983.

OECD, *Economic Outlook*, July and December annually.

OECD, *Economic Survey of France, of Germany, of Italy, of Japan, of United States, of United Kingdom*, annual.

OECD, *Historical Statistics*, annual since 1982.

OECD, *Labour Force Statistics*, annual.

OECD, *Main Economic Indicators*, monthly.

OECD, *National Accounts of Member Countries*, 2 vols., annual.

OECD, *Trade by Commodities*, annual.

ORGANIZATION FOR EUROPEAN ECONOMIC COOPERATION (OEEC), *Statistics of National Product and Expenditure No. 2, 1938 and 1947–55*, Paris, 1957.

OEEC, *The Problem of Rising Prices*, Paris, 1961.

Oriental Economist, Tokyo, monthly.

PARBONI, R., *The Dollar and its Rivals*, New Left Books, London, 1981.

PATRICK, H. (ed.), *Japanese Industrialisation*, University of California Press, 1976.

PATRICK, H. AND ROSOVSKY, H. (eds.), *Asia's New Giant*, Brookings, Washington, 1976.

PETIT, P., 'The Origins of French Planning – A Reappraisal', *Contributions to Political Economy*, March 1984.

PIORE, M., 'American Labour and the Industrial Crisis', *Challenge*, March/April 1982.

PLUTO PRESS, *Thatcher's Britain. A Guide to the Ruins*, Pluto Press, London, 1983.

PORTES, R., 'East, West and South: the role of the centrally planned economies in the International Economy', in S. Grassman and E. Lundberg (eds.), *The World Economic Order: Past and Prospects*, Macmillan, London, 1981.

POSNER, C. (ed.), *Reflections on the Revolution in France: 1968*, Pelican, Harmondsworth, 1970.

POSNER, M. AND WOOLF, S., *Italian Public Enterprise*, Gerald Duckworth, London, 1967.

PRAIS, S., *The Evolution of Giant Firms in the UK*, Cambridge University Press, 1976.

PRAIS, S., *Productivity and Industrial Structure*, Cambridge University Press, 1981.

PREIS, A., *Labor's Giant Step*, Pathfinder Press, New York, 1964.

PRITT, D., *The Labour Government 1945–51*, Lawrence and Wishart, London, 1963.

RAY, G., 'Labour Costs and International Competitiveness', *National Institute Economic Review*, August 1972.

RAY, G., 'Labour Costs in OECD countries 1964–75', *National Institute Economic Review*, November 1976.

REGGIO, G., 'Italy', in G. Spitaels (ed.), *La Crise des relations industrielles en Europe*, de Tempel, Bruges, 1968.

RIMLINGER, G., *Welfare Policy and Industrialisation in Europe, America and Russia*, Wiley, New York, 1971.

RIOUX, J.-P., *La France de la Quatrième République: l'ardeur et la nécessité*, Seuil, Paris, 1980.

ROBINSON, H., 'The Downfall of the Dollar', *The Socialist Register*, London, 1973.

ROGOW, A., *The Labour Government and British Industry*, Blackwell, Oxford, 1955.

ROSS, G., *Workers and Communists in France*, University of California Press, 1982.

ROUSSEAS, S., *The Political Economy of Reaganomics*, Sharpe, New York, 1982.

ROWTHORN, R., *Capitalism, Conflict and Inflation*, Lawrence and Wishart, London, 1980.

ROWTHORN, R. AND HYMER, S., *International Big Business 1957–67*, Cambridge University Press, 1971.

ROY, A., 'Labour Productivity in 1980 – an International Comparison', *National Institute Economic Review*, August 1982.

SABEL, C., *Work and Politics*, Cambridge University Press, 1982.

SACHS, J., 'Real Wages and Unemployment in the OECD Countries', *Brookings Papers on Economic Activity*, **1**, 1983.

SAGA, I., 'Labour Relations in Japan: the Case of the Nissan Motor Company', mimeo, Tokyo, n.d.

SAINT-JOURS, Y., 'France', in P. Kohler and H. Zacher (eds.), *The Evolution of Social Insurance 1881–1981*.

SALTER, W., *Productivity and Technical Change*, Cambridge University Press, 1966.

SALVATI, B. 'The Rebirth of Italian Trade Unionism', in S. Woolf (ed.), *The Rebirth of Modern Italy*.

SALVATI, M., *Il Sistemo Economico Italiano: Analisi di Una Crisi*, Il Mulino, Bologna, 1975.

SAMPSON, A., *The Seven Sisters*, Penguin, Harmondsworth, 1975.

SAMPSON, A., *The Money Lenders*, Coronet, London, 1982.

SAMUELSON, P., 'Full Employment After the War', in S. Harris (ed.), *Post-war Economic Problems*.

SARGENT, J., 'Capital Accumulation and Productivity Growth', in R. Matthews (ed.), *Slower Growth in the Western World*.

SCHMIDT, E., *Die verhinderte Neuordnung 1945–52*, Europaische Verlaganstalt, 1970.

SCHMIDT, U. AND FICHTER, T., *Der Erzwungene Kapitalismus: Klassenkämpfe in den Westzonen 1945–48*, Wagenbach, Berlin, 1971.

SCHUMPETER, J., 'Capitalism in the Post-war World', in S. Harris (ed.), *Post-war Economic Problems*.

SEABROOK, J., *Unemployment*, Quartet, London, 1982.

SHINOHARA, M., *Structural Changes in Japan's Economic Development*, Tokyo, 1970.

SHONFIELD, A., *Modern Capitalism*, Oxford University Press, 1965.

SIMPSON, E., 'Inflation and Deflation and Employment in Italy', *Review of Economic Studies*, **44**, 1949–50.

Socialist Economic Review, London, annual since 1981.

SOSKICE, D., 'Strike Waves and Wage Explosions 1968–70: an Economic Interpretation', in C. Crouch and A. Pizzorno (eds.), *The Resurgence of Class Conflict in Western Europe*.

SOSKICE, D., 'The UK Economy and Industrial Relations', *Industrial Relations*, Fall 1984.

SPIRO, H., *The Politics of German Co-determination*, Harvard University Press, 1958.

STEINDL, J., *Maturity and Stagnation in American Capitalism*, Blackwell, Oxford, 1952.

STEINDL, J., 'The Role of Household Saving in Modern Economy', *Banca Nazionale del Lavoro Review*, 1982.

STEWART, M., *Controlling the Economic Future*, Wheatsheaf Books, Brighton, 1983.

STRANGE, S., *Sterling and British Policy*, Oxford University Press, 1971.

SUTCLIFFE, B., *Hard Times*, Pluto Press, London, 1983.

SWEEZY, P., *The Present as History*, Monthly Review Press, New York, 1955.

TAIRA, K., *Economic Development and the Labor Market in Japan*, Columbia University Press, 1970.

TEW, B., *The Evolution of the International Monetary System*, Hutchinson, London, 1977.

TEW, B. AND HENDERSON, R. (eds.), *Studies of Company Finance*, Cambridge University Press, 1959.

TOTSUKA, H., 'Japanese Trade Union Attitudes towards Rationalisation', mimeo, Tokyo, n.d.

TROTSKY, L., 'The Curve of Capitalist Development', *Bulletin of the Conference of Socialist Economists*, Spring 1973.

TSURU, S., *Essays on the Japanese Economy*, Kinokuniya Bookstore, Tokyo, 1958.

TURNER, L., *Oil Companies in the International System*, Allen and Unwin, London, 1983.

UK GOVERNMENT, *British Labour Statistics, Historical Abstract*, Department of Employment and Productivity, London, 1971.

UK GOVERNMENT, *Economic Survey*, HM Treasury, London, annual, 1947–62.

UK GOVERNMENT, *Employment Gazette*, Department of Employment, monthly.

UK GOVERNMENT, *National Income and Expenditure*, Central Statistical Office, London, various issues.

UNIR, *Histoire du PCF*, Paris, n.d.

UNITED NATIONS, *Statistical Yearbook,* New York, annual.

UNITED NATIONS, *World Economic Review*, New York, annual.

UNITED NATIONS, *Yearbook of National Accounts Statistics*, New York, annual.

UNITED NATIONS CONFERENCE FOR TRADE AND INDUSTRY (UNCTAD), *Commodity Issues*, 1983.

UNCTAD, *International Trade and Monetary Issues*, 1983.

UNCTAD, *Production and Trade in Services*, 1983.

UNCTAD, *Protectionism, Trade Relations and Structural Adjustment*, 1983.

UNCTAD, *Trade in Manufactures and Semi-Manufactures of Developing Countries*, 1983.

UNCTAD, *Trade and Development Report*, Geneva, annual, from 1981.

UNITED NATIONS ECONOMIC COMMISSION FOR EUROPE (UNECE), *Economic Survey of Europe Since the War: a Reappraisal of Problems and Prospects,* Geneva, 1953.

UNECE, 'Reciprocal Trading Arrangements in East-West Trade', *Economic Bulletin for Europe*, June 1982.

UNECE, 'Recent Developments in East-West Trade', *Economic Bulletin for Europe*, December 1982.

UNECE, *Economic Survey of Europe*, Geneva, annual.

US GOVERNMENT, *Balance of Payments, Statistical Supplement*, Department of Commerce, Washington, 1962.

US GOVERNMENT, *Long-term Economic Growth 1860–1970*, Department of Commerce, 1973.

US GOVERNMENT, *The National Income and Product Accounts of the United States 1929–76*, Department of Commerce, 1981.

US GOVERNMENT, *Underlying Data for Indices of Output Per Hour etc.*, Bureau of Labor Statistics, May 1983.

US GOVERNMENT, *Economic Report of The President*, annual.

US GOVERNMENT, *Survey of Current Business*, Department of Commerce, monthly.

VAN PARYS, P., 'The Falling Rate of Profit Theory of Crisis', *Review of Radical Political Economy*, Spring 1980.

VATTER, H., *The US Economy in the 1950s*, Norton, New York, 1965.

WALLICH, H., *Mainsprings of the German Revival*, Yale University Press, 1955.

WEISSKOPF, T., 'Marxian Crisis Theory and the Rate of Profit in the Postwar US Economy', *Cambridge Journal of Economics*, December 1979.

WERTH, A., *France 1940–55*, Robert Hale, London, 1956.

WILLIAMSON, J., *The Failure of International Monetary Reform*, Nelson, London, 1977.

WILSON, T. (ed.), *Pensions, Inflation and Growth*, Heinemann, London, 1974.

WOOLCOCK, S., 'Textiles and Clothing', in L. Turner and N. McMullen (eds.), *The Newly Industrialising Countries*, Allen and Unwin, London, 1982.

WOOLF, S. (ed.), *The Rebirth of Modern Italy*, Longman, London, 1972.

WORLD BANK, *World Tables*, Johns Hopkins Press, 1980.

WORLD BANK, *World Debt Tables 1982/83*, Washington, 1983.

WORSWICK, D AND ADY, P., *The British Economy 1945–50*, Oxford University Press, 1952.

YAMAMOTO, K., 'The Production Control Struggle', *Annals of the Institute of Social Science*, Tokyo University, 1972.

YAMAMOTO, K., 'Mass Demonstration Movements in Japan', *Capital and Class*, Winter 1980/81.

YAMAMOTO, K., 'Labour-Management Relations at Nissan Motor Co. Ltd', *Annals of the Institute of Social Science*, Tokyo University, 1980.

YAMAMURA, K., *Economic Policy in Postwar Japan*, University of California Press, 1967.

YERGIN, D., *Shattered Peace: the Origins of the Cold War and the National Security State*, Penguin, Harmondsworth, 1980.

ZINK, H., *The United States in Germany 1944–55*, Van Nostrand, Princeton, 1957.

ZOLLNER, D., 'Germany', in P. Kohler and H. Zacher (eds.), *The Evolution of Social Insurance 1881–1981*.

Index

For the main entries, see also under individual countries.

ACCs, definitions   457, 462–3
accumulation   125, 161, 168–9, 219, 235, 241–4, 246, 257, 269, 340–4, 452
   effect on productivity   348
Acheson, Dean   114
Adenauer, Konrad   148, 163, 196
agriculture   236–7
   protection   376
Anglo-US loan   53, 97–8

balance of payments   338
Bank for Reconstruction   52, 119; *see also* World Bank
Bank of England   409
Benn, Tony   436, 440–1, 447
Beveridge report   194
Beveridge scheme   195
Bismarck   194, 196
Boeckler, Hans   85, 141, 142
borrowing   265–6, 345–6
bottlenecks
   fuel   29–30
   transport   28–9
Bretton Woods system   54, 227
   abandoned   294
budget deficits   71, 181, 266, 319, 338–9, 404, 429
Burns, Arthur   432
business confidence   161, 315–18
buy-back agreements   352
Byrnes, James   47

Callaghan, James   427
Camus, Albert   42–3
capacity utilization   250, 256–7
capital stock

asset lives   458
   definitions   457
   growth, *see* accumulation
   measurement of   253
   postwar   27–8, 45
capitalism, and social relations   30–1
capitalist control   31, 70, 126, 193, 239, 275, 396–401
Chevènement, J.-P.   445, 447
China, civil war   46
Churchill, Winston   194
   spheres of influence   48
Clayton, William   50, 120
colonial revolution   155
Committee of European Economic Cooperation   119
commodities boom   159, 303–7
Communist parties   110–11
   popular front policy   61–8
concentration
   aggregate   216–18
   by plant size   393
   decline within industries   226
consensus politics   193–4, 402
consumer prices   259
consumption   175, 177, 335–7, 451
convertibility of European currencies   227
credit   265–8
credit crisis   451
credit squeeze   407–8
Crosland, Anthony   193
'crowding out'   404
Czechoslovakia   64–8
   Communist Party   64–8
   nationalization   65–7

Czechoslovakia – cont.
  resistance programme 65
  works councils 65, 67

de Gaulle, Charles 91, 95, 284, 285,
    287–8
deindustrialization 327–8
Delors, Jacques 203
depreciation, definitions of 459
deregulation 415–16, 417
Deutscher, Isaac 62
devaluation 158–9
Dodge, Joseph 138
dollar 54–5
  devaluation 232, 293–7
  gold backing 231, 291
  gold convertibility 228, 230–1
  shortage 54–5, 107–8
  US defence of 232, 371
  world money 227–34, 298, 369
Eastern bloc, economic relations
    with West 351–3
economic collapse, conditions
    for 450–1
economic recovery
  conditions for 450
  possibility of 424–5
employment 236, 269, 324
  females 244, 326–7
  full 239
  growth 168, 325
  immigration 244
  industrial, decline of 327–8
  natural rate of 404
  obstacles to raising 427–31
  service sector 237–8
  state sector 238
Euromarkets 292
Europe
  accumulation 164, 219, 365–6
  attitudes to international monetary
    reform 296, 299–300
  balance of payments 271
  competitiveness 158
  consumption 164
  deficit with USA 107
  deflation 274–5

dependence on USA 45, 108
disease 22
dollar shortage 108
economic policies 270
employers' offensive 275
employment 327
food shortage 30
fuel bottlenecks 29–30
government spending 264
import restrictions 375
imports from USA 109, 122,
    125–6
incomes policies 274–5
inflation 290–1
monetary conditions 301–2
planning and Marshall Aid 120
production 108
productivity 126–7, 250, 219–20,
    367
profit rate 255, 320, 340–1
profit share 246
profits squeeze 274
public sector workers 275–6
reconstruction plans 119
stagnation 163
starvation 22
take-home pay 264
trade 371–4
unemployment 290
US aid 51, 119–21
wage explosions 273
European Recovery
    Programme 119; *see also*
    Marshall Aid
exchange controls 54–5, 429
exchange rates 54–5, 367–71, 429
exports 179–80
  'voluntary' restraints 375, 377

Fabius, Laurent 447
family allowances 195
Fforde, J. S. 409
Fiat, labour relations 277–8, 380–1
financial assets, wartime
    accumulation 70
food shortage 30
foreign exchange reserves,

composition of 369
foreign investment in LDCs 393–4
France 42–4, 91–6, 162, 202–6,
    282–90, 431–48
  accumulation 125
  accumulation and planning 204–5
  Auroux report 438–9
  austerity measures 435
  banks 445
  Barre Plan 379
  black market 93, 94
  budget deficit 128, 433–4
  CFDT 282–5, 289–90
  CGT 91, 96, 129–31, 282–7,
    289–90
  coalition government 91
  Communist Party 91, 95–6, 130,
    282, 289–90
  deflationary policy 128, 286–7,
    433
  devaluation 433
  dismissals procedures 379
  economic planning 202–6
  elections 43, 286
  employers' organization
    (CNPF) 131
  expansion policies 433
  financial assets 93
  Grenelle agreements 285
  industrial democracy 438–9
  industrial policy 433–8
  inflation 286, 287
  Interim plan 445–7
  labour force 26
  living standards 93–4
  Marshall Aid 203
  May 1968 282–90
  Mitterrand government (1981–)
    426–48
  monetary reform 93
  Monnet Plan 93, 96, 203
  nationalization 91, 92, 443–7
  peasant incomes 93, 94
  plan contracts 445–6
  postwar capital stock 27
  production 92
  productivity 94
  profits 92, 94–5, 128, 286
  protectionism 434
  reorganization of steel and
    textiles 379
  reconstruction 91–6
  resistance programme 43
  social security contributions 435
  Socialist Party 91, 96, 438
  strikes 96, 129–31, 162, 282–4,
    287–8, 289–90
  students 282–5, 288
  trade union split 130–1
  trade unions 91, 96, 129–31, 206,
    283–5, 288–9, 438
  trade unions and planning 206
  transport bottlenecks 29
  unemployment 286, 433–4
  wages 128, 286–7, 435
  war damage 26
  wartime investment 27
  working time reductions 434
Friedman, Milton 407

Galbraith, J. K. 414
GATT 54
Germany 37, 39–41, 58–60, 80–6,
    140–9, 162–3, 199–202
  accumulation 124–5, 147, 160
  antifascist committees 39
  black market 80, 82, 83, 143, 145
  bottlenecks 80–1
  Christian Democrats (CDU) 41,
    142
  codetermination 148, 199–202
  coal exports 81
  Communist Party (KPD) 40, 60,
    83, 85, 148
  concerted action programme 379
  devaluation 146
  economic policies 270
  elections 83, 148
  employment 146, 327–8
  exchange rate policy 296
  exports 146
  food shortage 22, 80, 82, 84, 141
  IG Metall 146, 148, 271
  industrial democracy 199

Germany – cont.
  investment   83, 145, 146–7, 160
  labour force   25–6
  level of industry plan   59
  living standards   82, 145
  Marshall Aid   140–1, 142, 147–8
  monetary policy   145
  monetary reform   141–3, 147
  nationalization   142, 148
  nationalization demands   40–1
  occupation authorities   39
  occupation policy   58–60, 80,
    84–5, 142–4
  partition   140
  postwar capital stock   27
  production   80, 140
  production abroad   394
  productivity   81, 144
  profits   83, 144
  rationalization   146
  reconstruction   80–6
  refugees   22
  reparations   59
  Social Democratic Party
    (SPD)   40, 142, 145
  Socialist Free Union   40
  socialization of industry   83
  strikes   84, 145, 163, 379
  trade union funds   146
  trade unions   40, 60, 83, 85, 146
  transport bottlenecks   28–9, 81
  unemployment   145
  US aid   120
  US monopoly policy   59–60
  US policy   148
  US trade union policy   60
  wages   143, 145, 146
  war damage   26
  wartime investment   27
  works councils   39–40, 85, 142,
    148, 200, 201
gold   227–8
  price   232–4, 292, 303
Gold Pool   231
government expenditure   181, 195,
  264, 338–9
government financing   181

grain   304–7

Hayek, F. A.   403, 404, 405–6
Healey, Denis   441
Herstatt Bank collapse   317
Holland, Stuart   440
hours of work   168, 244

IMF   119, 122
  debt policy   452
  foundation of   54
  policies to debtors   363–4
  recycling programme   316–17
import controls   356–60, 375–7, 429
import penetration of ACC
  markets   373–4
income distribution and postwar
  shortages   70–2
incomes policies   274–5
India, implications of
  independence   46
industrial democracy   199–202,
  436–9
industrial policies   206–11, 439–48
industrial relations, Japanese
  influence on West   382–3, 391
inflation   72, 160, 264–8, 269, 302,
  319, 348–50, 427–8
interest rates, effects of   408
international competition   251–3,
  256–7, 371–4, 429
international debt   361–4, 452
international monetary
  system   53–5, 227–35, 291–300,
  367–71
international relations
  between advanced
    countries   44–6, 364–77
  colonies   46–7
  USSR   47–9, 106, 110–11, 351–3,
    423
investment   160, 314–15, 339–40,
  451
  conditions for   430
  demand   182
  financing   182
  wartime   26–7

investment goods, relative
 prices 254
Italy 41–2, 86–91, 132–6, 276–82
 1970 Workers' Charter 282
 accumulation 125
 attack on union strength 133–4
 ban on dismissals 133
 black market 132
 borrowing difficulties 316
 budget deficit 88
 capitalist control 135–6
 Christian Democrats 86, 278
 coalition government 90–1
 Communist Party (PCI) 86,
 89–91, 134, 278, 380
 deflationary policy 132, 135, 279
 elections 278
 employers 42
 employers' policies 277–9
 financial assets 88
 government expenditure 132
 historic compromise 380
 Hot Autumn 276–82
 inflation 88
 investment 87
 labour force 26
 living standards 88, 89
 Marshall Aid 135
 migrant workers 280–1
 monetary policy 132
 nationalization 86
 production 135
 productivity 87, 88, 135, 279
 profits 87, 88, 132, 135, 278, 279,
 280
 reconstruction 86–91
 redundancy pay and
 conditions 379
 resistance movement 41–2
 share prices 132
 shopfloor control 133
 Socialist Party 278
 strikes 41–2, 90, 134, 162, 280–1,
 380–1
 subcontracting 394–5
 trade union split 134–5
 trade unions 276–7, 281–2

 transport bottlenecks 29
 unemployment 278
 US aid 89
 wage explosion 279
 wages 87
 war damage 26
 wartime investment 27
 works councils 86, 90

Japan 37–9, 72–80, 136–40, 183–92,
 206–10, 382–91
 accumulation 125, 161, 184, 186,
 364–6
 attack on union strength 139–40
 attitude to international monetary
 reform 296, 299–300
 balance of payments 184, 271
 black market 21, 137
 capital levy 76
 capital per worker 186
 Communist Party 38, 79
 competitive weakness 184
 computers 209–10
 consultation 384
 demonstrations 77, 78
 Densan wages system 76
 Dodge line 138
 economic conditions 162
 economic policies 270
 education and culture 383–4
 elections 78–9
 employers' tactics 190–2
 employment 185, 327–8
 exchange rate policy 296
 exports 73
 food shortage 30, 73–4
 foreign technology 209
 fuel bottlenecks 30
 government spending 264
 harassment of workers 387–91
 housing shortage 21
 IMF-JC 391
 import penetration 215
 industrial policy 206–10
 industrial relations 382–91
 inflation 74, 76, 137
 international competition 253

Japan – cont.
investment 75, 137, 184
investment finance 206
Korean war boom 184
labour force 25–6, 185
labour market 185
lifetime employment 391
living standards 382
materials stockpiling 304
MITI 206–10
monetary conditions 302
motor industry 209
Nissan workers union 384–90
occupation policy 77
oil crisis, effect of 313–14
postwar capital stock 27–8
postwar production 73
product wages 185–6
production control 38–9, 77
productivity 140, 184, 186, 250, 367
profits 74, 136, 140, 185, 187, 246, 382–3
quality circles 385
rationalization 210
reconstruction 72–80
red purge 140
redundancies 76, 140
reparations 56
savings 185
shipbuilding 207
Socialist Party 78, 80
starvation 21
steel 207–9
stockbuilding 137
strikes 77, 78, 136, 190–1, 384
subcontracting 395–6
surplus labour 136
take-home pay 264
technical change 186
trade 371–4
trade unions 37, 56, 76–8, 190–1, 383–91
transport bottlenecks 28–9
unemployment 383
US aid 51, 74
US monopoly policy 56–8

US occupation policy 55–8, 73, 136, 138
US trade union policy 56–7
wages 74, 76, 140, 382
wages system 191–2
war damage 26
wartime investment 26
Japan Development Bank 206
job vacancies 240
joint ventures 377
Jones, J. M. 108, 112

Kalecki, Michal 239
Kennan, George 110, 138
Keynes, Maynard 54, 109, 203
Keynesianism 181, 427–31
Korean war 158–9
Korean war boom 159, 160, 163

labour
demand for 241–4, 257
flexibility 397–9
intensity of 250
shortage 244, 246
underutilization of 126
labour costs, levels relative to USA 220
labour force 244–5, 326
postwar 25
labour movement, defeats 155, 378–81
labour shortage 235, 239–45
Lambsdorff, Otto 334
'least developed countries' 354–5
Leigh-Pemberton, Robin 403
Lend-Lease 45, 51, 52, 53, 97–8
Leonhard, Wolfgang 63, 67
Less Developed Countries (LDCs) 355, 393–4
accumulation 353–4
debts 361–4
economic relations with West 353–5
terms of trade 355
trade 358
libertarianism 403–4
living standards 259–64

long boom 126, 156, 167–8

MacArthur, Douglas 55–6, 58, 77, 78, 131
Marshall Aid 106–12, 118–22, 125–6, 154, 161
  concessions by recipients 121–2
  US exports 113–14
Marshall, George 106
Marx, Karl 167
Mauroy, Pierre 447
Meaney, George 130
military spending 159, 181, 264, 423
mini-boom (1972–3) 300–4
Mitterrand, François 131, 202, 206, 445, 447
monetarism 404, 451
monetary policy 266–8, 406, 407–10
Morgenthau, Henry 50

National Health Service 99, 196
nationalization 428–9
new technology
  employment effects 332–4, 348
  plant size 393
Newly Industrializing Countries (NICs) 357–61
  accumulation 357, 361
  trade balances 358–9
Nixon, Richard 292, 293
non-tariff barriers 359–61

OECD
  analysis of response to 1979 oil price rise 350
  explanation of end of boom 308
oil 53
oil companies 309, 313
oil crisis 308, 309–14
  and economic policies 310
oil production cutback 309
OPEC 309–14
  balance of payments surplus 361
  imports 355–6
  internal accumulation 355–6
  lending 316
  market for exports 338

oil price increases 310
oil revenue 310
output-capital ratio 33, 170–2, 253–4, 320
overaccumulation 235, 251, 257, 269–71, 273–4, 311

Part, Sir Anthony 441
participation rate 326–7
peasantry 70
pensions 194–5, 196
peoples' democracies, theory of 61–2
planning 211, 429
political consensus 193–4, 211
Pompidou, Georges 283
poverty 197–8
Prior, James 421
privatization 407, 415, 416–18
product wages 245, 251, 334–5
production 167, 323
  crash (1974–5) 314–15
  postwar 45
  relative to prewar 123–4
productivity 126, 237, 248–50, 429–30
  growth 168, 219
  levels relative to USA 212–14, 219
  slowdown 346–8
profits 32–3, 160, 170–1, 235, 252–3, 269, 302, 314–15, 319–20, 340–1
  accumulation 223–4
  determinants of rates 171
  determinants of shares 170–1
  effect on investment 70, 344
  impact of investment 70
  limitation to employment 427–8
  measurement of rates 170, 458–61
  measurement of shares 458–61
  rate of 33, 255–7
  share of 32–3, 170, 246–7
  squeeze 245–7
  taxation 258–9
protectionism 374–7, 451

quality circles 400

raw materials prices 251
Reaganomics 402–25
realization and exports 179–80
recession, effect on
     competitiveness 408
reconstruction 69, 104–5
relocation of production 393–6
restrictive practices 399
Ross, George 131

Samuelson, Paul 23
savings 177, 337
Schumpeter, Joseph 23
scrapping 174–5, 179, 235, 245,
     248, 251, 253
   effect on productivity 347–8
'second cold war' 423
self-employment 236–7
share prices 161, 317, 345
Shonfield, Andrew 202
Smithsonian Agreement 292–3
social insurance 194
special drawing rights (SDRs) 234,
     291
speculation 159, 303, 304
stagnation 452–3
Stalin, Joseph
   policy towards E. Europe 62–4,
     68
   policy towards W. Europe 61–2,
     68
   spheres of influence 48
steel 376
sterling convertibility 53
Stockman, David 413
strike waves 271–90
   key settlements 271
strikes 378
   by plant size 393
subcontracting 394–6
supply-side economics 404–5

tariffs
   effect of cuts 216
   postwar reductions 54–5

Tarnow, Fritz 83
tax cuts 407, 413–15
taxation 177, 181, 262
   and incentives 404–5
technical change 168–9
technology, catch up 250
Thatcherism 402–25
Thorez, Maurice 92, 95
Togliatti, Palmero 86, 89, 134
trade 44, 125–6, 214–15
   liberalization 214
   manufactured goods 357–8
trade barriers 157
trade union bashing 407, 418–23
trade unions 126
   effects of attacks on 422–3
   membership 238
Truman Doctrine 106, 115, 118
Truman, Harry 47, 59, 106, 111

underemployment 236–7
unemployment 159–60, 239, 319,
     323–7, 378–9
   costs of 426–7
   inadequacy of official data 324
   structure of 329–30
   youth 329–30
unemployment insurance 194, 196
United Kingdom 34–6, 96–105,
     149–52, 402–25, 426–8
   accumulation 125
   anti-trade union legislation 421–2
   balance of payments 97, 157
   British Leyland (BL) 397, 398–9,
     422–3
   Bullock report 437
   Butskellism 402
   CBI 441
   Chrysler 442
   colonial policy 98, 149
   Communist Party 152
   Communist witch hunt 151–3
   company liquidations 410
   competitiveness 409
   contracting out 417
   council house sales 417
   demobilization 98

United Kingdom – cont.
  dependence on USA 109–10
  devaluation 149, 150, 151
  economic planning 151
  employers' pressure 431
  Employment Acts 421
  financial assets 97, 99
  government spending
    cuts 410–11
  Heath government 420–1
  IMF agreement 432
  Imperial Preference 54
  incomes policy 149, 150, 151,
    434–5
  industrial democracy 437–8
  investment 102, 424
  labour force 25–6, 98
  Labour government (1945–50)
    35–6, 96–105, 149–52
  Labour government (1974–9)
    426–48
  Labour Party 152, 196
  living standards 99, 150
  local authority spending 411
  Lucas Aerospace Combine
    Committee 400–1
  Marshall Aid 151, 152
  military spending 423
  monetary squeeze 409–10
  National Enterprise Board
    (NEB) 440–2
  National Economic Development
    Council (NEDC) 442
  nationalization 36, 101–2, 439–41
  NGA dispute 422
  pensions 410
  planning agreements 440, 442
  postwar capital stock 27
  postwar controls 100–3
  privatization 416–18
  production 409–10
  productivity 424, 442
  profits 102, 151, 424
  profits taxation 258–9
  public expenditure cuts 410–11,
    432
  public sector unions 420

  rationalization 153
  reconstruction 96–105
  Social Contract 436
  social services 99–100, 150–1
  special employment
    schemes 432–3
  Sterling Area 97, 109, 122
  sterling balances 97
  sterling convertibility 149
  strikes 35, 103–4
  tax cuts 414–5
  trade union legislation 436
  trade unions 34
  Trades Union Congress
    (TUC) 60, 149, 422
  TUC-LP Liaison Committee 436
  unemployment 431–3
  unemployment benefit 410
  US aid 51
  US loan 97–8
  wages 34, 99, 149–50, 434–5
  war damage 26
  wartime investment 27
United States 31–4, 112–18,
    218–26, 228–32, 297–300, 402–25
  accelerated depreciation 413
  access to European markets 108
  accumulation 125, 161, 222–4,
    365–6
  aid to Europe 51, 52–4, 119–21
  aid to Japan 51, 74
  air controllers' strike 418–20
  anti-trust laws 419
  balance of payments 228–9,
    291–4, 297, 369
  balance of payments
    policy 294–5, 299–300, 369–70
  capital outflow 228–9, 291–4,
    297–9, 369
  Communist Party 117–18
  competitive pressure 224
  competitiveness 297, 410
  Congress of Industrial
    Organizations (CIO) 115, 118
  consumption 156
  deflationary policy 290
  deregulation 415–16

United States – cont.
  direct investment in   375–6
  dollar as reserve currency   228–32
  dollar devaluation   232, 293–7
  economic dominance of   50–2,
    212–13
  economic policies   269–70
  employment   113, 327–8
  Employment Act of 1946   33
  exports   114, 156
  financial power   230
  food stamps   412
  foreign investment   224–5, 230–1,
    369
  foreign profits and
    interest   230–1, 299, 369
  General Motors, work
    reorganization   398
  gold reserves   228, 230–1, 234,
    293
  government spending   223, 264
  grain stocks   303, 305, 307
  import penetration   215
  import restrictions   375–6
  inflation   271, 290
  international monetary reform
    232–4, 295–6, 299–300
  investment   156, 157, 159, 223,
    425
  job 'enlargement'   420
  labour force   25–6, 113
  liquid assets   113
  living standards   116
  Marshall Plan   156
  military spending   159, 423
  minimum wage laws   419
  monetary policy   291, 293–4
  multinational firms   225–6
  occupation policy   55–60
  oil companies   416
  oil crisis, effect of   314
  oil import policy   311–12
  output-capital ratio   223
  policy to the UK   53
  pollution controls   415–16
  postwar capital stock   27–8
  postwar strength   45–6

  poverty   412
  price control   116
  productivity   250, 267
  profits   32–3, 113, 156, 222–3,
    255–7, 271, 424–5
  profits from abroad   369
  recession   156, 157, 163, 410
  relations with USSR   48–9
  relative decline   218–19
  research and development   224
  savings   156, 337
  share prices   34
  shift to peacetime production
    112–13
  stockbuilding   159
  strike legislation   116
  strikes   31, 32, 115–16
  Taft-Hartley Act   115, 117
  take-home pay   264
  tax cuts   413–15
  trade   371–4
  trade balance   231–2, 297, 371–4
  trade policy   50–2, 375–6
  trade unions   31, 115, 117–18,
    418–20
  transport bottlenecks   29
  unemployment   157, 270, 290
  unemployment benefit   411
  wage cuts   419
  wages   31–2, 116, 413
  wartime investment   27
  welfare provision   411–12
  wheat exports   305–6
  'workfare' programmes   411
UNNRA   52, 107
USSR
  containment   154
  German reparations   48
  grain purchases   306–7
  policy towards Europe   60–8
  spheres of influence   48–9
  war casualties   48

wage explosions   271–90
wages   70–2, 160, 235, 348–50,
    427–8
  accumulation   174–7

Wages – cont.
  bargaining during oil crisis 381
  capitalist competition 178
  cause of unemployment 334–5
  determinants of 177–9
  devaluation 157
  labour shortage 178
  pressure on 70–2
  realization 174
  trade unions 179
war damage 24–6
Weidenbaum, Murray 415
welfare, and employers' control over
  labour 198–9

welfare cuts 407, 410–12
welfare state 193–9, 211, 238
Wilson, Harold 101, 441
work organization 396–401
workers' parties
  future options 448
  problems for 426–7
working class, development of 236
World Bank 119
world trade 371–4
World War I, economic and political
  aftermath 23

Fontana Paperbacks: Non-fiction

Fontana is a leading paperback publisher of non-fiction, both popular and academic. Below are some recent titles.

- ☐ WHAT DO WOMEN WANT? Luise Eichenbaum and Susie Orbach £1.75
- ☐ AVALONIAN QUEST Geoffrey Ashe £2.50
- ☐ WAR AND SOCIETY IN EUROPE, 1870–1970 Brian Bond £3.50
- ☐ MARRIAGE Maureen Green £2.75
- ☐ AMERICA AND THE AMERICANS Edmund Fawcett and Tony Thomas £2.95
- ☐ FRANCE, 1815–1914: THE BOURGEOIS CENTURY Roger Magraw £4.95
- ☐ RULES OF THE GAME Nicholas Mosley £2.50
- ☐ THIS IS THE SAS Tony Geraghty £4.95
- ☐ THE IMPENDING GLEAM Glen Baxter £2.95
- ☐ A BOOK OF AIR JOURNEYS Ludovic Kennedy (ed.) £3.95
- ☐ TRUE LOVE Posy Simmonds £2.95
- ☐ THE SUPPER BOOK Elizabeth Kent £2.95
- ☐ THE FONTANA BIOGRAPHICAL COMPANION TO MODERN THOUGHT Alan Bullock and R. B. Woodings (eds.) £6.95
- ☐ LIVING WITH LOSS Liz McNeill Taylor £1.75
- ☐ RASPUTIN Alex de Jonge £2.95
- ☐ THE PRIVATE EYE STORY Patrick Marnham £4.95
- ☐ BARTHES: SELECTED WRITINGS Susan Sontag (ed.) £4.95
- ☐ A POCKET POPPER David Miller (ed.) £4.95
- ☐ THE WRITINGS OF GANDHI Ronald Duncan (ed.) £2.50

You can buy Fontana paperbacks at your local bookshop or newsagent. Or you can order them from Fontana Paperbacks, Cash Sales Department, Box 29, Douglas, Isle of Man. Please send a cheque, postal or money order (not currency) worth the purchase price plus 15p per book for postage (maximum postage required is £3).

NAME (Block letters) _____

ADDRESS _____

_____

_____